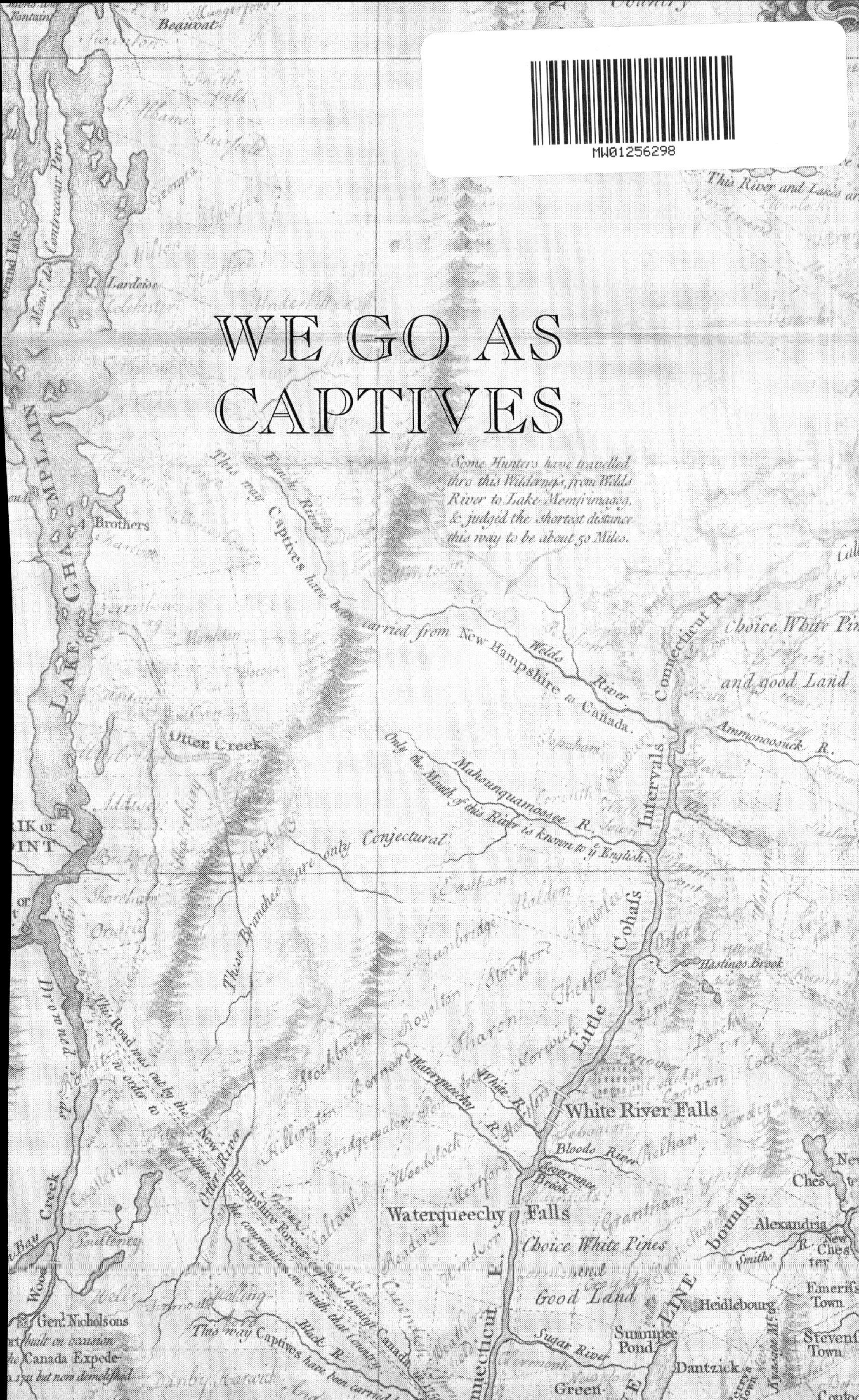

MW01256298
WE GO AS CAPTIVES
Some Hunters have travelled thro this Wildarness, from Welds River to Lake Memfrimagog, & judged the shortest distance this way to be about 50 Miles.
This way Captives have been carried from New Hampshire to Canada.
Welds River
Connecticut R.
Choice White Pines and good Land
Ammonoosuck R.
Intervals
Otter Creek
4 Brothers
Mahounquamossee R.
Only the Mouth of this River is known to ye English.
These Branches are only Conjectural
Little Cohass
Hastings Brook
White R.
Waterqueechy R.
White River Falls
Bloods River
Waterqueechy Falls
Choice White Pines and Good Land
Sugar River
Sunnipee Pond
Heidlebourg
Alexandria
Dantzick
Beauvat

VERMO

Leaperriere

Shelburne

St George

This way Captives have been carried from New Hampshire to Canada

French River

Waterford

Worster

Some Hunters have travelled thro this Wilderness, from Welds River, to Lake Memfrimagog, & judged the shortest distance this way to be about 50 Miles.

Shapoon I.

Brothers

Charlotte

Huntsbourg

Mons'. Robert

LAKE CHAMPLA

Middle sex

Durbury

Moretown

Berlin

No. Conn

Huntsbourg

Ferris bourg

Barnet

Peacham

Ryegate

Welds River

Connecticut

dial River were Hampshire, before undary between

Mons'. de

Pocock

Contracoeuse

Panton

New Heaven

Otter Creek

Topsham

Weybridge

Middle bury

Only the Mouth of this River is known to y English.

Mahsunquamosse R.

Newbury

Corinth

Waits town

Intervals

Addison

Ft. FREDERIK or CROWN POINT

Water bury

Salisbury

Bridport

These Branches are only Conjectural

Ticonderoga or Carolong Ft.

Shoreham

Orwell

2d. Narrows

Eastham

Malden

Fairlee

Cohass

Piermont

Orford

Tunbridge

Stratford

Thetford

Leister

Drown'd Lands

Sudbury

The Road was cut by the Hampshire Forces employ'd against Canada in 1759 to facilitate the communication with that Country

Neshobe

Royalton

Sharon

Norwich

Little

Lime

LAKE GEORGE

Durham

Stock bridge

Bernard

Waterqueechy R.

Pomfret

White R.

Hartford

Hanover

Dartmouth College

Canaan

Hubbardton

Pittford

Killington

White River Falls

1st. Narrows

Bridge water

Woodstock

Lebanon

Bloods River

Relhan

Castleton

Rutland

Otter River

New

Sugar River

Brook

Plainfield

Grantham

Shrews bury

Hertford

Waterqueechy Falls

Clarendon

Saltash

Poultney

Windsor

Choice White Pines and Good Land

Reading

Cavendish

South Bay

Wood Creek

Wells

Corinth

Gen'. Nicholsons Fort built on occasion of the Canada Expedetion 1711 but now demolished

Tinmouth

Wallingford

This way Captives have been carried by the Indians.

Black R.

Weathersfield

Croydon

Sunnipee Pond

n Henry

Clermont

Newport

Green

Danby

Harwich

Pawlet

CURVE LINE

Great Falls

Ft. Edward

Flamstead

Unity

Little Sugar R.

Rupert

Dorset

Brumley

Connecticut R.

Lempster

No. 8 New Concord

Thomlinson

Rockingham

No. 4

Ackworth

Charles Town

2d. Carrying Place

Sandgate

Manchester

Winhall

Kill

1st. Carrying Place

Saxtons R.

Westminster

COUNTY

Alstead

Marlow

Sunderland

West River

Batten Kill

Townshend

No. 7

Limerick

OF

Arlington

Stratton

Pultney

Walpole

Gilsum

Ashuelot R.

Shaftsbury

Glassenbury

New Fane

No. 6

Dublin

Fulham

Westmoreland

Keene

CHESHIRE

Seatcook R.

Bennington

Woodford

Draper

New Marlborough

Bratleborough

Chesterfield

Swansey

No. 5

Monadnock Mountains

Daniel Van Antwerpen

1784 Map of
Northern New England
Library of Congress

1. Zadock Steele, 1835, age 77, by Joseph Whyte.
Courtesy of Jennifer Kafka-Smith.

WE GO AS CAPTIVES

The Royalton Raid and the Shadow War on the Revolutionary Frontier

by Neil Goodwin

BARRE AND MONTPELIER

2010

This book is dedicated to

Margot

Seth

Kathy

Sage

VERMONT

Some Hunters have travelled thro this Wilderness, from Welds River, to Lake Memfrimagog, & judged the shortest distance this way to be about 50 Miles.

NB. Connecticut River has been actually

Leaperriere
Bolton
Worster
Lunenbourg
Shelburne
St. George
This way Captives have been carried from New Hampshire to Canada
Waterford
Onion River
Middle sex
Durbury
Moretown
Berlin
4 Brothers
Charlotte
Hinesbourg
Ferrisbourg
Mons. de Contracoeuse
Pocock
Panton
New Heaven
Otter Creek
Weybridge
Addison
Middlebury
Salisbury
Water bury
Bridport
Shoreham
Orwell
Leister
Neshobe
Durham
Hubbardton
Pittford
Castleton
Rutland
Poultney
Wells
Wood Creek
Gen. Nicholsons built on occasion Canada Expedition but now demolished
Tinmouth
Wallingford
Danby
Harwich
Pawlet
Rupert
Dorset
Brumley
Sandgate
Manchester
Winhall
Arlington
Sunderland
Stratton
Shafts bury
Glassenbury
New Fane
Bennington
Woodford
These Branches are only Conjectural
This Road was cut by the New Hampshire Forces employed against Canada in 1759
Otter River
Clarendon
The communication with that country
Stock bridge
Killington
Bridgewater
Bernard
Pomfret
Woodstock
Hertford
Shrewsbury
Saltash
Waterqueechy Falls
Waterqueechy R.
Reading
Windsor
Cavendish
Weathersfield
This way Captives have been carried by the Indians
Black R.
Flamstead
Thomlinson
Rockingham
Seatons R.
Westminster
Townshend
West River
Pultney
Fulham
Bratleborough
Walpole
Westmoreland
Chesterfield
New borough
Topsham
Only the Mouth of this River is known to ye English
Mahsunquamosse R.
Corinth
Newbury
Waits town
Intervals
Peacham
Barnet
Ryegate
Welds River
Connecticut R.
Eastham
Malden
Fairlee
Cohass
Tunbridge
Stratford
Thetford
Royalton
Sharon
Norwich
Little
Hartford
White R.
Choice White Pines and good Land
Lyman
Gunth
Loring
Bath
Landaff
Franconia
Ammonoosuck R.
Haverhill
Lincoln
Umpammonoosuck R.
Fairfield
Piermont
Warren
Orford
Wentworth
Hastings Brook
Rumney
Lime
Dorchester
Cockermouth
Hanover
Dartmouth College
Canaan
White River Falls
Cardigan
Lebanon
Bloods River
Relhan
Grafton
New Plymouth
Sugar River
Brook
Plainfield
Grantham
Choice White Pines and Good Land
Corinth
Protectworth
Bounds
Alexandria
New Chester
Smiths R.
Croydon
Heidlebourg
New Britain
Salisbury
Sunnipee Pond
Clermont
Newport
Green
Dantzick
Perry's Town
Kyasage Mt.
Boscawen
Rye Town
Unity
Curve Line
Little Sugar R.
Lempster
No. 8
Ackworth
No. 4
Charles Town
New Concord
Marlow
Alstead
No. 7
Gilsum
Limerick
Ashuelot R.
No. 6
Dublin
Keene
Swansey
No. 5
Monadnick Mountains
Cheshire County
Of
Hillsborough County
Hillsborough
Henneker
New Hopkinton
Contoocook R.
Mason
Wears Town
Proprietors Lands reserv'd
New Boston
Peterborough
Lindeborough
Pennigewasset River
New Chester
Dummers

CONTENTS

PART IV: THE RIVER

PART V: GONE

PART VI: AFTER THE WAR

ILLUSTRATIONS AND MAPS

ILLUSTRATIONS

MAPS

Among the evils resulting from the destruction of Royalton, my own captivity was far from being the least. I found myself, within the space of seven days, removed from my home and from all my relatives the distance of about three hundred miles, and presented with no other prospect for the future than a captivity for life, a final separation from all earthly friends, and situated in an enemy's country.

Zadock Steele's Narrative

VERMONT

Some Hunters have travelled thro' this Wilderness, from Welds River, to Lake Memsrimagog, & judged the shortest distance this way to be about 50 Miles.

This way Captives have been carried from New Hampshire to Canada

Only the Mouth of this River is known to ye English

These Branches are only Conjectural

The Road was cut by the New Hampshire Forces employed against Canada in 1759 the communication with that Country

This way Captives have been carried by the Indians

Genl. Nicholsons built on occasion Canada Expedi^n but now demolished

Choice White Pines and good Land

Choice White Pines and Good Land

Monsr. de Contracoeuse

Leaperriere
Bolton
Worster
Lunenbourg
LAKE CHAMPLAIN
Shelburne
S^t. George
French River
Waterford
Middlesex
Brothers
Charlotte
Hunesbourg
Duxbury
Moretown
Berlin
Barnet
Connecticut R.
Ferrisbourg
Peacham
Ryegate
Welds River
Lyman
Gunth
Loring
Pocock
Bath
Landaff
Franconia
Panton
New Heaven
Topsham
Ammonoosuck R.
Otter Creek
Weybridge
Middlebury
Mahsunquamassee R.
Newbury
Haverhill
Lincoln
Addison
Corinth
Waitstown
Intervals
Umpammonoosuck R.
Fairfield
Waterbury
Salisbury
Bridport
Eastham
Malden
Pierment
Warren
Shoreham
Fairlee
Cohass
Orwell
Tunbridge
Strafford
Thetford
Orford
Wentworth
Hastings Brook
Leicester
Royalton
Sharon
Rumney
Neshobe
Little
Lime
Dorchester
Cockermouth
Stockbridge
Norwich
Hanover
Dunbar
Bernard
Pomfret
White R.
Hartford
Dartmouth College
Canaan
Waterqueechy R.
White River Falls
Cardigan
Hubbardton
Pittsford
Killington
Lebanan
New Plymouth
Bridgewater
Woodstock
Bloods River
Relhan
Grafton
Castleton
Rutland
Otter River
Severrunce Brook
Hertford
Plainfield
Shrewsbury
New Chester
Clarendon
Waterqueechy Falls
Grantham
Saltash
Windsor
Protectworth
bounds
Alexandria
Poultney
Reading
Corinth
Smiths R.
New Chester
Cavendish
Connecticut R.
Wood Creek
Wells
Tinmouth
Wallingford
Weathersfield
Croydon
LINE
Heidlebourg
New Britain
Sugar River
Sunnipee Pond
Salisbury
Black R.
Clermont
Newport
Dantzick
Danby
Harwich
Green
Perry's Town
Kyasage M^t.
Boscawen
Pawlet
CURVE
Flamstead
Unity
Rye Town
Rupert
Dorset
Bromley
Little Sugar R.
Lempster
N°. 8 New Concord
Thomlinson
N°. 4 Charles Town
Ackworth
COUNTY
Rockingham
Hills borough
Henniker
New Hopkinton
Contoocook R.
Manchester
Winhall
Sandgate
Saxtons R.
Westminster
Alstead
Marlow
N°. 7
Mason
Wears Town
Sunderland
West River
Limerick
Townshend
Walpole
Gilsum
Ashuelot R.
OF
Proprietors Lands reserv'd
Arlington
Stratton
Pultney
N°. 6 1/2
Dublin
New Boston
Shaftsbury
Glassenbury
New Fane
Westmoreland
Fulham
Keene
CHESHIRE
Monadnock Mountains
HILLSBOROUGH
COUNTY
Peterborough
Lyndeborough
Bennington
Woodford
Bratleborough
Chesterfield
Swansey
N°. 5.

PREFACE

My interest in the Royalton Raid in general and the Zadock Steele narrative in particular is personal. I had lived in Royalton for 20 years before I first saw a copy of Zadock Steele's book about the 1780 Revolutionary War raid and his subsequent capture and two-year imprisonment in Canada. The little book was called *The Indian Captive, or A Narrative of the Captivity and Sufferings of Zadock Steele, Related by Himself.* It was an 1818 first edition and once I had begun, I could not put it down. In due course I started to look for the key locations, routes of travel, and missing pieces of the story.

Zadock's account had fascinating characters and elements of powerful drama. Most vivid were the people in the story. Zadock Steele himself wrote with a distinctive voice and persona but was at the same time typical of thousands of frontier-dwellers. Lieutenant Richard Houghton, the British officer who led the raiding party, was a hardened, professional soldier with an unusual aptitude and taste for combat on the frontier in the Indian service. Hannah Handy was the unforgettable heroine of the raid. The Mohawk and Abenaki members of the war party were seen at first through the standard colonial prism of racism, but, with the passage of time, appeared in quite a different light to Zadock and the other captives. A full cross-section of revolutionary American society made up the population of the Canadian prisons where hundreds were incarcerated: northerners, southerners, immigrant ethnic groups, soldiers, civilians, women and children, even a few captured African slaves. The events form a natural dramatic trajectory: surprise attack, flight, capture, and sudden death; a forced march followed by a transformative tribal adoption ceremony; the subsequent imprisonment by the British followed by a daring escape and safe return home.

My purpose in writing this book is, at one level, simply to reconstruct an accurate historical reality based on one individual's experience and point of view. Underneath its subjectivity, its occasional purple prose, and its standard Revolutionary, anti-British boilerplate, Zadock Steele's account is a remarkably accurate guide to what happened to him and his fellow captives. But it is more than that. It is a vivid picture of daily life on the Revolutionary frontier in a time of war. It is about the ingenuity that war demands—the compromises, the flexibility, and the occasional abandonment of ideology, principles, and allegiance.

As is so often the case, however, the more closely one looks at the life of an individual like Zadock Steele, the more his experience of the Revolution becomes a lens through which to view the entire War of Independence and the issues that drove it: loyalist vs. revolutionary; the crucial importance of France; the strategic position of Canada; the sovereignty of the individual states and their relationship to a central government; the settlement of new land; what to do about the native peoples; should prisoners be considered legitimate combatants or traitors to the king. Did it matter if they were abused by their guards, and to what extent did they become pawns in the larger Revolutionary picture?

As important as the geopolitical background are the natural and human environments that emerge from Zadock's narrative and other primary and secondary sources: frontier life, diet, and religion; the nature of the original forest and how it was cleared for farming; the weather; Native culture; the intricacies of British military structure; the treatment of prisoners by the Indians; medical care; the bitterness of persecuted loyalists; dislike and distrust between Americans from different regions.

To discover the universality of Zadock Steele's experience and to bring objectivity and accuracy to this book required a thorough comparison with the archival historical record and with diaries, narratives, other oral histories and scholarly secondary sources. I have worked with a variety of documents to corroborate, correct, reveal, or elaborate on events that Steele described, alluded to, or, for that matter, forgot, ignored, or eliminated.

I relied heavily on the Haldimand Papers, gathered by General Frederick Haldimand, Canada's Governor General and British Commander-in-Chief of the Northern Department from 1778 to 1784. They contain the thousands of documents that passed through his office or were accumulated by those under his far-flung command. Other British, Canadian, and American official records, local histories, contemporaneous newspapers, letters, diaries, manuscript collections, and journals serve to develop supporting characters and historical and political context and detail. Thus fleshed out, the Steele narrative provides a view of the complex world that captive American men, women, and children shared with British and German soldiers, loyalists, Mohawks, Abenakis, French Canadians, turncoats, and spies for both sides.

In spite of all that has been written about the American Revolution, the particular subject of this book appears to remain unexplored. No scholarship on either the northern frontier captive narratives or the British prison and detention system in Canada during the Revolutionary period came to light in the course of my research. Virtually nothing has been written about the experience shared by Zadock Steele and hundreds of others taken captive in the American backcountry during the Revolution. This book focuses primarily on a single story, but there are many others and there is no lack of primary source material. The field appears rich with unexploited documentation that describes the lives of people along the outer edges of colonial settlement during the Revolutionary period.

OTHER NARRATIVES

Among these sources are personal journals, pension affidavits, diaries, letters, and oral histories that relate the experiences of prisoners in Canada. The great majority of these people were captured by Indian allies of the British in raids on northern frontiers exposed to attack.

Of the men captured with Zadock in the raid on Royalton, only two others wrote their own extended narratives: Abijah Hutchinson and George Avery, who published in 1843 and 1846, respectively.[1] Their witness complements the Steele story, confirming his observations, adding details of personal experience that differ from Steele's and provide counterpoint to his narrative. While Hutchinson and Steele had very similar prisoner experiences, Avery was separated from them soon after capture, which led to a completely different sequence of events. Both Steele and Hutchinson made their way back to their central Vermont homesteads after the war, where they were neighbors for years and where they doubtless compared notes. It is possible that both Avery (who settled in nearby Plainfield, New Hampshire, after the war) and Hutchinson read Steele's narrative, but there is nothing in either text to suggest that they borrowed from one another or from Steele.

Josiah Hollister, captured in a similar raid on Ballston, New York, on the same date as Steele, Avery, and Hutchinson, and imprisoned with them for two years, wrote his own captivity narrative.[2] The Hollister text is invaluable for the names of other prisoners, British prison guards, and soldiers that it contains, but most of all for its recall of the place called Prison Island, where Hollister shared quarters with Steele and Hutchinson and some 200 other prisoners in 1781–1782. Among these was a remarkable character named John Fitch, destined for postwar fame (in 1790) as the inventor and builder of the first steamboat. He wrote an invaluable autobiography with several chapters on his captivity and confinement on Prison Island.[3] The only other narrative by one of the Prison Island captives was written by Nathaniel Segar of Bethel, Maine.[4]

These and many other Revolutionary veterans may have borrowed from the widely read account written by Ethan Allen in 1779.[5] As the first Revolutionary War captivity narrative into print, Allen's created a compelling *persona*: the defiant Yankee hero who assured the reader that American republican virtue could triumph over British arrogance and tyranny. The theme of active, civic "republican virtue," so central to Allen's tale, is muted in Steele's, and subordinate to personal outrage at being captured while minding his own business at home. Of course, once Zadock was captured, his conduct, culminating in escape, became a statement of his commitment to defy the British no matter what the cost—and that has its own persuasive political message.

THE TEXT AND ITS PUBLICATION

Ironically, as much as Zadock Steele's narrative tells us about his experiences, it also conceals much about the man. The opening page has this apology for his meager abilities:

> *I had been favored with very little opportunity to acquire an education; as the state of the colonies afforded little encouragement to schools, and caused a universal depression of literature in general.*
>
> *Long have I deeply regretted the want of that knowledge of letters requisite to prepare for the press a narrative of my own sufferings.*

Zadock says he's going to write the narrative anyway, and begins with a wry, even elegant turn of phrase:

> *Among the evils resulting from the destruction of Royalton, my own captivity was far from being the least.*

This, of course, is not how an 18th-century Vermont yeoman farmer would talk. He would have been more likely to say something like:

> *They burnt Royalton to the ground. No good came of it. Worst part was I got caught.*

Zadock's son, Horace, a newspaperman, was instrumental in the publication, transcription, and occasional embellishment of Zadock's detailed and vividly recalled oral history. Horace was, in 1826, the editor of *The Patriot and State Gazette, Montpelier,* for which he wrote editorials supporting presidential aspirant Andrew Jackson and attacking his rival, President John Quincy Adams. Horace's journalistic style is forceful, rhetorical, opinionated, and at times hyperbolic. His letter to the Secretary of War urging the granting of Zadock's pension application is equally forceful and reasoned. Zadock's narrative varies from flowery, moralistic, and antiquated (even for 1818), to straightforward declarative description. Comparing the writing of father and son is not entirely conclusive in determining the degree of shared or shifting authorship. The title page says Zadock wrote it himself, but the copyright belongs to Horace, and the book is referred to as "by Horace Steele" in Zadock's pension application of 1833.

Zadock's narrative begins by saying that it was written "to preserve in memory the sufferings of our fathers," with "no hope of pecuniary gain," and to "furnish a lesson of instruction to my fellow men and to future generations."[6]

As Robert Denn notes in his Ph.D. dissertation, *Prison Narratives of the American Revolution*, many veterans wrote their stories in hopes of earning money to alleviate financial difficulties. Even though Zadock disclaims any interest in "pecuniary gain" from his book, he could easily have attached his narrative to his 1818 pension application — he certainly mentions it in later affidavits.[7] Although apparently not attached, the *Narrative* would have been a dramatic testament to his record of service even though he was a man of property at the time. His 1818 pension application was granted, but two years later he was stricken from the pension rolls because he was not indigent enough to qualify under the 1820 Pension Act.[8] In 1829, 1832, and 1833, because of reduced circumstances, he reapplied to the war office to be reinstated, documenting his few assets and referring each time to his narrative.

Horace wrote a long letter to the Secretary of War in 1829 in support of Zadock's appeal for the reinstatement of his cancelled 1818 pension, which, Horace notes, would allow him (Horace) to be repaid a debt owed him by his father. Horace is not only a polished writer, but his own father's creditor as well. He reminds the War Office that, as a strong and very public political advocate of the by-then incumbent Andrew Jackson, he would consider it only right to have his request granted. We may never know whether it was owing to Zadock's insolvency or Horace's line of political credit, but this time the petition was granted. By then, ironically, Zadock Steele had been living in the border town of Stanstead, Québec, for at least 12 years.[9]

Thousands of Vermonters left the state for better land and opportunity in the early 19th century, and, like Zadock, a great many settled in the rich farmland of the St. Lawrence Valley of Canada. The timing of the publication of Steele's book, his first pension application, and his move to Canada is worth noting. There is a reference to "the present time, 1816" at the end of Zadock's book, published in 1818. He had bought his land in Canada in 1817, but was listed as a Brookfield resident on the 1820 census. Even though, according to local Canadian town records, Zadock moved to Canada in 1817, he declared under oath (in his pension application of 1820) that he was a "resident citizen of the United States on March 18, 1818," and indeed the census records bear it out. In the 1832 and 1833 depositions he stated his Canadian residency, and it clearly did not disqualify him at that time, though it apparently would have in 1820.[10] Are the dates of the book, the first pension application and the move to Canada coincidence? And were Zadock and Horace making sure that Zadock's Revolutionary bonafides were well established before he moved to Canada? It seems a legitimate, if, so far, an irresolvable question. Vermonters, many of them loyalists, were flocking to Canada in great numbers, and any suspicion that Zadock was a closet loyalist would certainly have disqualified him from receiving a pension. What was more, Zadock's son had married the daughter of a prominent Scottish-Canadian surgeon, an association that might well have made Zadock want to inoculate himself against patriots' doubts about his sympathies, especially in the wake of the renewed bitterness toward England following the War of 1812.

THE CAPTIVITY GENRE

Zadock's text is neither a diary nor a journal, but a narrative written many years after the war. There are hundreds of eyewitness accounts of the American Revolution, and many, like this one, recount the prisoner of war experience in particular. Of these, some were written as diaries while events unfolded and some long afterward. The latter fall into an identifiable genre and were often written (as Zadock Steele's apparently was) to preserve the history of a family elder's experience. Some were written in hopes of making money. Some were written to establish a record of military service in order to receive a pension. The bulk of these narratives appeared in the early 19th century at a time of rising American nationalism, when there was an interest in the raw materials of national history and a wish to recall what was seen as a golden age of sacrifice and civic virtue at the time of the country's founding.[11]

As Zadock and Horace prepared this book for publication they may have shrewdly framed the narrative with a marketing strategy in mind. As Denn points out, many other Revolutionary War narratives were appearing in the early 19th century and they were inevitably competing with one another. Instead of entering the marketplace as just one more tale of republican virtue confronting the British in the military/political arena, Zadock's is called *"The Indian Captive."* After all, Mary Rowlandson's, John Williams's, Mary Jemison's and many other Indian captivity narratives continued to be bestsellers.[12] In fact, there is nothing in the title to suggest it is a Revolutionary War story. Like the accounts written by other prisoners (Webster, Hubbell, and Scudder), Zadock Steele takes advantage of the sure-fire "brand" of the Indian captivity narrative: a private citizen's thrilling story of attack and capture by "savage Indians." At least that is what the title page suggests.

Zadock borrowed from the Indian captivity genre in the choice of his title, trading on its sensationalism — and at the same time joining a rare hybrid genre that combines Indian surprise attack and captivity in a Revolutionary War setting. He borrows the flowery, hyperbolic writing style, and his story contains the stock elements of terrifying attack and a long, dangerous journey into an alien world. Unusual for a Revolutionary narrative but standard in Indian captivity tales, there are literary and biblical references every few pages; not surprisingly, nearly a quarter of those come from the Book of Job.[13]

There is no way of knowing how many copies of Zadock's book were sold in his lifetime, but judging from its frequency of republication, the book must have become regionally quite well known. In the years since 1818, it has been published at least eleven times.[14] It was first republished in 1854 as part of a collection entitled "Indian Narratives." The mid-19th century was a time of increased contact with native peoples on the western frontier. There was an accompanying fascination with what were considered "Indian barbarities," along with the awareness that, in certain places, captivity by Indians was still a distinct possibility. Steele's original version contained a section on the "Burning of Royalton" that preceded his own captivity account. Later versions sometimes include the whole text, but just as often, only the "Burning" or only the "Captivity."

Steele's account of his own experience was well-rehearsed by the time he wrote it down, but, since he was captured a day after the Royalton attack, he was not an eyewitness to the "Burning" and had to reconstruct it from the memories of others. Steele was to spend two years in captivity with those who were eyewitnesses to the raid so he had ample opportunity to hear each man's account of what had happened. Moreover, he returned to Royalton to consult with those not captured for their versions of events. His narrative acknowledges in particular "Elias Stevens, Col. Edson and others." These 1818 interviews with villagers resulted in a very detailed, moment-by-moment account of the raid. It was one of the most sensational British attacks on Vermont of the entire war and nothing like it had happened east of the Green Mountains, so the events were burned into the collective memories of successive generations.

Interest in the events on the northern frontier of Vermont were of particular interest to the people of Connecticut, where the majority of Vermonters originated. Almost the entire town of Royalton came from a small cluster of towns in southeastern Connecticut, so it is no wonder that newspapers in that state were the first to print the story of the raid.

The Connecticut Journal, New Haven, November 30, 1780.

"On the 16th of October, a party of Indians and Tories, consisting of about 300, made a descent upon the White River. They proceeded as far down as Royalton, the most of which they destroyed. This was a flourishing town consisting of between 40 and 50 families, and a number of valuable buildings, the most of which they laid in ashes — murdered several of the inhabitants and made prisoners of all the rest."

PROLOGUE

BEFORE THE RAID

LIVING WITH WAR

It's not as if an attack was unexpected. The people of central Vermont were in a more or less constant state of alert. In every year since 1775, when the war for American independence began, there had been attacks from Canada.

During the summer and early fall of 1780, small British and Indian raiding parties began crossing the Green Mountains from Lake Champlain. They had never done this before; they had never come over the mountains or so close to the Connecticut River Valley. In early October, spies had brought reliable information to the garrison town of Newbury, Vermont, that a massive British force was gathering at St. John's, just a few miles north of the Canadian border, and that British shipping on Lake Champlain was on the increase.[1] This was bound to mean trouble.

A few scouts sent out on patrol in mid-October from Newbury had spotted a massive war party approaching and rushed back to spread the alarm. Everyone assumed the attack would fall on or near this strategic Connecticut River Valley community — so warning of the immediate danger went to nearby villages but never reached Royalton, some 40 miles away and of little strategic value. If it had, everyone would have fled to the nearest fortified blockhouse, common to many settlements on the frontier.

The Revolution in the northern and western hinterlands was a different kind of war from the one fought by massive armies on the heavily contested battlefields of the mid-Atlantic and southern colonies. In the backcountry from Maine to Illinois, hundreds of miles from the Atlantic coast, it was a war of stealth and lightning raids, a private war of retribution and revenge, a shadow war of spies and double agents. Even though the conflict is commonly thought of as a rebellion to replace British government with self-government, it was in fact a civil war as well, and like all civil wars it was especially brutal on non-combatants.

Some of these were loyalists: colonials who refused to rebel against King George. Political loyalties divided communities and pitted neighbors and family members against one another when they would not jettison one ideology for another. Rebel "Committees of Correspondence" brutally persecuted people who were loyal to the king. For loyalists there was no such thing as freedom of speech. [2] Some people were non-combatant—more or less neutral villagers who were sympathetic to neither side. Others were the indigenous people who had once traveled, hunted, traded, and made their own wars here. This was a conflict not of the natives' making, but one which they would have little choice but to join.

These were largely unsung men, women, and children who lived with the brutal realities and terrifying uncertainties of war at home, day in and day out for eight long years. Only a handful of these experiences was ever recorded.

What follows is one such story, its narrative spine based on the Zadock Steele memoir. It is one of the longest and most detailed of all Revolutionary captivity stories; but, although there were tens of thousands of prisoners taken in the war, Zadock Steele's account describes an underexamined facet of the Revolution: the experience of the people living with war on the northern frontiers—the loyalists, the members of militias, the non-combatants, the native peoples, and most central to this story, the prisoners taken by both sides.

Although these people lived in a backwater of the Revolution, their lives, as universal as they are singular, are a window on a much larger world. They tell us of the strategic importance and the brutal reality of a second front in the Revolution—the vulnerable northern frontier. Here the military role of indigenous peoples was crucial. Living side by side with the dedicated rebels and the more numerous indifferent citizens, there was an often hidden population of loyalists and spies.

In the unique and uncertain status of Vermont, we learn what a fragile union the early United States truly was. Moreover, the unfolding of events in Vermont before, during, and after the Revolution reveals that this small and sparsely populated region was a microcosm of the greater Revolutionary drama. Vermont was not one of the 13 states, but an independent republic, vulnerable to intense pressure from Great Britain to become neutral or even re-enter the British Empire.

In the friction between New York and Vermont, and among the various cultures in British prisoner-of-war camps, we see the durable regional characters and folkways that were established so early in colonial America. And finally, we see in Zadock's narrative of captivity and in his life story the veterans' preoccupation with establishing a record of their accomplishments and sacrifices, and the readiness of the public to preserve and absorb these raw materials of national identity.

ZADOCK STEELE

The son of an officer in the French and Indian War (also called the Seven Years' War, 1754-1763), Zadock Steele was born and raised on a farm in Ellington, Connecticut, near Hartford, along with his 12 brothers and sisters. Steele believed it was the civic duty of "every friend to the rights of man to be actively employed" in the Revolutionary cause.[3] But, like the vast majority of other citizen-soldiers, compelling personal matters eventually drew him home and away from the army before the end of the war.[4] Steele enlisted three times: in 1776, 1777, and 1778.[5] After his third term of service, he felt he had done his duty and made no apology for going home, although as everyone knew, the Continental Army was hard pressed to fill its ranks.[6] There is no reason to believe that Zadock's revolutionary zeal had flagged; it would soon be put to a test that he had never imagined.

Steele's father, James, and his three brothers, Aaron, James Jr., and Samuel, took up the cause for independence and entered the army as well.[7] Aaron, his oldest brother, was killed in battle at Chatham, New Jersey, and his father became so ill he could no longer serve. Zadock's younger brothers, Samuel and James Jr., however, remained in the army, the latter in training as a doctor.

With his father incapacitated, one brother dead, and two others in the war, Zadock—now the eldest son—took on new responsibilities. Chief among them were the prospects for the farm on which the family depended for sustenance. In Connecticut, agricultural land was becoming exhausted and overcrowded, and with warfare to the south and the west, Vermont was the only place in New England with so much unsettled land. The vast majority of Americans at the time were farmers and land was an invaluable but increasingly finite resource. James Sr., like many of his Connecticut neighbors, had acquired property on the central Vermont frontier, where townships were being organized and surveyed. James Steele would have heard of the fertile northern Connecticut and Champlain Valleys from veterans returning from the northern campaigns of the French and Indian War. The conflict had taken them to outposts such as Crown Point, Ticonderoga, the headwaters of the Connecticut River, and beyond.[8]

Between 1778 and 1780 much of the country had turned its attention away from the Revolution, confident that the British were about to withdraw. This was a widespread misconception fed by misleading newspaper accounts of negotiations between the Continental Congress and representatives from England.[9] Whatever their sympathies and however they may have seen the progress of the war, people were moving north, driven by a pressing need to find and settle new land. Between 1762 and 1770, Vermont's population had grown from about 400 to 5,000; by 1776 it had risen to 20,000, and by 1780, it stood at 30,000.[10] In spite of the risk of an attack from Canada, 10,000 people (most from Connecticut) had migrated to Vermont in those four war-torn years.

During the winter of 1779–1780, the Steele family made a decision to begin clearing and settling their plot of Vermont land, which now embodied their hopes for a better future no matter what the outcome of the war. So in the spring of 1780, Zadock set off on foot with a hired boy and a team of horses for a summer of back-breaking labor on the frontier. From Ellington, it would take him at least two weeks to walk the 140 miles to the new homestead in Randolph, a town just north of Royalton.

It is safe to assume that much value was placed on education in the Steele family. Zadock's grandfather, Stephen, was a minister, having graduated from Yale in 1718.[11] Zadock's uncle, Elisha, was also a Yale graduate; and Zadock's brother James was to be a doctor. Even though Zadock, in the opening page of his narrative, apologized for his lack of schooling, he may have had more of it than many colonial farmers. He could read and write, and knew enough arithmetic to conduct the business of farming. As might be expected of the grandson of an evangelical "new light" Yankee preacher, Zadock knew his Bible, and would fill his narrative with passages of scripture and excerpts from obscure British religious narrative verse.

Zadock had a dry, ironic Yankee wit that lay concealed most of the time beneath the stoic Calvinism of his Puritan upbringing. He kept his own counsel, was an obedient son and a dutiful soldier. Like other men and women of the time, he was accustomed to long days of hard physical labor, indifferent medical care, hunger, going barefoot most of the time, owning little clothing, hunting for his food, slaughtering and butchering animals, and to long, frequent church services driven by withering sermons. He did what was expected of him. He was stubborn. He was very sure of himself, but his self-confidence was a private matter, for his family would not have encouraged him to display it. He was not given to cockiness; he knew better than that. He was the third son of a tough Yankee farmer and soldier who himself was the son of an evangelical Puritan divine. Vanity and pride were not tolerated among his kind.

Zadock's reverence for learning may have been his most lasting legacy to his family of 11 children, all of whom would be raised on the farm in Randolph and, later, Brookfield, Vermont. One son, Hiram, would serve as a captain in the Civil War, then become a judge in New York state; Horace would become a lawyer and newspaperman; James, a lawyer and businessman; and Roswell would become a merchant. Another son, Solomon, a teacher and a magistrate, would marry Eliza Whyte, daughter of a distinguished Scottish surgeon, Dr. Joseph Whyte. The doctor, an accomplished artist and would paint a portrait of the patriarch Zadock in 1835. In this fine likeness, Zadock takes the viewer's measure with a shrewd, level gaze, leavened with a suggestion of mischief, irony, and humor. Although it may be artistic license, Zadock looks every inch the prosperous citizen, rather than the near-pauper his 1832 pension affidavit describes. There is in the portrait the beginning of a private smile—intelligent, generous, tolerant, inquisitive even in old age. He looks like a man who is hard to take unawares, a man who is not easily shaken.

THE WAR, FROM 1775 TO 1780

Although by 1780, the year of the Royalton Raid, most of the war's heavy fighting had moved south, conflict in the north country had been continuous since 1775. In fact, the region was as significant strategically as it had ever been.

It could be said, only half facetiously, that the American Revolution began and ended on Lake Champlain. In 1775 the lake was the site of the first rebel offensive victory: the capture of Fort Ticonderoga. In September 1783, the last of the rebel prisoners of war were released on the shores of Lake Champlain, not far from Ticonderoga, almost a year after the terms of a peace treaty had been negotiated in Paris.[12]

The Hudson River–Lake Champlain–St. Lawrence River–Great Lakes waterway was considered the most important transportation and communications route in North America: a "canal leading from New England and New York to the very bowels of Canada."[13] At one end of it sat New York City, British military headquarters in North America. At the other end were Montréal and Québec, British military headquarters of the Northern Department. The British controlled the Hudson River below West Point, and after 1777 they were unchallenged on Lake Champlain, the St. Lawrence River, and the Great Lakes. Throughout most of the war George Washington's headquarters were on the Hudson River near West Point (out of British control), giving the revolutionaries an opening from New England to the rest of the states and, most importantly, to Philadelphia, the seat of the Continental Congress.

In the Champlain Valley there was a movement afoot to take some action against the British as news of the April 1775 engagements at Lexington and Concord spread. Strategically located on the Hudson/Champlain waterway, Fort Ticonderoga made an easy mark and was captured by Ethan Allen, Benedict Arnold, and the Green Mountain Boys on May 10.

Following the June 1775 Battle of Bunker Hill just outside Boston, the Continental Congress decided on a bold offensive move: to invade and seize Canada—a pre-emptive strike in the fall of 1775 that would deprive the British of a base for attacking the rebellion from the north. In spite of some early successes, the invading American forces were forced to retreat the following year. Though the move postponed a British invasion from Canada, its failure awakened deep fears of a British counter-invasion accompanied by "ravages of Indians against the frontier."[14] In the meantime, Washington had managed to drive out the British forces occupying Boston. The American taste of success was short-lived and Washington very nearly lost the whole war at New York City in the summer of 1776.

The Battle of Trenton, New Jersey, in December 1776, was a crucial and altogether unexpected triumph for Washington and the Continental Army. Realizing at that point that the rebels constituted a force to be reckoned with, Britain's strategy for 1777 was to stage a pincer movement that would cut the colonies in two along the Champlain-Hudson waterway, thus isolating New England, the hotbed of rebellion, from the rest of the "revolted colonies."

The plan that followed was to initiate the series of events that eventually led to the Royalton Raid. The British decided to send one force south from Canada and another north from New York City. They would meet near Albany and the British could isolate New England from the rest of the states and turn their attention south of New York, where they would break the back of the rebellion and teach the colonies a lesson they would never forget. Initially successful, the British invasion from Canada, under General John Burgoyne, met with disaster in two decisive battles near Saratoga, New York, one on September 19 and the other on October 4. The lower jaw of the pincer never closed from the south, and Burgoyne and his entire army went down to defeat. Great Britain had to abandon its strategy for victory in the north and consider the possibility that she might very well lose the war.

The rebels, on the other hand, began to feel that they stood a good chance of winning. The rebel officer Nathaniel Green was nothing if not confident, saying, "We cannot conquer the British at once, but they cannot conquer us at all," while other rebels were heard to say, "[I]f Great Britain can't conquer us they can't govern us."[15]

Although the British still held New York City and soon regained naval command of Lake Champlain, they could neither control all of the vital waterway nor isolate New England. The principal military enterprise moved south to campaigns in New Jersey, Georgia, Virginia, the Carolinas, and the Ohio River Valley.

There were to be fundamental changes in the management of the war in Canada, too. On June 25, 1778, General Frederick Haldimand was appointed as the new military commander-in-chief and governor-general of Canada. Haldimand devised a three-part strategy: to prevent an American re-invasion of Canada; to establish an intelligence network to gather information and move couriers and agents in and out of the 13 rebellious colonies; and to send fast-moving war parties against strategic rebel frontier communities and forts, such as those in western Pennsylvania, northern New York, and New England. These raids would not decide the outcome of the war, Haldimand calculated, but they could be devastating on a local scale and would create a costly northern front for the revolutionaries to defend.

2. Lt. Gen. Sir Frederick Haldimand
Public Archives of Canada, Copy Neg. CO-18298.

The British filled the ranks of these raiding parties with British regular soldiers, German regiments, loyalists who had fled the colonies, French Canadians, and, perhaps most notably, with native warriors. These last would serve as shock troops with fearsome (if only partially deserved) reputations for savagery in battle. Perhaps of greater tactical importance, their tracking and woodcraft skills and intimate familiarity with the wilderness would be invaluable.[16] At a strategic level, neither side wanted to face Indians in battle, and as long as they could be enlisted as allies or committed to neutrality, they would not be opponents.

INDIANS

Native troops served on both sides in the American Revolution from virtually the beginning. Stockbridge warriors from western Massachusetts fought on the rebel side as early as the battle of Bunker Hill, killing British sentries with bows and arrows.[17] Solomon, a Stockbridge chief, declared at a 1775 meeting of many tribes at Albany:

> *When I ...considered and fully understood what this great king was going to do to us and what business he had sent his warriors on... I put him aside, I denied his authority, fire rose in my face, I took up my hatchet... I now bring it to you. My friends must take hold of it and rise up against the red coats that they may not do as they please...; they began this mischief, they have got proud and haughty, let us humble them; my tomahawk is sharp and already stained with their blood.*[18]

Solomon went on to say to the American representatives:

> *Wherever you go we will be by your side...our bones will lay with yours...If we are conquered, our lands go with yours, but if we are victorious, we hope you will help us to recover our rights.*[19]

But most native peoples were quick to see the American Revolution as a civil war among Englishmen, and, thinking at first that they had little at stake, wanted nothing to do with it. In May 1775, while attending the same Albany meeting as Solomon, a New York Mohawk chief named Little Abraham declared, "White people may settle [their] own quarrels; we shall never meddle as long as we are let alone."[20]

In Maine, with news of revolution spreading like wildfire, an Abenaki woman was heard to say on May 16, 1775:

> *[T]he men could not hunt, eat or sleep; keep calling together every night. Every night all night. O, straing English men kill one another. I think the world is coming to an end.*[21]

In many ways, the colonial world had become the Indians' world. In the more than 150 years since contact in this region, the two cultures — the European and the Amerindian — had developed complex commercial, kinship, religious, military, and political relationships. Many natives had come to know and trust British officials, such as Sir William Johnson, a Mohawk Valley land baron and the head of the British Indian Department. His protégé, the influential, Dartmouth-educated Mohawk chief, Joseph Brant, predictably would side with the British, relying on their assurances to protect Indian lands from encroaching settlers. He told the British that "whoever gained the most Indians, would win the continent."[22]

From the British point of view, the loyalty of Indian tribes from the Northeast, the Deep South, the Ohio River Valley, and the Great Lakes would be strategically crucial. Native peoples could provide a buffer between the populations in the 13 states and British Canada, and, if inclined, they could furnish manpower for frontier raids.

Of these peoples, one group was of greater significance than any other. Comprised of the Mohawk, Onondaga, Oneida, Cayuga, Seneca, and Tuscarora tribes, the Six Nations of the Iroquois Confederacy of upstate New York formed the most populous and powerful Indian federation in the region. Their ancestral land stretched from Lake Champlain west to Niagara Falls, territory that both the British and the rebels saw as one of the paths for victory in the larger conflict. If either side was to attempt an invasion across the U.S.-Canadian border, they would have to go through Iroquois country, making the alignment of the Iroquois of the utmost importance to both Great Britain and the United States.[23]

There was another group with close ethnic, cultural and political ties to the Six Nations; called "The Canada Indians" by the British, it supplied many of the warriors for raids on Vermont and the Champlain Valley. Also known as the Seven Nations, these people lived in seven discrete and widely separated settlements in the St. Lawrence River Valley. Each village contained a mix of native peoples drawn from Canada, New England, New York, and even farther south and west: 1. *Oswegatchie* (consisting of Cayuga and Onondaga); 2. St. Regis or *Akwesasne* (consisting of Abenaki, Cayuga, and Onondaga); 3. Lake of the Two Mountains or *Oka* (consisting of Iroquois, Algonquin, and Nippissing); 4. *Caughnawaga/Kahnawake* or Sault St. Louis (consisting of Mohawk, Oneida, and Onondaga); 5. St. Francis or *Odanak* (Abenaki); 6. Becancour (Abenaki); 7. Lorette (Huron).[24]

3. Abenaki Couple, an 18th-century watercolor by an unknown artist. Courtesy of the City of Montréal Records Management & Archives, Montréal, Canada.

Of the Seven Nations, the largest and most politically influential community was Kahnawake—the source of most of the warriors in the war party that attacked Royalton. Although the tribe's name was commonly spelled "Caughnawaga" in 18th-century documents, this book will use "Kahnawake," the spelling that predates "Caughnawaga" and is now preferred by the tribe.[25] Living on the south bank of the St. Lawrence River directly opposite Montréal, the people of Kahnawake were primarily Iroquoian, originally from New York State. Some came from a Mohawk village called Kahnawake, so that's what they called their new home in Canada. As early as 1670, they came north from the Mohawk Valley, where they had first encountered and been converted by Jesuit missionaries.[26] By 1778 Kahnawake had a population of over 700, with at least 300 warriors, nearly all unfriendly to the rebel cause.[27] It was the site of the council fire of the Seven Nations, the place where delegates from other villages came for debates and discussions that affected all of them.

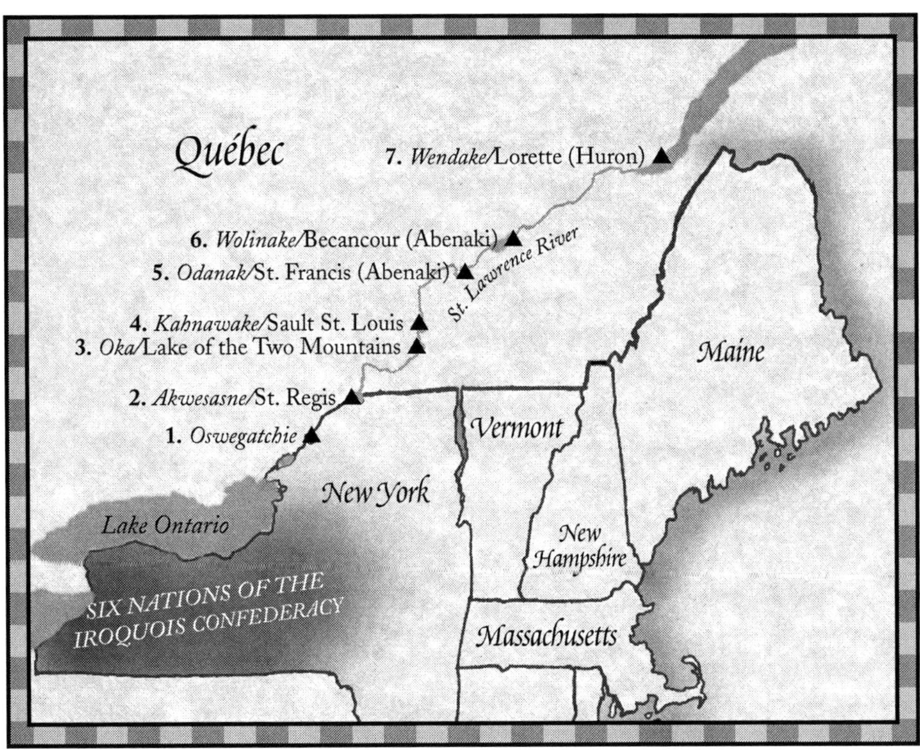

MAP 1. The Villages of the Seven Nations of Canada.

Like virtually all the native peoples of the Northeast, the Kahnawakes had been swept up in a series of wars between Great Britain and France that permanently fractured Indian cultures throughout the region. As soon as the century of British-French warfare that had displaced so many Indians was over in 1760, settlers from southern New England began flooding north into a large and promising section of country that had long been a battleground in the intercolonial wars. Bounded on the west by the Champlain Valley, on the east by the Connecticut River Valley and New Hampshire's White Mountains, the region that was eventually to become Vermont appeared to be sparsely inhabited. The new settlers found scattered, seminomadic family bands of Abenaki hunters, a fraction of the numbers that once had lived here—reduced by warfare and, perhaps more devastating, epidemics of European diseases.[28] As empty as it seemed, these newcomers had not discovered virgin territory, but, as the historian Francis Jennings evocatively named it, "a widowed land."[29] Within 15 years, the natives who had been driven out of these ancestral lands found themselves caught in the crossfire of another war—the American Revolution.

In the intense competition for the loyalty of native peoples, the British prevailed. They formed alliances with several Canadian tribes, four of the six Iroquois nations of New York, and many others farther south and west in the Ohio River Valley. The British considered the Indians amply compensated for their allegiance with gifts of weapons and supplies, and therefore more or less within the British chain of command. But it was far more complicated than that.[30] The Indians were not mercenaries and when they entered the fight and took sides, they did so for their own reasons—often because they saw ways in which they could take advantage of the war to advance their own aims.[31] Paramount among these was the protection of ancestral rights to land.

Indians in general saw the British as guarantors of their territorial rights and the American colonists as invaders determined to steal their land. One of the provisions of the 1774 Québec Act that American colonists had hated most was the prohibition on settlement of land west and northwest of the Appalachian Mountains. This was Indian country, protected by the British from incursion and settlement but coveted by settlers determined to move west. Native peoples in this unsettled country, like those of the Six Nations, continued to live by traditional ways and controlled vast territories, and they fully intended to keep possession of their land. For the Seven Nations of Canada, especially the Abenakis, whose homelands were in northern New England, the hope was that with a British victory they might one day reoccupy these grounds.

VERMONT

But even as the Revolution began, it was too late; the land rush after 1760 to the area that was to become Vermont was irreversible. Because this region, so long a battleground, had not been colonized, the matter of who had jurisdiction remained unresolved: was it New Hampshire, New York, or perhaps even Massachusetts?

New Hampshire's governor decided that the land between Lake Champlain and the Connecticut River was his to dispose of and began to distribute large parcels to speculators. By 1764, 112 townships totaling three million acres had been granted and the area became known as the New Hampshire Grants. (It was not to assume the name of Vermont for another 13 years.) Enraged, New York claimed jurisdiction and successfully petitioned the king of England in 1765 to settle the boundary dispute in its favor; the New Hampshire Grants then officially became part of New York, and over the next ten years that colony made land grants amounting to half a million acres.[32]

People continued to pour in and by 1775 there were 20,000 settlers in the New Hampshire Grants, the majority from Connecticut, with large numbers from

Massachusetts as well.[33] These people, accustomed to the democratic New England town meeting, became resentful of New York's quasi-feudal, autocratic brand of governance. Nor did they want to be governed by New Hampshire. Most of the people of the Grants wanted to govern themselves, and among the most vociferous was the fiery Connecticut land speculator Ethan Allen. As already noted, his attack on Fort Ticonderoga was to be the first successful offensive action of the colonial resistance.[34]

Herein lies a remarkable irony. Despite this early, eager entry into the rebellion and its strategic position along the porous northern border with Canada, Vermont was never to be a part of the United States during the Revolutionary War. Many of its inhabitants wanted the territory to become the 14th state, independent of New York, New Hampshire, *and* Great Britain, thereby asserting the same right that the other 13 colonies claimed in the Declaration of Independence: that a government derives its legitimacy "from the consent of the governed."

New York refused to allow the disputed territory to secede. Defiant, the Grants renamed itself "Vermont" and on June 4, 1777, became an independent republic. At the same time, a massive British offensive was under way. General John Burgoyne and an invasion army of 7,000 troops were moving south from Canada across Lake Champlain. Vermont's act neither endeared it to Congress nor exempted it from the approaching attack. Even though Burgoyne went down to defeat at Saratoga, New York, in the fall of 1777, the Champlain Valley remained a battleground and Vermonters a thorn in the British side. General Haldimand considered them to be

> *[v]ery formidable enemies, having been from their earliest contests ...continually in arms. They are in every respect better provided than the Continental Troops and their principals more determined.*[35]

By 1780 most of the northern population had been driven to southern Vermont or even farther south by British raids from Canada, and the north had become a dangerous no-man's land. A diagonal line of forts stretched across central Vermont from the southern end of Lake Champlain to Newbury. This line marked the frontier, and Vermont's governing council warned settlers it could not defend them north of it.[36] To live above the line was to live in constant danger of attack from Canada.

Of greater strategic import than these cross-border hit-and-run raids was another large-scale invasion, and both the rebels and the British in Canada continued to make their respective plans for a massive assault as the war progressed. The Champlain Valley, northern Vermont, and the Connecticut River Valley were the routes of choice for both sides. To that end, forward posts and accurate intelligence were of the utmost importance. The British Secret Service operated an espionage network from an outpost called the Loyal Blockhouse on North Hero Island in Lake Champlain.

High on the Connecticut River, Newbury, Vermont, was the northernmost settlement of any size in New England and the rebel counterpart to the Loyal Blockhouse. It was the home of General Jacob Bayley, an influential militia officer and public figure who corresponded heavily with George Washington, with whom he had served in the early years of the war. Bayley operated an espionage network from Newbury that gathered information about British military operations and, equally worrisome to the British, collaborated with a French-Canadian faction in Québec dedicated to the overthrow of British rule in Canada.[37] In early 1779 a large barracks and warehouses for provisions were being built at Newbury in readiness for an influx of rebel troops.[38] In a rare example of Indian alliance with the revolutionaries, there was a detachment of 50 Abenaki scouts stationed at Newbury commanded by Lewis Vincent, a Kahnawake graduate of Dartmouth.[39] For the British no place was a more disquieting source of trouble on the northern frontier than this town, also known by its Abenaki name, Coös or Cowass.

In spite of its supply depot, the settlement was not well defended and the few troops there were poorly armed and clothed. The people felt vulnerable and the place was gripped with anxiety.[40] Throughout 1780, Bayley and other leaders in both Vermont and New Hampshire had been writing to Washington, urging him to mount a reinvasion of Canada and pleading with him to send more troops to protect the northern frontier.[41] Accompanying these entreaties were offers of immense reserves of grain and other provisions that could be used to feed continental troops posted to the upper Connecticut River Valley, or elsewhere for that matter.[42] Washington not only advised them to keep their food supplies and to use local militias to guard them, but he declared his armies too short of men and arms to reinforce the northern frontiers, whether New England, New York, or Pennsylvania—all equally exposed and under-defended. He had in fact just sent an emergency request to the governors of Massachusetts, Connecticut, and New Hampshire for the loan of 5,000 muskets with ammunition to be sent at once to Fishkill, New York, adjacent to Continental Army headquarters.[43]

In spite of Bayley's express worries about being attacked, Congress had ordered the withdrawal of the small number of Continental Army troops at Newbury and other frontier posts for redeployment to other theaters of the war.[44] The fact that Vermont was not one of the United States and that it was involved in a bitter dispute about sovereignty with both New York and New Hampshire made matters complicated. As commander-in-chief, Washington's hands were tied with respect to devoting Continental Army troops or materiel to the defense of an independent republic, no matter how closely Vermont and U.S. interests were aligned. Without approval from the Continental Congress there was little he could do.[45] Though Washington was well aware of the strategic importance of northern Vermont and the rest of the frontier, he did not share Bayley's sense of urgency about the threat from Canada.

In a letter written in March 1780, Washington told Bayley that his spies in Canada had led him to believe that there was little danger of trouble from that quarter. Since then, Bayley had written regularly to Washington about the massing of British troops on the border and warships in Lake Champlain.[46]

Bayley's intelligence was sound—better than Washington's. The British offensive in the north had in fact taken a ferocious turn. New York, Pennsylvania, and Virginia had already been hit hard early in the summer, and more of the same was on the way—it was part of a British strategy to terrorize the hinterland. Frederick Haldimand, the British commander-in-chief in Canada, had been planning all summer "to send a strong detachment into the enemy's country by way of Lake Champlain...in order to destroy their provisions of grain and other supplies expected from that frontier."[47] Well-planned assaults were poised to strike settlements along the New York frontier at Lake George and in the Mohawk Valley north of Albany.

Although the party moving into Vermont was substantial in size, it was an offshoot of the overall British plan to attack New York. The Vermont raid was an 11th hour improvisation designed to redistribute and reassign the unexpectedly large number of Indian warriors who answered the call to fill the ranks of the New York raids. It was, the British reckoned, an unexpected and fortuitous opportunity to create an additional mission to strike the stronghold on the upper Connecticut River Valley.

What was more, Bayley represented a prize captive. Knowing Vermont's troubled relationship with the Continental Congress, the British Secret Service was brewing a plan to tempt Vermont into neutrality or possibly even to subvert its revolutionary loyalty.[48] Bayley was a powerful arch-rebel and the British saw him as a serious, perhaps even insurmountable, obstacle to any such plans for meddling in Vermont's internal affairs.

* * *

The British knew they could do a great deal of damage if they attacked Newbury.[49] So it is with Newbury that this story begins, for Newbury was the original target of the war party that sacked Royalton.

In September 1780, when General Bayley learned through his spies about the force gathering at St. John's, just north of the border, he dispatched scouting parties to find out where it was headed and reported the situation to Washington:

> *Two men we sent to Onion River was taken or killed.*[50] *Two days after, two others discovered the enemy advancing but our commander took no notice of it for three days.*

For some reason an officer identified by Bayley only as "our commander" who "took no notice of it for three days" had apparently no idea of the true size of the offensive and the threat it posed. Perhaps he thought it was a false alarm, but the townspeople were in a state of extreme apprehension.[51]

> *When the people were so urgent he* (the "commander") *sent five men who were lost in the woods and gave no intelligence, but as I could not be satisfied with their ability I sent three of the inhabitants who returned and gave intelligence that the enemy was advancing in a large body towards this place, and another smaller body towards the river 40 miles below.*[52]

But when the British officer in charge of the approaching raiding party realized he had been discovered he made a quick decision and ordered the entire command to change course and avoid Newbury.

By the time Bayley's scouts reported back to Newbury, the British force had moved south and it was too late to spread the word to any but the closest settlements, leaving Royalton and other towns on the White River in the dark and at risk.

PART I
THE RAID

VERMONT

Some Hunters have travelled thro this Wilderness, from Welds River, to Lake Memfrimagog, & judged the shortest distance this way to be about 50 Miles.

This way Captives have been carried from New Hampshire to Canada

Only the Mouth of this River is known to ye English

These Branches are only Conjectural

This Road was cut by the New Hampshire Forces employd against Canada in 1759

the communication with that County

This way Captives have been carried by the Indians

Gen.l Nicholsons built on occasion of the Canada Expedition but now demolished

N.B. Connecticut River has been actually

Choice White Pines and good Land

Choice White Pines and Good Land

LAKE CHAMPLAIN

Leaperriere
Bolton
Worster
Lunenbourg
Shelburne
S.t George
French River
Waterford
Middlesex
Brothers
Charlotte
Hinesbourg
Durbury
Moretown
Berlin
Barnet
Ferrisbourg
Mons.r de Contracoeuse
Pocock
Peacham
Welds River
Ryegate
Connecticut R.
Lyman
Gunsth
Loring
Bath
Landaff
Franconia
Ammonoosuck R.
Panton
New Heaven
Otter Creek
Topsham
Weybridge
Middlebury
Newbury
Havenhill
Lincoln
Mahsunquamosse R.
Corinth
Waits town
Intervals
Addison
Waterbury
Salisbury
Fairfield
Umpammonoosuck R.
Bridport
Shoreham
Eastham
Malden
Cohass
Fairlee
Piermont
Warren
Orwell
Stratford
Tunbridge
Thetford
Orford
Wentworth
Hastings Brook
Leister
Royalton
Sharon
Little
Lime
Dorchester
Rumney
Neshobe
Sudbury
Drowned Lands
Dunham
Stockbridge
Norwich
Hanover
Cockermouth
Bernard
Pomfret
Hartford
White R.
Dartmouth College
Canaan
Waterqueechy R.
Hubbardton
Pittsford
Killington
White River Falls
Cardigan
Lebanon
New Plymouth
Bridgewater
Woodstock
Bloods River
Relhan
Grafton
Castleton
Rutland
Otter River
Severance Brook
New Chester
Hertford
Plainfield
Shrewsbury
Waterqueechy Falls
Grantham
Clarendon
Saltash
Windsor
Protectworth
bounds
Alexandria
Poultney
Reading
Cavendish
Corinth
Smiths R.
New Chester
Wood Creek
Wells
Tinmouth
Wallingford
Weathersfield
Croydon
Heidlebourg
New Britain
Black R.
Connecticut
Sugar River
Sunnapee Pond
Salisbury
LINE
Clermont
Newport
Dantzick
Perrys Town
Kyasarge M.t
Boscawen
Danby
Harwich
Green
Pawlet
CURVE
Plamstead
Unity
Rye Town
Little Sugar R.
Rupert
Dorset
Brumley
Lempster
N.o 8
COUNTY
Contoocook R.
Thomlinson
Rockingham
N.o 4
Ackworth
New Concord
New Hopkinton
Manchester
Winhall
Charles Town
Sandgate
Hillsborough
Henniker
Seatons R.
Westminster
Alstead
Marlow
Weare Town
Arlington
Sunderland
West River
Walpole
OF
N.o 7
Mason
Stratton
Townshend
Gilsum
Limerick
Proprietors Lands reserved
Shaftsbury
Glassenbury
New Fane
Pultney
Ashuelot R.
N.o 6
Dublin
New Boston
Fulham
Westmoreland
HILLSBOROUGH
Keene
CHESHIRE
Monadnock Mountains
Peterborough
Lyndeborough
Bennington
Woodford
New Marlborough
Bratleborough
Chesterfield
Swansey
N.o 5
Pemigewasset River

CHAPTER 1

ZADOCK

"Being in my twenty-second year, I came to Randolph, in the State of Vermont."

Zadock Steele Narrative

OCTOBER 15, 1780. Zadock Steele was alone in the woods for the first time all year. Just the day before, the hired boy had set out for Connecticut the way he had come—the way they had both come six months ago. It was April then and they had walked, driving the team of horses ahead of them, drawing the wagon laden with food, tools, weapons, and seed for planting. The distance was about 140 miles and it had taken two weeks to reach Randolph, stopping for the night at farmhouses, sleeping in barns. They had followed the Connecticut River, crossing it once on a ferry so they could go north on the west side.

Once Zadock and the boy had passed out of Massachusetts and entered Vermont, the road became rougher, in places impassable owing to the runoff of spring melt water. Where the mud had very nearly swallowed them whole, they had emptied the wagon and put their shoulders to the wheel to help the horses, cutting saplings to lay in the way to keep the wheels from sinking deeper into the mud. When the road vanished altogether, they seized their axes and felled trees to make a new passage. They had toiled north up the river like this. There were occasional settlements where they could put up for the night, but just as often they had camped and slept rough.

Then they had reached the White River, 70 miles into Vermont, and for another 35 miles followed it west. The two young men were used to the tidy farms, cleared land, and tilled fields of Connecticut. Now they were seeing how Connecticut must have looked when it was first settled. There were occasional clearings with low-slung log cabins, crude shelters, bottomless black mud in livestock pens, untethered swine rooting in the woods where they ran wild most of the year. Along the banks of the White River many huge trees had been felled to make way for new families, coming all the time.

Where people had made their pitch, they cut some trees near the dwellings, but beyond that they girdled them, killing them, so that Zadock and the boy passed through stands of immense dead trees. After a couple of years the settlers would burn the trees where they stood or would topple them with teams of oxen and then burn them. The remains lay in charred ruins as Zadock and the boy passed by, some still hot and smoking. Fire had enriched the soil and for a few years the harvests were known to be good.[1] The people had drawn the unburned roots aside and formed them into ragged lines as fencing for pastures.[2] Where trees were felled on steep slopes, banks were already eroding. But these were a migrant people and if the soil gave out or washed away, as it had in Connecticut, they would move on, abandoning one homestead to begin another.[3]

Sometimes they had traveled along the bank or the beach where the river was shallow and wide. Whenever the river passed through a steep-sided canyon, they had had to veer away following a muddy track that climbed high into the hills before taking them back to the river.[4]

The last settlement of any size they had gone through was Royalton. There were at least 40 families there in widely separated clearings. Royalton had not lost its raw look, but it already had a grist mill, a saw mill, and a blacksmith.[5] After that came Bethel, another six miles up the White. It was an outpost with a new blockhouse and a few families in cabins and hovels, no more. They had turned north a few miles before reaching it and followed the Second Branch of the White River for ten miles. The forest grew right to the edge of the river and it towered over them.

Along the Second Branch they had crossed into the township of Randolph—hardly more than an idea, a rectangle six miles square on a survey map with no fort, no mill, no meeting house, only a few clearings and huts. When Zadock and the boy had come to the ax slash on the tree they had been looking for, just where a swift creek spilled out from a narrow drainage, they had turned west, following the watercourse and then veering into the forest to follow a faint track marked by blazes until they came to the place.[6]

Here they had found the unfinished log cabin left by the man from whom Zadock's father had bought the land. Here they had spent the summer, living on the food they had brought and what they could gather, hunt down, or catch; clearing and burning brush; girdling the immense trees; tilling the soil where a little sunlight spilled into their clearing; planting subsistence crops; cutting firewood; laying in feed for the horses; finishing the cabin, making it fit for winter. It was a beginning.

4. Typical 18th-Century Homestead, from *A Vermont Settler's Story*, by Seth Hubbell.

Now it was October, the end of the season. As in the spring, on some days the sky was nearly black with flights of passenger pigeons flying south. The boy was walking back to Connecticut, but Zadock was going to spend the winter at the cabin, alone except for the horses and the nearest neighbors, six miles away. In Randolph there had been a congenial company all summer of other young men from Ellington, Connecticut. For five days a week they had camped in the woods on their plots, building, clearing, planting, and spending weekends with families in Royalton, 12 miles away, where they had attended divine services. They all planned to go south to Connecticut for the winter.[7]

Zadock had spent all of his 21 years in his family's crowded Connecticut household or among fellow soldiers in the Continental Army. He had never lived alone. He had never had to endure the cold of a northern winter, though the winter of 1776-1777, in the field with the army in New Jersey, had been severe enough. Many told him it was just as bad as Valley Forge the following year. Zadock was under no illusions as to the prodigious amount of work, ingenuity, and resourcefulness it would take to keep from freezing or starving. Even a minor injury could be a death warrant if it should lead to infection or prevent the gathering of firewood.

Young men like Zadock usually spent only summers for two or three years before making a permanent home in Vermont. But by spending the winter here Zadock would be able to make an early start on planting in the spring. Then his father and the family would come north and settle, leaving the war behind.

Zadock had not dwelt on the war that summer. It had become a distant memory; setting aside provision for winter was the task at hand, and if he failed in this, the war would hardly matter.

It was known that sometimes there were Mohawks or, more often, Abenakis in the woods. Some were passing through from Canadian villages, but there were a few Abenaki families who had never left, and they befriended some of the settlers. They would appear without warning at a man's door demanding hospitality—something Zadock and the others on the frontier were not

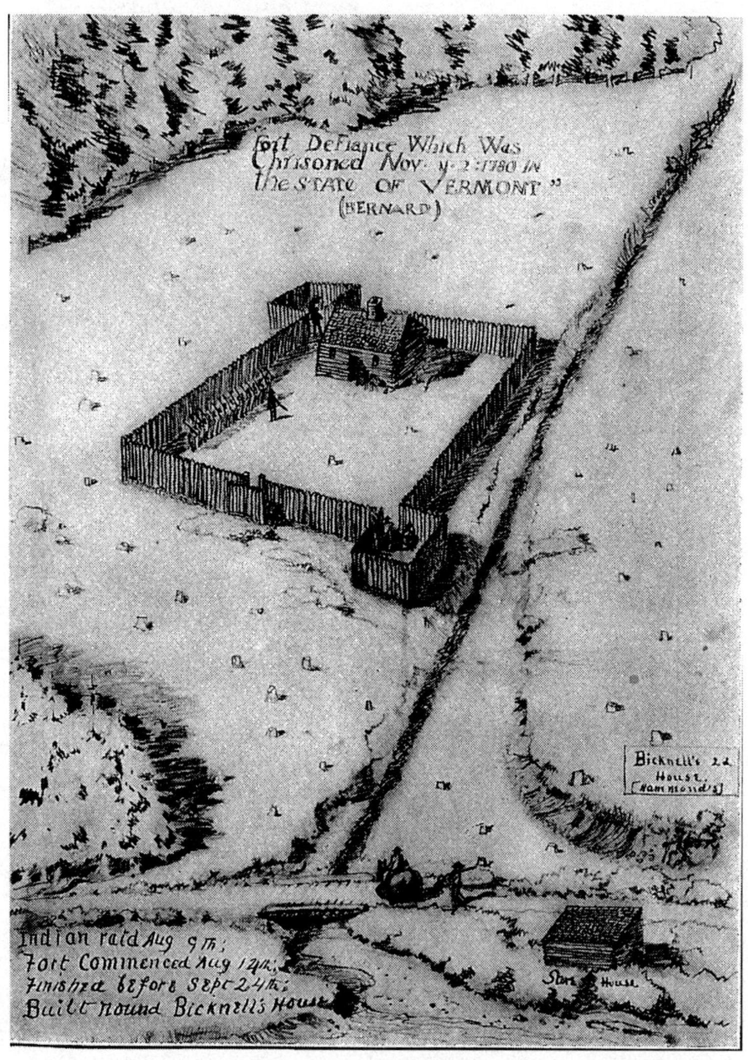

5. Fort Defiance at Barnard, Vermont, from *History of Royalton*, by Evelyn Lovejoy.

6. American Militiamen as seen by a German Observer at the Time of the Revolution, probably wearing fringed jackets and trousers. Their hats are inscribed "CONGRESS", so they are not Vermonters, but they would bear a resemblance to Vermont militia. From *Canada Invaded*, by George Stanley, the H.K. Bird Collection.

unaccustomed to. They had all grown up in the company of the remnants of Pequot, Mohegan, and other tribes that once populated Connecticut. The town of Lebanon, Connecticut, where Zadock's Royalton neighbors, the Hutchinsons, hailed from, was the site of Moor's Indian Charity School before it moved to Hanover, New Hampshire, in 1770 and became Dartmouth College. The Hutchinson boys even had several friends among the Indian student body at Moor's.[8]

The colonists on the Vermont frontier never fully trusted the Indians who would sometimes appear, apparently out of nowhere, because so many of them were known to have joined with the British. This was deeply troubling to these settlers. They had grown up with family stories and the Puritan tradition that Indians were steeped in satanic evil, that they were capable of mindless brutality and were beyond the reach of reason or human feeling. If the Indians had reasons beyond primitive savagery to fight on the side of the British, the people here did not know what they might be.

What they did know was that Indian and Tory raiding parties had descended on Vermont two years prior. All the people living on the Onion River to the north had been burned out and driven south in August 1778, and then two months later a much larger war party had swept down Lake Champlain and struck all the farms on the Otter Creek, burning everything as far as Middlebury and taking many prisoners back to Canada.[9] In anticipation of further such attacks, in the fall of 1780 a force of 150 Vermonters was gathering at newly built forts in the Champlain Valley towns of Pittsford and Castleton, the most likely area for a major British offensive against Vermont.[10]

On the other hand, attacks by either Indians or the British were unknown on the east slope of the Green Mountains—at least prior to 1780, when small enemy scouting parties were encountered in midsummer by local Vermont militias sent out to probe the forest.[11] And then, in the middle of September a shudder had rippled through the settlements along the White River Valley. There had been surprise attacks on two neighboring towns. Zadock remembered it well:

> *[H]earing that several of the inhabitants of Barnard and Bethel was taken prisoners by the Indians and caryed to Canedy, I, with others then in town, formed in a milishe company, chose our own officers, kept gareson and scouted up and down the wood, joyning the troops for Bethel fort.*[12]

The local militia was a mere handful of men, capable of not a great deal more than patrolling the forest and sounding the alarm at the approach of the enemy. Still, with militia on guard at Bethel and other frontier towns, the people of Royalton had reason to feel they would at least have timely warning of danger. In fact they had felt safe enough to dismantle their fort and transport the timbers to Bethel, where it had been reassembled in response to the September alarm. They did not grow complacent, but the people of Royalton at least felt they were no longer on the vulnerable, ragged edge of settlement.

* * *

On the night of October 15th the Havens family was up late celebrating and making ready for the marriage of Lorenza Havens to Thomas Pember, now boarding with them and awaiting the arrival of his father from Connecticut. The patriarch Robert Havens was Royalton's first settler and had lived there for nine years. He had gone to bed with a mind to his sheep, still foraging but out of sight back in the forest as the sun set. He would fetch them in the morning.

Elias Stevens, a prominent citizen and one of Zadock's prime informants, had told his wife, Sarah, that he would be up at dawn and would drive his team of oxen two miles down the White River to a clearing where he would be pulling stumps. He wanted them out and hauled off before frost turned the earth to iron.

Hannah Handy's mind was occupied with a dozen different things. With less and less daylight as October lengthened, there was hardly enough time for the household chores. As she stirred a kettle over the cooking fire, she considered her son Michael, now ten and able to do nearly half a man's work every day. As for Lucretia, who was three, it would be only a few more years before she could do most of a woman's work herself.

George Avery, who lived just over the town line in the neighboring village of Sharon and later wrote a memoir of his own, was 21 years old and had recently finished a season in the Connecticut militia, stationed in Milford, Connecticut.[13] He was at once naive, cocky, and impulsive.

> *I had left my parents care and theire good rules and admonitions,* he wrote. *I was an unsteady youth, a giddy youth with vain expectations to be something in the world.*[14] *I lived a careless loose life with other comerads of the same cast.*

His carefree life notwithstanding, his normally sound and peaceful sleep was plagued that night by nightmares.

> *I dreamed I was beset by serpents the most hideous and numerous that I ever saw, and awoke in the horrible fright; I was soone asleep again, and dreamed of being besett by Indians and as frightfully awakened as before. But haveing no faith in dreams, my fears soone vanished.*[15]

Lieutenant Richard Houghton, of His Britannic Majesty's 53rd Regiment of Foot, knew he had a long night ahead. He had been marching with his scattered and unruly command for nearly two weeks. He and the raiding party were camped in what he hoped was silence and secrecy on a hilltop in Tunbridge, poised to move at dawn. He had sent out scouts to reconnoiter and they were under strict orders to refrain from violence and to return by dark. They were to build no fires and make no sound all night long. They would attack at first light. They would sweep down the First Branch of the White River, striking every house. Any gunfire would immediately warn the inhabitants down stream, so the attack would be silent—not a shot, not a yell. The surprise and terror would be shocking, overwhelming.

CHAPTER 2

ATTACK

"They were committing ravages, killing the inhabitants, destroying property, burning all the buildings, killing the cattle, pillaging the houses, and taking captives."[1]

ROYALTON, VERMONT, OCTOBER 16, 1780, 8:00 AM. Elias Stevens—running hard. His dog, cutting back and forth, behind and to the side, thinking, maybe, it's a game. Stones in the track, polished roots, hardened ruts from wagon wheels. The dog slicing in front of Stevens, too close, Stevens going down, then up again quickly.

Two hundred sixty-five Indian warriors behind Stevens, making no noise, except for the sound of their running, a strange thudding and rustling. The raid had begun an hour ago. Stevens, trying to return to his house and wife, had encountered women and children running, the Indians still upriver, but not far and coming fast. He had turned and joined the townsfolk in flight, not knowing what might have befallen his family, house, livestock.

* * *

After it was all over—after the burning, the slaughtering, the killing, the scalping, the plundering, the taking of prisoners, after that was all over—Robert Havens remembered hearing just at daybreak a sound like sheep or cattle racing through water, yet not quite like that. He remembered the rising sun, then a dog barking, then this sound, the likes of which he had never heard before. Havens, on a hill looking after his sheep when it began, could see some of his neighbors' dwellings. They squatted in small, ragged clearings in the otherwise unbroken hardwood forest along both banks of the First Branch, stretching about two miles downstream to the junction of the Branch and the White River itself. People had built in the narrow bottoms and benches along the Branch and the River, where they would be able to plant and tend crops most easily. Back from the watercourses the land rose sharply into steep shoulders and gullies forested with immense and ancient trees, now ablaze with autumn color. Robert Havens, Royalton's first settler, had come here only nine years before.[2] The harvest had been good this year, his sheep flock was now expanding and he had a fat hog to butcher for the coming wedding of his daughter to Tom Pember.

Havens, watching his house from just above, was wondering if wolves had set the dogs to barking and the livestock to running. Then he saw the Indians pouring into his dooryard from the forest. Some rushed into the house; Havens heard the cries of his wife and sons. Unarmed, Havens did not go to their rescue, instead finding a downed hollow tree and concealing himself within it. He knew that single-handed counter-attack would have been a death warrant. He also knew that any men the Indians captured they would take with them as prisoners. Dead or captive—either way he would have been useless to his family. Nor did he try to spread the alarm: The raiders stayed at his house all day and at 62 years of age he was not as agile as he once had been, so in the end Havens kept to his hiding place and listened to the cries of his neighbors as the attack tore through the settlement.[3]

Before concealing himself, Havens had seen a flash of polished brass or maybe silver—the gorget of a British officer. Because of the small British and Indian scouting parties lurking in the forest, Havens and the other settlers knew perfectly well that the war had not passed them by. But a force of this size was unheard of. The people of Royalton had no idea of the scale of the British autumn offensive in the north. Assaults like this were at the same moment descending on settlements along the New York frontier at Lake George and in the Mohawk Valley north of Albany.

* * *

In Royalton the attack moved very fast. Witnesses later remembered that the Indians had been so silent that only a few settlers were able to flee to spread the alarm. One villager later wrote, "Like the messenger of death, they were scarcely seen till felt."[4]

No one could tell how many Indians there were. They had spread out and seemed to be everywhere at once. Each time they came to a house, a few would burst in and the main body would move on to the next, so that their progress seemed relentless. A few people were able to stay in front of the headlong attack and warn the households they came to, telling the people in each one to drop everything and run.

When the Indians racing down the First Branch reached its junction with the White River, they formed two groups, one going upstream and another downstream. Some settlers fled along the White toward Bethel, where they knew there was a fort. Others fled downstream, where there were more settlements, more people, and scattered companies of militia. They thought, perhaps, that they could outrun the pursuit in that direction.

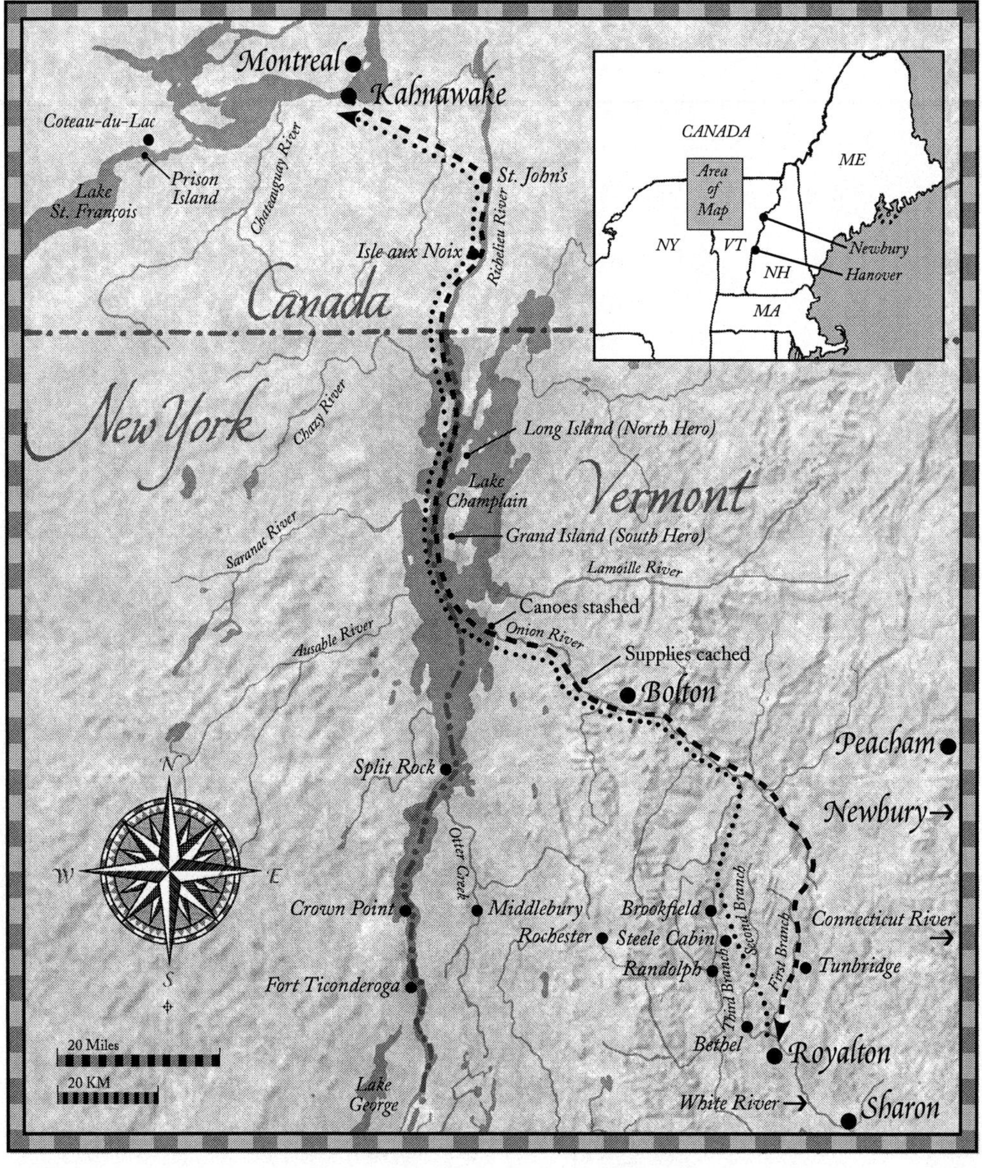

MAP 2. Route of the Raiding Party between Kahnawake and Royalton.

Royalton, 9:00 am. Daniel Havens, Robert's son, and his soon-to-be brother-in-law, Thomas Pember, were going out to look after their flock of sheep. As they entered the barnyard, they saw a body of Indians pouring out of the forest and coming at them fast. One witness remembered later that

> *Mr. Thomas Pember stept at the door and cry'd "may the lord have mercy on us, there is a thousand Indians upon us."* [5]

Daniel and Thomas turned and ran. Daniel jumped down the bank of the river and ducked under a log where he remained concealed. The pursuing Indians rushed past. Thomas Pember was a fast runner and stuck to the road, where he might have outrun the pursuit, but one Indian hit him with a short spear. Pember kept running but could not keep it up. He fell, still alive, and the warriors were upon him. One man grabbed a fistful of his hair, pulled it tight, then carved a five-inch circle with his knife around the top of Pember's head, leaned down, fastened his teeth onto the loosened flap of skin and reared back, ripping off the scalp, leaving a bloody circle on the dying man's head. [6] Daniel slipped unseen down the bank to look for cover so he could move downstream and warn the rest of the town.

* * *

Lieutenant Richard Houghton came hard on the heels of the first Indians who spilled into the small room of the Havens house and he came face to face with a frail and terrified Mrs. Havens. She was ill with consumption. When her condition became apparent to him, Houghton saw to it that the warriors carried her out of the house and clothed her in a quilt and her husband's hat and shoes.

Houghton was a perfect gentleman by all accounts—considering his assignment was to destroy the town. A pale, lean, hard-looking man, he spoke with the cultivated accent of the English landed gentry. He hadn't shaved for two weeks and he walked with a limp. [7] Five months before, while running through the woods in New York state on a similar raid, he had impaled his foot on a long sliver of wood. Sharp as a knife, it had gone right through his moccasin and cut deep into the sole of his foot, disabling him and keeping him out of combat. [8] After that he had barely been able to walk, and it was a long time before he could again march all day.

Houghton was an officer in the regular British army's 53rd or Shropshire Regiment and he had seen a great deal of fighting since his arrival from a posting in Ireland in 1776. He had been attached to the Indian service almost as soon as he had arrived in Canada, and he had served under General John Burgoyne in the 1777 invasion of the Champlain Valley.

Assigned to one of the contingents of Mohawk warriors used by the British in that campaign, Houghton had seen heavy action. While trying to herd a party of inebriated Indians out of harm's way during the siege of Fort Ticonderoga in July, Houghton had been seriously wounded. Wounded again in September at Saratoga, he had been evacuated to the rear.

Since then, the 53rd had been stationed in Canada without seeing any combat. Houghton had not been interested in sedentary garrison life and had sought the most active service available—one that attracted few other regular officers. In a "memorial" written to General Haldimand following the Royalton raid, he was to point out that he had passed up attractive, career-advancing assignments in Europe so that he could be in the thick of things in Canada.[9] He had been the Assistant Superintendent at the Mohawk village of Kahnawake since 1778.[10] Serving in one of the most demanding and unorthodox roles for a lieutenant in the regular British army, Houghton earned high praise from his superior, Col. John Campbell, who reported to Haldimand how much he valued Houghton's activity, his zeal, and "the pleasure of his acquaintance."[11]

Houghton was not the only white man. There were five altogether. Three were French Canadians who ran with the Indians and spoke with them in a rapid mixture of French and at least two Native languages. These men were not in uniform, but were dressed in the hybrid clothing of Canadian woodsmen—blanket coats, leggings, and moccasins. Each had a tomahawk and a short sword, a bag for lead ball, a powder horn, and a pack consisting of a blanket and a pemmican pouch. The Indians carried much the same equipment, but most wore only a shirt of tanned leather or cloth on their upper body, some were bare-chested. Their heads were shaved except for a scalp lock wound with feathers, and there were streaks of red paint on their faces and bodies.[12]

The fifth white man spoke quietly and urgently with Houghton and the three Canadians. If the Havens women thought they had seen him before, they would not have been mistaken: He was Richard Hamilton, and he knew the place intimately because he had been in Royalton and other frontier settlements recently under an assumed identity.

He had crossed paths with Houghton before as well; both were at the 1777 battle of Saratoga, Hamilton as a grenadier of the British 21st Regiment. Houghton's misfortune had been to be wounded, while Hamilton's was to be one of the several thousand captured in the British defeat. But by the summer of 1779 he was free, either through release or escape or enlistment with American forces. He was known to have been in Newbury during the summer of 1779, and he may well have been one of a group of 50 such "enlistees" in an American military company at Newbury.[13] It was common practice among prisoners from Burgoyne's defeat at Saratoga to take an oath of loyalty to the American cause in order to enlist in rebel units and then escape at the first opportunity.

During the summer of 1780, Hamilton had slipped away from Newbury, visiting Royalton, among other places. He had then left the Royalton area with four other men, as the villagers remembered and retold it over time, saying they were going north to survey some land.[14] That was the last Hamilton had been seen in the village until the morning of October 16.

* * *

It was frigid that morning and Lorenza Havens was outdoors, barefoot in her nightgown. Encouraged and emboldened by Houghton's solicitude toward her mother, she spoke up and asked the Lieutenant to bring her something to wear. He went back into the house among the ransacking Indians and brought her a quilt, green on one side and red on the other. Knowing the Indians' taste for anything red, Houghton advised her that if she wanted to keep the quilt from being stolen, she needed to put it on green side out.[15]

In spite of his disdain for the Revolution, Lt. Houghton had a good deal more in common with these colonial settlers than he had with the French Canadians or his Mohawk and Abenaki warriors. Eyewitnesses that day remembered and later recounted the way in which he advised the women on how to handle the Indians. Let them have what they want, he counseled, and he interceded when he thought the women's resistance to the pillaging might lead to violence on their persons. Having brought the war into their homes, it was in Houghton's interest to keep the women from harm when he could, for he was under orders to prevent his Indians from committing atrocities.[16]

Of course, it was precisely because of the settlers' terror of Indian atrocity that they were used so effectively by the British in frontier raids. For both Mohawks and Abenakis, warfare was a traditional determinant of manhood, status, and cultural identity. Training for warfare was an integral part of their upbringing; their skills were honed and the warrior persona became part of their very being. Among the measures of prowess were the things they would take with them from Royalton: plunder, captives, and scalps from slain enemies.[17]

Although Lt. Houghton had been fighting alongside Indians for nearly five years, he had never thought of them as a reliable fighting force, and he often said as much in reports to superiors.[18] This, of course, reveals more about limited British understanding of the natives' motivations for involvement in the Revolution than it does about the Indians' abilities in combat. Other seasoned officers shared Houghton's skepticism, saying that the best way to get Indians to fight the rebels was to draw them into the line of fire so that some Indian blood would be shed.

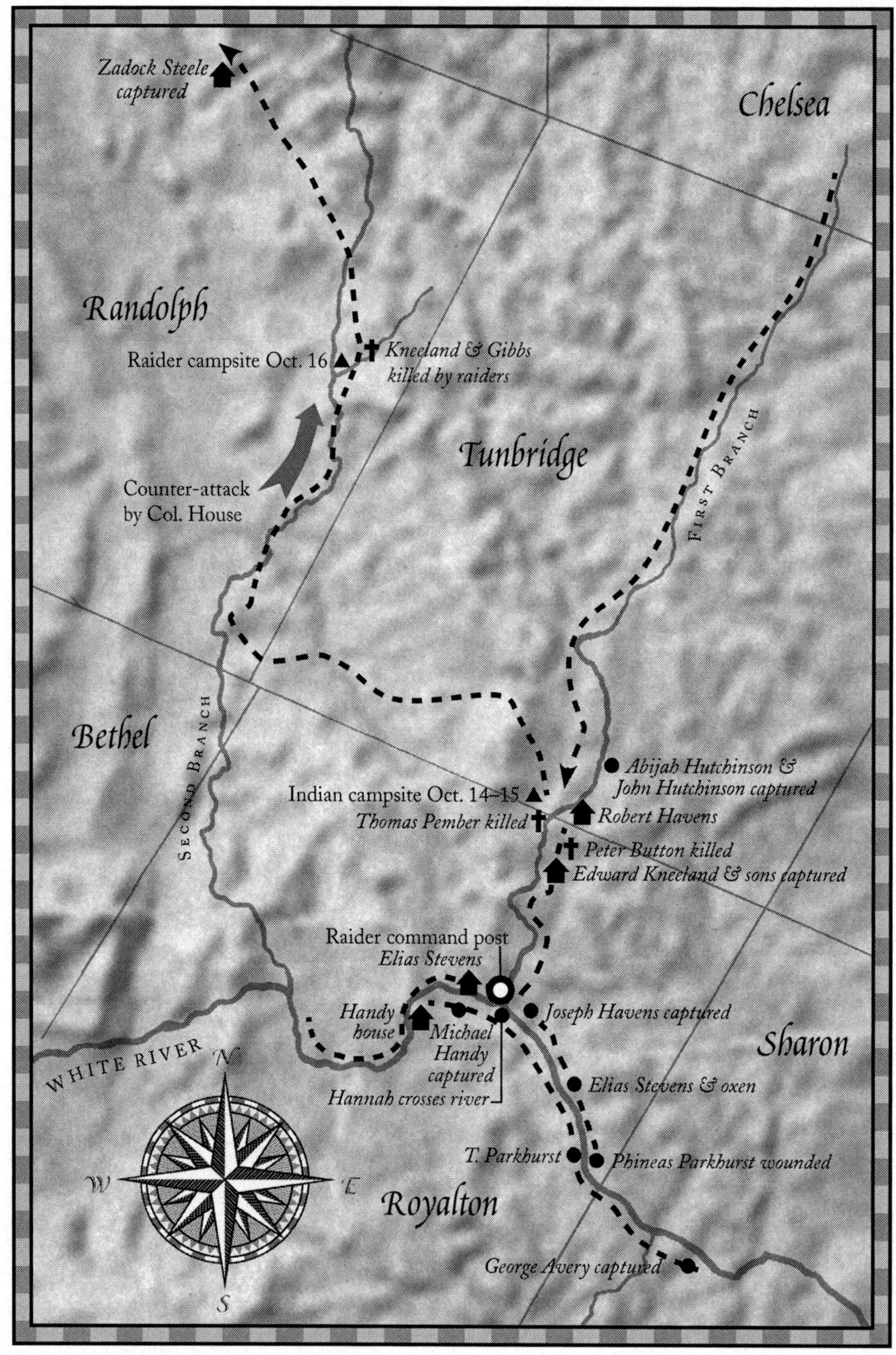

MAP 3. Key Events of the Royalton Raid.

The revenge they would then seek would "outdo all bribery."[19] That insight, cynical as it was, reflects a certain primitive understanding of Indian ways.

Even so, Houghton was drawn to the Indians and had never sought another assignment. By conventional European standards their violence might be unpredictable, but Houghton had come to understand how to use it and when to count on it. He knew from experience there would be killing, scalping, and terrifying threats of mayhem, but he also knew the women had no reason to fear sexual molestation—though it had been a favorite colonial *bête noir* since the beginning of European settlement.

Rape was taboo. Warfare and sexual activity were mutually exclusive. All potential captives were likely to become adoptees with full Indian family status; to rape them, even before adoption, was in the native view to commit incest, an unthinkable sin.[20] Houghton also knew there was virtually no chance that the Indians would torture any captives. Except in isolated cases of Indian outrage at white atrocities against Indians, torture of whites during the Revolution was extremely rare.[21]

The alarm had not yet spread far and the raiders moving downstream still had the advantage of surprise. The houses were far apart, so commotion at one was not heard at the next. Not a shot had been fired so far. People at morning chores and errands or still in bed in the early minutes of the attack were caught unawares. So far, men found indoors with nowhere to run were spared, and merely captured. Thomas Pember, who had run, was killed; and when Peter Button was surprised carrying his wheat to the mill, he unwisely bolted down the road away from the raiders. They pursued, speared, killed, and scalped him: another who would not spread the alarm.

But there was one the attackers knew had not been accounted for. Daniel Havens, who had run from the house with Thomas Pember, had managed to get away and he raced downstream ahead of the raiders. Reaching the house of Elias Stevens, he found Mrs. Stevens still in bed with one child and warned her to run, calling out, "The Indians are as thick as the devil at our house."[22]

Then he was out the back door in a shot and across the river in the Stevens canoe beached on the shore. From the other side he saw the war party burst through the front door of the Stevens house—Sarah Stevens and her two children still there. The raiders ransacked the place, making first for the feather bed, which they hauled out through the door. Sarah put up a fight to save it, but soon the mattress was slit and the door yard was a blizzard of feathers. A deranged act of petty vandalism, she might have thought, but the warriors knew that the mattress ticking would make a stout sack for carrying plunder. Sarah Stevens was rooted to the spot until, warned to leave or burn with her house, she escaped into the woods with the two children. There she watched while the Indians took burning logs from her fireplace and used them to set the house ablaze.

The raiders swept two miles of the First Branch from the Tunbridge town line to the White River. They captured 14 and killed two. They rousted five women from their beds, several with small children, and hounded them into the woods. Once they reached the junction of the First Branch and the White, Lt. Houghton established a rendezvous point in a meadow by the Stevens house. From here the marauders sped up- and downstream on both sides of the river, sacking and destroying the homesteads as they went. As the alarm spread, most families fled along the river, while some simply went to ground in the forest. There was no organized defense, no counter-attack.

* * *

ROYALTON, 10:00 AM. The Indians were looking for men and boys to capture, and they appeared to have no interest in gratuitous bloodshed, having killed and scalped only two men. They neither harmed nor captured any women. It was not as if Indian warriors had not captured, and at times killed and scalped, English women before—they had been doing so for 150 years, most recently in 1778 at Cherry Valley, New York, which Iroquois warriors had attacked to avenge rebel outrages committed against neighboring Indian communities.[23]

But at Royalton, the raiders were not harming the women, and that meant the women would have the most intimate contact with them. Some of the women did not shrink from the Indians, and these were the ones who became so well-remembered in oral history. They appeared to have a curious standing, almost an immunity. The raiders would haul the women from their beds, grab articles of clothing, shoes, and jewelry and the women would snatch them back, risking death—or so the raiders would have had them believe. When there was no escape and further resistance was pointless, the women wisely did not run unless told to do so. They often stood and watched as their homes were destroyed.

Robert and Hannah Handy and their two children lived a short distance upstream of the mouth of the First Branch and on the opposite, or south side of the White River. Little is known of Robert or of what he did that day, but his wife Hannah was to earn a place in the history of the raid and the town that has been preserved and passed down from generation to generation.

Of Robert, this much we do know: Alerted to the raid, he reacted as so many of the men did this day. His first duty was to spread the alarm. He told Hannah that he would ride to the fort at Bethel, four miles upstream, and get the militia to turn out and get people into the safety of the fort. Then he told her to run with the children to the security of a neighbor's house, and off he rode. Many people had found safety in the woods that day; so would Hannah and the children. He was certain of it.

Handsome, attractive—as many agreed when they later retold the story among themselves and to Zadock Steele—remembered for her blue eyes and her warmth, Hannah was 27 years old and had lived on the frontier all her life. Her ten-year-old son, Michael, hurried ahead of her, but three-year-old Lucretia was too small to keep up as they left their house so Hannah carried her. Robert urged his horse upstream and she and the children hurried into the woods. Hannah did not know where the raiders were.

Downstream, where Daniel Havens and others had already spread the alarm, there were many more raiders and they were moving fast. At dawn, Elias Stevens had been working his plot of land along the White River and had been warned early by a man pounding towards him on a lathered horse, shouting, "For God's sake turn out your oxen for the Indians are at the mill!"[24]

Stevens had quickly driven his oxen into the thick brush along the side of the clearing, hoping the Indians would overlook them. He had caught up his horse, mounted, and sped upstream toward his house where he knew Sarah and the two children must still be. On the way he had met others in flight who passed him in terror; Stevens had finally decided he must turn back, leaving wife and child to fend for themselves. He was now galloping downstream on the rough road, one of a fleeing, ragged mob of women and children. Stevens pulled to a halt at the Parkhurst home, where his widowed mother lived, now remarried to Mr. Parkhurst. His stepsister, Molly, was milking a cow as he leapt down, telling her what had happened and that she must flee.

With the raiders bearing down, he put Molly and his mother on his own horse and sent them at a gallop after the disappearing villagers. He was afoot, his dog bounding along beside him, the Indians not far behind. One of the few men on horseback spreading the alarm was Phineas Parkhurst, Molly's brother, now coming into sight across the river riding hard downstream.

Phineas rode to the water's edge, saw his mother, and prepared to cross. The Indians were by now at his house, and, seeing him on the opposite shore, showed themselves and beckoned to him to come across. He wheeled his horse away from the water and it lunged up the bank. An Indian raised his musket and got off a shot—the only gunfire of the raid so far—and it took Phineas low in the back. The ball plowed through muscle and glanced off bone, missed vital organs and came to rest just under the skin on the front of his rib cage. He could feel its weight and found that if he held it tight with one hand and kept it still as his horse bolted down the road, it lessened the fiery pain. His mother saw him lurch as the half-inch ball tore into him. Her only relief was that he was mounted and that if he got far enough he might live.[25]

Phineas made it to Tilden's Tavern in Hartford, ten miles down the White River. The people there fired the alarm gun to summon the militia. Phineas remounted and continued, fording the Connecticut River at its junction with the White, and rode another four miles to Lebanon, New Hampshire, where he found Dr. Laban Gates, the only physician for miles around. The doctor extracted the ball from the boy's abdomen, dressed the wound, and duly sent Vermont a bill for his services.[26]

Stevens's dog had been with him all morning and loped easily beside him, then cut in front of him. Stevens, trying to avoid the dog, went down, then scrambled up, legs pumping hard. The dog pranced in front of him again and Stevens tripped again. The townsfolk pulled away up ahead and Stevens plunged into the woods before his pursuers could see him; he was into the trees and out of sight as they raced past.

The fleeing townspeople were by now well into the neighboring town of Sharon, and were nearing the cabin that George Avery shared with some other young men. He had shaken off the memory of the night's bad dreams, and begun the day noticing nothing out of the ordinary.

> *That morning I went to a neighbor for our bread, while my mates cooked breakfast. When I returned I met my companions affrighted running to the woods. I thought of going to the camp and save my cloaths. I made light of it, and told them I would get my breakfast first.*[27]

But then his nightmares proved all too true:

> *I saw others flying for safety, but turning I was surprised by the sight of two Indians very near me.*
>
> *The foremost one with tomohok in hand we were face to face suddenly both stopped. He waved his hand "Come, Come." I answered the Indian, "Come." and took to my heeles and ran for escape, followed the road on the River bank but a little, Jumped into the bushes on its bank out of his sight and made for foarding the River. The two followed me; the tommahok one caught me in the back of the collar and gave me a few blows with his instrument and a few greeting words.*
>
> *Here I was as really affrighted as I was in my dreams but a few hours before. The two Indians stripped me of my outside garments. They took me by each arm and I ran between them, to return to theire company which they left that were destroying Horses and cattle and had taken prisoners.*[28]

With Avery and other prisoners in tow, the south-bank raiders turned and worked back toward the Stevens' meadow at the mouth of the First Branch, their rendezvous. As they moved, they put every dwelling, barn, and shed to the torch, taking special care to destroy all food supplies. All the grain, corn, hay, fruit, vegetables, nuts, berries—all of it went up in flames.

It was at this point that the rising din of panicked people was drowned out by an eruption of gunfire. Shots echoed up and down the valley. If the prisoners and those hiding in the woods could hear it and thought that the counter-attack had begun, that the militia from surrounding towns had arrived, it was a vain hope. The raiders had commenced a great slaughter—all the cattle, sheep and swine to be found—all were shot. The alarm had been spread; anyone who heard the shooting already knew of the raid, and this was by far the most efficient way to effect the carnage that was, along with the capture of prisoners, the main object of British frontier raids such as this.

CHAPTER 3

HANNAH

"I'll follow you to Canada"

ROYALTON, 11:00 AM. Hannah Handy, with her children Michael and Lucretia, was hurrying upriver toward the safety of a neighbor's house. What she did not know was that one raiding party had already moved swiftly upstream beyond her house on the other side of the river and waded to the south side. They were now coming toward her on the path, running fast. She saw them too late, and in a flash they were upon her and Michael was theirs.

Though there had been no Indian raids in New England for 20 years, Hannah, like all her neighbors, had grown up hearing of the French and Indian wars. She clutched her daughter, sensing that perhaps the girl was safe from capture, though a hundred years earlier neither of them would have been. Lucretia was trying to hide in her mother's skirts, telling her to *"keep away the Indians."* [1] Hannah was no stranger to Indians, and from time to time she and Robert had even shared a night's shelter and food with a passing Mohawk or Abenaki, as they would have with any traveler. Hannah believed she even recognized one old man in the raiding party. [2] In the moments before they raced off with her boy, she challenged Michael's captor.

> *"What will you do with him?"*
> *"Take him to Canada and make a soldier of him."*
>
> *"A good deal you will. He will not be able to make the journey and it will be the tomahawk for him. I'll follow you to Canada before I will give up my boy."* [3]

The raiding party rushed off with Michael. Hannah, clutching Lucretia, hurried after. She later told Zadock Steele that she then met some white men along the path and stopped them to ask what the Indians would do with her son; with gratuitous cruelty they told her that he would be killed. [4] She believed them and this belief stoked her growing rage. Hannah kept moving and came out at the White River across from the Elias Stevens place, where she could see the raiding party gathering in a meadow on the opposite bank. There were some still on the south side waiting to cross. As both she and her daughter, Lucretia, told the story in later years, when Hannah moved to the bank and made ready to wade the river, an Indian approached her. He was the old man she thought she had recognized earlier, and he signed to her that he would carry her daughter across while Hannah waded. Lucretia would have none of it, saying she did not "*want to ride the old Indian.*"[5]

The river was unusually low that October, but even so, it was swift and there would be holes and hollows, and in the end Hannah made a calculated, desperate decision. She bid Lucretia not to argue, but to do as she was told. Hannah handed Lucretia to the Indian, not doubting she would be safe. They set out: the old man first, then Hannah. The raiders gathered on each shore, watching and waiting. Halfway across, where the water was deeper and swifter, the footing more uncertain, Hannah stopped and could go no further. The old man motioned to her to wait by a big rock and kept going with Lucretia. He put her down on the shore among the other Indians and came back for Hannah. Steadied by the big rock, he settled her on his back and with her arms locked across his chest and the river tugging on her skirts, they crossed.

The old man deposited Hannah on the north shore by Lucretia. Taking her daughter by the hand, she marched into the crowd of raiders, looking for the officer in charge. Her son was nowhere to be seen, but she found Lt. Houghton and demanded to know what he would do with Michael. He reassured her that it was contrary to policy to harm women and children, and that the boy would be trained as a soldier. With mounting fury and mindless of the risk, she later told Zadock, Hannah commenced a tongue lashing of Lt. Houghton that he would not soon forget, demanding that he make the Indians release Michael. Because of the force and detail with which Zadock retold Hannah's story, it is safe to assume that she herself recalled and perhaps even relived the vehemence with which she acted at the time. Hannah was known as a vivid and persuasive woman and her fury must have been a thing to behold.

Hannah remembered Houghton's words: "Madam, they are an ungovernable race. They do as they please."[6]

Hannah told Houghton that this was nonsense: that he was their commander, that they would do as he bid, or they should if he had any mettle as an officer; that, in any case, if any harm should come to her son, the boy's blood would be on Houghton's hands and for that there would be no escape from eternal damnation. What kind of a man would allow such a barbarity to take place when it placed his very honor as a civilized gentleman at risk? She was by no means done with him, she remembered, but paused in case an answer might be forthcoming.

Lt. Houghton could by now see that Hannah Handy was not to be denied and that as an enraged mother she was fearless of both him and the rest of the raiders—all of them now wholly attentive to this gathering drama. As much to put an end to the scene as anything else, Houghton relented and promised to restore Michael to her as soon as he and his captors should appear.

As good as his word, when they crossed the river Houghton commenced an extensive and heated negotiation that involved a French-Canadian interpreter, a bilingual Mohawk, and Michael's affronted Indian captor. Houghton gained Michael's release. Her family reunited, Hannah set off upriver for a shallower ford, but before she had gone far, Houghton called her back, advising her to remain close until the entire party had gone so that no one would try to take the boy again.

As the other raiding parties returned, Hannah saw that they were bringing in many prisoners—men who were her husband's friends and neighbors. Among them were many boys, some, like the two Downer brothers, clinging to their father, Ephraim, who also had been taken prisoner. There was only one thing she could do, and she went to Houghton again.

"Let them go. Let the children go."

She gave no credence to Houghton's claims that such a demand was beyond his powers—that prisoners, once taken, had always been a captor's property by inviolable Indian right and ancient custom. Houghton knew the Indians well; he had been living and raiding with them for four years, and he told Hannah they were intractable. In fact, Houghton had a fair amount of influence over them, more than he let on. He knew just how far he could push them and had been very persuasive with them on other occasions.[7] Hannah pressed her case and, in the end, again Houghton apparently could not resist her—or perhaps he decided it was not worth the trouble. He may even have found her fearlessness admirable, as, no doubt, did the Indian onlookers, in spite of the fact that her persuasiveness would cost them dearly in captives to bring home.

* * *

Houghton managed to persuade the Indians to release the boys, but Hannah had no idea what a contentious issue this was between the British and their native allies. What Houghton had told her about the difficulty of separating warriors from their captives was true. The taking of captives was an ancient Indian practice, followed in order to increase tribal membership, often by replacing specific individuals who had died or had been killed in battle.[8] In fact, before the arrival of Europeans there was rarely any concrete purpose to warfare except for the taking of captives.[9] Bringing captives back from a raid such as this, like scalping, was a testament to a warrior's prowess in battle and an essential component to the collective mourning of the deaths of tribal members. To deprive a warrior of his captive was a grave transgression for Houghton to commit.

The British had to make it worthwhile for the Indians to be part of these raids, so they let them plunder the settlements, supplied them with weapons, food, finery, and rum, and allowed them to take captives. If the Indians decided not to adopt captives upon their return, they knew they could sell them to the British for hard cash. Taking prisoners served British purposes, too: It deprived frontier communities and militias of manpower. But it had become official British policy not to allow the Indians to adopt prisoners once they had been captured. The Indians were to be told that captured rebels were "*the king's undutiful children... must be delivered up to be corrected by their father as he shall think fit.*" [10]

Hannah may have had at least one ally in the raiding party, and he could have been aiding Houghton's efforts to free the captive children. When her daughter, Lucretia, retold the story in later years, she vividly remembered her certainty that the old man who carried her across the river was already known to the family and that he had interceded on behalf of the release of the children. Like so many other strands of oral history, this one was passed down in Hannah's and Lucretia's families, told to Zadock Steele, and preserved in a series of letters written by Hannah's descendants.[11] Though there is no way of knowing who the old Indian was or if he helped in securing the release of the boys, at least one member of the raiding party *was* predisposed to sympathy with the villagers.

In 1704 a French-led Kahnawake war party had attacked the Massachusetts frontier settlement of Deerfield and captured a three-year-old girl, Eunice Williams. She had remained with her captors, married a Kahnawake man and raised a family. Her grandson, *Tehoragwanegen*, also called Thomas Williams, was one of the members of the Royalton war party, and, according to a biography written in later years, was a close friend and confidant of Lt. Houghton. *Tehoragwanegen* claimed to have protected some women from abuse and to have saved the life of an old man during the course of the Royalton raid. Though there is no way to corroborate this, apparently Eunice had instructed him to join war parties such as this in order to protect women and children in settlements under attack.[12]

When Eunice had been carried to Canada 76 years earlier, her captors had brought her up the White River past the very spot where Hannah and Lt. Houghton were now facing off while Eunice's own grandson looked on. Quite possibly, he was aware of the irony in witnessing a situation so like the one that had brought his own grandmother to Canada.

* * *

Still on the north bank of the White River at the mouth of the First Branch, surrounded by 265 warriors and some 30 hapless men and youths, Hannah moved in a ring of power. The nine children she had freed crowded close, clinging to her skirts as she waited for the war party to leave, not knowing if Houghton's fragile agreement with her would last long enough to protect the little brood.

She had not been able to gain the release of all the children. The Indian who had caught a boy named Garner Rix refused to give him up. Impressed with Garner's resistance and with the way he had attacked his captors with his little club, the man saw the boy as a valuable trophy possessing warrior potential. So Garner, 13 years old, was to go to Canada, as were two other boys.

Hannah gradually edged her clutch of boys away from the milling, noisy crowd of warriors. She must have known that every moment of proximity risked recapture and that by now she had pressed her luck and influence with the lieutenant to their limits. The children would do as she directed, but they also must have been riveted by the spectacle, the likes of which they had never seen. Besides the typical bush outfits worn by the British officers and the French Canadians, the war party carried an assortment of weapons that included muskets, bayonets, scalping knives, tomahawks, and a type of spear called a "spontoon." There were even a few short swords. The only item distinguishing Lt. Houghton's rank was the silver gorget he wore around his neck.

7. Iroquois (Mohawk) Warrior, Public Archives of Canada, Ref. # R9266.

The Indians blurred into a noisy riot of color and motion: painted faces, tattoos, shaven skulls with scalp locks, silver and brass nose rings, ear rings, bracelets, and arm rings. They wore loin cloths, leggings, and moccasins with rows of small metal cylinders packed with deer hair. As the warriors moved, these made a curious sound—as if high notes were being struck and muffled at the same time. Some warriors had buckskin hunting shirts; others had cloth shirts of checked muslin or even silk; some were bare-chested.

Hannah reached the river, slipping upstream along the bank while the party of raiders left the meadow and went back up the First Branch. She found a shallow ford and crossed twice, each time carrying one of the smallest boys while the others crossed with their arms linked. Safe on the other side, they walked three miles downstream until dark, then moved off the trail and found a place to hide in the woods for the night. Along the way Hannah saw some of the damage to the town, but in the gathering dusk didn't know yet how devastating it truly was.

One hundred fifty head of cattle and all the sheep and pigs were lost. Those not shot had been burned alive when the barns were set on fire. Household furniture had gone up in flames and the raiders had made off with 30 horses, along with pots, kettles, axes, hoes, shovels, tongs, sickles, scythes, chains, bedding, women's silk and lace finery, side saddles, warming pans, plates, mirrors, and one blacksmith's anvil.[13] It was mid-October and the raid had destroyed virtually all of the settlement's sustenance and shelter for the coming winter.

8. Soldiers of Lt. Richard Houghton's Regiment, the 53rd, in the uniform he would have worn on formal occasions. Public Archives of Canada, Accession # 1937-419.

CHAPTER 4

GOING NORTH

"What mischief we done"

OCTOBER 17, HOUGHTON'S FIRST CAMP, 2:00 AM. The raiding party left Royalton at about two in the afternoon and moved back up the First Branch for a short distance through the township of Tunbridge, then turned west over the hills and came down into the valley of the Second Branch in Randolph. They were going north along a somewhat different route from the one by which they had arrived. Houghton's matter-of-fact report of the operation made it clear to his superiors just how unprepared Royalton had been for such an attack.

> *We burnt close to a Stocaded Fort wherein there was a Captain and 60 men but they could not turn out after us. I marched from the settlements that evening and encamped in the wood about two o'clock in the morning.*[1]

Houghton deployed a perimeter guard, and the Indians spread out, made camp, started fires, and secured the captives.[2] George Avery later remembered how his first bewildering night as a captive began:

> *They encamped in Randolph Woods the 16th of Octr 1780 About 350* (sic) *Indians and 26 prisoners. The Indians made fiers and shelters of Hemlock boughs to encamp by for the night.*
>
> *The prisoners had different masters at different camps. The prisoners were stripped of outer garments by their masters and collected at the chief officer's encampment. We stood huddled together, the fier between us and the officer.*[3]

The encampment covered about five forested acres and the 26 prisoners were scattered among some 20 fires and shelters—around each of which was a group of 15 to 20 raiders. Houghton had his own encampment and he summoned the prisoners to appear at his camp so he could get a head count and take the measure of the captives. He gave them instructions, warnings, and even a few words of reassurance. Avery remembered that each prisoner had a different Indian captor and each was subject to different treatment:

> *An Indian came to a prisoner took him by the hand to lead him off. The head officer told the prisoner to go and bade fare well; A prisner nearby me whispers, I believe he will in another world. I asked why. He replied He had contenental cloth and was a soldier when taken. By this I was frightened.*[4]

It's safe to assume that this was young David Waller, who later declared in his pension application that he was wearing "continental cloth." The only coat he owned was the uniform jacket of a Continental Soldier, marking him as a potential rebel combatant, not a simple unarmed civilian.[5] When Avery saw him disappear into the gloom under close guard, his recent nightmare seemed more and more prophetic:

> *Then others were led off in the same way. I think my turn might be about the 6th or 7th. I am not able to express [my feelings] in any other way but by confusion in thoughts, like one to die violently. I expect I became quite frantick. When I was led a short distance through woods to the camp where the Indians were cooking, all looked calm and peaceable to my view and astonishment.*
>
> *The silly phantick thought struck my mind. They'l fat me before they kill me. Soone however they brought a strong belt to bind me, then took me to a booth (or shelter). I was laid down under it feet to the fier. Stakes drove down in the ground each side of me, my belt tied to them stakes. Thus I was staked to the ground.*
>
> *Still here is no Safety. They gave me here of their supper but I cannot tell the relish of it that night. After supper 4 Indians lay on my belt that tied me to the stakes, two upon each side of me so that I could not move but that they all would feele the belt move. When I looked at the fier there was the guard: an Indian Smoking.*[6]

The Royalton captives received treatment from the Indians that was by turns humane and utterly capricious. Each campfire group was autonomous in its behavior, its accountability, and its treatment of the prisoners. Most of the captives were probably separated from one another and had little chance to offer encouragement or to plan an escape. All they could do was hope to survive the night.

It was three in the morning, the fires were blazing, and the raiding party was in a high state of excitement. Food was cooking, plunder was heaped around the fires, tethered horses were stamping and blowing in the underbrush, only just beginning to settle.

There were so many in the raiding party that the captives had probably not seen all of the warriors—or all of the non-Indians for that matter. But now, by the light of the fires, some of the Royalton men were beginning to realize they had seen the British soldier, Richard Hamilton, before and knew him by name.

They had also seen some of the Indians before. Besides the men that Hannah and other women had recognized, there was one warrior who stood out. In dress and speech he appeared to be fully Indian, but he spoke fluent English with Houghton, and Houghton called him Philips. At least one of the captives, Old Edward Kneeland, may once have met this man, as it is a near certainty that Philips had passed up and down the White River on more than one occasion.[7] Philips was clearly one of the leaders of the Kahnawake war party, but he had not been born an Indian.

* * *

His Mohawk name was *Sanorese.*[8] But before that his name had been Philips when, as just a youth on a colonial farm in New York State, he had been captured more than 30 years earlier. When given a chance to be exchanged in 1750, he had demurred, apparently preferring life among the Kahnawake.[9] Since then, positioned advantageously, he had served as an interpreter and go-between, facilitating Indian-European interchange, communication, and commerce, while gaining power and economic advantage for himself. Eventually he became one of the most respected and influential of all the tribe's adopted captives.[10]

Philips had kept a foot in both worlds and had seen to it that his children did, too. He had a son named Talbot, who for the past five years had been a student at Dartmouth College.[11] Talbot was one of the few Canadian Indian boys whose parents Eleazar Wheelock, Dartmouth's founder, had managed to win over in his mission to educate Indian children. Although many Indian children had attended the school when it was in Lebanon, Connecticut, all but a handful had rejected it once they realized that even at this institution there was no escape from the virulent racism of the American colonies.[12]

The ultimate goal of Wheelock, and indeed of most Protestant missionaries, was to turn the "insufferably proud" Indians into Englishmen and their land into privately owned property.[13] The Indians that lasted at Moor's and later at Dartmouth in Hanover were not beguiled by their experience. A letter from a spokesman for the Onondaga Iroquois delivered a stinging rejection, not only of Wheelock's school but Protestant methods in general:

> *Brother do you think we are altogether ignorant of your methods of instruction...? We understand not only your speech, but your manner of teaching Indians....*

9. The Reverend Eleazar Wheelock (1711-1779), First President of Dartmouth College (1769-1779). Artist: Joseph Steward, commissioned by the Trustees of Dartmouth College. Hood Museum of Art, Dartmouth College, Hanover, N.H.

> *Brother take care. You must learn of the French ministers if you want to understand and know how to treat Indians. They don't speak roughly nor do they for every little mistake take up a club and flog them.*[14]

Wheelock was persistent if nothing else and focused his attentions on the somewhat more acculturated Indian children of the Seven Nations of Canada,

10. The Founding of Dartmouth College, courtesy of Dartmouth College Libraries. A somewhat romanticized view from J.W. Barber's *Historical, Poetical and Pictorial American Scenes*. New Haven, 1852.

and in particular on children descended from white captives, such as the Philips boys, saying that

> *[t]hough they were born among the Indians and have been exposed to their national vices, they appear to be as sprightly as English children are...the most promising set of Youths I have ever seen from the Indian country.* [15]

Although Wheelock gradually lost interest in converting and educating "full blooded Indians," he and his son John, who succeeded him as Dartmouth's president, maintained relations with Philips and others like him in Canada. It was only one of many ironies of the position of the Indians in the Revolution that

John Wheelock had recently applied to the Continental Congress for a continuation of the financial assistance it had been providing for the Philips boy and three other Canadian Indians.[16] Wheelock's assertion to Congress was that this educational experience might nourish pro-rebel sympathies, and might "redound to the benefit of the states," thus mitigating against hostilities and building a "bulwark against a herd of savages."[17] George Washington was fully in agreement and, as of March 1780, was quite sure that supporting the native boys at Dartmouth would help to "cultivate the friendship of these people. If the large number of native people on the Royalton raid was any measure, Wheelock's efforts appear to have failed utterly.

Philips had many reasons to join this war party. He was a man of considerable influence at Kahnawake and he had become so fully transculturated that he lived by Mohawk measures of status and warrior prowess. That alone would have been reason enough for most Kahnawake warriors to partake in the attack. But Philips may also have seen in this raid the added benefit of an opportunity to communicate somehow with his son at Dartmouth. After all, peacetime visits by assimilated captives in Canada to their New England families had been quite common in the past.[18]

Old Edward Kneeland knew he had little value as a captive and might well be tomahawked on the grueling march, as lagging captives so often were. In a transcribed statement he was to make following the raid, he declared that he had "interceded with Capt. Philips to be released." Kneeland apparently had approached Philips, perhaps to make the case that he was too weak and ill to survive the trip to Montréal, and had asked if there was any chance he might be released.[19] In Kneeland's plea, Philips saw a chance of his own: If Kneeland were released, he could conceivably deliver a letter to Talbot Philips at the college. All Philips had to do was to convince Houghton to set Kneeland free.[20] Houghton was in the Indians' debt over the release of the children to Hannah Handy. If the Indians were willing to liberate Kneeland, Houghton would have no real reason to keep him captive, so he agreed to let Kneeland go in the morning. Houghton even agreed to pen the letter if Philips would dictate it.[21]

* * *

OCTOBER 17, 4:00 AM, HOUGHTON'S FIRST CAMP. The war party knew that the trail they had left would not be hard to follow and that the glow of the campfires could be seen from a distance. They fully expected a spirited pursuit, but they settled in for the night, ready to pull out at dawn or sooner if they had to.

The local militias had indeed gathered, rapidly and in substantial numbers. Under clear night skies and the glow of a nearly full moon they set out in groups from surrounding towns to try to overtake the raiders. [22]

At two in the morning, October 17th, some 364 men under the command of Col. House of Hanover, New Hampshire, were closing on the raiders' encampment. Houghton's sentries, posted a mile out, saw them coming, allowed the advance guard to pass, then fired on the main force of pursuers from ambush. [23] There was a brisk exchange of shots in the dark, with little apparent damage done by either side. Then the militia stood down and the raiding party wasted no time in breaking camp.[24]

George Avery, staked to the ground, was awakened by the gunfire and the sudden commotion of the Indians as they made ready to fight and retreat at a moment's notice. Avery saw his life now hanging by a thread.

> *The Indians in confusion and rage unstaked theire prisoners. My belt was taken and put round my neck and tied to a sapplin. Another I see bound to a tree while they packed up. Theire eyes looked like wildfier. One uttered to his prisoner as tho death at hand.*[25]

Col. House ordered his militia to back off after the skirmish. It was to be a controversial decision. Many would criticize him for not pressing the attack. The break in the firing gave the war party time to get organized. Apparently Houghton then coolly decided that, even though surrounded and outnumbered, he was not outmaneuvered. He may have seen that there was some advantage in keeping his promise to release Kneeland and write the letter to Talbot Philips, because he would have Kneeland deliver another message as well.

According to several eyewitnesses, Kneeland was to tell Col. House that if there were to be any further attack or pursuit all the prisoners would be killed instantly. [26] What was more, Kneeland had to pledge his word of honor "not to take up arms" against the king for the duration of the war. Kneeland's two sons were still prisoners of the raiding party, so he had ample incentive to deliver the message forcefully. He owed Philips a debt of gratitude for brokering his release, so the letter to Talbot was in good hands.[27]

Houghton was later to write of the skirmish with the settlers' militias, "I had but one Indian wounded. What mischief we done them I cant say" but then went on to guess that "we killed a good many of them." [28] In fact, Houghton's gunners had killed none, though one militia man had been hit.[29] On the other hand, at least one of the Indians had been seriously wounded in the exchange, and though Houghton reported him as "only wounded," he died before the war party returned home. [30]

Despite the hint of swagger in Houghton's report, his ability was at this moment being severely tested. His force was encamped following a ferocious raid and now he himself was under surprise counter-attack in the dead of night in enemy territory. Even though the American militia had backed off, Houghton knew he and his volatile warriors would have to retreat while it was still dark, without losing their plunder or their food supplies, without taking any more casualties, without compromising discipline—and all the while keeping track of 26 headstrong prisoners.

* * *

At one of the campfires, where Nathaniel Gilbert and Joseph Kneeland were staked down side by side, a member of the war party approached with the news that everyone would be leaving very soon, very fast. Witnesses later described what followed and it has been preserved in family traditions. Kneeland apparently refused to march, certain that the attacking militia would soon rescue the prisoners. One Indian, presumably his captor, walked over and in a motion that was so fluid it appeared to be part of the man's walking stride, a tomahawk flashed in the flickering light and ended Kneeland's life in mid-sentence.[31]

Nathaniel Gilbert had never seen a man killed, had never heard a sound quite like that of a tomahawk ripping into bone. For this 14-year-old boy it was a stunning experience, made yet more terrifying by the briskly executed act of scalping. The Indian wasted neither time nor motion. Then, tucking the scalp into his belt, the Indian moved toward Nathaniel, circled him once, considered him and made sure his bonds were secure, then busied himself with a pile of plunder. When it appeared to Nathaniel that he was not to be killed, he found his tongue and, as he told it later in his life, asked this Indian why he had killed Joseph. The man simply replied that Kneeland was too strong-looking to be made to go peacefully to Canada, so he dispatched him rather than risk the chance of his escape in the confusion of the coming retreat.[32] Other witnesses that night said that Joseph might have begun to make trouble for himself by being overly insistent that the Indians give his younger brother, Edward, some clothes. Joseph had been complaining that his brother was barefoot and nearly naked, that the weather was getting colder, and that there were plenty of extra clothes for him to wear.

Giles Gibbs, another man taken at the Kneeland house, suffered a similar fate and was found the next morning at the campground scalped, tied to a tree, and, according to tradition, with a tomahawk firmly buried in his head. If that was indeed the case, the man who killed him had to work around it to take Gibbs's scalp.[33] Word circulated among the other captives and was preserved in oral history that he was killed to retaliate for the warrior seriously wounded in the exchange of gunfire.

The executions of Kneeland and Gibbs were vivid object lessons for the rest of the captives, not to mention the militia who would move into the camp at first light and discover them. Lt. Houghton would later report that he took advantage of the lull in the firing and began a stealthy and well-organized withdrawal from his encampment in the dark. The raiders managed to carry much of their plunder, but had to abandon most of their provisions, not to mention the food cooking on twenty campfires.[34]

It was clear to George Avery and the other prisoners that a successful retreat was their best chance at survival and that if the militia were to attack again, he and his mates would not fare well.

> *I was loosed from the Sapplin, loaded with a pack and led by the halter on my neck and my leader with tommahok in hand. Each master of a prisoner (as I understood afterward) had orders to kill his prisoner if closely persued. life and death is set before us.*[35]

As the encampment emptied of raiders, Col. House did not make a move to pursue. No doubt he carefully considered the message brought by old Edward Kneeland, and waited with his men in the frigid darkness. At dawn, House entered the deserted camp, found the bodies of Kneeland and Gibbs, 30 abandoned horses, the war party's provisions and the plunder too heavy to carry easily.

Houghton and his Kahnawake and Abenaki warriors had handily outmaneuvered a superior force. One man, Jonathan Carpenter, who had eagerly joined the pursuit, noted dryly in his diary:

> *[W]e returned home in peace, and our Savage Enemy gone with flying Coulers into Canida which is a poor story for a whig to tell.*[36]

CHAPTER 5

ZADOCK TAKEN

"The cause of my captivity"

RANDOLPH, STEELE CABIN, OCTOBER 17. By 1780, settlers had scattered farther north and west of Royalton, in the newly chartered and settled towns of Bethel, Randolph, and Brookfield.

Of these, only Bethel had a fort, recently hauled in pieces from Royalton. Called Fort Fortitude, it was manned by a company of 50 militia under Capt. Jesse Safford.[1] Ten miles of virgin forest separated Zadock from the fort, but he had by now got used to the immense and endless woodland out of which he had hacked a small clearing. A few felled trees—maple, beech, ash, basswood, and butternut—lay around his cabin like giants that had dropped to the ground, now charred from a season of burning. Beyond them other towering trees, girdled by Zadock and the boy, stood leafless all summer, allowing them to plant a small crop of Indian corn, pumpkins, winter vegetables, and some winter rye among the shadows on the rich earth. Now Zadock faced a frigid six-month season of almost complete solitude. It was a journey of six miles on a blazed trail to his nearest neighbor. If he was daunted by the isolation, the coming winter, or the dangers of a frontier the likes of which he had never before experienced, his narrative gives no hint of it.

The militia in which Zadock served had established alarm posts in order to alert settlers in case of attack, and when word came of the raid on Royalton, he got busy spreading the alarm to his few, scattered neighbors.[2] There was no time for these people to reach the Bethel fort, so the best thing for them to do was to hide deep in the forest, far from watercourses and trails. A counter-attack or any offensive action was out of the question.

> *It was expected they would follow up either the second or third branch on their return to Canada*, Zadock wrote in his narrative. *I was assisting the settlers on the third branch in Randolph to move their families into the woods. I then requested that one of them should accompany me to notify the Brookfield settlers. Unable to*

persuade any to go, I started alone. I had only time to arrive at my own dwelling, before I was overtaken by night. As there was no road and nothing but marked trees to guide my way, I tarried all night. Having prepared some food for breakfast I lay down to sleep, little knowing what awaited my waking. [3]

Zadock believed he would be safe from discovery and attack because his place was on high ground, and therefore well out of the way of the raiding party as long as they did what Indians had always done while traveling: follow the river and its tributaries.

The next town north of Randolph was Brookfield, its three or four families living along the river directly in the path of the raiding party. To warn them he would have to walk several miles through the forest following a blazed trail before he could reach even the first of the Brookfield clearings. He set out at dawn, but was forced to turn back by a violent storm. [4]

Certain that he was well out of the path of the war party, but equally certain that it would not spare the unsuspecting people of Brookfield, he had no choice but to wait out the storm.

Soon after I arrived within doors I heard a shocking cry in the surrounding woods. I ran to the door and beheld a company of Indians, consisting of not less than three hundred in number, not ten rods distant. There was no way of escape. I had only to stand still, wait their approach, and receive my miserable destiny. Their leader came up and told me I must go with them. They asked me if any other persons were to be found near that place. I told them it was probable there were none to be found. [5]

From Zadock's cabin the raiding party was headed northwest over the hills, so he could safely assume no other settlers would be encountered and captured in Brookfield. As dangerous as it was known to be between his hut and the Canadian border, there were still a few families in utterly isolated homesteads, and at least one of them, the Browns of the Lamoille Valley town of Jericho, would be added to the band of captives as the war party hurried north. [6]

After taking every thing they found worthy to carry with them, they set the house on fire and marched on.

One of them took a bag of grass seed upon his back, and, cutting a hole in the bag, scattered the seed as he marched.

The chief who came up to me could talk English very well—he became my master. They took all my clothes, and furnished me with blankets sufficient to defend me against the cold. [7]

Zadock soon came to know this man as Captain Thomo.[8] He was Thomas Orakrenton, a Kahnawake warrior and no stranger to Vermont. He had spent his boyhood hunting and fishing along the shores of Lake Champlain, and was likely to have been with Lt. Houghton in attacks along the Otter Creek in 1778.[9] Thomo took possession of Zadock as his personal captive and hustled him off to join the rest of the war party. Thrown in with the other captives, Zadock soon learned the details of the raid and the counter-attack and the circumstances that led to his capture.

> *The Indians had been put to rout by a party of Americans, about two hundred and fifty in number, commanded by Colonel John House.*
>
> *They took a course which brought them directly to my dwelling. Had they pursue[d] their intended course up the stream, the defenseless inhabitants of Brookfield would doubtless have shared the miserable fate of the inhabitants of Royalton.*
>
> *This prevention, which was the cause of my captivity, was probably the only good that Colonel House effected; and this he did unwittingly, for which he can claim no thanks from me.*[10]

Surrounded as he was, his life most likely in the balance, Zadock still could not resist a moment of bargaining, testing his rapport with Captain Thomo.

> *Soon after we started from my house my master...discovered that I had a pair of silver buckles in my shoes, and attempted to take them from me; but, by promising to let him have them when we arrived at our journey's end, I persuaded him to let me keep them.*[11]

VERMONT

Some Hunters have travelled thro' this Wilderness, from Welds River, to Lake Memsrimagog, & judged the shortest distance this way to be about 50 Miles.

This way Captives have been carried from New Hampshire to Canada

Only the Mouth of this River is known to y English

These Branches are only Conjectural

The Road was cut by the New Hampshire Forces employed against Canada in 1759 with the communication to that country

This way Captives have been carried by the Indians

Mons.
Leaperriere
Bolton
Worster
Lunenbourg
Shelburne
St George
French River
Waterford
Middlesex
Duxbury
4 Brothers
Charlotte
Hinesbourg
Moretown
Berlin
N. Connecticut River has been actually
Called
Ferrisbourg
Hinesbourg
Pocock
Mons. de
Contracoeuse
Panton
New Heaven
Otter Creek
Weybridge
Middlebury
Addison
Water bury
Salisbury
RIK or
OINT
Bridport
Shoreham
Orwell
Leister
Neshobe
Dunbar
Hubbardton
Pittford
Castleton
Rutland
Otter River
Clarendon
Poultney
Wells
Bay
Wood Creek
Drowned Lands
Gen. Nicholsons
built on occasion of the Canada Expedition but now demolished
Tinmouth
Wallingford
Black R.
Danby
Harwich
Pawlet
ward
Rupert
Dorset
Brumley
Sandgate
Manchester
Winhall
ing Place
g Place
Sunderland
Arlington
West River
Stratton
Shaftsbury
Glassenbury
New Fane
Benningtion
Woodford
R
Peacham
Welds River
Ryegate
Barnet
Topsham
Canada
Newbury
Mahsunquamosse R.
Corinth
Waits town
Intervals
Connecticut R.
Choice White Pines
and good Land
Lyman
Gunth
Loring
Bath
Landaff
wait
Franconia
Ammonoosuck R.
Haverhill
Lincoln
Umpammonoosuck R.
Fairfield
Eastham
Malden
Fairlee
Cohass
Little
Piermont
Warren
Orford
Wentworth
Hastings Brook
Rumney
Tunbridge
Strafford
Thetford
Royalton
Sharon
Norwich
Lime
Dorchester
Cockermouth
Stockbridge
Bernard
Pomfret
Waterqueechy R.
White R.
Hartford
Hanover
Dartmouth College
Canaan
White River Falls
Cardigan
New Plymouth
River
Killington
Bridgewater
Woodstock
Lebanon
Bloods River
Relhan
Grafton
New Chester
Hertford
Sugar Brook
Plainfield
Grantham
Shrowsbury
Waterqueechy Falls
Saltash
Windsor
Reading
Choice White Pines and Good Land
Corinth
Protectworth
bounds
Alexandria
Smiths R.
New Chester
New Britain
Salisbury
Cavendish
Weathersfield
Connecticut R.
Croydon
LINE
Heidlebourg
Sunapee Pond
Sugar River
Clermont
Newport
Green
Dantzick
Perrys Town
Kyasarge Mts.
Boscawen
CURVE
Unity
Rye Town
Plamstead
Little Sugar R.
Thomlinson
Lempster
No. 8 New Concord
Contoocook R.
New Hopkinton
Rockingham
No. 4
Ackworth
Charles Town
COUNTY
COUNTY
Hillsborough
Henneker
Saxtons R.
Westminster
Alstead
Marlow
Mason
Wears Town
OF
No. 7
Townshend
Walpole
Gilsum
OF
Limerick
Proprietors Lands reserved
Ashuelot R.
HILLSBOROU
Pulteney
Westmoreland
No. 6
Dublin
CHESHIRE
New Boston
Piscataq
Fulham
Keene
Monadnock Mountains
Peterborough
Lyndeborough
Bratleborough
Chesterfield
Swansey
No. 5
New
borough

PART II
ANOTHER WORLD

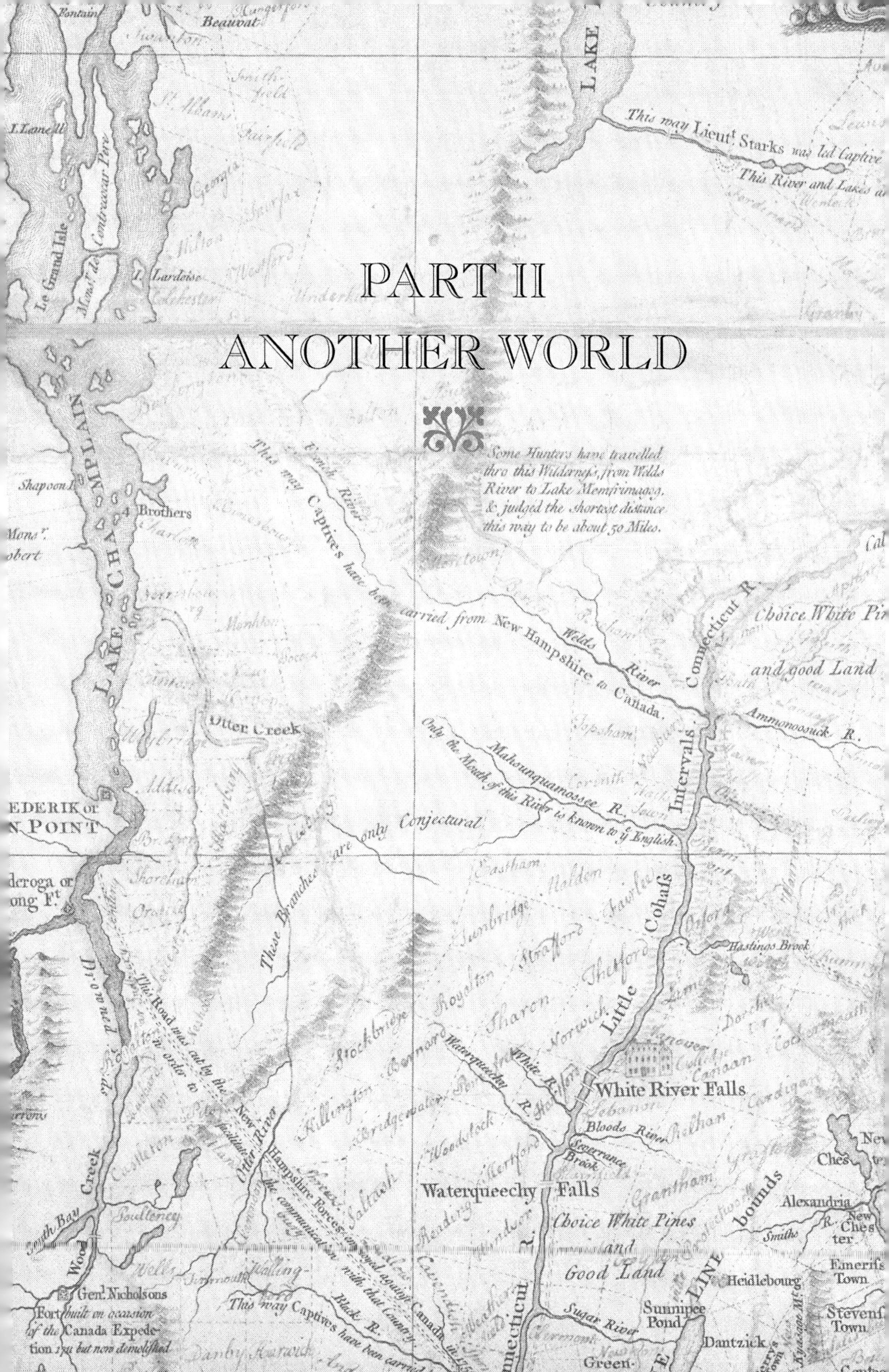

VERMONT

Some Hunters have travelled thro this Wilderness, from Welds River, to Lake Memfrimagog, & judged the shortest distance this way to be about 50 Miles.

N.B. Connecticut River has been actu...

LAKE CHAMPLAIN

Leaperriere
Shelburne
Brothers
Charlotte
St George
This way
French River
Waterford
Middle sex
Dudbury
Worster
Bolton
Lunenbourg
Hunesbourg
Captives have been carried from New Hampshire to Canada
Dunstown
Berlin
Ferris bourg
Monsr. de
Pocock
Contracocuse
Panton
New Heaven
Otter Creek
Weybridge
Addison
Middlebury
Salisbury
Water bury
Bridport
Shoreham
Orwell
Leister
Neshobe
Dunbar
Hubbardton
Pittford
Castleton
Rutland
Clarendon
Poultney
Wells
Gen. Nicholsons built on occasion Canada Expedetion but now demolished
Tynmouth
Wallingford
This Road was cut by the New England Militia
These Branches are only Conjectural
Otter River
Hampshire Forces employed against Canada in 1759. the communication with that country
This way Captives have been carried by the Indians
Black R.
Danby
Harwich
Pawlet
Rupert
Dorset
Brumley
Manchester
Winhall
Sandgate
Sunderland
West River
Arlington
Stratton
Shaftsbury
Glassenbury
New Fane
Bennington
Woodford
Wood Creek
Drowned Lands
Barnet
Peacham
Ryegate
Welds River
Topsham
Newbury
Corinth
Waits town
Mahsunquamosse R.
Only the Mouth of this River is known to y English
Connecticut R.
Intervals
Cohass
Little
Choice White Pines and good Land
Lyman
Gunth
Loring
Bath
Landaff
Franconia
Ammonoosuck R.
Haverhill
Lincoln
Upper Ammonoosuck R.
Fairfield
Eastham
Malden
Fairlee
Piermont
Warren
Tunbridge
Strafford
Thetford
Orford
Wentworth
Hastings Brook
Rumney
Royalton
Sharon
Lime
Dorchester
Cockermouth
Stockbridge
Bernard
Pomfret
Norwich
Hanover
Dartmouth College
Canaan
White River Falls
Hartford
White R.
Waterqueechy R.
Killington
Bridgewater
Woodstock
Lebanon
Relhan
Cardigan
Bloods River
Severance Brook
Grafton
New Plymouth
New Chester
Hertford
Plainfield
Grantham
Shrewsbury
Saltash
Reading
Windsor
Waterqueechy Falls
Choice White Pines and Good Land
Corinth
Protectworth
bounds
LINE
Alexandria
Smiths R.
New Chester
New Britain
Salisbury
Heidlebourg
Croydon
Cavendish
Weathersfield
Sunnipee Pond
Sugar River
Clermont
Newport
Dantzick
Perry's Town
Kyasage Mt.
Boscawen
Green
Unity
CURVE
Rye Town
Flamstead
Little Sugar R.
Lempster
Ackworth
No. 4
Charles Town
Rockingham
Thomlinson
No. 8
New Concord
COUNTY
Contoocook R.
New Hopkinton
Henniker
Hillsborough
Saxtons R.
Westminster
Walpole
Alstead
Marlow
No. 7
Mason
Wears Town
OF
Townshend
Pultney
Limerick
Gilsum
Proprietors Lands reserved
HILLSBOROUGH
New Boston
Ashuelot R.
No. 6
Dublin
Westmoreland
Fulham
Keene
CHESHIRE
Monadnock Mountains
Peterborough
Lyndeborough
Contoocook
Chesterfield
Swansey
No. 5
Bratleborough
New Marlborough
Pemigewasset River

CHAPTER 6

CAPTIVITY

"Mine enemies are lively"

EN ROUTE TO CANADA, OCTOBER 17. Even though it was moving fast as it approached Zadock's cabin, the war party had not passed up opportunities to take captives. Zadock was actually the fifth Randolph prisoner of the new day,[1] but once they had taken him and fired his hut, the warriors wasted no time. By nightfall they had covered 20 miles, camping in the snow near the Onion River.

> *[T]hey had told me before we encamped that if they were overtaken by the Americans they should kill every prisoner,* Zadock later wrote*; and they seemed, in view of their danger, more desirous to keep us within reach of the tomahawk, and secure us against a flight in case the Americans should approach. I watched with trembling fear and anxious expectation during the night, seeking an opportunity to escape, which I found utterly impossible.*[2]

Zadock didn't realize that Colonel House had abandoned the pursuit. In addition to the warning carried by Edward Kneeland, the bodies found by Col. House may well have served the intended purpose: *turn back or there will be more of these.* It was well known to generations of frontier-dwellers in New England that Indians preferred to kill captives rather than lose them.[3] Zadock and the others were certainly looking for a chance to escape, but that would have meant taking a grave risk. Less than 100 years before, both Kahnawake and, less often, Abenaki warriors had been known to torture or burn to death captives who tried to escape—a much less likely outcome now, due to Jesuit and British influence—but instant death would have been a near certainty.[4]

The Royalton prisoners now added their number to an immense host of English captives who had been brought north since the late 17th century. Of the more than 1,600 already carried from the New England frontier to Canada, hundreds had followed precisely the same route the Royalton prisoners were now taking. The largest single group had been captured in the 1704 raid on Deerfield, Massachusetts, conducted by 48 French soldiers and over 200 warriors, the largest percentage from Kahnawake.[5] One hundred nine men, women, and children had been captured, but 20 of them had never made it to Canada. Very young children or adult women weakened by childbirth or old age, having become too exhausted to keep up, were killed on the trail by the warriors.[6]

The Deerfield raid had been an extension of Queen Anne's War, one of the many conflicts between France and Great Britain, but the Indians had had their own reasons for taking part. Abenakis had joined the raid because of English encroachment on Abenaki land in northern New England. Kahnawake Mohawks had joined the raid to take scalps, plunder, and captives—specifically to replace people lost to a 1701 smallpox epidemic.[7] With that in mind, warriors often took pains to carry and feed young captives who might make promising adoptees.[8] As with the Royalton raid, a large body of local Deerfield militia had gathered for pursuit, in spite of the known jeopardy in which it placed the captives. Then as now, the pursuit had not been pressed for more than a day.[9]

Captivity by Indians had been, from the earliest days, one of the defining experiences of the New England frontier. Zadock and the others from Royalton had grown up hearing about hapless citizens abducted from their homes by "savages" from the north, and now it had happened to them.[10] Widely read by the general public, narratives written by such victims had a predictably ideological and partisan agenda. They were cautionary tales that celebrated the moral and physical fiber of New Englanders in a life and death struggle against the satanic evil seen in the American Indian as well as the "wilderness" that was his natural habitat. That these Indians had been in league with French Catholics made the captives' situation even more dire. If prisoners had managed to survive the march to Canada, they faced pressure from priests to convert to Catholicism. This posed an even greater peril than simple Indian captivity, for it would have jeopardized a Puritan Protestant's immortal soul.[11]

One of the most widely read captivity narratives was written by the Reverend John Williams, taken in the Deerfield raid.[12] As some of the Royalton men must have known, he had returned from captivity without his daughter, Eunice, to write his narrative. *The Redeemed Captive Returning To Zion* was likely to have been one of the seminal texts of Zadock's boyhood. His grandfather, the Rev. Stephen Steele, who had presided for 40 years at the Tolland, Connecticut, Congregational church, was succeeded in his ministry in 1759 by none other than the Reverend Nathan Williams, the grandson of John Williams of Deerfield.[13]

As Zadock was hurried north he may even have been considering the words of

John Williams, who had followed exactly the same paths and river valleys 76 years ago. What he did not know, of course, was that somewhere not far from his side was another Williams descendent: Lt. Houghton's trusted comrade in arms, *Tehoragwanegen*, Eunice's Kahnawake grandson, Thomas Williams.

Two days into their captivity, the Royalton captives had seen little to disabuse them of their standard image of Indian savagery: Pember, Button, Kneeland, and Gibbs—killed and scalped; houses and harvest burned; livestock slaughtered. On the other hand, no women had been harmed and most of the children had been released to Hannah Handy, albeit grudgingly.

Weakened by sickness and a life of hard work, old Edward Kneeland would not have been able to keep up, as everyone knew, and would almost certainly have been dispatched with a tomahawk blow, like his son, Joseph. So his release, even though it had served the purposes of Houghton and Philips, might have been seen as humane by some of the captives. Still, to recognize Indian humanity at this point would have required overcoming a prime tenet of New England Puritanism: any hint of Indian decency was due to divine intervention and not to the goodness of the savage.[14] What was more, there was a divine purpose: captivity by Indians was seen as a test of faith and an imperative to atone for sin. It was a trial that George Avery could only hope would lead to a kind of redemption.

> *I had at this time the Holy Bible and Watts Hymn Book in my bosom, that we used to read and meditate, which I took from a house that the Indians burned. The Indians would take these from my bosom to see what I had, and return them. These books was read by us on our Journey to Canada and consoling to use when prisoners. We had no where to look but to God in our troubles. In one of our stops, reading the 38th psalm as applicable in part to our case.*[15]

The 38th Psalm echoes the Puritan creed that misfortune is both penance and trial, and deliverance must come from a provident almighty. The Psalm closes with this reminder and plea:

> *But mine enemies are lively and they are strong. Forsake me not, O Lord: O my God be not far from me. Make haste to help me, O Lord, my salvation.*

* * *

Since escape appeared out of the question, Zadock and the other prisoners knew that the more distance Houghton and the warriors put between themselves and Royalton, the less chance there would be of summary executions, at least as long as the captives did their captors' bidding. Each of the captives had become the property of a specific captor and that was what would determine their fate and the nature of the coming ordeal of travel.[16] As Zadock vividly remembered, there was one trial no captive escaped:

> *They compelled many of the prisoners to carry their packs, enormous in size and extremely heavy, as they were filled with the plunder of pillaged houses and every thing which attracted their curiosity or desire to possess—pots, spiders, frying pans, and old side saddles.*
>
> *Looking glasses, which by the intention or carelessness of the prisoners became broken in a short time.*[17]

The youngest of the captives was Garner Rix, 13 years old. No matter how Hannah Handy had pleaded with Lt. Houghton, there had been no release for Garner. The testing of the boy's mettle began right away and the experience became firmly embedded in family oral history and repeated by his grandson on anniversaries of the raid in later years. His keeper loaded him with a massive pack that was so heavy he could barely carry it. When he collapsed, his captor, in an act of charity, relieved him of a part of it.[18]

David Waller, 14, did not fare as well. It was not unusual on previous raids for the Indians to bring moccasins with them for captives to wear on the march north.[19] Not this time. David later remembered that he was

> *barfooted and marched toward Canada and the next day October 17th 1780 there came a snow. [He] had no shoes and he froze his feet, and the Brittish put a pack on his back and not withstanding his feet was so badly off they marched him for days.*[20]

None of these men had been captured by Indians before, so they probably did not understand the extent to which they were now merchandise in an economic and cultural enterprise that had been evolving since long before Europeans arrived on this continent. In previous centuries Abenakis had been primarily hunters and gatherers, and Mohawks primarily agricultural; and they each had taken captives for adoption, slavery, and ritual torture. With increased European contact and Indian involvement in the Anglo-French warfare, Abenaki and Mohawk capturing practices had evolved by the early 18th century to accommodate not only the needs of the respective tribes for new membership, servitude, and revenge, but also the market for adult English male slaves and servants to the French in Canada. Even though adult men were the least suitable for Indian adoption, they had been captured during the French and Indian wars in far greater numbers than women or children, and had been sold in Canada to French families and to convents to enhance a diminished labor force. This had also become a mitigating factor in the practice of ritual torture: captives were simply worth more alive than dead.[21]

Allied now with the British instead of the French, the Indians were continuing in the same business. Captives unsuitable for permanent adoption or enslavement were kept alive to be sold to the British for money or exchanged for supplies, weapons, and rum.[22]

Because the captives had heard the stories of redeemed Indian prisoners, many of them first-hand, they knew that if they survived the trip to the tribe's village they would probably be safe, for the passage north was the most dangerous part of the experience. What was more, the captives were in the power of people they saw as utterly capricious, implacable, and alien. At this point the Royalton prisoners quite simply did not understand their captors.

What they perceived as unpredictability was really much more complicated. The Indian war party was as diverse a group of men as the people of Royalton had ever seen in one place. They were multicultural and multilingual: All spoke more than one language—English and/or French and anywhere from one to three Indian languages. Most were Roman Catholic, but their religion was a complicated hybrid, to say the least.[23] In one of many accommodations, the Jesuits at Kahnawake had obtained a special dispensation to say mass in Mohawk because they could not force all the people to learn French.[24]

The Kahnawakes for most of the 18th century and the preceding one had traveled regularly to Albany, conducting a thriving commerce with Dutch fur buyers (where they probably had picked up a smattering of that language, too). Kahnawake men followed the Saint Lawrence River and Great Lakes waterway as far as the Mississippi. The war party itself was a mixture of Kahnawake and St. Francis Indians, and those tribes themselves were a complex amalgamation of various tribes and descendants of European captives and adoptees—English, French, Dutch, and German.

Because this civil war, the American Revolution, was not their fight, the Indians as individuals had different reasons for being in the war party. Added to that were internal rivalries between the tribes represented in the war party. There was competition among them for captives, scalps, and plunder, and the attendant glory awaiting them upon return home. Finally, there was the political tension between the Indians and the British officers over control of the members of the party. With all that potential for friction in a single company of warriors, the resulting mixture was combustible.

The volatile Indians were by turns terrifying and teasing, so the captives could not tell the difference between a kind of playfulness and deadly ferocity. As much as they were helplessly enraged by the destruction of their property, harvest, and livestock and the waste of their labor, they had been utterly baffled as the warriors slit open feather beds in fits of glee, seized women's dresses and jewelry, and strangest of all, stole all of the mirrors in the village and loaded their prisoners with them.

Years later, Abijah Hutchinson's account of the march to Canada was recorded by his grandson. It is not nearly as detailed as Zadock's, but in it there are vivid moments of recall. Along with several others, Abijah Hutchinson was laden with looking glasses tied to his back with ropes and withes of bark. After two days of bearing this weight he was so exhausted and the load so unmanageable that he was nearly unable to continue. What was worse, an old wound was taking its toll. After serving at the Battle of Bunker hill, Abijah had gone to sea in a privateer out of Boston and in a naval battle had sustained a crippling injury to the knee from a flying shard of wood. By now he was limping badly. [25]

Oblivious of all but his load and his bare feet, Abijah paid no attention to the close appraisal that two of the warriors had been giving him. All of the Indians amused themselves by taking the measure of their captives. One member of the war party, who had been watching Hutchinson, approached and forced a pint of rum on him, insisting that he drink it, all of it at once, that it would make him strong.

The situation could have become ugly no matter what he did. If he refused, his defiance would be a death-warrant. If he drank the pint of rum—if it didn't kill him outright—the intoxication was likely to incapacitate him. He knew he would then be dispatched rather than abandoned to escape back to Royalton with crucial intelligence as to the war party's course of travel.

Abijah chose defiance. He refused the rum and the Indian was on him in a flash, thrusting the bottle toward his mouth while Abijah pushed back. A struggle ensued and the Indian, forgetting the rum, grabbed Abijah by the throat with one hand, forcing him to the ground. A tomahawk appeared in the other hand and a moment later it flashed down, missed its mark, and struck the ground, shattering a rock beside Abijah's head.

The blow had been deflected by the hand of another Indian who had been following Abijah. The assailant whirled around. Abijah saw standing above him a familiar face: his boyhood Indian friend from Lebanon, Connecticut, a boy who had gone to Moor's Indian Charity School. Abijah guessed that his old friend had recognized him earlier, and, knowing how easily a trivial matter could turn to one of life and death, had resolved to watch his back. The Indian reprimanded Abijah's assailant, redistributed Abijah's load, and saw to it that he and the other captives were given a decent meal, then apparently showed Abijah no further favor.

The records of Dartmouth College show a number of Indian boys enrolled between 1766 and 1772 when Hutchinson would have known them. The only Canada Indians were Mohawks, so that's probably what the long-lost, well-met friend was. There are several possibilities, but a likely candidate is a boy named Paulus (or Ograshuskon), mentioned in correspondence between British officers in June 1780, that confirms his presence in Montréal and his association with the British military.[26]

Although Zadock may not have witnessed this near-disaster, he was learning that Indians could not be measured by conventional settler stereotypes. Even so, on the heels of the murders of Kneeland and Gibbs, the flare-ups of gratuitous violence, and the brutal pace, he was entirely unprepared for Indian benevolence and generosity when it appeared.

> *On the morning of the 18th*, he wrote, *they first ordered me to eat my breakfast, urging me to eat as much as I wanted; while, on account of the loss of their provisions at Randolph, they had scarce half an allowance for themselves. I knew not whether to attribute this conduct to their feelings of charity and generosity, a desire to secure my friendship, or a wish to preserve my life under a prospect of procuring gain. Indeed, they seemed at all times to be willing to "feed the hungry." Their food, however, was very unsavory, insomuch that nothing but extreme hunger would have induced me to eat of it, though I always had a share of their best.*[27]

THE ONION RIVER, OCTOBER 19. Zadock also remembered, "They often traveled with the utmost celerity in their power" to test his strength and endurance. When they found Zadock was "able to keep pace with them," they viewed him with new-found respect and interest. Zadock and the other captives had been so toughened by their daily lives that the forced march to Canada along well-worn Indian trails was not greatly more taxing than their own, far longer, migrations north from Connecticut and Massachusetts on foot. At least one of the captives, Joseph Havens, had been on this very trail along the Onion River in February, one of the regular patrols sent north looking for the enemy—"chasing the Indians," as he later wrote.[28]

As the party descended the Onion River Valley toward Lake Champlain, it passed through stands of immense white pine trees that grew along the river. The late light, slanting in shafts through the leafless hardwood forest, made the snow-covered ground glow, but the pine groves the party passed through were nearly dark as night. An occasional trunk was six feet in diameter with a crown that soared 200 feet above the earth.[29] Every night since the captives had left Royalton, they heard wolves howling. They never saw one, but they knew wolves were watching, never far. The men saw their tracks in the snow each morning, as they had with regularity back in Royalton, where packs preyed heavily on livestock. It was no comfort that only the wolves reminded them of home.[30]

Zadock and the others had certainly heard of the abandonment of the Onion River Valley. Word of the devastation here had filtered south, but seeing it firsthand must have been a sobering experience.

Developed by the Allen brothers and their speculative Onion River Land Company, the bottom lands and meadows of the valley had been settled and thriving in the early 1770s, but now they were abandoned. The British and their Canada Indian allies, under the command of Lt. Houghton and Major John Peters, had swept up the valley two years ago. A staunch and notorious Vermont loyalist, the Yale-educated Peters had owned property near Newbury before the war, until he was driven out and fled to Canada. There he eagerly formed a corps with other Vermont loyalists, called the Queen's Loyal Rangers, for raids on the frontier.[31] Peters had initially been ordered to destroy the settlement of Newbury, but he had been pulled back by messenger at the last minute, and instead, he and Houghton had wiped out the Onion River settlement.[32]

As the ragged Royalton party passed the overgrown clearings, the pastures and gardens gone to seed, the vacant burn-out cabins and sheds, disintegrating masonry, shreds of fabric, shattered crocks, charred nubs of furniture, and bleached bones of slaughtered animals, they saw what their own ruined homes would look like within a year.

CHAPTER 7

THE LAKE

"I got thirty-two prisoners and four scalps"

LAKE CHAMPLAIN, OCTOBER 20. As the Onion River spilled out of the Green Mountains, the valley broadened, the land flattened, and the water slowed and snaked in lazy meanders through fertile intervales seeking the lake.

A well-used path ascended from the mouth of the river at the lake, worn by centuries of Indian travel and a decade of busy settler traffic that was now stilled by the War. After passing through a vast marsh and then a dense, gnarled forest, the river poured into the lake from a narrow opening in a shore strewn with massive driftwood trunks and roots.

The war party had left bateaux and big canoes here and had pulled them out of sight into the trees. A British vessel, the *Carleton,* was moored off the mouth of Onion River where it had been since the night of October 19th.[1] To Zadock it must have been a sobering reminder of the reach of British power to see a heavily armed warship riding at anchor on Vermont's inland ocean.

The raiding party was home free. They launched their boats while the *Carleton* covered them from just offshore. The British controlled Lake Champlain and their ships moved about on it with impunity, even though they were frequently challenged by rebel militia along its shores as little as 30 miles south of the mouth of the Onion River. In any case, it was only the water they ruled; except for a few isolated outposts at the northern end of the lake, there was no permanent British presence along the shoreline.

From here it was a matter of only two days for the war party, in an armada of canoes and other vessels, to travel north to St. John's, the British military headquarters between Lake Champlain and Montréal.

11. View of St. John's, 1776, Public Archives of Canada, Copy Neg. # C001507.

ST. JOHN'S, OCTOBER 23. The 32 men and boys from Royalton and the surrounding area would soon be joining hundreds of others streaming north who had been captured during the great October raids on the northern frontiers. They were forced from forts, farms and isolated settlements along the length of the back country, from New England to the Ohio Valley, and now they were entering the British prison system. Only a day behind Houghton's party in reaching St. John's was a ship with 60 captives from attacks on rebel posts and towns in the Lake George area: Fort Ann, Fort Edward, Fort George, and Ballston, New York. These were soon to be joined by another raiding party with 40 more New York captives. It made for a very nearly unmanageable overnight crowd in the British garrison town of more than 370 Indian warriors and more than 130 hapless prisoners.[2]

Until their arrival at St. John's, all the captives had more or less shared a common fate, but this was a processing center and from here they would be going in dramatically different directions. Of the 32 brought in by Houghton's war party most were marched overland to Kahnawake. At least one, Abijah Hutchinson, was taken by his Abenaki captors to the village of St. Francis. Once there, he was sold on October 27th, nine days after capture, to the British Commissary of Prisoners for "a half-Joe," worth eight dollars, the standard bounty for rebel captives. From St. Francis he was taken to join hundreds of others in the vast stone building outside the city of Montréal known as the Provost. Some of them had been captured as recently as himself, and others as long ago as 1777.[3]

Even though an official British policy had been set down in June 1780, opposing the Indian practice of adoption, the officers at St. John's must have viewed the departure of all these Vermont and New York captives under the custody of the Indians with some relief.[4] The British had virtually no place to put the captured rebels.

Lt. Richard Houghton took his leave of the war party at this point, but not before he reported to the commanding officer at St. John's, Captain Monsell. The captain fired off a quick dispatch to headquarters with the news that Houghton had just arrived and "brought in 32 prisoners and some scalps. He has destroyed a great number of houses, barns, corn."[5] In short order, Houghton made a terse report to General Haldimand on the events of the raid that concluded:

> *I burned twenty eight dwelling Houses, thirty two Barns full of grain and one new barn not quite finished, one Saw and one G[rai]ns Mill killed all the black Cattle, sheep, Piggs &c of which there was a great quantity, there was but very little hay.*
>
> *I have the honor to be Your most obedt. Humb. Servant, Richard Houghton, Indn Residt. (at Kahnawake)*
>
> *P. S. I got 32 Prisoners & 4 scalps. the Country was alarmed by Whitcomb the day before I got there.*[6]

It was the report of an experienced officer and betrayed no reflection, no shadow of the devastation his raid had visited upon 40 families; nor (quite understandably) of Hannah Handy's defiance; nor of the summary executions of Kneeland and Gibbs, Button, and Pember—except to note the acquisition of their scalps; nor of the rigors of the forced march, his troubling old injuries, or the fate of the captives, whom he would never see again.[7] By this time, Lt. Houghton had seen a great deal of bloodshed; he was used to war. It was a way of life.[8]

On October 25, Haldimand wrote a long letter to the British Foreign Secretary, Lord Germain, in which he enthusiastically praised the exploits of Maj. Carleton and John Johnson in New York and those of Lt. Houghton in Vermont.[9] But Houghton's exploits would come back ironically to haunt the British command.

Adorned with paint and wearing not a stitch of his own clothing, George Avery, like the other captives, was set by his master on the last leg of the journey toward the humiliation and uncertainty of ceremonial entry into the Indian village. The road the Royalton prisoners followed led straight across the dead flat of the St. Lawrence Valley, and in an extended ragged procession they shared the rutted, muddy route with 40 other mostly barefoot captives from New York and a few hundred warriors who were in a state of high excitement and advanced inebriation. For Avery it was a vivid memory, dryly recalled:

> *The Indians this day (Sabbath) take up their march for their Home Cahnawaga, many of them very drunk and often those loaded down with theire plundered goods sowsed down in mud as road was much soaked by the snows melting off at this time. Some of those loaded drunken Indians in this plight were three days traveling 25 miles. I was taken by my Master Indian to Cahnawaga at his home.*[10]

Even before the village was in sight, they heard the water. The St. Lawrence River, as it approached Montréal, dropped dramatically in a series of violent rapids, and it was the raging water tumbling past that gave the place its French name, Sault St. Louis, or the Falls of St. Louis. Since settling here in 1670, the Kahnawakes had become legendary river men and runners of rapids.

The first thing the captives saw of the village was a towering steeple on a magnificent stone church at least as grand as anything they had seen in New England. In form it was a familiar sight that might have given them a sense of relief—the possibility that they might have been within a circle of civilization once more. Except, of course, that this was a Catholic church, embodying everything these New Englanders held most suspect.

Although a vast wilderness separated Kahnawake from Royalton, both places were part of a single world whose extremities were joined by traffic in captives, commerce, and competing religions. Eleazar Wheelock of Dartmouth had sent more than one missionary to Kahnawake to pry the people from the Catholicism that had first taken hold among them in the 17th century. Most recently, in 1773, Wheelock had dispatched young Thomas Kendall to preach and recruit boys for his college.[11] When Kendall had arrived in the spring of 1773 he had with him introductions to village elders from Wheelock. One of the first people he had met was John Stacey, an Englishman who had been captured as a boy in 1756 in New York and adopted into the tribe. He had eventually decided to stay for good, married a Kahnawake woman (possibly a captive herself) and now operated a trading post at the village.[12] Stacey, like Philips of the raiding party, lived with a foot in both worlds; in answer to Wheelock's urging, he had sent his son Thomas to Dartmouth.[13] As the Royalton captives arrived, young Thomas Stacey was by all accounts still at Dartmouth, along with Talbot Philips.[14] And if it weren't for their attendance at Dartmouth, they would almost certainly have been among the Royalton raiders.

Like any good missionary, Kendall had been persistent and had worked hard to cultivate friendships, particularly with the influential Philips/*Sanorese*, now returning from the Royalton Raid to a triumphant reception. There was an outside chance that, if the war party had gone only a little farther downstream into the village of Sharon, Philips and the Reverend Kendall might have come face to face once again. Thomas Kendall, having returned to Dartmouth well before the war, had been living as a preacher and missionary in Sharon since 1778 and was there at the time of the raid.[15] Back in Vermont, Kendall was no doubt surveying the smoking ruins of the village, knowing full well where the warriors had come from, and wondering perhaps how many of them had been his eager students in Bible class only a few years earlier.

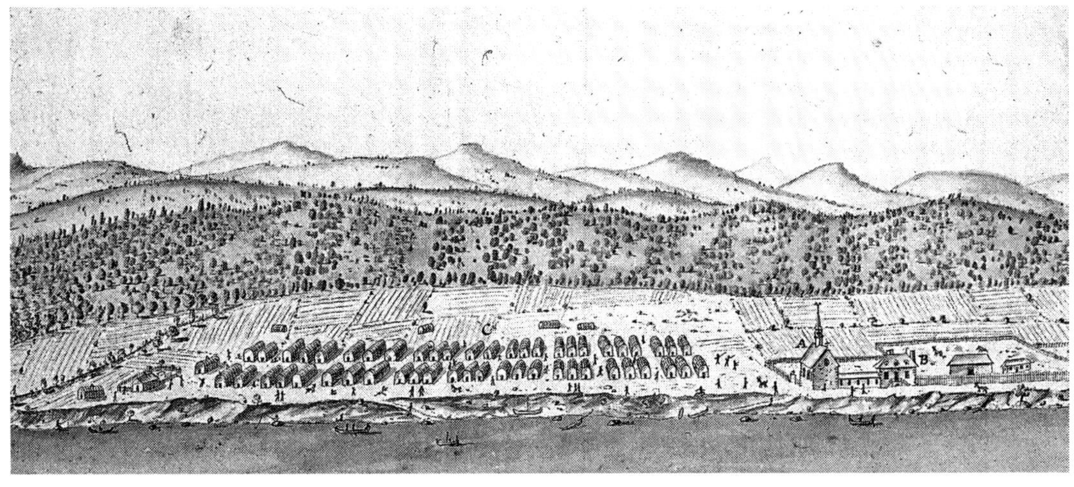

12. View of Kahnawake, Bibliothèque Nationale de France, Microfilm P-183974.

There were at least 300 fighting men at Kahnawake and two-thirds of them were members of this war party; most of the rest were with the war party that had gone to New York State.[16] The return of a large force like this was an event of great importance to the village. Even before the procession arrived, each warrior with a scalp painted the flesh side red and displayed it proudly, and each in turn voiced a short, shrill, ear-splitting yell.[17] After the fourth scalp call, each warrior with a prisoner gave a much longer shout of a different pitch, signifying a captive.[18] When the inventory was complete, the entire body of warriors erupted in a sudden cacophony of shouts signifying a transport of exultation and triumph. They were answered by the rattle of celebratory musket fire from the village and then the war party and its spoils and trophies poured into the village.

13. Indians Poling up the Rapids of the St. Lawrence, Public Archives of Canada, Copy Neg. # C-024163.

CHAPTER 8

KAHNAWAKE

"The ceremony of my own adoption afforded no small degree of diversion"

OCTOBER 23. It was a scene that had repeated itself in this place for well over a century: captives from the English colonies paraded into the village, halters around their necks and no expectations for the future. Zadock and the others did not know that it had been a long time since captives had been tortured to death at Kahnawake, or even forced to run the gauntlet. Not knowing that, they had every reason to fear the worst.

The crowd would have pressed in around him, most of them women, children, and old men. The throng would have taken the measure of the new captives, assessing the value of their remaining possessions, their monetary value through sale to the British, the desirability for adoption—especially the boys. Even in the army, Zadock would never have felt quite like this, like an item of livestock. Hands would have reached out to touch his hair, to pinch his flesh, to clutch at what clothing he had left. Faces would have been thrust in front of his, as if to test his nerve.

As Zadock met the gaze of the people of the village, he might have noticed what he had overlooked in the painted faces and shaven skulls of the warriors: here and there a pair of blue, brown, or green eyes and light-colored hair and skin, while from their tongues came the effortless, incomprehensible Mohawk language, salted, perhaps, with phrases in English and French. Some of them would have been the descendants of the seven girls and five boys captured by Kahnawake warriors in the 1704 Deerfield raid who had been adopted and had never gone back to New England. Maybe recalling her own arrival, Eunice Williams, now 83, was in the village, quite possibly a witness herself to the scene. She would soon be joined by her grandson, Thomas, who would surely tell her of the raid and of his part in it, conceivably reassuring her of his attention to the safety of the settlers.

The wardrobes of the throng were eclectic: the women wore cloth or buckskin leggings under knee-length skirts; many had cloth shirts and colorful sashes and hood-like caps; there was an assortment of moccasins and leather shoes. The men wore silver bracelets and arm bands; ears were pierced for rings, lobes stretched; there were rings in noses and many faces were tattooed. The crowd was a riot of color and style: glints of silver, splashes of blue and buff from snatched Continental Army uniforms, shoulders wrapped in the geometric patterns of quilts, bits of frothy lace, creamy silk, homespun wool, cotton and linen shirts and breeches, colored ribbons, and cocked hats.[1]

On the way to the village the prisoners would have seen a few tidy farms of French-Canadian settlers, ironically people much like themselves: descendants of European immigrants, some of them not unsympathetic to the rebel cause. And the captives must have wondered: if they could only slip away and somehow be taken in by these other white people—escape, salvation, redemption might be a possibility. But they also would have seen these Canadians mingling with the Kahnawake villagers, speaking with them in French, gossiping, grinning, gesturing, and exchanging items of barter. The French would have been eyeing the youngest captives with as keen an interest as the Indian women. They even might have seen the priest, Père Huguet, hovering on the margins of the scene; and they would have realized that they had entered a remarkably complicated world.

At one end of the village was the great stone church and along the banks of the river two rows of houses. Like so much else in the lives of the Kahnawake people, their dwellings were resourceful improvisations. Some were built as they had always been, with log walls and barrel-vaulted bark roofs, but in recent years more of the people had been building houses that combined timber and masonry construction, learned from the French Canadians and encouraged by the Jesuit priests.[2]

In front of them on the river bank sat birch bark canoes, some ten feet, others as much as 30 feet in length. Beyond the houses were horse pens and planted fields where just recently corn, squash, pumpkins, beans, and potatoes had been harvested. Across the river the prisoners could see the great stone walls fortifying Montréal, the cultivated fields surrounding it, and the waterfront bristling with a forest of rigging, spars, and masts. Heavily laden vessels were making ready, before the river froze, to sail downstream, home to England. Montréal was a place where Zadock and Avery and the others might have felt quite at home, but just across the river, Kahnawake was a separate world, byzantine in its political complexity, and nearly as perplexing to the British as it was to the Royalton captives.

Though it had supplied warriors for the British attack on Royalton, Kahnawake, even more than the other villages of the Seven Nations, was riven with factions that disagreed on allegiance in this war. Most of them suspected that the outcome of the conflict would leave them worse off than they had been at its outset, no matter who should win. What the British wanted was the Indians' allegiance; and with some exceptions, some maddening reversals, and the constant countercurrent of factionalism and intrigue, allegiance was largely what they got. However, it cost the British mightily in supplies, equipment, time, uncertainty, and mistrust.[3]

Just as the Royalton captives arrived, two Kahnawake couriers were slipping across the border into Canada after an arduous cross-country journey from Rhode Island. One was *Horatouskon*, a notorious pro-rebel Oneida spy, and the other, *Hogatagete,* a Kahnawake man.[4] They had gone to meet the French General Rochambeau and to view his army of 5,000 men and the fleet of French warships anchored (and blockaded by the British) in Newport harbor since July 1780. The couriers brought a proclamation urging the French Canadians and the Seven Nations of Canada to join the French in their alliance with the rebels, especially in the event of a joint French-American invasion of Canada.

The British knew whom they could not trust, but were unable to penetrate effectively the intertribal network or frustrate the movement of spies and emissaries that regularly crossed the border. Nevertheless, informers in the village had told the British of the spies' arrival, and orders had gone out to seize the incendiary French proclamation, and to take the couriers dead or alive.[5]

When not raiding the frontier, Lt. Houghton was the Assistant Superintendent at Kahnawake and one of Haldimand's most forceful and effective agents in the Indian community. He would soon turn his attention to just who these couriers were and to the full import of the intelligence they had brought.[6] To complicate matters further, Haldimand was convinced that the Jesuit priest, Père Huguet, was influencing the Kahnawake to remain neutral.[7] Kahnawake was a magnet for Mohawks of all political stripes, and it was where lengthy, oration-filled councils with the British were conducted.[8] The Iroquois of the Six Nations (of New York State) considered Kahnawake to be their northern capital, an "extension of Iroquois political and economic sovereignty."[9]

* * *

This intrigue and maneuvering would have been well beyond Zadock's ken or concern as he and the others were hurried down the main thoroughfare of the village. They did not remain together. Each was taken by his captor or custodian to a separate house where he remained in deep uncertainty. Zadock spent his days in the dark interior of the dwelling, breathing the smoky air, peering through the gloom or out the door into the glare of the day, never alone. People entering, leaving, bringing him the food he was sure he would never learn to love, touching up his painted face as needed to signify his captive status, sometimes with blue-eyed children staring at him, men and women inscrutably considering him and his future with them. For Zadock, life as a Kahnawake captive was unimaginable. It became all the more so when Philips came to see him.

> *Some days after we arrived at Kahnawake,* Zadock later recalled, *an old man by the name of Philips—whose visage indicated the trials, sorrows, and afflictions of a long and wretched captivity—presented to me a solemn and awful token of what I myself might expect to suffer.*
>
> *Mr. Philips was taken prisoner in the western part of the State of New York, by the Indians, in his youthful days, and, having been adopted into one of their families, had always lived with them. He had retained his knowledge of the English language, and served as an interpreter for the tribe.*[10]

It is not surprising that Zadock did not recognize Philips from the raid, since there had been 265 face-painted warriors in the party moving in single file, making many separate camps at night, separated on the lake in different boats, and going by different routes to this and other villages.

It is perhaps more surprising how deceived Zadock was by the man's appearance. Philips's life as a captive may have aged him severely—at least, if Zadock remembered him clearly—but he was only 47 years old, having been born in 1733.[11] Boys were far less likely than girls to make the choice that Philips had made at the age of 14, but it had led to a vastly different and probably more appealing life than that of a farmer in one of the German or Dutch settlements of the Mohawk Valley. He had risen in the tribal hierarchy to a position of influence, helped by a canny political instinct and an ability to use his captive status to gain favor with both French and British authorities. Like many captives, Philips had married another captive—a woman from the St. Regis village named Anna Tarbell, who gave him 11 children. As we know, one of them, Talbot, was studying at Dartmouth; another, John, had become a youthful Sachem, or chief of the Kahnawake.[12]

Philips made sure that Zadock knew his background and his English name. There was not much happening in the village that Philips did not know about, and now he had come to tell Zadock that, like the other prisoners, he was about to become one of them, "to fill the place of one whom they had lost on their expedition to Royalton."[13]

The captives, especially the boys, were viewed as prime material for building the tribe, and no matter what the British policy against adoption may have been, the village elders were not about to forgo this ancient ritual, so integral to the return of a war party.[14] Zadock had been reassured by Philips of the benign nature of the proceedings. Once Zadock realized he was truly out of danger, his native Yankee skepticism relented, making room even for a measure of distraction from his misfortune.

> *The ceremony of my own adoption afforded no small degree of diversion—a spectacle of barbarism assuming the appearance of civilization. All the Indians, both male and female, together with the prisoners, assembled and formed a circle, within which one of their chiefs, standing upon a stage erected for the purpose, harangued the audience in the Indian tongue.*
>
> *Although I could not understand his language, yet I could plainly discover a great share of native eloquence. His speech was of considerable length, and its effect obviously manifested weight of argument, solemnity of thought, and human sensibility. I was placed near by his side, and had a fair view of the whole circle.*[15]

Following the ceremony, the captives were separated again, but in the eyes of the Kahnawake people the process had transformed the identities of the captives. Once adopted into the tribe, a prisoner was no longer who he once had been; he would frequently inhabit the identity of a tribal member who had died, sometimes recently, sometimes in the past. Thus, an adoptee eventually assumed the social position, rights, and responsibilities of the one whose place he was taking. If a prisoner replaced a person of influence, wisdom, and courage, great things were expected of him and he would be treated with deference. From someone who was replacing a person of low esteem, nothing of value would be expected and he was generally used accordingly.[16]

There had been a time among the Kahnawake when an adoptee would have undergone an elaborate three-part physical transformation as well. The first would have been the running of the gauntlet, an experience that varied from benign to lethally violent and was meant to beat the "whiteness" out of captives. The second was a ritual cleansing, first in a sweat bath, followed by a kind of baptism to wash out all the white blood. The third part completed the metamorphosis, with all the head hair plucked save for a small, circular scalp-lock; the nose and earlobes slit for rings or plugs; the face tattooed and painted; the body painted and then clothed in new clothes, even jewels. But for Zadock and his Royalton mates, today's was to be a short-form ceremony.[17]

George Avery was still not aware of what was about to happen to him, except that for the moment it would apparently be free of violence; it was not until he was informed by a fellow adoptee that he realized what his new status was to be.

Later, he wrote that he was troubled by one particular aspect of the ceremony:

> *But what I saw afterward which was more affecting. That they displayed the Scalps of our prisoners (those they killed) in the same seremony.*[18]

The scalps that Avery found so disquieting had for the Indians powerful symbolic as well as intrinsic properties. It was not only a valuable trophy, testifying to a man's prowess in battle, but a scalp could also serve as a substitute for a captive taken to replace a relative killed in battle.[19] Zadock, Avery, and the others now experienced what adopted captives for centuries had discovered: once taken into the tribe in this way, they were treated with elaborate, even loving, kindness. Reports of this outcome may have made their way back to the New England colonies via people who had gone through the experience, but such accounts got neither much attention nor credence, nor did they make much headway against ingrained colonist attitudes.

Discovering they were to be neither abused nor enslaved, the Royalton captives, as had so many before them, embraced their new status, at least for the time being.[20] In the past, those who had remained for long periods of time with their captors came to wonder at the completeness with which the Indians accepted so many of them as equals—so unlike the treatment accorded to Indians living among British colonists in New England.[21] Of course, it did not always end well; the lot of a captive who became a slave was a miserable one and could end with humiliation, physical abuse, and worse, but that was not to be the case here.[22]

John Stacey, like Philips, was making the rounds of the prisoners. He had been at times on the British payroll as a commissary in the Québec Indian Department, so he would have been an important source of information for the British about prisoners and their treatment.[23] The British were neither able nor inclined to prevent adoption ceremonies, but they were intent on removing captives eventually from Indian custody, knowing that they could only do so through careful negotiation and never by decree.[24] To further that policy, Stacey's role seems to have been to facilitate redemption, ransoming and indenturing the captives as frequently as possible.

One of the first things he apparently did was to arrange to have the youngest boys taken in by local families. Although the British had no problem with holding such young captives *per se,* they were not eager to feed, clothe, and care for them. If local families would take them on as servants, they would provide the boys with room and board. Beyond a certain age, the British saw the boys, as they did all rebel prisoners—as potential recruits; and enlistment in the king's service was made an attractive alternative to living with the savages or rotting indefinitely in prison.[25]

The youngest Royalton boys were not offered enlistment, but those over 15 were. Like all the captives, the boys at first lived with Kahnawake families. Nathaniel Gilbert, who was 15, moved in with a motherly woman for a period of several months, but in March of 1781 the prospect of enlistment was attractive enough to entice him—though no others. He became a member of one of the loyalist regiments being assembled in Canada, the 2nd Battalion of the King's Royal Regiment of New York.[26]

The remaining Royalton men bided their time, and Zadock found that life among the Kahnawake was bearable, if disorienting. He had splendid new clothes but also a new, insistent, English-speaking mother who expected more warmth than Zadock could summon. Her cuisine was repellent and her affections were self-defeating. To Zadock's dismay, her attentions were redoubled when she discovered how fine a singing voice he had; but by way of balance, his talents gained him privileges.

> *An old squaw came and took me by the hand and led me to her wigwam, where she dressed me in a red coat, with a ruffle in my bosom, and ordered me to call her mother. She could speak English tolerably well; but was very poor, and therefore unable to furnish me with very sumptuous fare. my new mother endeavored to endear the affections of her newly-adopted yet ill-natured son.*
>
> *I found the appellation of mother highly pleased the tawny jade, which proportionably increased my disgust; and added disquietude to affliction and sorrow.*
>
> *As I was blessed with an excellent voice for singing, I received much better treatment from my new mother, as well as from other Indians.*
>
> *I was allowed the privilege of visiting any part of the village in the daytime, and was received with marks of fraternal affection and treated with all the civility an Indian is capable to bestow.*[27]

As is customary, Zadock was handed over to the custody of a woman—very likely one who had lost a family member, most likely a son. Even so, neither Zadock nor Simeon Belknap, a Randolph neighbor whose sense of mischief appeared to have remained intact, made especially compliant new members of the Kahnawake community.

> *A prisoner, by the name of Belknap, was set about hewing some poles for a stable door while his Indian master held them for him. ...the workman, [Belknap],*

> *laughing in his sleeves, hew[ed] quite round the stick. Thinking that Belknap knew no better, the Indian endeavored to instruct him.*
>
> *After trying several poles the Indian, filled with impatience for this untractable pupil, with his eyes on fire, left him and called his interpreter to make his wishes ...known. ...Belknap declared, that he did well understand the wishes of the Indian, and was determined to avoid doing his will.* [28]

Belknap was not the only defiant prisoner. The men from Royalton and the Mohawk Valley were proving so recalcitrant that the Kahnawake villagers were soon only too willing to get rid of them. Most were clearly going to be useless as adoptees, but they still had some monetary value as chattel. Zadock wrote:

> *After a few weeks, finding the prisoners very incorrigible, and wishing for the reward they might obtain for them, information was given the prisoners that they might be delivered over to the British at Montreal as prisoners of war, or continue with the Indians, as they should choose.* [29]

Escape from Kahnawake appeared to Zadock not to be an option. The captives were very closely watched, the route by which they had come to the village from Lake Champlain was heavily patrolled by the British, and winter was closing in. It was November. The days were short and frigid; ice was forming in the lakes and ponds; snow would soon be piling up, and flight was as fruitless as recapture was certain.

John Stacey was busy as a go-between and expediter in the village. Zadock resigned himself to indefinite Indian captivity, but now that the Kahnawakes wished to part with him and the others, he asked Stacey for advice.

> *He appeared to be a man of integrity and veracity... I was advised by Mr. Stacy to be delivered into the hands of the British. He said I might doubtless obtain leave to dwell in some family of a private gentleman until I should be exchanged.* [30]

Zadock pictured himself rescued and redeemed by Providence and British magnanimity, as all the remaining captives must have done as well. John Stacey had, of course, told Zadock and the others what they wanted to hear, and there was some substance in the hope he held out for them. Some of the younger captives had already been placed in households. It was common for captured American officers to be likewise housed under conditions of parole: They would give their word of honor not to try to escape and in return would be treated less as captives than as guests who had no way home. Such men enjoyed a remarkable degree of freedom and independence, and were even permitted into the social fabric of the city, dining from time to time with British officers and benefactors who took it on themselves to come to the aid of destitute prisoners of war.[31]

Captives on both sides were pawns in the ongoing traffic of prisoner exchange. Women and children ended up as servants in the households of officers and professional civilians. As of November 1780, the British held about 550 prisoners of war in and around Montréal, and that included 26 women and children—nearly all from Virginia and Pennsylvania—the youngest of whom was but a year-and-a-half old.[32]

And so Zadock and all but the youngsters of Royalton joined this company of taken people.

> *I made choice to be given up to the British,* Zadock wrote. *All the captives did likewise. We were all conducted to Montreal, by the Indians, in the latter part of November 1780, and there "sold for a half Joe"* [33] *each. Most of the captives were young, and remarkably robust, healthy, and vigorous. I was now almost twenty-two years of age. To be compelled to spend the vigor of my days in useless confinement was a source of grief and pain to my mind; but I could see no way of escape. The wisdom of God I found to be unsearchable indeed.*[34]

CHAPTER 9

WRONG RAID, WRONG PLACE, WRONG TIME

"Lieut. Houghton acted for the best, but..."

THE ROYALTON RAID was never meant to be. It was a last-minute tactical and logistical improvisation that had unintended political consequences which threatened to jeopardize a top-secret geo-political realignment under discussion between the British Foreign Office, General Frederick Haldimand, and the government of Vermont.

All year Haldimand had been receiving credible intelligence that Washington was again planning an invasion of Canada, to be preceded by a military occupation of Vermont as a base of operations.[1] In fact, Washington had no such plans, but was releasing disinformation to make the British think he did.[2]

Taken in, Haldimand doubted that Vermont would stand for such a move. Vermont had become one of the wild cards of the Revolution, and Haldimand was intensely interested in what its people and its government thought about the rebellion and in what the Continental Congress was planning to do about the thorny Vermont question. He had informants and spies placed in Vermont who encouraged him in believing that Vermont's alienation from the United States was increasing and might eventually be irreversible: A British agent named William Marsh wrote to him that:

> *New York represented in Congress that they (Vermont) were disobedient, fractious, riotous and rebellious to the United States of America....these people might be brought into the [British] fold if promised a separate colony and promotion of leaders.*[3]

Well aware of the tension between the independent republic of Vermont and the Continental Congress, the British government saw a way to drive a wedge between the two and persuade Vermont to declare its loyalty to Great Britain. As early as 1779, the British Secretary of State for America, Lord Germain, had been discussing ways to lure Vermont back to the side of Great Britain.

In 1780 Germain had written to Haldimand that this was an essential goal to be pursued no matter what the cost.[4] Furthermore, Germain was urgently encouraged to win over Vermont by Benedict Arnold, whose treason had been discovered only days before the Royalton Raid. In a letter written by Arnold to Lord Germain October 28, 1780, his plan for winning the war would begin with attacks up the Hudson River to cut off New England from the rest of the states. He urged measures to bring Vermont over to the British side by offering it self-government, which was more than the Continental Congress was prepared to do.[5]

In late September, Vermont's Governor Thomas Chittenden had written to Haldimand proposing to exchange British prisoners for Vermonters held by the British in Canada.[6] On October 22, Haldimand duly responded, inviting Chittenden to nominate a "proper person with full power" to attend a meeting on the subject.[7] In due course, representatives were appointed by the governor and his council.[8] Believing that Vermont might be receptive to reunion, Haldimand saw an opportunity to initiate secret negotiations to bring the breakaway republic over to the British side. The perfectly plausible cover story would be prisoner-exchange negotiations—a ploy under discussion in British intelligence circles since August.[9] Making the ruse even more believable was the fact that in August, Washington himself had suggested discussions between Vermont and Canada on the subject of prisoners. Not fully trusting the Vermont government, Washington insisted in a letter to Chittenden that this was the only subject he was to discuss with Haldimand.[10]

14. Governor Thomas Chittenden, Special Collections, University of Vermont Libraries.

In a coincidence of supreme historical irony, the details of this meeting were being hammered out at precisely the same time as Lt. Houghton and his 265 warriors were returning from their own rendezvous with history at Royalton.

By the time Houghton got to St. John's from Royalton with his Vermont prisoners, the place and time of the meeting had been set; by the time the Kahnawakes were adopting Zadock and the others, the meeting was under way. The negotiations opened on October 28, 1780, at Castleton, in western Vermont, far from Royalton. The principals were Justus Sherwood, the head of the British Secret Service in Canada, and none other than the once arch-rebel, Ethan Allen, the hero of Ticonderoga and arguably the most famous Revolutionary ex-prisoner-of-war to date.[11]

It would seem that the last thing Haldimand would have approved was a military operation that would jeopardize this crucial diplomatic undertaking, but that is just what he seems to have done. Haldimand had understood Houghton's assigned mission and told Col. Campbell, who had ordered it, that he hoped "it would have good effect."[12]

What seems likely is that the chance to "detach Vermont" arose serendipitously in the midst of the planning and execution of the massive campaign against the New York frontier. Chittenden's letter of late September gave Haldimand an opening, but he didn't take immediate advantage of it. Perhaps preoccupied with the details of the New York offensive, Haldimand did not reply to the letter for a month, but during that time the idea of a reunion between Vermont and Great Britain was no doubt taking shape. Justus Sherwood had been convinced for months that Vermont could be brought over and said as much to senior military figures.

On October 22, two weeks after approving Houghton's mission, Haldimand sent Justus Sherwood to Vermont. Sherwood's assignment was to persuade Ethan Allen to come back into the British fold and to bring Vermont with him. Well before the time they sat down to talk in Castleton on October 28, news of the Royalton Raid had arrived in Bennington, where the state government was in session.[13] Allen read letters to the assembly "about the approach of the enemy" that almost certainly described the Royalton Raid as well as the massive British force on Lake Champlain, and without delay the assembly voted to put Vermont on a "war footing."[14]

Houghton had written his report to Frederick Haldimand on October 26th, carefully summarizing the damage he had done. Even though Haldimand must have known that there would be trouble once reports of the raid reached Governor Chittenden, he sent to Houghton by return mail his "perfect approbation of your conduct in that affair."[15]

So by early November, just as Zadock and his mates were leaving Kahnawake Village for the uncertainties of British custody, the lieutenant must have been feeling that he could take pride in a difficult job well done.

Or could he?

A week and a half later, once the political implications of the raid became clear, Capt. Robert Mathews, Haldimand's secretary, wrote to Houghton's commanding officer, Col. John Campbell:

> *I am Commanded by His Excellency General Haldimand to signify to You his desire that you will not Send or permit any Scouts to go out to the Eastward of the Hudson's River, or to any Part which Can be Considered belonging to the State of Vermont, until further orders. Lieut. Houghton acted for the best, but it was very unfortunate that he Changed his Route, or appeared at all in that Quarter, as they have made proposals for an Exchange of Prisoners, which His Excellency has paid some attention to.*[16]

Campbell did not know even then what was going on behind the scenes—that a prisoner exchange was cover for secret negotiations with the State of Vermont. Haldimand was pursuing a dual policy, one part of which was aimed at wooing Vermont's allegiance and the other at destroying potential bases for an American invasion of Canada via the Connecticut River and Lake Champlain. In spite of intelligence to the contrary, Haldimand suspected that a great many Vermonters were in fact committed to the Revolution. The people of the upper Connecticut River Valley in particular would do all they could to support an invasion of Canada, and they relentlessly pressed George Washington to act.[17] The garrison town of Newbury was crucial to any such military operation, with its troops, key officers such as Bayley and Whitcomb, and depots of provisions, the original object of what became the Royalton Raid.[18]

Back in November 1779, at least one senior British officer, Major Christopher Carleton, had proposed a massive invasion of Vermont for 1780 that would have wiped out Newbury along with several other Connecticut River towns.[19] Whatever Haldimand may have thought of Carleton's idea, he had shelved it in favor of a massive campaign against upstate New York in the summer and fall of 1780.[20] An attack on Vermont was not part of the scheme. Late in the summer, Haldimand told his field commanders to begin planning the assault using combined British and Indian war parties. On September 21st, Haldimand wrote to Col. Campbell, who was in charge of the Canada Indian Department at St. John's, to gather

> *as many Indians, from 50 to 100, as will cheerfully offer themselves...The usual Preparations...must be laid aside—and no more sent than those in Your neighborhood who Can easily be Collected, and who will march in a few Hours*

notice. They must be at the Isle aux Noix the 30th Instant, where you will meet them with whatever light articles of Cloathing may be absolutely necessary to fit them out. [21]

The notice went out to Houghton at Kahnawake and to officers at other Canadian Indian villages to gather a force of no more than 100 warriors for the expedition to New York State. [22] Then two unexpected things happened.

One was the arrival of new intelligence. The second was the arrival of too many Indians.

All year long, couriers, spies, fleeing Tories, and escaped British prisoners had been arriving at St. John's. If they had intelligence to report, they were exhaustively debriefed. On the 22nd of September a routine report had recorded the arrival of Richard Hamilton, last seen in Royalton heading north claiming to be a surveyor. In fact, he had gone north, but he and his party had crossed the border into Canada, where he had been picked up by a British patrol and brought to St. John's. [23] He had given the debriefing officer fresh information about road building and military strength along the frontier. He knew that Jesse Safford was the captain of a militia company, though he mistakenly thought he was at Barnard when Safford was actually at Royalton at the time. Otherwise, he had accurately memorized details of the settlements, numbers of families, state of preparedness, quantity of arms. He knew the condition of crops and livestock, and the potential of the fall harvest. He had an intimate knowledge of Newbury and Royalton. Within days, British field commanders would have a very special mission for him.

From the 23rd of September until the 27th, troops gathered at Isle aux Noix, just north of Lake Champlain, until there were 875 British solders, including Houghton. There were 138 Fort Hunter Mohawks and St. Regis warriors. [24] There were none from Kahnawake or St. Francis—yet. [25]

On the 27th of September, though, Kahnawake and St. Francis warriors began pouring into St. John's in answer to Campbell's summons. By the 30th there were well over 300 of them, all eager to join the British expedition against upstate New York. Campbell and his superior, General Powell, had a serious problem on their hands. Powell sent an urgent dispatch to Haldimand that

Col. Campbell is arrived with upwards of 300 Indians, and as your exclly has proposed that not more than 100 should be employed in this service, I told him the rest had better return as more than those ordered might do more harm than good. He replyed that most of them would insist upon being employed. [26]

This was a volatile situation and it took all the persuasive skills possessed by (most likely) Houghton and his French Canadians to resolve it. The warriors had been called away from preparations for the coming hunting season, and they had set their minds on this warrior enterprise. They had been offered an opportunity for plunder, for captives, and for the display of prowess, and they were not about to stand down. The British knew they could not send some of them to New York without deeply offending those not sent. As officers in the Indian department knew all too well—and as one of them wrote—"...it requires more patience to conduct Indians than most gentlemen are possessed of." [27]

Senior officers on the ground had to devise a plan for the extra warriors. There were simply too many to send with the planned attack on New York state; it was too large a number to control, and control of Indian warriors during an attack was of major concern to the British. General Powell knew that Haldimand had always wanted to strike a blow against the rebels in the settlements along the upper Connecticut River, and fresh intelligence had just come in from that very quarter. [28] Its bearer, Richard Hamilton, was at hand, so Hamilton became part of the solution to the troublesome superabundance of Indians. A scheme was hatched involving him and Richard Houghton in command of a second attack or a "second road"; the first, and much larger, would head for New York as originally planned. Houghton's command was to drive farther eastward into New England than any raid had gone to date. Col. Campbell reported to Frederick Haldimand that there were

> *assembled many more warriors than what was wanted. Therefore to comply as nearly as possible with your intentions, sir, I persuaded them after near 24 hours passed in councilling, to take two roads instead of one... The second leads to the Connecticut River or near Dartmouth [College]. The party for this service left the island late in this day. It consists of 265 warriors conducted by Lt. Houghton, Mssrs la Magdaline, Verneuile Lorimier, and la Mothe. There are not as many officers on this occasion but the second party was quite unexpected and there was not time to make provision accordingly.* [29]

There was supposed to have been another British officer, Lt. Wills Crofts, the superintendent at the Abenaki village of St. Francis. He had brought 30 warriors with him from St. Francis to Isle aux Noix and had been ready to accompany them, but he wrote to Haldimand that he had been injured and was unavailable. [30] Crofts went on to note that this left Houghton, who was "not in a good state of health," in charge of a large party of warriors with no other British officer to assist him. Perhaps Houghton's old wounds from Saratoga were bothering him. Perhaps the injury to his foot early in 1780 had never healed properly. Whatever Houghton's problem was, he would breathe not a word of it in his reports.

So the unusual command was formed: Houghton, the warriors, three French-Canadian officer-interpreters, and Richard Hamilton, all approved by General

Powell.[31] Hamilton was central to the formation of this war party and its mission on the upper Connecticut because he knew the country and he knew the loyalists. The British knew that such raids were most effective when accompanied by men who knew the place to be attacked and its inhabitants and dwellings.[32]

Hamilton would have been able to slip into Newbury village after dark, knock on a loyalist door or two, identify himself, ask where Ben Whitcomb was (or any other likely candidate for capture, such as General Bayley), what the exact state of the defenses was, and warn loyalists that an attack was coming. At this point, there had been no thought of attacking Royalton—only Newbury, or, because of the reference to "Dartmouth" in Campbell's letter to Haldimand, possibly even Hanover, New Hampshire.[33] The prospect of an Indian attack was far more terrifying to the people of Hanover than an invasion of British regulars and, within a year of the start of the war, Wheelock had seen to it that his students were armed.[34]

During the 24-hour negotiations mentioned in Campbell's letter, the British and the Indians jointly shaped this mission. The Indians learned of Hamilton and were allowed to take him along, provided they brought him back safely; the British did not want him falling into enemy hands. Hamilton himself knew as well as anyone the risk he would be taking in going back to these settlements, where he would almost certainly be identified and, if captured, most likely killed.[35] So on the 4th of October, confident they were doing the right thing, General Powell and Colonel Campbell, the senior officers at Isle au Noix, watched Lieutenant Houghton and his armada take leave. As the intimidating, unruly command moved off, the senior officers on the shore might well have had some misgivings as to what the warriors might do once in action. They had no idea that the raid would turn out to have political as well as military ramifications.

It wasn't until November 9th, a month after hoping it would "have good effect," that Haldimand realized how easily the raid on civilian Vermonters might ignite a diplomatic crisis. He had every reason to worry about the consequences of the assault on Royalton. At the very least it sent a mixed message to Vermont with regard to the delicate negotiations underway at that moment. In the month that had elapsed since Haldimand's note to Powell expressing approval of the planned raid, a great deal had happened on the diplomatic front. There had been a flurry of correspondence between British and Vermont officials not only setting the negotiations for reunion in motion, but also articulating a general agreement about a cessation of hostilities on the northern frontier as long as the talks were in session.

To make it clear beyond any doubt, Haldimand fired off two letters on November 9, one to Maj. Carleton and one to Col. Campbell, with a message that was now consistent with policy: hands off Vermont until further notice. In his letter to Carleton he ruefully acknowledged that the "truce was broke," but that an "accommodation" of some kind with the "principal men of Vermont" appeared to be in the offing. "Hostilities," he commanded, "will be avoided as much as possible towards that state."[36]

Even though word of the raid on Royalton that broke the truce had reached Ethan Allen, the Vermonter's late October letters to the British make no specific mention of the attack. Concerned primarily with the possibility of negotiations, he only pressed for a cessation of hostilities on the northern frontier by both sides.[37] Allen's uncharacteristic equanimity is understandable if it meant that the importance of the coming negotiations silenced a normal reaction of outrage. But there might have been another factor. Within the secessionist republic of Vermont there was an internal secession brewing. The towns of the Upper Valley, including Royalton and Newbury, no longer considered themselves to be part of Vermont as of February 8, 1780, because of a dispute with the state government over the eastern boundary of Vermont in the Connecticut River Valley. If this matter was not settled favorably, declared a petition to Continental Congress, the towns of the Upper Valley would oppose recognition of Vermont as the 14th state.[38]

What's more, there were serious policy and religious disagreements and bad blood between Jacob Bayley and Ethan Allen and their respective coteries. Was the Chittenden-Allen faction, as a result, indifferent to the attack on Royalton, basically giving the British a pass on the attack while it pursued its own agenda? Or, perhaps thinking strategically, did Allen consider the cessation of hostilities and the promise of leverage with the British more important than recriminations over a frontier raid?

The British had just demonstrated a fearsome military capability that the Americans were nearly powerless to resist. Allen had told no one, except his brother Ira, the true nature of his talk with Sherwood, and the latter's journal indicates that while Allen was not ready to embrace union with Great Britain, he was intrigued with the possibilities inherent in such a discussion and seemed to keep the door open.[39] Allen reassured the British that "no hostilities shall be commenced from his quarter."[40] He dispatched orders on October 31 to a number of officers, including Jesse Safford, who was now posted at the new Bethel fort, not to engage in any offensive military actions until further notice—though, like everyone else in the White River Valley, Safford must have been thirsting for revenge.[41]

Haldimand was perfectly aware that, if discovered, the cessation of hostilities linked with the secret negotiations constituted an intelligence bonanza for the United States. He knew that as soon as Washington got wind of a separate truce between the British and Vermont "it will lead him to suspect and the whole scheme may be frustrated."[42]

As hard as Haldimand and Allen tried to keep the substance of the talks with Justus Sherwood secret, the cat very nearly got out of the bag. The subject of talks had been presented to the Vermont Assembly as "prisoner exchange" and had been approved as such. Copies of Allen's orders to field officers in Vermont to stand down reached Albany and the Connecticut River Valley within a day, and Philip Schuyler quickly suspected that the prisoner exchange parley was to "cover some design of the enemy." Schuyler informed Washington of the meeting and Washington answered that if Schuyler found "palpable proofs" that Allen was in collusion with the British, Schuyler was to arrest Allen immediately.[43]

The shock of Benedict Arnold's betrayal, discovered only a month earlier, had shaken Washington and the rebel leadership to the core. Now they were facing the possibility that the other hero of Ticonderoga might be selling out to the British, too. In spite of his suspect meeting with Justus Sherwood, however, its exact purpose was not exposed, and Allen's rebel *bona fides* remained more or less intact for the time being. From then on, though, Ethan Allen, Vermont, and its government were never fully trusted by the Continental Congress—or, for that matter, by Haldimand, who would before long come to understand the full extent of Allen's opportunism.

The uncertainty about Ethan Allen's frame of mind remains to this day. Ever since he sat down to listen to Justus Sherwood's proposition, the nature of the ensuing two years of negotiations between Vermont and Frederick Haldimand and the subsequent drama of the Allen brothers' dialogue with Great Britain that followed the Revolution has been the subject of debate involving not only Vermont, but also the broader picture of the formation of the young United States.

Ambiguous from the outset, these negotiations, as long as they lasted, would amount to a sort of stalemate that ironically suited both Haldimand and the Chittenden-Allen faction in Vermont. While they were talking (which they did until the war was over), Haldimand would not mount a major invasion of Vermont and Vermont's government would more or less stay out of the fight. Nevertheless, the no-man's-land north of the frontier became the locus of an ever-intensifying shadow war between small raiding parties from both sides intent on taking captives and spreading espionage networks. In fact, the fragile mid-November truce did not last out the month; Carleton informed Allen on November 15 that Haldimand was about to withdraw from "the cessation of arms."[44] Then, in March 1781, the British Secret Service made a daring raid on Peacham, north of Newbury, in a probable attempt to capture Bayley or Whitcomb.

In spite of these skirmishes, the dialogue continued intermittently and in different venues; and as long as Vermont was an independent republic the question of its allegiance remained in play. Allen and Chittenden did not speak for Jacob Bayley during or after the war, however, and Bayley and the more militant rebels of the quasi-breakaway Upper Valley were eager for action against the British. In light of this, Haldimand was happy to sideline at least some Vermont fighters whose effectiveness he and his officers knew all too well. He was as uneasy about Vermont as Burgoyne had been in 1777, when the latter wrote:

> *The Hampshire Grants in particular, a country unpeopled and almost unknown in the last war, now abounds in the most active and rebellious race in the continent, and hangs like a gathering storm on my left.*[45]

By the same token, Washington regretted that Vermont was not firmly one of the United States and would soon write to Philip Schuyler,

> *it is greatly to be regretted they are not, by some means or another, added to our scale; as their numbers, strength, and resources, would certainly preponderate very considerably, and make the Enemy extremely cautious how they advanced far in that quarter.*[46]

VERMONT

Some Hunters have travelled thro' this Wilderness, from Wells River, to Lake Memfrimagog, & judged the shortest distance this way to be about 50 Miles.

NB. Connecticut River has been actually

Lunenbourg

Leaperriere
Shelburne
St. George
Brothers
Charlotte
Huntsbourg
Hinesbourg
Ferrisbourg
Mons. de
Pocock
Contracoeuse
Panton
New Heaven
Otter Creek
Weybridge
Addison
Middlebury
Water bury
Salisbury
Bridport
Shoreham
Orwell
Leister
Nefhobe
Dunbar
Hubbardton
Pittford
Castleton
Rutland
Clarendon
Poultney
Wells
Gen. Nicholsons
built on occasion
Canada Expedition
but now demolished
Tinmouth
Wallingford
This way Captives have been carried by the Indians
Black R.
Danby
Harwich
Pawlet
Rupert
Dorset
Brumley
Sandgate
Manchester
Winhall
Sunderland
West River
Arlington
Stratton
Shaftsbury
Glassenbury
New Fane
Bennington
Woodford
Wood Creek
Bay Creek
Drowned Lands

Bolton
Worster
This way Captives have been carried from New Hampshire to Canada
French River
Waterford
Middlesex
Danbury
Dixtown
Berlin
Barnet
Peacham
Ryegate
Wells River
Topsham
Newbury
Corinth
Waits town
Only the Mouth of this River is known to y English
Mahsunquamosse R.
These Branches are only Conjectural
Eastham
Malden
Tunbridge
Stratford
Fairlee
Thetford
Royalton
Sharon
Norwich
Little Cohass
Intervals
Stockbridge
Bernard
Pomfret
Waterqueechy R.
White R.
Hartford
Killington
Bridgewater
Woodstock
Hertford
Shrewsbury
Saltash
Waterqueechy Falls
Windsor
Reading
Cavendish
Weathersfield
Hampshire Forces employed against Canada in 1759
The communication with that Country
Connecticut R.
Plamstead
Thomlinson
Rockingham
No. 4
Charles Town
Saxtons R.
Westminster
Townshend
Walpole
Pultney
Westmoreland
Fulham
Bratleborough
Chesterfield
New
Road cut by the Hampshire Militia

Connecticut R.
Choice White Pines and good Land
Lyman
Gunth
Loring
Bath
Landaff
Franconia
Ammonoosuck R.
Haverhill
Lincoln
Fairfield
Unpammonoosuck R.
Piermont
Warren
Orford
Wentworth
Hastings Brook
Rumney
Lime
Dorchester
Cockermouth
Hanover
Dartmouth College
Canaan
White River Falls
Cardigan
New Plymouth
Lebanon
Bloods River
Relhan
Grafton
Severance Brook
Plainfield
Grantham
New Chester
Choice White Pines and Good Land
Protectworth
bounds
Alexandria
Smiths R.
New Chester
Corinth
Croydon
LINE
Heidlebourg
New Britain
Sugar River
Sunnipee Pond
Clermont
Newport
Greenfield
Dantzick
Perrys Town
Kyasage Mt.
Salisbury
Boscawen
Unity
Little Sugar R.
CURVE
Rye Town
Lempster
No. 8
New Concord
Ackworth
COUNTY
Contoocook R.
Hills borough
Hopkinton
Henniker
Alstead
Marlow
No. 7
OF
Limerick
Mason
Wears Town
Gilsum
Ashuelot R.
Proprietors Lands reserv'd
No. 6 1/2
Dublin
New Boston
Keene
CHESHIRE
HILLSBOROUGH COUNTY
Monadnock
Peterborough
Lyndeborough
No. 5
Swansey

PART III
THE PRISON

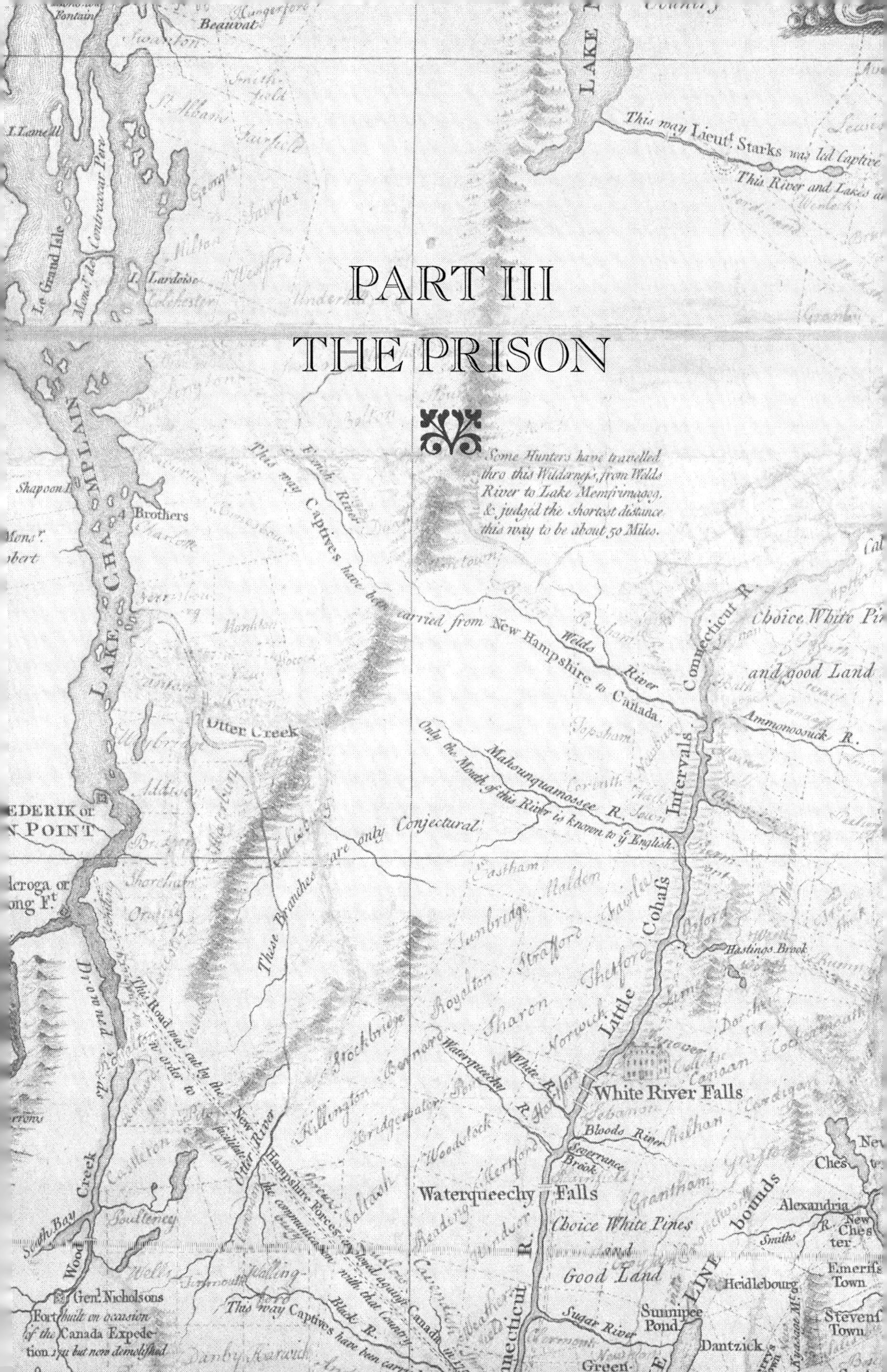

VERMONT

Some Hunters have travelled thro this Wilderness, from Welds River, to Lake Memsrimagog, & judged the shortest distance this way to be about 50 Miles.

NB. Connecticut River has been actua...

This way Captives have been carried from New Hampshire to Canada.

Only the Mouth of this River is known to y English.

These Branches are only Conjectural.

The Road was cut by the New Hampshire Forces employed against Canada in 1759 to facilitate the communication with that Country.

This way Captives have been carried by the Indians.

Gen. Nicholsons built on occasion the Canada Expedition but now demolished

Choice White Pines and good Land

LAKE CHAMPLAIN

Leaperriere
Shelburne
St George
Brothers
Charlotte
Hinesbourg
Ferrisbourg
Mons. de
Pocock
Contracoeuse
Panton
New Heaven
Otter Creek
Weybridge
Middlebury
Addison
Waterbury
Salisbury
Bridport
Shoreham
Orwell
Leister
Sudbury
Neshobe
Dunbar
Hubbardton
Pittford
Rutland
Castleton
Otter River
Clarendon
Poultney
Wells
Wood Creek
Bay
Drowned Lands
Tinmouth
Wallingford
Danby
Harwich
Pawlet
Dorset
Brumley
Rupert
Sandgate
Manchester
Winhall
Sunderland
West River
Stratton
Arlington
Shaftsbury
Glassenbury
New Fane
Bennington
Woodford
Bolton
Worster
Waterford
French River
Middlesex
Duxbury
Moretown
Berlin
Barnet
Peacham
Ryegate
Welds River
Topsham
Newbury
Corinth
Watstown
Mahounquamosscoe R.
Eastham
Malden
Fairlee
Tunbridge
Strafford
Thetford
Royalton
Sharon
Norwich
Little Cohass
Stockbridge
Bernard
Pomfret
Waterqueechy R.
White R.
Hartford
Killington
Bridgewater
Woodstock
Hertford
Shrewsbury
Saltash
Waterqueechy Falls
Reading
Windsor
Cavendish
Weathersfield
Black R.
Plamstead
Thomlinson
Rockingham
Saxtons R.
Westminster
Townshend
Pultney
Fulham
Walpole
Westmoreland
Chesterfield
Bratleborough
Connecticut R.
Intervals
Lyman
Gunth
Bath
Landaff
Franconia
Ammonoosuck R.
Haverhill
Lincoln
Upper Ammonoosuck R.
Fairfield
Piermont
Warren
Orford
Wentworth
Hastings Brook
Rumney
Lime
Dorchester
Cockermouth
Hanover
Dartmouth College
Canaan
White River Falls
Cardigan
Plymouth
Lebanan
Bloods River
Relhan
Grafton
Severance Brook
Plainfield
Grantham
New Chester
Alexandria
Protectworth
Smiths R.
Corinth
Croydon
Heidlebourg
New Britain
Salisbury
Sugar River
Sunnipee Pond
Clermont
Newport
Green
Dantzick
Perrys Town
Kyasage Mt.
Boscawen
Unity
Little Sugar R.
Rye Town
Lempster
Acworth
No. 4 Charles Town
No. 8 New Concord
Contoocook R.
Hopkinton
Hills borough
Henckers
Alstead
Marlow
No. 7
Mason
Wears Town
Limerick
Ashuelot R.
Gilsum
Proprietors Lands reserv'd
No. 6
Dublin
New Boston
Keene
Swansey
No. 5
Monadnock Mountains
Peterborough
Lyndesborough
CURVE LINE
bounds
COUNTY OF CHESHIRE
COUNTY OF HILLSBOROUGH

CHAPTER 10

MONTRÉAL

"Made captives by the Indians in different parts of America"

NOVEMBER 9. This was the day the captives were to be released by the Kahnawake to the British. Every morning for more than a month the prisoners had watched the spires of the old French Colonial city rising out of the smoke of countless chimneys on the other side of the St. Lawrence. Underneath the night fog that settled over the river, the water surged through the narrows in front of the village, making for a mile-wide stretch of treacherous, roaring rapids. There had been hard frosts nearly every night and by dawn the hoar blurred the hard edges of things and the ice on standing water crackled under the captives' feet as they moved to the river bank.[1]

Birch bark canoes that could hold 20 people were by the shore, ghostlike in the lifting mist. The prisoners were loaded and launched, deliverance just ahead, just below these rapids, just across the river, only a mile away in the city. But deliverance was hardly what awaited them; those crossing from Kahnawake that day would be entering the ranks of a vast captive multitude in Montréal.

Once on the other side, they were herded like cattle by their captors toward the city—a long, ragged line lurching and shambling along a muddy road between the tidy fields of the French farmers, passing the occasional church and, every half mile or so, crosses, some 20 feet high, fitted with small enclosed shrines containing crucifixion scenes of wax figures protected from the weather by a pane of glass. In front of them, devout Canadians, who never passed one without pausing to kneel and say brief prayers, looked up from their devotions to consider the passing men.[2] By now the French Canadians were used to such tableaux and the sight endeared neither the British nor the Mohawks to them. But that didn't necessarily mean they all felt sympathy for the American captives either. The inhabitants of Canada could not forget that these rebels and their forebears had been eagerly killing French Canadians up until 20 years ago, when the wars had finally ended with France's loss of Canada to Great Britain.

As Zadock and the rest of the Royalton captives moved along the road that ran between the recently harvested fields toward Montréal, the corn and wheat stubble and the roadside weeds were touched with frost. Zadock's Royalton neighbor, Joseph Havens, must have been remembering the last time he had been in Canada. It had been 1776 and he had marched north with a force of men to come to the aid of the American army besieging Québec City.[3] It had been a disaster. British reinforcements had arrived by ship from England and the invaders had had to retreat. Made ghastly by a smallpox epidemic that had killed 20 men a day, it had been a hellish march in the heat of summer from Québec to Lake Champlain, and then home—for Joseph Havens, 500 miles in all. As a survivor of that ordeal, what he had faced so far as a captive of the Kahnawake had been far easier.

* * *

The city of Montréal was situated at the bottom of the Lachine rapids, a stretch of water that dropped sharply for several miles over an unbroken series of outcrops, shelves, and ledges of bedrock, forming a continuous cataract that had claimed many lives. No shipping of any size could go farther upstream, but below the rapids the river widened to form a vast lake where dozens of ships rode at anchor, lighters busily plying the water between them and the waterfront. The British military operation was almost entirely dependent on supplies shipped from England: food, clothing, weapons, tools, implements, textiles, and a multitude of domestic luxuries. The fleet preparing for the fall crossing to England was being loaded with raw materials, timber, bales of beaver pelts and other furs, and the crucial dispatches that were the only direct line of communication between Canada and England. Soon the river would freeze and then no ships would appear until late the following spring. Frederick Haldimand's last-minute dispatches going out in the fall fleet had full and glowing reports of the raids on New York and Vermont.[4]

Less than a mile from one end to the other, Montréal was dense, compact, urban—like a fortified European city surrounded by open fields and farms. It was a wartime city: The British military was a dominant presence, reinforced by their German allies, the Brunswicker Regiments under General Friedrich Adolphus Riedesel. Most of the structures were now of stone; originally of wood, the first buildings had been lost to fire one by one and rebuilt with stone. As if the walls weren't secure enough, many of the houses were themselves fortified with heavy wooden and iron shutters and doors, locked and barred at night.

The people of Montréal were by now accustomed to sights such as the captives presented. There were nearly a hundred of them, herded by their Mohawk captors through the narrow streets. The prisoners were poorly shod, if shod at all, and if

15. An East View of Montréal, Public Archives of Canada, Copy Neg. # C-041692.

they were lucky they had a blanket against the chill.[5] What clothes they had were what remained once they had been stripped at capture. By contrast, the Mohawk warriors had put on their finest for the delivery of their prisoners to the British: French and English leather shoes and boots, fine shirts and coats, silver jewelry, gorgets and medals—all provided by the English as part of the annual tribute paid to the Mohawks and other tribes to ensure their allegiance and cooperation.[6]

Allied first with the French and now with the English, Iroquois and Abenakis were part of the daily scene in Montréal. Kahnawake had always been the closest village and the people of Montréal had come to take its residents for granted as traders, guides to the fur trade, expert river men, occasional in-laws—and today as traders in human chattel.[7]

As the procession halted in the city's largest public space and the British Commissary of Prisoners, Richard Murray, took possession of the new arrivals, the people of Montréal were witness to a drama that had become a regular occurrence. Murray paid the bounty of half a Joe for each prisoner. For Zadock the die was cast; he'd made a gamble that he could find a way out of the misery of the ranks of common prisoners and into a better situation. He recalled:

> *We found at the city of Montreal about one hundred and seventy prisoners, some of whom were made captives by the Indians in different parts of America, and others had been taken prisoners of war in forts by capitulation and by conquest. Here we could see women and children.*[8]

The scale of the coordinated series of late-1780 military assaults was only now becoming clear to Zadock. There were dozens of children and women, some with infants, captured in Pennsylvania and Virginia. They had journeyed hundreds of miles; that any had survived was remarkable.[9]

General Allan MacLean, commander of the Montréal garrison, was improvising quarters for captives just as Zadock was arriving. The only large, vacant, more or less available building in Montréal that the British could utilize was the Recollet Church. Zadock spent his first few nights there as a guest of the British government, while space was being cleared in a large stone warehouse about a mile downstream of the city to accommodate a more or less permanent facility.[10]

This place was for captured enlisted men and penniless civilian farmers like Zadock. For prisoners higher on the socio-economic scale, things were quite different. Officers on both sides expected comfortable housing in a private home, having given their word of honor as gentlemen not to try to escape. This, of course, was exactly what Zadock had had in mind when he had opted for captivity among the British rather than the Mohawks: release on parole as a servant in the house of a private family for the duration of the war.

The prison Zadock was about to enter came to be known as the Provost, and it made a grim and vivid impression on all those who were herded inside. In spite of the fact that most them were American Revolutionary prisoners, captured in a common cause, Zadock took their measure and found he would not normally seek the company of this "complicated collection of people of different habits, comprising almost every kind of foul and vicious character."[11]

The prisoners all occupied rooms on the second story, where they used one room by day and then were confined in a much smaller one by night. There were several such rooms, holding at times as many as 50 men. They were guarded by 24 Hessian soldiers under the command of a sergeant. There were complaints that one of the corporals made a regular practice of beating the prisoners and when these complaints reached Richard Murray (the commissary of prisoners), the corporal was quickly removed from guard duty.[12] The British command would not tolerate deliberate abuse if reported and verified.

Zadock knew that the daily food allowance was supposed to be one pound of bread and one pound of fresh beef per day, supplemented with dried peas and oatmeal from which to make porridge, but he was convinced that the guards were taking a cut for themselves. There was a daily commerce among the prisoners and visitors and even among some of the guards. If Zadock had been given what was rightfully his, he would have been able to use a portion of it to trade, essentially as currency, for other articles with people on the outside—perhaps a bit of extra clothing, some soap, some tobacco. But with nothing extra to trade, he had to consume what little he received.

They were furnished a gallon of water per day and three pints of spruce beer.[13] Bitter, astringent, powerfully aromatic, and mildly alcoholic, spruce beer was a staple drink for soldiers and prisoners alike. It was thought to prevent scurvy, even though doctors did not yet know what caused the disease or why spruce beer might be a remedy for it.[14]

These rations were issued every Monday and they were meant to be equal to two-thirds of the daily ration of a British soldier.[15] The men complained bitterly that the rations were shorted because they invariably ran out by the end of the week and went hungry Saturday and Sunday.

> *[We were]...obliged to pound up the beef bones and boil them for broth,* Zadock wrote. *We had no butter, cheese, flour, nor any kind of sauce during the winter. We were kept almost totally without firewood, having scarcely enough to enable us to cook our meat.*[16]

The only way to cook their food was over a fire in the Brunswicker guard room on the first floor, so there was a constant procession of hungry men moving up and down with food to heat over the fire. The Germans eventually lost patience with this process and drove the prisoners from the fire. The Germans were isolated by language in this French- and English-speaking world, but there were some New Yorkers who were of German descent and were able to talk the guards into letting the men come back to use their fire for cooking.[17]

CHAPTER 11

THE PROVOST

"Less than a common slave"

November, Montréal. William Jones, the British officer in charge of the Provost, was, most prisoners agreed, a kind and decent man. He was known personally to some of the New York captives because of his marriage to an Albany woman.[1] It was his duty to see to it that the prisoners were supplied with food, bedding, clothing, firewood, and medical attention. It was a huge task, similar to problems of prisoner treatment wherever the war was being fought.

At the outset of the Revolution, the British had been reluctant to recognize captured rebels as prisoners of war, seeing them as traitors who should be strung up rather than coddled in prison. These issues were debated throughout the war by the Continental Congress, Washington, and the representatives of the British government, but while they were locked in debate the parties had to arrive at practical ways of handling the sheer numbers of captives. As the rebels accumulated British prisoners, the English gradually showed more willingness to negotiate equitable terms of prisoner treatment, though it was by no means uniform and was frequently inhumane on both sides.

The number of Americans imprisoned by the British varied greatly during the course of the war and lists are inconsistent, but at the end of 1780 there were at least 5,000 captured combatant soldiers and seamen.[2] The British held captured revolutionaries in different places on both sides of the Atlantic and for varying lengths of time. Some went briefly to St. Augustine, Florida, others to Senegal, Portugal, Guernsey, Antigua, Barbados, and England, as well as to the infamous floating prison hulks in New York Harbor.

But by 1780 there were so many British soldiers in captivity in the colonies that the English had really no choice but to deal with those they captured in such a way as to protect their own men held by the rebels.[3]

Washington and the British carried on a lengthy correspondence about the treatment of prisoners, in Canada as well as in other locations. Both sides had much to complain about. Washington protested the British practice of housing prisoners of war with common criminals, and he detested the British practice of indiscriminately capturing civilians—such as most of those held in Canada. Although he had no problem with severe treatment of loyalists who were collaborating with the British, Washington saw no point in abusing or interning harmless loyalist civilians.[4]

There was a general agreement on rations and clothing for prisoners, though no one would claim they were generous, or, for that matter, honestly or evenly administered. Once prisoners were in the British detention system, routine medical care was indifferent to nonexistent, though if ill enough to be moved out of prison and into a hospital, a prisoner's chance of recovery was quite good. British hospitals were clean and efficiently run.

* * *

By 1780 there were about 550 American prisoners in the Canadian prison systems. About 12 percent were officers, 73 percent were men, mostly civilian, and the rest were women and children.[5] Virtually all women and children were released to private households and lodgings in the Montréal or Québec area, where they worked as servants for room and board, removing them from official responsibility for subsistence. To further ease the drain on supplies, the British released many of the women and children and old men to their homes "out of humanity" before the end of the war.

Officers were given food, but were expected to pay for items such as clothing and various "necessities." If they could not have money sent from home, the British commissary of prisoners loaned it upon guarantee of repayment at the war's end.[6]

Most civilian prisoners held in Canada were in a kind of limbo. Washington and the Continental Congress were not willing to allow the exchange of captive British soldiers for captive American civilians. Nor did they allow individual states to make separate deals with the British for prisoner exchange.[7] It was all to be done through a central authority. Prisoners in Canada were perfectly aware of this problem, and those who could write did all they could through correspondence to secure their exchange or release on parole. If paroled they had to promise on their word of honor not to take up arms again, and to return voluntarily to detention if called.

To maintain hundreds of captives in Canada was a massive logistical and administrative undertaking, though by no means the problem it presented in New

York, where there were thousands of American prisoners, scores of whom died every day.[8] It was not unusual for Provost Marshal Jones to dip into his own pocket to pay for firewood and soap for the men, "without which," he wrote Haldimand, "the situation would be intolerable."[9] He did the same thing for the captive women and children, finding them clothing and, on at least one occasion, money to pay for a nurse to look after a very sick child.[10]

In spite of having dozens of "check shirts" and pairs of moccasins made, hundreds of cords of wood cut and hauled, and daily deliveries of water, for Zadock and many of his mates the prison experience was a grim one.[11] "Many of the prisoners as well as myself had only one shirt, and were obliged to go without any while we washed that," Zadock wrote. "Indolence and disregard for cleanliness prevented many from doing this.[12]

While some spent their days playing cards, others were more enterprising. One New Yorker established a small fabrication business. There was demand on the outside for certain items, and he acquired materials and simple tools and before long was making oars, brooms, and baskets.[13] With the money he made he was able to buy the greatest luxuries of all: rum and tobacco.[14] Prisoners with special skills were actually in demand; one of them, William Bostwick, made pocket money repairing shoes and found himself on the British military payroll, even as he remained a prisoner.[15]

Ingenuity was a way of not giving up, and perhaps even more important, it was a way of passing the endless, empty hours. With the temperature dropping and his clothes growing more threadbare with each passing day—and none forthcoming from the British—Abijah Hutchinson, Zadock's Vermont neighbor, considered the old Indian blanket he had been issued, took its measure, and went to work. First, he made a sewing needle from a splinter of firewood. Then he unraveled his woolen knee-length stockings, giving him a large ball of yarn. Devising his own patterns, he cut the blanket into pieces and sewed them together, making of them a complete suit that would serve him through the winter.[16]

George Lawe, the commissary of prisoners, leased iron stoves from a local merchant for heating the rooms in the Provost with wood hauled in from the countryside by local contractors during the late summer and fall.[17] But the deliveries of wood appear to have come to a halt after January. Throughout January there was one blizzard after another, sometimes so ferocious that people could not stand up out of doors. At least one prisoner, William Scudder, remembered the winter as the severest he had ever seen, with five feet of snow "on the level."[18] The great river was frozen solid and the cold penetrated and seized the stone walls of the Provost and never left.[19] For the British, too, essentials such as food and clothing, rum, tobacco, weapons, and gunpowder were in very short supply.[20] This meant that by midwinter everyone was suffering, especially Zadock and his mates in the prison. "Pinched with hunger, half naked, and chilled with the cold, we were forced to have recourse to our beds, and occupy them a great part of the time," Zadock noted.[21]

Britain's Indian allies did not get their annual bounteous tribute of gifts. The Indian department was reduced to buying blankets for the tribes from local merchants at high prices.[22] Blankets for prisoners, in especially short supply, were a low priority, and Zadock believed the worst, his already low opinion of the British dipping lower still:

> *Our beds consisted principally of blankets, which they brought from the hospital in all their filth. This was an apparent manifestation of their disregard at least for the prisoners, if not a malevolent design to introduce that contagion which should spread disease, desolation, and death throughout our camp.*
>
> *[T]hey were the habitations of filthy vermin. [and] caused a general and universal prevalence of the itch.*[23]

This widespread, psoriasis-like affliction caused lesions and scabs and could lead to skin loss. Unless the men could obtain the hog's lard, pine tar, or sulfur used to cure it, they had to live with it.[24] Every evening after eating and before being moved out of the day room into the confined night room, the men repeated what had become a daily task: picking lice out of their clothes and bedding and one another's hair.[25] To their credit, the English did what they could for the prisoners, considering the privations that the entire British military establishment faced. Though firewood was in desperately short supply, large quantities of soap and water and dozens of brooms and shovels were sent to the Provost, but not much ground was ever gained against the lice.[26]

CHAPTER 12
WINTER

"Scurvy among the prisoners"

FEBRUARY 1781. The St. Lawrence was taken—frozen solid from Lake Ontario to the Atlantic Ocean, a solid ribbon of ice a thousand miles long except where there were rapids and waterfalls, where it churned and boiled as if alive. As the pale winter sun rose in front of Montréal each day, the river seemed to catch fire. The Lachine rapids never froze, but threw off spray and vapor that coalesced in the frigid air, forming a river-hiding, incandescent cloud, backlit by sunrise.

The river was still a thoroughfare, though it was now a bridge instead of a great divide as in other seasons. People flocked to the ice and traveled on it in sleighs. The British officers started a skating club and listened to stories about great feats of skating: the Tory, Philo, who had skated north across Lake Champlain from Vermont to Canada in January 1778 to help lead a British and Indian attack on rebel settlements in Shelburne, near the mouth of the Onion River; the three Indians who had raced on skates 140 miles to Québec.[1] Because the river was so heavily traveled, all the parishes on the banks were required to set rows of pine trees in holes in the ice, marking the way for safe travel, day or night. Even so, treacherous spots of thin ice claimed lives every year. The ice thickened during the winter, but the river heaved it from time to time, fracturing it, thrusting great shelves of it into a chaotic landscape of ravines, tilted slabs, and toppled blocks. The thunderous icequakes could be heard for miles at night and must surely have troubled the sleep of the prisoners in the Provost.

Prisoners housed within Montréal heard the sounds of a city more lively in many ways in the winter than during the summer. The British and Hessian soldiers had time on their hands and they were learning from the French Canadians the pleasures of the northern winter.[2] Life spilled out into the streets from houses and taverns in French, English, and German, from time to time mixing with Indian scalp-yells echoing off the stone walls.[3]

The British admired the Canadians' capacity for recreation and amusement, and hardly a night went by in the city and its suburbs without parties and dances. By day, excursions on brightly painted horse-drawn sleighs called carioles skimmed back and forth on the frozen river—often to a favorite rendezvous near Point aux Trembles at the house of a Dutch woman famous for her sausages and bottled porter.[4]

* * *

16. A View of the St. Lawrence in the Winter, Public Archives of Canada, Ref. # R9266.

After spending four months imprisoned together, the 200 inmates in the Montréal Provost would probably have found that they had even less in common with each other than when they arrived. Though virtually all of them had at some point taken up arms for the cause of independence, men from New England, New York, Pennsylvania, and Virginia were almost as different from one another as if they had been of distinct nationalities—which, of course many of them were: German, Dutch, Highland and Lowland Scots, Scots-Irish, Celtic Irish and Anglo-Irish. What was more, like any prison population, this group had devolved into its own factions: turncoats, informers, survivors, steadfast rebels, opportunists, entrepreneurs, natural-born politicians, peacemakers, and troublemakers. By now, perhaps the one thing they all had left in common was the desire to escape.

The British had underestimated the impulse to break out of prison before, and one nonplussed major had written, following escapes by some Vermonters in May of 1780:

> *Eight of them made off. I am really ashamed. When any of those prisoners undertake to make their escape, they show more ingenuity to effect it than I had any apprehension of.*[5]

But no one in his right mind tried to escape in the middle of a Canadian winter. The men were weakened and demoralized by the cold, by the diet and, worst of all, by the near impossibility of hundreds of miles of overland travel in the dead of winter. Still, that did not keep some from plotting.

The network formed by New York prisoners was by far the most extensive. Among them was a man named John Simpson, who had been receiving regular visits from a group of nine fellow New Yorkers. They had been captured but had quickly enlisted in a loyalist regiment, now upriver for training at a fort known as Coteau-du-Lac. They were planning to desert and escape back to New York. Back at the Provost, John Simpson had been talking and rumors were beginning to circulate about this plan. It was thought that some prisoners in the Provost might have been planning to escape with these nine soldiers at Coteau-du-Lac.[6]

The plan was as violent as it was desperate: the nine men had decided to surprise and overpower the other soldiers at Coteau-du-Lac, kill them and the officers, burn the post to the ground and escape through the Adirondack Mountains in upstate New York.[7] They had bribed an Indian who frequented the fort to guide them back to the Mohawk Valley.[8]

The plan was fully developed and the men were irrevocably committed to its execution, but the confidentiality of such a plot could not remain a secret for long in an atmosphere where it had to compete with old grudges, regional intolerances, and ruthless self-service. Someone who had learned of the plot in all its incriminating detail informed on the conspiracy, and the nine men were arrested at Coteau-du-Lac before they could take any action. By the 28th of May they were in the Provost themselves, awaiting a British court martial and the terrible punishments it was sure to hand down.[9]

Zadock surely took notice of these new additions to the Provost population, for their presence served as a dire warning of the cost of betraying the pledge of enlistment with the British. But Zadock had problems of his own. He had passed the winter in deepening depression, "brought low," he said, "through oppression, affliction, and sorrow," spending most of his time in bed, beset by lice, the penetrating cold, and relentless hunger. However, the first British supply fleet of the year had managed to evade the American privateers in the Atlantic, and in early May sailed up a finally ice-free St. Lawrence River with vast quantities of supplies and staples of the British military diet.[10]

> *[W]e were supplied with salt pork, bread, oatmeal and peas in abundance. As we had long been almost starved, our avidity for the food may more easily be imagined than described. Let it suffice us to say, that none ate sparingly. This sudden repletion of our wants produced the scurvy among the prisoners which threatened death to everyone.*[11]

It was probably not the sudden feasting, but rather the sudden lack of dietary vitamins that brought on the scurvy, compounded possibly with beri-beri and pellagra, other vitamin-deficiency conditions. The prisoners had been fed fresh meat, spruce beer, and very likely enough vitamin-rich winter vegetables, such as carrots, cabbage, turnips, or onions, to keep them scurvy-free. With the new food supply this vitamin source may well have been eliminated and the illness could no longer be kept at bay.[12]

Zadock was not affected severely enough for a trip to the hospital, but at least seven prisoners from Royalton were, and by the beginning of summer their illness was severe enough for full-time medical attention. Zadock might well have wished to be a little sicker, because, when his Vermont neighbors were taken to the hospital, they received first class treatment—as they nearly always did. Col. Thomas Johnson, a rebel prisoner from Peacham, Vermont, with a good deal of liberty to move about, paid them a visit and noted it in his diary:

> *June 26 went to the grand hospital to see the sick and lame. Saw 7 prisoners from Royalton. Rooms, bedding, attention, provisions of the best and neatest kind.*[13]

While the British medical system had ample resources to look after their captive patients, the general prison population was showing signs of growing evermore unhealthy and unmanageable.

The people of Montréal were all too aware of this growing body of desperate, potentially violent and not very well-confined men in their midst; and Zadock sensed that it made them uneasy, writing:

> *[The] citizens of Montreal, alarmed, perhaps, for their own safety, seemed to feel anxious for our relief. Conscious that they had all partially contributed to increase our miseries, they furnished us with green herbs and every thing which was adapted to our disorders. By these means our health was fully restored.*
>
> *After our recovery we were allowed the privilege of a yard, of some rods square in extent, by which we were enabled to exercise for the preservation of our health.*[14]

And, of course, this relaxation of security was just the opportunity that escape-prone prisoners in the Provost had been waiting for. The ice was long gone from the river, the days were long, the weather mild, vigilance relaxed. It was the season for escapes. There was one escape from the Montréal Provost on May 17th that Thomas Johnson heard about and noted in his diary, followed by a six-man outbreak in early June.[15] Zadock's brief taste of daily liberty came to an abrupt halt:

At length some of the prisoners made their escape,...which occasioned all the rest to be put into close confinement and kept under lock and key. We were supplied, however, with all the comforts of life, so far as our close confinement would permit.[16]

June 1781. As grim as reconfinement was for the remaining prisoners in the provost, there was a vastly more sobering spectacle unfolding in Montréal. The nine New York prisoners who had enlisted with the British and had been caught plotting a bloody mutiny at Coteau-du-Lac had been on trial since the first of June. On the 25th of June the court, a blue-ribbon panel of high-ranking officers, delivered its verdict. The desperate plan of these nine simple Mohawk Valley farmers was viewed by the British as the gravest kind of criminal betrayal. The court exonerated three, but decided to make an example of six men that would leave a lasting impression:

For "exciting and concealing a mutiny" six of the men are to receive 1000 lashes each and to serve his majesty in foreign parts for life in breach of the articles of war.[17]

The entire King's Royal Regiment of New York was assembled at Coteau-du-Lac to witness the punishment of these six fellow-soldiers. It would take more than an hour to inflict a thousand lashes on one man, and it was rare that anyone survived such an ordeal. Those few who did were disfigured and usually crippled for life. Even so, in the British army such punishment was not unusual. By contrast, the Continental Army rarely imposed sentences of more than one hundred lashes—an increase from 39 after 1776. Washington was in favor of 500 but the Continental Congress would not allow it.[18]

At least two men died under the lash.[19] The regiment was forced to stand and watch as the punishment continued throughout the day. The court briskly concluded its decision with the instruction that the guilty were

to be sent down to Québec as soon as they can undertake the journey after the infliction of their corporal punishments.[20]

And then the men disappeared from sight, bound presumably to "foreign parts" on his majesty's service as the sentence decreed, providing they lived that long.[21]

CHAPTER 13

EXCHANGE 1781

"No prisoners will be delivered who are in the Continental Army or of the United States"

July 1781. Zadock and the other prisoners were in frequent contact with visiting captive officers on parole, with guards, prison officials, and even Montréal citizens. Through this network the men had almost certainly heard rumors during the summer that there might be a prisoner exchange between the British and Vermont. The issue was still part of the ever-unresolved, often-stalled negotiations between Haldimand and the Allen brothers.

Not content with the promise of such rumors, prisoners from all states were petitioning Haldimand for release, many on the grounds that they had been taken unarmed from their farms and that their families were suffering. They knew that Congress would not exchange British soldiers for American civilians.[1] If Congress were to do that it would have given the British incentive to capture more—an easy matter—and thereby acquire human currency for the redemption of valuable soldiers. Congress and Washington wouldn't make such exchanges and hundreds of civilian captives were trapped with no way home.

Eventually Washington relented and allowed individual states to try to repatriate captive civilians as best they could.[2] But Washington didn't want individual states to be negotiating unilaterally with the British for release of their captured soldiers; he wanted prisoner exchange to be centralized.[3]

The one exception was Vermont. Because Congress had refused it admission to the union, Vermont did not feel bound by anything Congress or Washington had to say on the subject of prisoner exchange. Indeed, by 1780 Washington had already invited Ethan Allen to talk directly with the British about prisoner exchange. Moreover, Haldimand wanted to stay on the good side of Vermont, so the Vermont prisoners were in play and the word was getting around.

While Haldimand was willing to consider sending back Vermont prisoners, owing to the recent rash of escapes he was at the same time looking for a way of confining captives more closely. Virtually all of those who had broken out in early June were recaptured by the end of July—three near Yamaska on the 15th, and the party of six on the 23rd.[4] These six very nearly made it to Newbury, but, careless in lighting a fire, they were discovered and retaken by a British scouting party operating in the no-man's land of northern Vermont.

When the six were brought back to Montréal they went temporarily to the Provost, but Haldimand had other arrangements in store for captives prone to escape. Upriver at the Coteau-du-Lac garrison there was an island in the middle of the mile-wide St. Lawrence surrounded by violent rapids. What could be better for a prison than an island from which escape would be virtually impossible, and which was isolated from all casual contact with the local population and prisoners on parole? So in the middle of July, Haldimand instructed his engineers to begin work at once on the construction of barracks on the small nameless island facing the blockhouse on the shore.[5]

Although Haldimand had no confidence that Chittenden and Ethan Allen would negotiate re-union with the British in good faith, the discussions continued. Because they created a sort of *de facto* truce, these talks served both sides. As long as the negotiators were in dialogue, there would be no devastating British attacks on Vermont. By the same token, the British could enjoy a free hand in using Lake Champlain to attack New York State without fear of interference from the Vermont militias.[6]

Only vaguely aware of these geopolitical forces, the prisoners were nevertheless about to benefit from them dramatically—even though the discussions of union between Britain and Vermont were so far inconclusive. Ira Allen, taking Ethan's place in the talks, had brought about something concrete: A Vermont prisoner exchange was underway. The terms were very clear. In exchange for Vermonters, the British would accept only regular army British soldiers. Most important, since this was a transaction designed to benefit only Vermont, the British negotiator insisted, "[N]o prisoners will be delivered [by the British] who are in the Continental Army or are from any of the United States."[7]

Accordingly, a list of 19 British soldiers held prisoner by the state of Vermont was drawn up. In return, a group of 18 Vermont prisoners would be selected and presented by the British.

Prisoners were exhaustively accounted for in lengthy and usually complete lists, updated every few months. Inexplicably, the early 1781 inventories failed to name four of the Royalton captives: Zadock Steele, David Stone, John Parks,

17. Ira Allen, Special Collections, University of Vermont Libraries.

and Simeon Belknap. They simply were not on the British rolls—and if you were a prisoner hoping for exchange, that meant your chances for release and freedom were nonexistent.[8]

The British letter of agreement on the exchange of prisoners noted first that the Vermont men were not truly released, but simply on parole, honor-bound to return to captivity in Canada if recalled. The 19 British soldiers were likewise exchanged on the condition that they not bear arms against Vermont until truly exchanged or released. The letter noted also that in this exchange the British were in debt to Vermont by 22 men, and that they would send the balance when more Vermonters could be located among the prisoners the British were holding.[9] Since the British were giving up civilians for soldiers of the regular British army from the 34th and 53rd regiments, it is likely that they were not exchanging on a one-to-one basis. Rather, there was an exchange rate or equivalency, so that 19 British soldiers were worth 40 (18 plus 22) Vermont civilians. The British were as good as their word. A few days later they came up with 13 more Vermont captives. This group made an addition to the 18 that had left only a few days earlier, among whom were 16 of the Royalton captives.[10]

Incomplete as the returning Vermont group was, Haldimand understood that their release was seen by the government of Vermont as a genuine gesture of good faith. He noted in a letter to Sherwood that "sending prisoners back had a good effect on the people of Vermont," and added that he was optimistic about the prospects for union with Vermont.[11]

He might have been congratulating himself on the prisoner exchange, but in what appears to be a self-defeating move as hopes for the outcome of the secret negotiations were rising, Haldimand was planning kidnapping raids on eastern Vermont. This time he had his eye on no less a quarry than General Jacob Bayley. Bayley was an archrival of Ethan Allen and violently opposed any talk of re-union with Great Britain, of which well-founded suspicions abounded. In fact in September 1781, Bayley had been assigned by the Continental Congress "to counteract what is being done by [the British] Government" to bring about a reunion of Vermont with Canada."[12] Although an attack on Newbury would certainly inflame some of the Connecticut Valley people against the British, the capture of Bayley would remove a considerable obstacle to the secret designs of the Vermont government, which was situated across the Green Mountains in the Champlain Valley. There were several other political issues that divided the east and west sides of the fractious little republic, and Bayley would not be missed by the Ethan Allen junta.[13]

Haldimand felt, however, that prospects for union with Vermont were promising only "as long as the war goes well in the Chesapeake."[14] Haldimand had been receiving intelligence throughout the fall from the Secret Service about Washington's troop movements, the massing of French and American troops and warships near Yorktown, Virginia, and in Chesapeake Bay. It was clear that a great battle was in the offing.[15] On the 20th of October French and American armies overcame British positions at Yorktown, Virginia, and Lord Cornwallis and his forces suffered a crushing defeat. Word had gone out from Haldimand's headquarters instructing the Secret Service to get all rebel newspapers after the 18th of October and to learn "what you can of our southern army but in particular of Lord Cornwallis."[16]

As serious as this defeat was, it was by no means the end of the violence. The British were making plans for further offensives in addition to raids on Vermont. So far that year, in the American back country, Iroquois warriors had conducted 64 separate attacks on frontier settlements in Pennsylvania, New York, and Ohio where the fighting had been steadily escalating.[17]

PART IV
THE RIVER

VERMONT

Some Hunters have travelled thro this Wilderness, from Welds River, to Lake Memsrimagog, & judged the shortest distance this way to be about 50 Miles.

N.B. Connecticut River has been actually surveyed

Leaperriere
Bolton
Worster
Shelburne
St. George
French River
Waterford
Middlesex
Brothers
Charlotte
Hunesbourg
Danbury
Moretown
Berlin
Barnet
Lunenbourg
Called
Ferrisbourg
Hunesbourg
Mons. de
Pocock
Contracoeuse
Panton
New Heaven
Otter Creek
Peacham
Welds River
Ryegate
Topsham
Canada
Connecticut R.
Choice White Pines and good Land
Lyman
Gunth
Loring
Bath
Landaff
Franconia
Ammonoosuck R.
Haverhill
Lincoln
Weybridge
Middlebury
Addison
Waterbury
Salisbury
Bridport
Shoreham
Orwell
Only the Mouth of this River is known to ye English
Mahunquamosse R.
Corinth
Newbury
Waits town
Intervals
Umpammonoosuck R.
Fairfield
Lake Champlain
This way Captives have been carried from New Hampshire to Canada
These Branches are only Conjectural
Eastham
Malden
Fairlee
Cohass
Piermont
Warren
Orford
Peeauhick
Wentworth
Hastings Brook
Rumney
Leister
Drowned Lands
Tunbridge
Stratford
Thetford
Little
Royalton
Sharon
Norwich
Lime
Dorchester
Cockermouth
Neshobe
Richbury
Dunbar
The Road was cut by the New Hampshire Forces employed against Canada in 1759 to facilitate the communication with that country
Stockbridge
Bernard
Pomfret
White R.
Waterqueechy R.
Hartford
Hanover
Dartmouth College
Canaan
White River Falls
Cardigan
Plymouth
River
Hubbardton
Pittsford
Rutland
Killington
Bridgewater
Woodstock
Lebanan
Bloods River
Relhan
Grafton
Castleton
Otter River
Hertford
Sevarrance Brook
Plainfield
Grantham
New Chester
Shrewsbury
Clarendon
Waterqueechy Falls
Windsor
Protectworth
bounds
Alexandria
Poultney
Saltash
Reading
Choice White Pines and Good Land
Corinth
Smiths R.
New Chester
Wood Creek
Bay
Wells
Tinmouth
Wallingford
Cavendish
Weathersfield
Croydon
LINE
Heidlebourg
New Britain
Genl. Nicholsons Fort built on occasion of the Canada Expedition but now demolished
This way Captives have been carried by the Indians
Black R.
Sugar River
Sunnipee Pond
Salisbury
Clermont
Newport
Green
Dantzick
Perrys Town
Kyasage Mt
Boscawen
Danby
Harwich
Pawlet
Flamstead
Connecticut R.
Unity
CURVE
Rye Town
Edward
Rupert
Dorset
Bromley
Little Sugar R.
Lempster
No. 8 New Concord
No. 4 Charles Town
Ackworth
COUNTY
Contoocook R.
New Hopkinton
Manchester
Winhall
Thomlinson
Rockingham
Hillsborough
Heneker
Sandgate
Sextons R.
Westminster
Alstead
Marlow
Wears Town
Arlington
Sunderland
West River
Stratton
Townshend
Walpole
No. 7
Limerick
Mason
OF
Proprietors Lands reserved
Shaftsbury
Glassenbury
New Fane
Pultney
Gilsum
Ashuelot R.
No. 6
Dublin
HILLSBOROUGH
New Boston
Fulham
Westmoreland
Keene
CHESHIRE
Monadnock Mountains
Contoocook R.
Peterborough
Lyndeborough
Benington
Woodford
Bratleborough
Chesterfield
Swansey
No. 5

CHAPTER 14

PRISON ISLAND

"Impossible that any person should escape"

AUTUMN 1781. There were now two groups of Vermonters going home. One was the group that included 16 Royalton men. The second was a group of 14 men from other parts of Vermont.[1] Those from the Royalton raid who remained in captivity seemed to have fallen through the cracks.

The names of Zadock Steele, Simeon Belknap, David Stone, Jonathan Parks, and Abijah Hutchinson were not called out at the Provost when the others were summoned. Abijah saw his brother John called and saw him go, along with the other Royalton men, not understanding why these were released and he was not. The British would at times refuse to exchange prisoners—usually for escape attempts or bad behavior—but there is no indication any of these men had accumulated such a record.

One possibility was that Steele, Belknap, Stone, Parks, and Hutchinson were considered poor risks for keeping parole. The 18 Vermonters had been released on their word of honor to return to confinement in Canada if called by the British commissary of prisoners. Perhaps these five refused to do so, but there is no hint in either British records or the written accounts of the captives.

Not only were Steele, Belknap, Stone, Parks, and Hutchinson not to be released, they were to be removed from the Montréal Provost to Coteau-du-Lac, the high-security facility that had been in preparation all summer. Rumor had it that this place was for the most violent, recalcitrant, hard-bitten, and escape-prone of the prisoners. There may have been some truth to this characterization of the prisoners going there, but the primary reason for removing them from Montréal was to make room for new prisoners.[2] Virtually emptying the Montréal Provost, the men were moved in mid-October to the new location. Already the site of considerable trouble for the British, Coteau-du-Lac was now to be a penal colony, adding to its combustibility.[3]

18. Passage of Amherst's Army down the Rapids at Prison Island toward Montréal, Public Archives of Canada, ICON3536.

The attempted mutiny at the post was common knowledge, so Zadock already knew a few things about the place, but he was stoic about the new quarters. He wrote:

> *In October 1781, all the prisoners were removed to an island in the River St. Lawrence, called Prison Island, about forty-five miles above the city of Montreal, and opposite to a place called Coteau du Lac.* [4]

Haldimand was aware, when he decided to make this island a prison in July 1781, that it was in the midst of an infamous stretch of rapids. When Lord Geoffrey Amherst had descended the St. Lawrence River in 1758 during the Seven Years' War, he came upon the violent white water in a small armada of craft and, before they could put ashore, the ferocious cataract had devoured them: 46 bateaux, 17 whaleboats and a rowing galley wrecked. Eighty-four men had drowned. [5]

The prisoners were marched the 45 miles from Montréal and when they arrived at Coteau-du-Lac they found a well-manned garrison with a blockhouse and a bustling and, by now, disciplined community of soldiers, Indians, voyageurs, loyalist families, tradesmen, quartermasters, clerks, and supply officers. There were large warehouses where supplies were stored during the winter for shipment

19. The Fort of Coteau-du-Lac and Rapids Seen from Prison Island
Public Archives of Canada, #C-1121278.

upriver in the spring—vast quantities of flour, salted meat, tea, Indian trade goods, and hundreds of barrels of rum. Coteau-du-Lac until recently had been the head of navigation: no boats could pass the rapids, so everything arriving by boat had to be unloaded, portaged above the rapids and reloaded into boats for the journey to the interior. In the spring of 1781 a canal with locks had been constructed, making this an important link in the chain of transport and communication to the interior.[6]

Zadock stood on the shore, surrounded by the ordinary business of daily life: women, children, shopkeepers, and sweating, cursing, bawling laborers. From there, across 500 yards of violent rushing water, he saw his immediate future. He could make out a group of buildings in a clearing in the forest that covered the island.

Zadock and 50 fellow prisoners were marched a mile upstream. Crews of boatmen towed whaleboats through the canal and up along the shore to the crowd of docile prisoners. A few of the men were loaded aboard the first boat; it cast off and the current swept it toward the murderous water. The oarsmen pulled hard for mid-river, then rode it downstream, still rowing hard, on a course for the rocks at the head of the island. The men in the boat saw the boulders rushing toward them and then the current snatched the boat violently, sucking it into a sluiceway that spilled the boat into flat, protected water on the

20. View of the Block Houses and Barracks at Coteau-du-Lac, Public Archives of Canada, Ref # R3908-0-0-E.

far side of this island—a small bay invisible from the fort or from upstream. This was the only way to reach the island from the shore.[7] The boat fetched up on the gravel shore and the men considered their new quarters. What they saw were 40 flat, low-lying acres of dense forest on a crescent-shaped island.[8] A party of 30 smartly uniformed and well-armed soldiers held them in place until all the boats arrived.

To return to the shore, each boat cast off into the current and plunged more or less out of control into the rapids. The helmsman had by now become expert in finding the one safe channel but he did not regain any real control of the boat until the river leveled out three miles downstream. From there the boat was towed back to the fort, through the canal, and along the shore a mile above the island to start all over. When all the men had made the crossing, they were marched a short distance from the boat landing to a clearing on the downstream end of the island.

Zadock saw an orderly compound of newly constructed log buildings surrounded by a low picket fence. Commanding the place was a two-story fortified blockhouse near the shore. Next to the blockhouse stood a tent of the type used as personal quarters for British soldiers. A young officer emerged and gave orders to the sergeant escorting the prisoners; he in turn bellowed the orders to the assembled men. Zadock heard the rules by which he would have to live, and immediately understood why the British were so confident that this prison without walls would contain him and the other men for an indefinite period of time:

> *This island was considered a very eligible place for the confinement of the prisoners. Indeed, it was thought impossible that any person destitute of boats should be able to escape without being drowned, as the water ran with the utmost velocity on each side of the island. We were, therefore, allowed the liberty of traversing the whole island.*[9]

The prisoners might have had the liberty of the island, but, at first glance, what separated them from real liberty might as well have been the North Atlantic.

Placed side by side were three log buildings that looked like barracks to Zadock—it was probably where he and the others prisoners would be living. Facing them were a number of smaller buildings and a larger one that looked like a storehouse.

As the men milled about in the enclosure, they gathered into familiar tribal clusters. Nearly half were from New York; other sizable groups were from Pennsylvania and Virginia.[10] There were 21 Vermonters, of whom five were from the Royalton raid. Many of the rest had been captured at Fort Ann, near Lake George, and there were a few unlucky enough to have been caught alone in the north by British or Indian patrols. There were a few individuals from Massachusetts, Delaware, and Connecticut.

The soldiers marched them into two of the three barracks, each of which had six rooms that slept 12 men in wooden bunks.[11] The final barracks remained empty.

And then the prisoners took stock.

All the guards were loyalists from the colonies, not Hessians as they had been at the Provost. Zadock and his Vermont neighbors, Abijah Hutchinson, Simeon Belknap, David Stone, and John Parks were thrown in with one Josiah Hollister and a few other New Yorkers. One was a man named John Sprague who, like Hollister, had been caught a year earlier in the October raids on Ballstown. They would have wasted no time in telling the Vermonters that the guards were New York Tories, virtually all of them from the Mohawk Valley and some of them men they once knew as neighbors. The question on the minds of all the men was whether this meant they could expect kinder or harsher treatment than they might from a more neutral corps. Hollister and Sprague would certainly have warned the Vermonters that it was probably going to be the latter, knowing full well what had been meted out to these self-same loyalists and their families back home in the Mohawk Valley. No one would have been surprised at this prediction. Vermonters had not spared their Tories either.

Zadock and his barracks-mates had all been captives for exactly one year—sharing the hardships of the Provost, seeing some of their mates die, some sent home. Rumors of a great rebel victory in Virginia were circulating, and with them, as always, the tantalizing chances of release. But instead of release, these men had been sent into a new level of confinement and isolation on an island which they now had to share with the men they had come most to loathe—the loyalists who had gone north to join the British. It was an incendiary situation, one made more so by virtue of the isolation. A minor incident could easily escalate and get out of hand.

One event had already caused an alarm on the island. Zadock and his contingent were not the first prisoners here. They were met by others, among them Robert Hopkins from New York, whom they recognized from the Montréal Provost. He had been here for a few weeks already and would probably have told them that only a few days earlier, he and the others had been amusing themselves by trading insults with one Lt. Simmons, the soft young engineer in charge of the construction still underway on the island. The exchange had offended the lieutenant greatly and he had immediately reported it to another officer. By the time the commissary of prisoners heard about it, the incident had become a full-fledged rebellion replete with "mutinous behavior" and "threatening and riotous expressions."[12] Major Gray, the senior officer of the regiment, had rushed over from the fort, expecting the worst. What he found, of course, was that the inexperienced and edgy soldiers had first reacted with indignation, then high dudgeon, then near-panic to prisoners who had posed no threat.

Even so, the Major was taking no chances. The large shore garrison, across impassable rapids, could be of little help in case of an emergency. The result of Gray's assessment was to place a heavily reinforced guard detail of 30 men and an officer, Lt. James McDonell, on the island. Ashore in the fort at Coteau-du-Lac were two captains, Joseph Anderson and Archibald McDonell, and 50 men.[13]

The Vermonters would have learned from Hollister and other New York prisoners that these loyalist officers were with the British forces who had descended on them and wrenched them from their Mohawk Valley homes in the massive October raids a year before.[14] They had not seen them since, and having to live under their control for the indefinite future did not bode well.

Within a few days, the prisoners took the measure of the two young officers with whom they would have the closest contact, the ones who would be living on the island. Lt. James McDonell, born in Scotland, was known to have been a large landowner in the Mohawk Valley—land he had by now lost to rebel confiscation, like so many other loyalists.[15] He was an experienced, professional officer who had held similar commands, but was bound to harbor unpleasant memories of some of these prisoners—and may well have had old scores to settle.

The prisoners heard that Lt. John Prentice, the other officer, had a reputation as a brawler and a bully with a particular grudge against French Canadians. He was something of an embarrassment to the regiment, but his father was the politically powerful Miles Prentice, the Provost of Québec, so young Prentice managed to get away with more than most.[16]

Twice a week the men were issued rations which they cooked in the fireplaces built into each room. Zadock was somewhat grateful for an improvement over his first year of imprisonment, remembering: "we were furnished with a full supply of wholesome food during our confinement on the island." The rest of it, though, was not promising. The log buildings rested on stone foundations and there was a crawl space beneath the wooden floors. The damp, icy wind came howling down the river, found its way into every opening and penetrated the rooms and everything in them with a dank, lingering chill. And it was only October.

The buildings were gathered at the downstream end of the island. The opposite end, broad and rounded and boulder-strewn, shouldered the river aside. Logs, whole trees and the snarled roots of stumps piled up here all summer. The men were free to move all over the island to gather firewood and forage for whatever driftwood fetched up on the shore. The fireplaces were in constant use and the embers glowed all night, flames leaping from time to time as a man would get up to settle another log among the coals.

The routine blurred the days: roll call, food, sleep, the arrival of the boat from the shore with supplies, and occasional new prisoners. The only variety came from fishing and scavenging for firewood—errands broken by careful exploration by those who believed there just might be a chance of escaping alive from the island.

They would slip through the underbrush close to the shore and consider every boulder, eddy, and embayment. They would take note of logs that might serve as rafts, committing their locations to memory. They would stand on the downstream shore eyeing the way the divided river swept past on both sides and wonder if there was any chance of surviving a plunge into the violence below, where the separated currents collided. As the men read the water, one thing was not lost on them: if it did not drown them, the flow would inevitably carry them to the heavily settled and constantly patrolled northern shore. This meant that, if they were not caught as soon as they landed, they would have to cross the mile-wide river before they could begin the trek south toward home.

It was a daunting prospect. Still, some of the men would return every day to study the river, to listen to it, to see how it changed from day to day, to gauge its dropping temperature, to consider the gamble.

* * *

OCTOBER 19. Charley was playing the fiddle on this night, as he did most nights for a few of the men and the soldiers and laborers, too.[17] It was virtually their only entertainment and usually one or two of the men would dance a jig to Charley's tunes. He was an old black man swept up by the Indians in one of the frontier raids and he and his fiddle had been billeted with the prisoners ever since capture—even though most Negroes were generally either released or sold into the service of British officers.

The night-sergeant came by to secure the barracks, sending the men to their respective rooms and the island's carpenter back to his bunk in the workshop. The fires were banked for the night.

The guard who patrolled the compound at regular intervals was making his rounds at two in the morning when he rounded a corner of one of the barracks and saw a bright glow coming through the chinks in the logs of a small adjacent workshop. A moment later, the carpenter burst through the door followed by a billow of smoke and a tongue of flame. The first thought in the guard's mind was that the prisoners had devised a diversionary action to cover an escape attempt. The fire quickly consumed the workshop and spread to the nearest barrack building, which was still unoccupied. Not only had the prisoners not set the fire, they surprised the guards by their good behavior as they stood watching the flames, probably grateful for the entertainment value of the spectacle.[18] The workshop and one of the barracks buildings were burned to the ground. Though the whole place had very nearly gone up in flames, no one was hurt.

It was clear that the buildings were all fire hazards, and Captain Anderson laid down some new rules. From then on there were to be no fires or even candles after nine o'clock at night, and he ordered that there be patrols every two hours to enforce the prohibition.[19]

When Frederick Haldimand's chief engineer, William Twiss, arrived in December to inspect the fire damage and the general state of the compound on Prison Island, he noted that there were neither signal flags nor a three-pounder cannon for alarm signals. The only method of communication with the shore was, at the time, by a volley of musket fire. Still, Twiss observed, "...the Coteau Island [is] extremely well arranged for the accommodation and security of prisoners of War and I think that Your Excellency will not hear of any making their escape from thence."[20]

In fact, the matter of escape was on everyone's mind. In November there were a series of escapes by officers on parole who had been housed with civilians in and around the city of Montréal. They were retaken, as they so often were, and word of these failed escape attempts was bound to circulate among all the prisoners, a sobering dose of reality to even the most ambitious, determined breakout plans.[21] Zadock, perhaps overcome by inertia, appears to have had no intention of trying to escape:

> *[T]ime soon rolled away,* he remembered, *till winter approached. The rapid current of the stream, roaring in a voice like thunder, bade us beware. Desperate indeed must be anyone knowingly to plunge himself into the jaws of death to escape.*[22]

Later in the fall came a grim reminder of just how futile escape from confinement could be. Getting out of prison was just the beginning. The one party that had escaped from the Provost during the summer and had been thought to have got clean away was finally brought ignominiously back. Its members had made it through the wilderness and into northern Vermont, then were discovered and caught only a day's travel from Newbury and freedom. When they were recaptured, they were not returned to their berths in Montréal: they were brought instead to Prison Island.[23]

* * *

Winter had closed in early; by the second week of December there were three feet of snow on the ground. The St. Lawrence River was icing up; Lake Champlain had seized; and no one had any illusions about going home. There was no shipping, no travel, and, under these conditions, no more prisoner exchanges.[24]

Word of the defeat of British forces under Cornwallis on the Chesapeake in mid-October had been making the rounds of the prison population; but no one, least of all the prisoners, knew yet what it meant as far as the course of the war was concerned.[25]

As far as Frederick Haldimand was concerned, the war was not over until he heard otherwise. Negotiations with Vermont were another matter. They appeared to have been thrown into limbo by the defeat of Cornwallis. Haldimand was on the verge of issuing a public proclamation containing the terms on which Vermont would be readmitted to the British empire as a separate Canadian province, but Ira Allen advised against it until the meaning of the defeat at Yorktown could be determined.[26]

That had been back in October. By the end of 1781, there was still little for Haldimand to go on. The other colonies might have been lost, but, believing Vermont might still be leaning toward re-union he was not prepared to lose her if she wanted to come over. Haldimand's orders from London were to make Vermont a top priority and to spare no expense in gaining her allegiance.[27]

But Haldimand's spies were sending him mixed messages about Vermont's intentions and he was proceeding with caution. He did not count on Vermont's allegiance nor could he even be sure of her neutrality; what was more, he was proceeding on the assumption that an American invasion of Canada was inevitable. Reports from his Secret Service were consistent on that score, but the one thing his network had not picked up was the closely guarded secret that the Continental Congress had, as of late 1781, lost all interest in Canada.[28]

CHAPTER 15

McDONELL, ANDERSON, AND McALPIN

Zadock's Narrative:

The captain of the guard, whose name was M'Daniel (Lt. James McDonell), was a Tory, and totally devoid of humanity.

I once saw one of the prisoners plunge into the river in the daytime and swim down the current the distance of three miles, but was discovered by M'Daniel soon after he started, who ordered him to be shot before he should ever reach shore; but a British soldier, possessing more humanity than his commander, waded into the river and took hold of the trembling prisoner, almost exhausted, declaring, "if the prisoner was shot, he, [the soldier] would [have to] be likewise." [1]

ZADOCK HAD WATCHED THIS SCENE soon after his arrival in October, when the water was bitterly cold but not yet frozen. He learned three valuable lessons: one, that escapes needed better planning; two, that McDonell was a dangerous hothead who could be faced down; and three, that some of the enlisted loyalist guards were decent fellows who were willing to cross McDonell under the right circumstances.

Even so, it was clear that help from the enlisted men would come at great risk; none of them had forgotten the thousand lashes inflicted the past summer on the soldiers who had planned the mutiny at Coteau-du-Lac. In any case there would be no more escapes anytime soon. While the slack water above the island and below it froze, the rapids surrounding the island never did. It was abundantly clear to Zadock that anyone jumping into the water who did not succumb to the cold would be swept beneath the ice to certain death. "The ice below the island rendered it utterly impossible to escape alive," he wrote. "We were, therefore, now forced into submission, and had only to consult together to promote our own happiness while we waited the return of spring." [2]

"Consulting together" meant presenting a united front in resisting the demands of the martinet on Prison Island who controlled the prisoners' lives. Lt. James McDonell had no day-to-day supervision from his captain, Joseph Anderson, who was across the river at the fort. So McDonell had a more or less free hand on the island, and he had decided to put Zadock and the prisoners to work. Zadock wrote.

> *In January we were ordered by McDonell to shovel the snow for a path, in which the guard were to travel while on their duty. we complied with the demand, thus sacrificing our rights on the altar of peace.*
>
> *[But] prisoners were possessed of certain inalienable rights, which we resolved to assert.*
>
> *[W]e unanimously agreed to disobey all similar orders.* [3]

The next time the prisoners were ordered to shovel snow, Zadock told McDonell that none of them would do it. McDonell put him in irons in an unheated holding cell for the rest of the day, then extended his sentence a few more hours until nine o'clock, when he was sent back to the barracks.

With Zadock out of the way, McDonell again commanded the men to shovel snow; some Dutchmen, who preferred shoveling snow to spending the day in shackles, picked up the shovels and cleared the paths as ordered. [4] It had become much colder since the order against fires had gone into effect after the conflagration, and the soldiers on patrol had relaxed the enforcement of the command. But no longer, and Zadock noted McDonell's command that from now on, the guards were to make sure orders were followed:

> *Accordingly the guard came into our barracks every night with large quantities of snow and put out all the fires, using as much caution not to leave a spark unquenched as though the lives of thousands and the wealth of a metropolis were at stake.* [5]

* * *

Like many New York loyalists, Lt. James McDonell was a highland Scot for whom loyalty to clan, clan chieftain, and king formed the only valid social and political contract. [6] Such men had no use for what they saw as faddish rebel rhetoric about "inalienable rights" and a society that revolved around self-indulgent individual liberties. [7] When he saw these loathsome novelties at work in defiance of his orders, the impulse to impose discipline was irresistible, even gratifying.

McDonell's time on the island was not long. At some point during the late fall he was promoted to captain and soon after that was assigned elsewhere and replaced. [8] His place on Prison Island was taken by a young ensign, probably the troublemaker John Prentice, but it wasn't long before he was joined by James McAlpin, a younger ensign deeply embittered by his loyalist family's treatment at the hands of rebels.

His father, Major Daniel McAlpin, and his family had been mercilessly persecuted by local rebels and the Albany Committee of Correspondence. Driven from his Saratoga home in 1776, the elderly major had been arrested, imprisoned, and then released late in the year. After a brief return to his home, he had been forced to flee with other loyalists into hiding in the Adirondacks in the bitter cold of January and February 1777. Daniel's wife Mary, two daughters, Mary and Isabella, and a teenage son James had remained at home.

Eventually the committee had removed Mary McAlpin and her family to Albany with only the clothes on their backs, sold off all of their possessions, and seized their land. McAlpin fled to Canada, where he was eventually joined by his family.[9] He then set about recruiting refugee loyalists for the King's Royal Regiment of New York, which would be sent again and again to attack settlements on the northern frontier.

When the old major died on July 22, 1780, influential friends, along with Mrs. McAlpin, petitioned Frederick Haldimand for a lieutenant's commission for McAlpin's young son, James. Stripped of all her property and wealth, she wanted for James the advantages, the polish, the discipline, and the manly training available to him in this new world only through the military profession.[10] Haldimand knew that the boy was too young to be a lieutenant, but was willing to make him an ensign and thereby give him a chance to prove himself with the discharge of a very real responsibility.[11]

So in January 1782, James was awarded command of the company of soldiers and the captives on Prison Island. Less experienced even than Prentice or McDonell and seething with vengeance, James McAlpin was as dangerous as he was immature. Zadock's first impression was not promising.

> *M'Daniel was called away, and succeeded by one M'Kelpin (McAlpin) in command. He was also a refugee, the son of a Tory, and had the appearance of a raw boy not more than eighteen or nineteen years old, whose very visage portended evil and bade the prisoners prepare for trouble.*
>
> *His father, he said, had received very ill treatment from the American army, and he had also shared with his father in the abuse for not engaging in the rebellion against the British government.*[12]

By early January, the snow was so deep and the river crossing so hazardous and so infrequently attempted that repairs to the burned buildings and construction of new barracks on the island had come to a halt for the season. Besides the ash-house and the officer's house and storage sheds, there were now four buildings containing rooms for the prisoners, of which 22 were now occupied by groups of men. The rough-hewn timbers were chinked with clay from pits on the island and the sills were banked with clay in an attempt to cut down on the icy drafts that whistled up through the cracks in the wooden floor.[13]

With plenty of blankets to go around and plenty of firewood to burn, Zadock was able to stay reasonably warm and adequately fed with salt pork and beef, and with spruce beer. He was given biscuits so hard they "str[uck] fire like a flint" and could only be eaten by boiling them in water with a strip of salt beef, making a kind of soup.[14] As always, there was a little money circulating for purchases and there seemed to be enough tobacco to go around. However, lack of clothes was a real problem and, as there had been none issued since the fall, the men had to make do with what they had brought to the island from the Provost in Montréal. Washing what they did have was virtually out of the question in the winter, so they were plagued with lice. Most serious of all, many had no shoes, and to leave the barracks they had either to risk frostbite or wrap their feet in strips of blanket or borrow shoes from a mate.[15]

The prisoners could assume that the departing James McDonell thoroughly briefed James McAlpin on his experience with the prisoners: the refusal to shovel snow, the posturing, the assertion of rights, the complaints about extinguishing fires, the abortive escapes, and in the end, the ease with which the prisoners were cowed when threatened with a bit of discipline. Young James must have felt he would have an easy time of it as long as he kept the upper hand. But when he saw the list of prisoners on the island and recognized the names, he realized that here were men he knew all too well, men who had deprived his family of home and property and who were now in his power.[16]

* * *

February 1782. The situation was ripe for exploitation: McAlpin was the only officer on the island.[17] His command of the British enlisted soldiers, no matter how much older or more experienced, was absolute. His control over the prisoners could not be challenged. His remove from the officers at the fort was distant enough to conceal his actions from day-to-day supervision. Among the 30 British soldiers under his command on the island, there were at least some who shared his experience and his bitterness.

McAlpin settled into his new command, took note of and sampled the supply of rum under his care and custody, and in small ways began to assert his authority.[18] In addition to the narratives of Zadock Steele and Josiah Hollister, what follows is reconstructed from pension records, British military archives, and oral histories collected in New York State.

> *His first steps towards tyranny and oppression met no opposition,* Zadock noted; *as we wished to enjoy peace, and were willing to yield a portion of our rights to the enjoyment of so invaluable a blessing. But our indulgence served only to stimulate him in the course of revengeful tyranny; and he seemed the more angry, as if "coals of fire were heaped upon his head."* [19]

Zadock believed McAlpin was "manifesting a desire to meet with opposition, by using every exertion to provoke to rage"—in short, to precipitate an act of insubordination.[20] But the prisoners knew better and did not resist his petty demands, driving McAlpin deeper into both resentment and the rum supply. The opportunity for a showdown arrived with a heavy February snowfall and, emboldened by rum, he followed the example set by McDonell before him. He ordered one of the prisoners to clean the snow away from his door yard. The man answered "that he was no servant, but a prisoner of war," Zadock wrote, "and that the officer had no right to order him to work."[21]

At once enraged and gratified, McAlpin ordered that the man be seized and brought inside. There, where no others could see and with the man pinioned, McAlpin drew a bayonet, held it at the man's throat, and ordered him to shovel or die. The prisoner remained defiant.

Losing control and fearful of losing face if he could not bend the prisoner to his will, McAlpin beat him with a rattan cane, 75 strokes. But that was not enough. The man still had to pay. In irons, he was consigned to the open-air ash house into which the fireplaces were emptied each day and where the mixed snow and cinders rose knee deep.

By now it was clear to Zadock what McAlpin planned to do. "As the prisoners discovered in him a determination to pursue compliance with more grievous burdens until he could meet a refusal to comply," he wrote, "we resolved to reject all further encroachments upon our rights. We refused to obey his arbitrary commands any longer."[22] Yet outright defiance on the part of the prisoners had to stop short of an outright insurrection.

The snow before McAlpin's house remained unshoveled, but prisoners were hardly in short supply. So others were called, one man from each of the 22 rooms in the barracks. and, each time, McAlpin was defied. All were ironed, some beaten first, and then chained to the posts in the ash house and left there without food, without water, without fire, without tobacco,—without end in sight. A guard was posted at the ash house door.

Gloating, perhaps, on his success in provoking and then punishing acts of insubordination, McAlpin sent for Charley, the black fiddler, that he might have some recreation, might even dance a few steps by way of celebration. Charley refused to play, wanting no part of McAlpin's triumph. McAlpin turned on him without warning and laid into Charley with his cane. When he was done, he clapped the old man in irons and threw him into the ash house with the others.[23]

Zadock, after his experience with McDonell, managed to keep a low profile under McAlpin's tenure and avoided the ash house. He and his barracks mates had heard all about McAlpin's experience at the hands of the Tory-baiters of New York and understood that McAlpin wanted everyone on the island to pay for it. He wrote:

> *It was [McAlpin's] avowed object to wreak his vengeance upon the prisoners for injuries, which he said he had received from men who were entire strangers to us, and in which abuse he well knew we took no agency or even had any knowledge.*[24]

By now McAlpin had been "drunk for near a week"—too drunk to consider the consequences of what he did.[25] The rest of the prisoners knew it was only a matter of time before the 22 in the ash house froze to death. Natural scavengers and opportunists, more or less free to move around the island to take advantage of the carelessness of construction workers, the prisoners had accumulated a few basic tools. Pooling resources, they assembled a kit containing a pair of pincers and a file. Wrapping it in a blanket, one man came straight up to the guard at the ash house door and said he wanted to pass the blanket to his mates within. The guard said he could not allow it, as the prisoners were not to have anything. "But," he said, "when I walk the other way, fling them in."[26]

Hands and fingers numb, hardly able to move, the men set to work on their fetters and during the night, shackles forced open and chains cut through, one after another slipped out a window of the ash house and back to their bunks.

Zadock saw to these men as they came back in during the night and did what he could about the frostbite that afflicted ears, noses, faces, and hands. David Carswell, a boy of just 18, had his feet frozen so thoroughly that they clattered like stones as he walked in from the outside across the wooden floor of the barracks room.[27] The men in the barracks did not know if they could save his feet.

McAlpin, well into his week-long bender, discovered at morning roll call that all had escaped from the ash house during the night. The collusion of the guard was an obvious possibility, but McAlpin's attention fell elsewhere. He had his soldiers seize the same 22 men again and chain them in an empty room in one of the barracks. It was not the ash house—open to the wind and weather—but there was no fire and there were to be no food, water, blankets, or tobacco.

For two days and two nights the men were thus confined. But the room they were in shared a common interior wall with one of the occupied barracks rooms, so the other prisoners conspired to relieve the men by means of a hole in the wall through which they passed a steady supply of heated stones, hot food, water, blankets, and tobacco.[28] The guards looked the other way, and among them there was talk about Ensign McAlpin, his consumption of rum, and the direction in which his measures were leading them all.

Two days passed and the men remained confined in the unheated room. McAlpin had been drunk for three days; the fourth was now beginning. The improvised sabotage of McAlpin's regime of punishment could not continue indefinitely. The men were willing to keep on passing the means of survival through the hole in the wall, but they agreed that an end must be brought to the cold-room confinement.

Lieutenant Robert Lyons of Pennsylvania was one of the very few, perhaps even the only officer among the prisoners, and he now went to the sergeant of the guard, known to be troubled by young Ensign McAlpin's behavior.[29] "It will not do," he said, "to have the men suffer at such a rate. What can be done?"

The sergeant agreed, and then took a perilous step in the direction of mutiny. He did not dare to face down an officer by himself, even one like McAlpin, but he would with another officer, albeit an American prisoner. So he told Lyons that he had to come too, and together they would warn Ensign McAlpin to mend his ways. It was a bold push, said the sergeant, but if McAlpin would not let the men go, he would arrest McAlpin and release the men himself. They entered his quarters and found him drunk and truculent inside. They pressed their case with an appeal to reason, humanity, and an officer's sense of justice. McAlpin reacted as if he'd been patronized. "How old do you suppose I be?" he asked.[30]

With no claim to authority based in age or experience, McAlpin's only source of power was his rank; and he was daring them to challenge it. McAlpin was irrational, inebriated, and the situation was explosive. Lyons and the sergeant tried to reason with the young man, but were met only with sneering insolence.

Lyons, losing patience, told McAlpin that this was no trifling matter, that he wanted direct answers, that the punishment had gone far enough. McAlpin finally relented, saying he would release the men. He dismissed Lyons, who returned to the barracks to spread the news of having achieved a measure of victory.

But McAlpin was not through. He sent for the 22 men, one at a time. Choosing a few of his soldiers whom he knew to share his taste for revenge, McAlpin had the men brought into the guard house.

> *Some were surrounded with soldiers,* Zadock recalled, *armed with guns and bayonets pointing directly at them, and so near as to render the prisoners unable to move without being pierced with the bayonets; while McAlpin whipped the prisoners and caned them.* [31]
>
> *...and one by the name of Herwood he hung by the neck until he was dead, to all appearances; however he came to again, and carried the mark of the rope for more than a month.* [32]
>
> *...other prisoners which was strung up were persons which routed his father's house and plundered his mother and sister of their body clothes.* [33]
>
> *...their hands were confined in irons and their faces black with death, when they were taken down, and the irons which had bound their hands jammed into their mouths till they were filled with blood.* [34]

Toward the end of his alcoholic rage, McAlpin beat a prisoner named Jonathan Allbright with a cane on his bare back, leaving welts, contusions, lacerations, and an abiding bitterness. And then after a week of this, he stopped. Sober, McAlpin realized that, though his rage may have run its course, what he had done had taken on a life of its own.

* * *

MARCH 1782. In due course Jonathan Allbright, who was from New York and may have been one of the Tory-baiters, went with his injuries to the resident surgeon's mate, Dr. Connor.[35] Remembered by several prisoners for his attention to their well-being, Connor earned the gratitude and respect of the men as "humane, inquisitive, industrious, and skillful."[36] When the good doctor saw Allbright's back, there was no way the abuse could be concealed.

McAlpin considered the consequences of what he had done. Hoping it was not too late to put things right, he called in the men he had abused and told them that word of how he had treated them must go no further, that he would mend his ways, and that if the General heard about this it would be the ruin of him.[37] Yet even if the men had been willing to do as he asked, it was too late. Dr. Connor knew, and would be sure to tell Captain Anderson. An uneasy peace settled on the island. The men remained sullen and insolent.[38]

Not yet out of boyhood, James McAlpin was out of his depth, and most likely, out of luck. He dared not lay a hand on any of the prisoners, nor was he about to press his luck with his own soldiers, knowing full well they would be called to testify against him if his conduct was officially investigated. Though he may have had allies among his men, he knew he could not count on the senior non-commissioned officer, Sergeant Perrigo, who had sided with the prisoners at times and might well turn on him. Though loyal to the king, Perrigo had much in common with the prisoners. He was a New Englander by birth, a farmer from Massachusetts who had once served in the rebel army and who had been captured by the British at the battle of Bennington in 1777. He may have enlisted in the king's service, but he was not likely to have forgotten his origins or his humanity.[39]

Above and below the island, where the river was wide and slow, solid ice now ran from shore to shore, so thick that it had become a bridge between the shores. But Prison Island was still surrounded by rapids and, if anything, more isolated than ever. Occasionally a longboat was able to cross from the fort with supplies and new prisoners; it would be watched by a few gaunt men wrapped in blankets, distracted from the daily task of gathering firewood, but they would make no move to approach the boat. They knew the soldiers would bring in the supplies, and if the fresh prisoners had news of the war, they would want to hear this in private.

There was in fact precious little news, for in the winter there was little communication with the outside world. The Québec and Montréal *Gazettes* had published virtually no news of the war of any kind except very stale reports: British victories in the Caribbean, Benedict Arnold's attack on New London, Connecticut, in September of 1781. There had been news in September in local Canadian newspapers of the convergence of troops and warships on the Chesapeake for the great battle.[40] Then came silence on the subject in the *Québec Gazette*—not a word of the outcome of the engagement. Although news of the British defeat at Yorktown had spread across the continent and through the Canadian prisons, the outcome of that action had not yet been reported in the local papers—nor, for that matter, had any news unfavorable to the British cause.

The supplies brought by the longboats to Prison Island eventually made their way into the barracks, where the salt pork, salt beef, biscuits, spruce beer, and other items were issued to the men. The men had come to take their ration of medicinal, slightly intoxicating spruce beer for granted, and would complain loudly about if it ran out.

Zadock had spent nearly a year in the Montréal Provost without getting scurvy, and he was managing again; but Josiah Hollister was felled again by the disease and he recalled:

> *My mouth was so sore that I could hardly eat anything. My gooms were covered with blood blisters so that they would bleede at the least touch. I felt myself in a critical situation, with no money to get anything for my comfort. Fregitt Patchen*

> *gave me a dollar, which I esteemed a greater favour than I should twenty dollars at any other time. With it I bought some tea and some onions, which I think proved a greate relief to me.* [41]

Just as in the Provost, Prison Island had its haves and its have-nots. Onions, carrots, cabbages, potatoes, turnips, tea, and other such items came across in the boat, and there was a busy market for them which was driven by barter as well as by a certain amount of currency.

The winter advanced in an uneasy standoff without incident, except for two events. One was a ferocious late March blizzard. The other, momentous for the prisoners and for the atmosphere on the island, was the abrupt and completely unexpected departure of Ensign James McAlpin.

He could not indefinitely escape the consequences of what he had done, and before long the news reached Prison Island that McAlpin had been relieved of duty and probably confined to quarters at the fort on the shore. For Zadock, McAlpin's tenure had been as brutal as it was short, and his replacement was a welcome change. He wrote:

> *[McAlpin] tarried not long on the island, though much longer than he was desired, when another took his office, who manifested a disposition for peace, establishing good order, appeared to have a regard to the laws of justice, humanity, and benevolence, restored tranquility among the prisoners, and reconciliation between them and the guard.* [42]

Captain Joseph Anderson had replaced McAlpin with his nephew and namesake, Ensign Joseph Anderson, and life on the island changed dramatically for the better. [43]

Peace and stability may have been reigning in the isolated, ice-bound world of Prison Island, but for Great Britain the picture was anything but propitious. It was April 1782, and the British were beginning to concede the war, or at least to resign themselves to a more defensive posture. Haldimand was to "avoid all measures of offensive war" or in any way to attempt to "reduce the revolted colonies to obedience by force." He was to authorize no more "predatory excursions" by Indians on the frontiers of the revolted provinces, especially in the case of Vermont whose people were, at all costs, not to be "exasperated," but won over if possible. [44] On April 22, 1782, London announced that all American prisoners were to be sent home from England and that Frederick Haldimand was to do the same with prisoners in Canada. Representatives from Great Britain and the United States had gone to Paris and were negotiating terms for a cessation of hostilities. The war was all but over.

Yet in spite of orders from the home office, the war was not over for the prisoners. What commenced now was a series of negotiations between representatives from both sides to determine the order and reciprocal numbers in which prisoners would be released. There were hundreds of women and children to be inventoried and some men were claiming to be from Vermont so as to take advantage of the early release promised to its captives. The process was to take months—not only because of the red tape, but also because of the logistics of moving large numbers of people safely by ship.[45] Furthermore, Haldimand was in no hurry to release men considered to be radical rebels likely to make trouble for loyalists wishing to remain in the United States.[46]

CHAPTER 16

NEW ARRIVALS

"Some thus succeeded in making their escape"

APRIL-MAY 1782. Long after all but the deepest drifts of snow had melted, the great river waited—still frozen solid but slowly softening—thawing by day and refreezing by night, eroding, fracturing in the heat of the sun. Then one late April day it rained long and hard. The water poured off the land, jumped the banks of creeks, tore at the earth, shattered and carried away the last of the small ice—and all this, multiplied by thousands, rushed into the tributaries of the St. Lawrence. This immense tide of water could not be contained and once in the river and under the ice it heaved and split the great slabs, tearing them from the banks. They hurtled downstream, until the river was a foaming brown torrent of tumbling blocks of ice, rocks, and entire trees. The spectacle was shrouded and its noise muffled by a dense fog that settled out of the warm wind.

Where the river narrowed, steepened, and shoaled as it did just above Prison Island, the ice plowed into the river bed until even the force of the water could no longer move it, and first one, then another and then another raft of ice came to a halt. They collided, they were upended, overturned, stacked into mountains, shouldered up out of the river bed onto benches, uprooting the willows, and then the whole thing stopped. And when the ice stopped, the river stopped for a time, until the pressure above the ice dams gathered such force that the dams burst, hurling the slabs of ice, the trees, and the angry water downstream again.

On Prison Island the noise was constant, thunderous, apocalyptic, and all the more unsettling because so little of it could be seen. It surged at them out of a thick fog that obscured land and sky and everything but the churning brown water and what it carried. The flood very nearly swept across the island, but the ice went aground on the rock-bound upstream shore, as it had for thousands of years, and though the slabs piled 20 feet high there, the raging water divided and rushed past.

The immense pile of ice at the head of Prison Island remained for weeks as the only reminder of winter and of the hated McDonell and McAlpin. For weeks, there had been no boat from the fort, but with the river finally free of floating ice, the boat returned. The men had had no new clothes since last fall and what they wore was by now in tatters. Many had been shoeless at the beginning of winter and now there were many more. Many were malnourished, or laid low by scurvy. Frostbite had taken its toll.

When the first boat of the spring arrived, it brought the usual supplies and the one item besides clothing that the men had been asking for all winter: seeds for vegetable gardens. But by now there were also familiar wild edible plants emerging on the island and Josiah Hollister did what he would be doing back home. "In the spring as soon as vegetables began to spring up, I used to gather greens, and by degrees my health was restored," he wrote.[1]

At the same time, he and Zadock and the others cleared a plot of ground outside the muddy compound and began spring planting. Zadock recalled:

> *In seed time we were allowed to sow garden seeds and plant. This gave us not only a more full supply but a greater variety of food, if kept in confinement another winter. It also gave the prisoners proper exercise to preserve health and prevent disease.*[2]

The possibility of another winter on the island weighed on Zadock's mind, as it did on everyone's. Rumors circulated about a prisoner exchange, but they were only rumors until late in May, when the boat came over from the fort with some 20 new men.[3] After they got out, Zadock heard the names of three other Vermont prisoners on the island called (not Royalton men), and they were sent to the boat.[4] He must have expected his to be called too, since it was common knowledge that Vermonters were handled differently from other prisoners.

On May 13th, a directive had been issued by Frederick Haldimand to Richard Murray, the Commissary of Prisoners, to forward "all prisoners whatever belonging to that district (Vermont) without loss of time to Chambly where further orders will be given concerning them."[5] In an effort to continue to treat Vermont with kid gloves, Murray was instructed to identify all Vermonters and have them released. He wrote that between Montréal and Prison Island there were 14 who could be set free.[6] But that list still did not include Zadock and the four others taken from the Royalton area, and they all waited in vain to be called.

When the boat left with three of their mates, they must have wondered if the British even knew they were there, and if so, whether they even believed them when they insisted they were from Vermont. As Zadock may well have heard, prisoners in Montréal and Québec sometimes falsely claimed to be from Vermont when they learned that Vermonters were going home; and the British were suspicious of anyone making that claim. When the boat next came from shore to take prisoners for release, it brought a new group. The fact that new prisoners were still arriving was not a good sign; to the men on the island their advent made it look as if the war would never end. When Zadock talked to the new arrivals, his fears were confirmed. They had been captured only a couple of months ago on the Ohio River, over 900 miles away. Like Zadock, these men had been taken by Indians—Delawares, who then had turned them over to the British at Detroit—and they had been traveling downriver for a month.

Zadock, curious about the new men, mingled with them and might well have overheard as one of them asked if there were any Connecticut men on the island. This individual was older than any of the other new arrivals and had a different look about him. Most of the others were a hard-bitten lot from the Pennsylvania frontier—men formed by a life of hard physical labor and frequent violence. John Fitch, on the other hand, had always lived by his wits. A compulsive inventor, he was a watchmaker and silversmith by trade, and had been an indifferently successful migrant entrepreneur in New Jersey and Pennsylvania since the beginning of the war. Zadock was one of several from Connecticut, so he soon made the acquaintance of the remarkable John Fitch. Fitch seemed pleased, even relieved, to find other New Englanders.[7]

With the precipitous depreciation of Continental currency, Fitch had decided to go farther west and see if there might not be a way to make a fortune speculating on land in Kentucky. Land was one of the few commodities whose worth was appreciating at that time and for which there was an insatiable demand. He also knew perfectly well that the Ohio River country was becoming more and more dangerous. Unwelcome settlers were pouring into the territory of native tribes, who were now willing to take up arms and join the British to fight this wholesale land theft. In the Ohio Valley, the fighting was as much over Indian land as it was between the rebels and the King.[8]

Fitch would certainly have heard of the dangers faced by any party of travelers on the Ohio River. But he probably did not know until later about an appalling atrocity committed in the Ohio Valley just as he was about to set out himself. In March 1782, on the Miskingum River, 300 American backwoodsmen had slaughtered 90 Delaware Indians, peaceful Christian converts—most of them women and children.[9]

Fitch and a small party of entrepreneurs gathered at Fort Pitt, noted and then disregarded any warnings they might have received, hired a boat, loaded it with provisions and weapons and set forth on March 19th, 1782. Predictably, Fitch and his companions were ambushed and captured by Delawares three days out on the

Ohio River. They were lucky not to have been killed, or worse. Three months later, Delawares in Ohio would capture a rebel officer and torture him to death on the Upper Sandusky River.[10]

Treated fairly well by the Delawares, considering that the blood was up among all the tribes of the Ohio because of the behavior of belligerent backwoodsmen, Fitch and his party were quickly marched to Detroit and sold to the British. From there, once the ice was out, he and 20 other men were loaded onto boats for the journey across lakes Erie and Ontario and down the St. Lawrence directly to Prison Island.

As Fitch soon found out, the majority of the men already on the island were New Englanders and New Yorkers and they considered Fitch's Pennsylvanian companions as foreign as Fitch himself had found them to be. From the moment he joined them at Fort Pitt, Fitch was at odds with his companions and their rough southern frontier ways. Slight of stature, older than the others, and unsure of himself in the backwoods, Fitch was a businessman, an artisan used to the world of commerce and enterprise. The Pennsylvanians thought of him as an ingratiating, overly cautious, priggish know-it-all.[11]

While among the Indians he had amused himself and his captors by cutting designs into their powder horns with the only tool of his trade salvaged from the chaos of the ambush—a steel engraving burin. He had been able to trade this skill with the Indians for favors, food, money, and bits of clothing. This had not endeared him to his ruffian fellow captives.

Fitch had only been in captivity two months so he had not been through what the other men of the island had. He had not lost his health or his restless initiative or as many of his clothes as the others. Once again among fellow Yankees, his spirits improved and as he considered his situation, he did what he had always done: look for opportunity.

As Fitch worked with the others on the vegetable gardens, he discovered that even in this place it might be possible to do some business. All he needed was to identify a market and then devise a way to serve it—perhaps he could even create demand where none yet existed. So he set to work. He knew he would need tools, so from a discarded splitting wedge, an augur, an old axe head, steel barrel hoops, a broken straight razor blade, a rusty jackknife, a worn-out file and a few other scraps of metal, Fitch fashioned some rudimentary tools and a miniature forge.

What he had in the back of his mind was a button factory. He knew something of button-making and thought there might be a market here. Besides, with the materials at hand he didn't know what else he could make.

He had had his eye on a discarded brass kettle, so with a little bargaining and with money he had earned back at Detroit, he bought it and cut it into button blanks. These he shaped with a shoemaker's hammer, fastening fronts and backs together with homemade solder, engraving designs with his burin. His brass buttons were such handsome, such useful, and such utterly unusual items to be found in a prison camp that soon he was selling brass buttons as fast as he could turn them out, to inmates and guards alike.

Fitch's factory was the most interesting thing on the island, and far from prohibiting his enterprise, the British soldiers were fascinated, spending long hours in his workshop, providing a ready market for his button production, even providing him with the materials for silver buttons. The enterprise expanded and Fitch undertook to make a rudimentary wooden clock using a pendulum, stone weights, and a simple escapement.[12] It worked so well that more were wanted and Fitch took on a staff. His first hire was James McCullough, a young Virginian with whom he had been captured. He took a liking to an ingenious Yankee from Maine named Nathaniel Segar and hired him as assistant in clock-making.[13] As demand grew, Fitch took on two other assistants, the Vermonter John Reynolds, and William Clark, a Virginian who had been taken on the Ohio River, not far from Fitch's place of capture.

Everyone on the island had spent the winter weighing the chances of successful escape, and now that the ice was out and the weather had moderated, some of the men who had been studying the river were eager to take their chances with escape. Not Zadock, though. He was biding his time, certain that his best chances lay in waiting to be exchanged. But he had been talking to the others, and exchange or no, some were convinced that nothing could be worse than even one more day of confinement and abuse on Prison Island.

> *[D]isaffected by our former treatment,* Zadock wrote, *many chose to hazard their lives by an attempt to swim down the rapids. Some thus succeeded in making their escape, while others only plunged themselves into the jaws of death.*[14]

Which is to say they got off the island, and then they were swept away in the violent water. Those who drowned were sometimes fished from the slack water three miles downstream. But those who did not drown: Did they reach the shore, cross the river, and avoid patrols, Indian war parties, and starvation? No one knew. Zadock wondered what became of them, and slowly began turning over plans in his own mind, an indefinite wait for exchange seeming less and less promising. His nature was methodical, whereas these escapes had been impulsive.

As spring turned to summer, escapes continued. New prisoners arrived even as some prisoners were being repatriated, but no one—at least, no one on Prison Island—knew when or if general release was imminent, so many men saw no point in waiting for exchange.[15] They still had the freedom of the island and it was not hard for a few to slip away and disappear. There was a good chance they would not be missed for hours because they were outdoors so much of the time, tending gardens, gathering firewood, keeping an inquisitive eye on John Fitch and his doings.

But every morning there was roll call and when the British realized the rapids were not instilling the fear and discretion they counted on, they took measures. They surrounded the barracks with a 12-foot-high palisade of posts set in the ground.

JUNE 1782. John Fitch considered these developments with a certain equanimity, or so his narrative indicates. Although what he wrote seems at times self-serving, much of it is in fact verified by what others wrote. Prison this may have been, but he was making the best of a bad thing. His little factory was turning out wooden clocks, which sold for four dollars apiece. He was well on his way to making 300 pairs of brass buttons and 80 pairs of silver ones. He had fashioned tools for repairing watches, in which he did a brisk business. He was apparently using his resources to buy necessaries for the sick prisoners and he also provided them with the bounty of his own vegetable garden: corn, squashes, peas, cucumbers, and other vegetables.[16]

From all of this industry and enterprise, Fitch reaped a harvest, as he wrote:

> *A superfine suit of clothing, plenty of coarse working clothes, and a good hammock of Russia sheeting, swung midway in the barrack, to escape the vermin which the dirty habits of... fellow-prisoners had introduced. ...five blankets, and two or three cords of wood, laid up for winter.*[17]

In some ways Fitch was better off than he ever had been; he was even planning for the coming winter. Fitch had economic independence, one of the era's most compelling definitions of freedom. He had a self-sustaining business. He paid no taxes, but shared his good fortune: nearly a Revolutionary ideal.

But Fitch also had enemies. Joseph Parkerson and Captain Hopkins, with whom he had been captured on the Ohio, had never liked him, had always resented his cleverness; and now this bad blood was causing real problems. Allegations of fraternization with the British and imperfect patriotism led to insults and open hostility. Fitch found a way to appeal to his fellow New Englanders for support and allegiance by pointing out that this hostility toward him was nothing more than southern envy of the Yankee qualities of industry, ingenuity, discipline, and cooperation. This case struck a chord and soon Fitch had the New Englanders rallying to his cause, creating an uneasy standoff between the two factions.[18]

Zadock did not appear to be especially interested in prison politics. He was a rationalist, a quintessential Yankee, and he was more concerned with his prospects for an successful escape as he watched the daily progress of the imposing palisade around the compound:

> *Several [of us]...resolved to effect our escape before they had completed the barricade.*
>
> *We accordingly collected some logs together on the lower part of the island for a raft.*
>
> *Our attempt to escape now became known to some of our fellow-prisoners by discovering our absence, who betrayed our object to our keepers thus courting favor. ...our suspicions were well founded, as they (the guards) then went and rolled all the logs off that part of the island.*[19]

In mid-June, five men who had managed to escape from Prison Island were recaptured and delivered back to the island. The British hoped that their recapture would discourage further escapes, but, although it may have done this, it also proved that it was possible to survive the rapids.[20] There was also another outcome, completely unexpected. One of the recaptured men, while being interrogated by the British, made the allegation that earlier in the year Ensign McAlpin had subjected several prisoners to prolonged physical abuse—in particular, a man named Jonathan Allbright.[21] It is even possible that the recaptured prisoner was Allbright himself, but British records name only four of this party of five.

In any case this prisoner had credibility and an investigation ensued that eventually led to an examination of the scars inflicted left by McAlpin's lash. It also led to another reliable witness in the person of Dr. Connor. The charges could not be ignored. Josiah Hollister remembered with satisfaction:

> *Dr. Conner, who examined into the matter [of Allbright's injuries] and reported him [McAlpin] to the General, who kept him under arrest.*[22]

If McAlpin was relieved of duty and possibly confined to quarters as a result of his February misbehavior, why was he not court-martialed right away? Captain Anderson, in command of Coteau-du-Lac, may have thought that his discipline of McAlpin was severe enough and that the matter would go no further, even though he must have known what a serious infraction this had been. Anderson may have failed to report the matter because it reflected poorly on himself, or perhaps because McAlpin was a fellow Scottish New York loyalist. A "certificate" describing Allbright's injuries, perhaps written by Dr. Connor, was submitted to Captain Anderson either when it happened or at some later date. In any case the document eventually went up the chain of command all the way to Haldimand's desk. It wasn't until McAlpin's behavior became thus known that the British opened an official investigation.[23]

A blue ribbon panel of very senior officers traveled to Prison Island on June 24th, and, after interviewing some of the soldiers who had been present throughout McAlpin's week-long descent into hell, could only conclude that these charges were probably true and, if so, McAlpin's behavior had been outrageous.[24] By the 2nd of July the opening drumbeats of dishonor began. As the official orders read:

> *A general court martial to assemble in Montreal on or before the 12th [of July] inst. for the trial of Ens. McAlpine put under an arrest by his Excellency Gen. Haldimand's order on complaint of several prisoners of which he had the care at Coteau du Lac of most barbarous and inhuman treatment.*[25]

CHAPTER 17

SUMMER OF DISCONTENT

"The willfullest set of men I ever saw"

JULY-AUGUST 1782. Whatever satisfaction the prisoners might have taken from the retribution McAlpin was about to face, they were once again under the control of the martinet James McDonell. The size of the detachment at the fort and island had been enlarged from 73 to 102 rank-and-file soldiers, three junior officers, seven sergeants, and two drummers.[1] In spite of McDonell's reputation for hotheadedness, his ability as an officer did not appear to have been questioned, and if he could impose some discipline it might even have discouraged the prisoners' chronic insubordination and tendency to escape.

Of course, precisely the opposite was more likely to happen, and as Josiah Hollister recalled, McDonell's authority was put to the test over an issue that could hardly have been more contentious.

> *On the fourth of July we had a mind to celebrate Independence. Accordingly we gathered some green bushes and stuck them in our hats and over the barrack room door, which greatly enraged the guard, particularly Lieut. McDanolds (McDonell), who commanded the guard. He ordered a sergeant to have them taken down. He came into our room and ordered the bush down.*[2]

John Fitch, occupying a unique position in the social order of the prison, had a private word with the sergeant. As Hollister wrote:

> *Fitch said: "Sergeant, it is the fourth of July. The boys have a mind to celebrate Independence." He replied: "I know it, and that is what makes me mad. I had as lief you would raise your flag on the block house."*
>
> *We all turned out to role call, with the green bushes in our hats. The Lieutenant asked the sergeant what it was best to do to us.*
>
> *The sergeant replied: "It is best to let them alone. If you know them, as well as I do, they are the willfullest set of men I ever saw.*[3]

Celebrating the Fourth of July was a thumb in the British eye, a reminder of their inability to put down this colonial rebellion. The loyalist soldiers guarding the island knew the war was nearly over and surely lost. The guards had been telling the men that they would be released sometime soon, if only they would be patient. As much as the men might have wanted to believe what they were being told, they remained unpersuaded. The pending trial of James McAlpin was a vivid reminder of the men's firm belief that the British were not to be trusted under any circumstances.

The trial began in Montréal on the 12th of July and lasted for days. McAlpin was charged under the Articles of War with "misbehaving in a scandalous infamous manner, such as is unbecoming the Character of an Officer and a Gentleman."[4]

This solemn proceeding lasted until the 29th of July, when the court made its finding and issued its verdict. Ensign James McAlpin was found guilty as charged and was dismissed from the service only two years after entering it.[5] Young James had been dealt a setback that could not have been more devastating. Nothing that his parents had wished for him was now possible; his prospects for the future were gravely diminished. Zadock was not impressed:

> *Complaint was made to the British provincial government against the base M'Kelpin, which resulted only in his exclusion from the service of the army with disgrace. Doubtless the court by which he was tried was strongly though unjustly biased in his favor, which greatly ameliorated his punishment.*[6]

Zadock may not have been convinced, but for someone of James's heritage, this was the gravest punishment, short of death, that a court martial could hand down for an officer.

Whatever vindication the men on the island might have felt, they had not all waited around for the verdict. By the time it came down, there had been more escapes from Prison Island: on July 11, seven jumped into the rapids;[7] on July 13, five more were gone.[8] Ten Mohawks were sent after them and recaptured some right away, returning them to Prison Island, where they were placed in irons.[9] Those not captured had either made good their escape or they had been drowned.

It was clear from these escapes that surviving the rapids was possible; the truly hard part was what came next, as those who were recaptured would attest. Stealing food from farms was risky: The inhabitants were as likely to turn against you as they were to help. Lieutenant Houghton had been sending out parties of Indian trackers and hunters from Kahnawake since early in the year in pursuit of escapees and to intercept rebel couriers and spies. A defensive line of outposts manned by Indian scouts had been deployed, reaching from the headwaters of the Chateauguay

River to Schroon Lake in the eastern Adirondacks.[10] And if escapees were not recaptured, there was always the prospect of becoming utterly lost in the wilderness of northern Vermont or New York State and starving to death.

Even so, Zadock and a few trusted friends made up their minds.

> *We were determined to use every exertion and watch for an opportunity to effect our escape from confinement,* Zadock later recalled. *We sought, but sought in vain. Time rolled away, till we found ourselves enclosed with pickets. We were not allowed to go without this enclosure unattended by the guard, and in the daytime only.*
>
> *The yard which was surrounded by the pickets was about ten or fifteen rods (240 feet) wide and nearly forty rods (640 feet) long, extending lengthwise of the stream. They completed the yard some time in the month of July 1782.*
>
> *We were allowed to hoe our corn and garden roots. But this afforded us no opportunity for escape, as it was impossible to swim the current on either side of the island undiscovered.*[11]

For obvious reasons there had never been a boat moored on the island; boats only came from the shore and then returned. Daytime escape without detection was virtually impossible. At night, everyone had to be in the barracks for roll call at nine o'clock and sentries patrolled the walled compound all night.[12] Zadock believed he and the others had been lulled into passive acceptance of the wall by promises of imminent release. As he put it, "Their object in giving us repeated encouragement of being exchanged was only to dally us with the fond hopes of soon seeing better days, and thus amuse our minds with fancied prospects."[13]

Another winter was unthinkable, but Zadock and his barracks mates had been slow off the mark. With the stockade finished, security was much tighter. Still, that did not hold back the indefatigable Fred Sammons, who was undeterred by the failure of other escape attempts. On August 18th, he and James McMullen, taking advantage of a guard's momentary inattention, flung themselves into the river and were swept out of sight before they could be missed.

With Sammons and McMullen added to the seven who had escaped only a few days prior, security on the island grew tighter than ever. Lt. McDonell and Capt. Anderson were drawing unwanted attention from their superiors.[14] The guards grew increasingly on edge and less cooperative than they once had been. "We had once paid several dollars to one of the guards to suffer us to pass through the gate, should he find an opportunity," Zadock wrote; "but never had the good fortune even to see him again."[15]

CHAPTER 18

THE PLAN

"Darkness at noon"

MID-AUGUST 1782. Zadock and the 11 other men in his room decided that impulsive, opportunistic escape was probably suicidal. Perhaps by watching what Fitch had been able to produce through organization and ingenuity, perhaps even by recalling the ideals of the Revolution itself, Zadock and his roommates decided on an ambitious coordinated enterprise.

> *The plan we adopted was in itself extremely precarious as to its success,* Zadock wrote.
>
> *Our plan was to dig a passage under ground that should extend beyond the pickets, about twenty feet from the barracks.*
>
> *Had we been confined upon the main land, liberty from the prison might have given us a passport to the wilderness. But now our freedom brought us to "troubled waters," which seemed to promise death inevitable to all who should attempt to pass the current even with well-fitted boats; while we had nothing in our power but logs, fastened together with ropes.*[1]

It was going to be a massive outbreak. The men decided there would be safety in numbers—in planning, in tunneling, in executing the escape itself, and during the weeks they would have to spend getting home through the wilderness. They had grown to trust one another and were convinced their best chance for success was to escape together. They spent hours estimating the distance from the barracks to the log palisade; the distance from there to the river bank; the safe depth to reach before digging horizontally; where to store the earth they dug; how to conceal what they did; how to keep it secret from other prisoners; how to stockpile food and equipment for the trip; where to secrete logs for rafts; how to shore up the tunnel; and what to dig with.

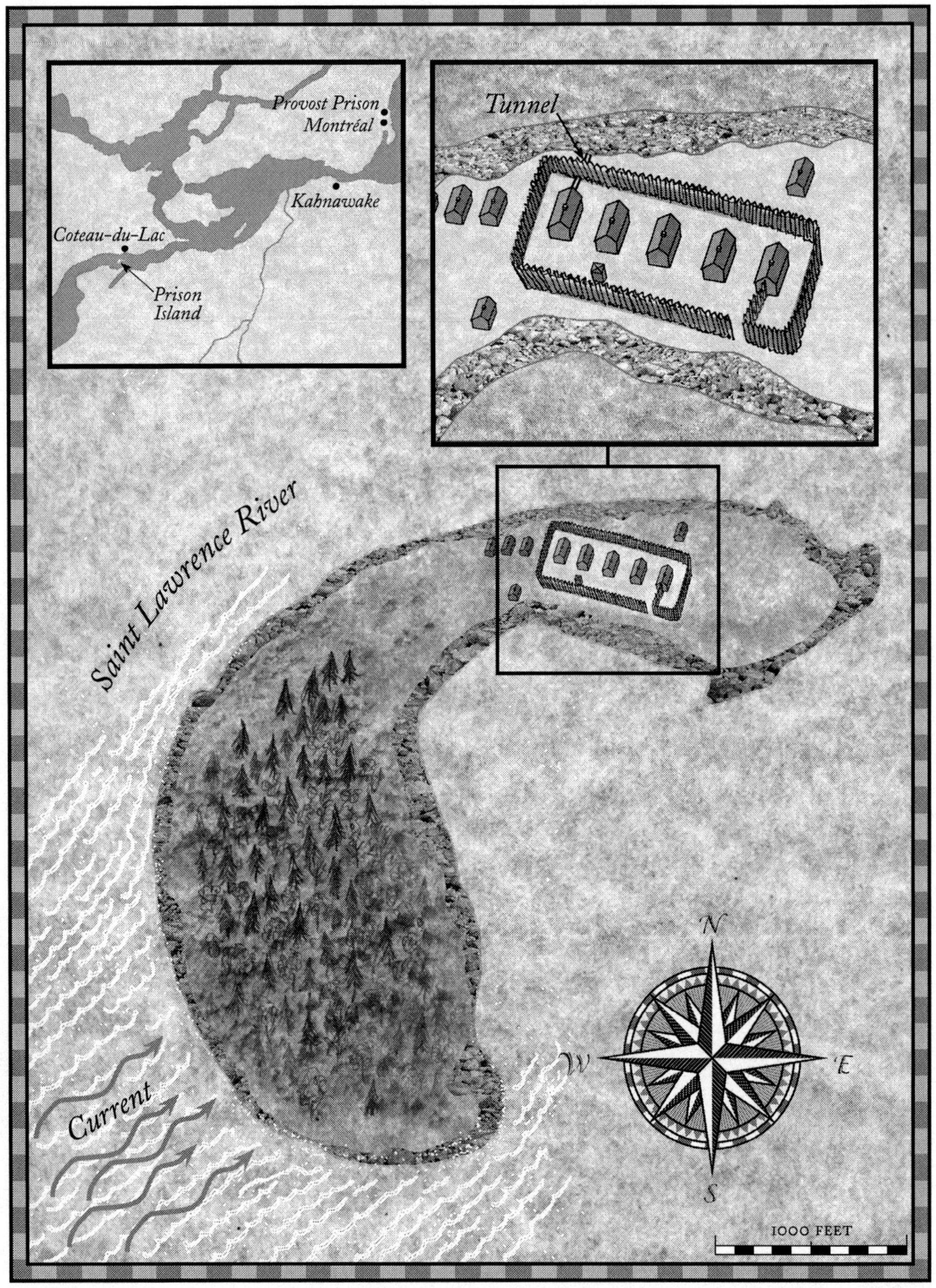

MAP 4. Prison Island.

Once the men in the room decided on a course of action, their first resolution was to keep their plans a "profound secret." After two years in prison, Zadock had learned that revolutionary loyalty was one of the most evanescent of bonds. He had come to assume that people looked out first for themselves, and if there was an advantage to be had from informing—either for preferential treatment from the guards or for settling old scores—it would almost certainly be exploited. So the first rule of the room was simple: no one beyond the door was to know of the plot.

The men in the room by then knew one another well enough to feel confident that this scheme might work. There were eight Vermonters, two New Yorkers, and two Virginians.

The Vermont neighbors Zadock Steele, Simeon Belknap, Abijah Hutchinson, David Stone, and John Parks had all been captured together. The three other Vermonters were John Hathaway and Joseph Bonette, who had been captured in October of 1780 and had been with Zadock in the Montréal Provost,[2] and Zarah Norton, a recent arrival who had been captured in July of 1782 at Corinth by one of the many British scouting parties still combing the north for captives and intelligence.[3]

The New Yorkers were Josiah Hollister and John Sprague, both captured in Ballstown at the same time as Zadock and who had also been with him in the Montréal Provost. The Virginians were William Clark, a surveyor, and James Burnett, a relatively recent captive picked up in Kentucky and, like John Fitch's party and most other recent captives, sent directly to Prison Island.[4]

They were mostly young men in their 20s or early 30s, who had come from frontier settlements, most from the north. Although they had spent much of their lives in the manual labor of the colonial American farmer, digging a 30-foot tunnel with their bare hands would probably try them as much as anything they had ever done.

Zadock's resolve not to tell anyone about his escape enterprise was child's play compared with the task of keeping the physical evidence of the operation from being discovered. He and his mates would have to keep quiet and they would have to avoid arousing suspicion through unexplained absences when guards came in unexpectedly. They would have to conceal the access to the tunnel. And the biggest problem would be the disposal of tons of excavated earth.

Confident that they could improvise solutions to these and other problems as they arose, the men began. Josiah Hollister's bunk was nearest the outside wall and he remembered the day they started:

> *We began to dig under the room I lived in. We began under the floor. ...It was under the berth I slept in that we went down under the floor, and so privately we carried it that the prisoners in the other rooms had no knowledge of it.*[5]

It was a lucky accident of construction that the bases of the bunks were enclosed, so the men could lift out the bottom of Hollister's bunk and then remove the floor boards beneath, giving them access to a dank, lightless crawl space with barely enough headroom to roll over. Even though the entrance was thus concealed, there had to be a man at the entrance to the tunnel while another dug, so they took the extra precaution of hanging blankets—which they had used during the summer to keep flies away—around the bunk.[6]

They decided that, if possible, they would work around the clock. And then the first men went down, taking with them the tool they would use for tunneling: a large jackknife with a broken blade. The bottom of the bunk and the bedding were replaced, Hollister crawled in for a nap, drew the hanging blankets together, and lay there listening to the scraping and scuffling as one man dug and the other spread the dirt around the crawl space.

A constant worry was that the noise could be heard all over the camp, but Zadock recalled the simple ruse they devised.

> *If any of our fellow-prisoners or the guard happened to come in while one was at work, others would drown the noise of his digging by making some noise with a stick or with their feet, which was easily done without being suspected of the design.*[7]

While working like this, any clothing the men wore would become suspiciously filthy, so they found a leather shirt, an old pair of trousers and a cap that they kept out of sight when they weren't being used. The men took turns wearing them.

Having planted gardens and observed construction crews digging trenches for the stockade wall, the men had been reasonably certain that the earth was deep and free of boulders, but they had no way to be sure until now. As the first man pecked at the soil in the dark under the barracks, he found what they had all hoped for: The soil contained a large proportion of clay, peppered with small round pebbles.[8] It was not sand or gravel, which would have made tunneling almost impossible without continuous shoring to prevent collapse.

Once they found that the earth would be relatively easy to dig through, "it became necessary," Zadock remembered, "for us to dig a perpendicular course of considerable depth before we could dig horizontally."[9]

The men had studied the most serious obstacles to tunneling: the stockade wall, made of tree trunks whose butts were set at least three feet into the earth; and a long, shallow trench just inside the wall from which had come a great quantity of soil that had been banked against the walls of the barracks to seal them from the winter weather. The tunnel would have to go well beneath these so that neither the heavy logs of the wall nor anyone walking above would break through.

Our progress was very slow, Zadock recorded*; one of us kept constantly digging except in the hours of sleep and time of taking refreshment.*[10]

Things were too quiet at night to risk working on the tunnel, so they changed their round-the-clock work plan. Men in the neighboring barracks and even the guards might have heard it. If men from a single room were unaccounted for at meal time day after day, that too would arouse suspicions.

Digging at the rate of a foot or two every day, the men deepened the shaft. It had to be wide enough for a man to sit or kneel while he loosened the earth under him; then he would reach down for a handful and dump it into a container. When the container was full, the man at the top of the opening would pull it up and spread it in the crawl space. It was tedious work, Zadock wrote:

[A]lternately following each other in our turns each one worked in this dreary cavern, groping in darkness at noon.[11]

When the shaft had descended far enough—at least nine feet—the men decided it was safe to dig horizontally. Easily disoriented in the total darkness, they first had to make sure of the direction the tunnel was to take. The opening of the tunnel had to be high enough so that a man kneeling on the bottom could ease forward into the opening and stretch out on his belly. Then he would have to crawl forward to the face of the drift, where he would peck away at the earth in front of him with the knife. Then, Zadock recalled:

After we had dug a quantity of earth loose, so that we had no room to dig more, we returned backwards, drawing or scraping the dirt we had dug with our hands and arms, which we put under the floor of the barracks.[12]

It took constant attention to make sure the tunnel was going in a straight line, toward the river, and, most important, that it was neither gradually climbing nor descending. With each foot of progress, Hutchinson recalled, the man laboring at the face of the tunnel would find himself fighting for breath, at times on the verge of blackout:

[F]inding it difficult to obtain air at so great a distance from the surface, for the safety of the person digging, a rope was fastened to his feet; and after laboring until exhausted, he was pulled back by his companions at the mouth of the hole.[13]

Even more worrisome than poor air circulation was a cave-in. They were burrowing through the earth with no shoring to support the walls and roof of the passageway. The only thing keeping the tunnel from collapsing was the cohesion of the clay in the soil. If the men maintained a steep vault in the roof, it would be somewhat less likely to collapse. But they all knew that a cave-in meant almost certain death. A trapped man's only hope of survival lay in rapid extrication by the lifeline tied to his feet and a man with the strength of ten on the other end.

Zadock and the others in the room would descend every day in turn to their enterprise—each day another in which they managed to cheat the odds of suffocation or discovery. As soon as each man had worked his shift and been dragged to the mouth of the hole, he would climb the nine-foot shaft and surface under Hollister's bunk, giving the signal to the minder of the entrance. He would lift the boards and emerge, caked with mud. He would strip off the leather shirt and filthy trousers and cap and pass them to the next man, who would quickly put them on before vanishing down the hole.[14] There was a large tub full of water in the middle of the room where the tunnelers washed off the caked clay and grime. So far the warning system had worked and no guard had yet burst into the room unannounced. Nor had anyone else found them out.

But the men knew that with every day the odds against them were growing. Discovery would almost certainly doom the project and land the men in chains in the guard house, along with the growing number of men who had escaped and been recaptured.

> *One day as I came out of the hole,* Hollister recalled, *and was stripping myself, a man by the name of Kelsey, who sat in his berth mending his cloaths, discovered me through a small hole, his berth being opposite mine.*
>
> *I thought I was secure from any discovery. I walked out to take the air after being two hours in the hole. Kelsey met me and asked how far I had got.*
>
> *I told him, "I am here."*
>
> *"But how far have you dug your hole?"*
>
> *I made very strange of it.*
>
> *He said: "You needn't make so strange of it. I saw you come out of the hole with your leather shirt on. I mean to be one of your party."*
>
> *I told him to keep it quiet, for there were Judases amongst us. I informed him I thought we had dug two-thirds of the way.*
>
> *The news soon went through the barracks, which made me fear we should be betrayed. But there was an Irishman amongst us, whose name I do not recollect, who was a true hearted fellow, who went to one Van Epps, who was set to watch and give information against the prisoners and told him.*

> *"You know what is going on, and if you make any discovery, I'll as sure cut your throat as you are now alive." He repeated it with so much earnestness that Van Epps promised he would make no discovery.*[15]

As word of the tunnel spread through the barracks, some believed that the guards would soon discover the tunnel, shut it down and tighten security so that subsequent escape would be virtually impossible. So those who yearned to break free but had no taste for dark cramped spaces and saw the tunnel as a death-trap made a dash for freedom while the now-swollen number of tunnelers dug what might well be their own grave.

At the beginning of September, two men plunged into the river in broad daylight. The guards saw them and fired five shots at the fast-disappearing heads, bobbing, sinking, resurfacing; all the shots went wide of the mark and soon the men were out of sight. Hot pursuit was mounted and before the fugitives had gone three miles, their trail was picked up and they were cornered, recaptured, brought back, and shackled in the guard house.[16] In short order, on the 2nd of September, three more tried their luck in the rapids, but this time only two were recaptured. Perhaps one had been drowned, but he might also have got clean away—the two who had been caught were not about to say which.[17]

Undaunted by this demonstration of the odds against success, William Knieskern followed these men into the rapids a few days later, riding on three brandy casks lashed together.[18] He was not seen again, so Alexander McNutt decided to try the same method, clinging to some wooden casks, but he was caught and brought back to the island. Even if they were unsuccessful, these escape attempts infuriated Lieutenant McDonell, who found resistance to his authority unspeakably offensive. As McNutt was dragged ashore, the lieutenant, in a blind rage, made ready to run the prisoner through with his sword; but Sgt. Perrigo took him aside and, risking a charge of insubordination himself, counseled restraint.[19]

Ensign McAlpin's fate for abuse of prisoners was fresh in everyone's mind, and McDonell, if found guilty of cold-blooded murder, would be dealt with even more harshly. The young sergeant had coolly saved the prisoner's life and quite possibly the hotheaded lieutenant's career.

Even as men were attempting escape and as Zadock and his barracks mates were burrowing deep below the prison compound, others were occasionally being released. One morning in early September the names of Robert Hopkins and Stephen Valentine, both captured in the great raids on New York state in the fall of 1780, were called and they were whisked off the island, to be sent home on parole, where they had agreed not to take up arms against the king.[20] Not being

Vermonters, but rather from New York, these two might well have been released through back-channel negotiations facilitated by influential connections. Their release was the subject of much correspondence between high-level officials and a special agent was sent from New York via Vermont to bring them home.

The prisoners watched them go and wondered — why them? Never knowing what to believe, they must also have wondered if, in fact, the guards had been telling them the truth—that the war was truly over and the men were being sent home. Some considering escape might have reconsidered, but those committed to the tunnel did not waver. In fact, now that knowledge of the tunnel was spreading, others were signing up to escape through it, too.

But not John Fitch. Fully prepared and provisioned for the coming winter on the island, he was content to observe the drama from a safe distance. As his own narrative indicates, he was not eager for a complicit role in the project, though he counseled the tunnelers from time to time. But his advice was guarded, tangential, suggestive, as if to maintain deniability in case informers were eavesdropping.

Zadock's dozen had already grown, and soon it was decided to let others in on the secret. He wrote:

> *We made known our object to all the prisoners who were stationed in our line of barracks and received their universal and respective promises not to divulge the secret to any of the prisoners who were stationed in the other line of barracks. Few would assist us, considering it labor in vain.*[21]

Now, instead of the original 12 and those in the adjoining room, there were six rooms with a dozen men, each of whom must keep the secret safe. Besides the fearsome Celt, probably Abraham Brannan, there would be others to enforce the pledge of silence.[22] Bringing in so many was a calculated risk, but widening the circle of knowledge also widened the brotherhood, the complicity, the solidarity; it put informers on notice that if the secret got out, none were safe; and it served to enlist a few more tunnelers. As the burrow lengthened, the work became more demanding, the air grew stale more quickly, exhaustion set in faster, and the earth was more difficult to dispose of.

Zadock and his expanded crew were now able to move faster and there was time to turn to other pressing matters, such as stockpiling food, clothing, and equipment. Speed was of the essence, for the longer they worked the greater the chance of discovery. So far the project had encountered no great obstacle, no misfortune, and by now it was passing beneath the long ditch that ran along the inside of the palisade.

CHAPTER 19

RAIN

"Our subterraneous way...half buried in mud and water"

SEPTEMBER 5, 1782. The morning of September 5th was hot and humid, and the men watched the clouds piling up in the west as the still air thickened with heat and the hum of mosquitoes and the rasp of cicadas. As the tunnelers rotated in and out of the hole in shifts, they came out to eye the building thunderheads. The sky blackened late in the day, and in the distant sky there were jagged streaks of lightning. The roar of the river drowned out the mutter of far-off thunder, but before night, the storm was upon them—violent and deafening and torrential. In the blue-white detonations of light they could see the water collecting, flowing, looking for a place to go. No one worked in the tunnel after sunset, but the men had only one thing in mind this night. In the morning, Zadock was down the hole at the first chance, and what he found was disheartening:

> *[R]ain filled the ditch (along the palisade) full of water, which soaked through the ground into our subterraneous way and filled the hole we had dug completely full.* [1]

The men considered abandoning the project altogether, but they were convinced that unless they escaped, their lot would be to spend another frigid and demeaning winter under the thumb of McDonell. With so much invested and with the tunnel so close to the palisade, a shutdown was unthinkable.

> *If we refrained from digging,* Zadock reasoned, *we seemed to be threatened with death on every side; and if we continued to dig, fear and trouble were before us. Our absence from the barracks exposed us to the danger of having our plan discovered. We chose rather to hazard our lives in an attempt to escape, though doubtful of success, than to risk the consequences of remaining in confinement.*
>
> *We now commenced dipping out the water into a barrel, which we emptied into a ditch that was made to convey our wash water from the barracks into the river.* [2]

Having decided to continue with the tunnel, the men faced a greater chance of discovery than ever before. Positioning a large wooden barrel on Hollister's bunk, they lowered a cooking pot into the shaft, hauled it up hour after hour, and emptied it into the cask. This was noisy, sloppy work, almost impossible to conceal, and never more so than when it was time to wrestle the brimming, heavy container out of the barracks to dispose of the water. "We dipped six barrels' full and emptied it into the ditch, besides a considerable quantity which we put into a clay pit under the barracks where they dug clay for their chimneys; and still there was much left in our way," Zadock recalled.[3]

There was no way to conceal this amount of water from the British sentries, but they never questioned it, never investigated, never suspected. Zadock could only assume that his plot was simply too audacious to be imagined—or could it possibly be that the guards knew, and were for some reason looking the other way? He later wrote:

> *The guard, no doubt, supposed we were washing, or they would have suspected us. Nor yet can I account for their stupidity while they saw we were in possession of such a quantity of water, which we brought out of, without carrying into, our barracks.*[4]

In any case, there was no time to lose. The tunnel was more dangerous than ever. Zadock lowered himself down the access shaft, entered the tunnel, and crawled through the water, soon churning it into a bone-chilling, soupy mire.

> *[W]e now were forced to enter upon our subterraneous labor entirely naked, to lie half buried in mud and water while digging.*[5]

And so in the darkness he resumed, hacking with the broken knife at the softened earth. Where the tunnel passed under the ditch, water continued to seep from the roof and the chances of a cave-in were the most severe. But, wet as it was, the clay held firm and, taking greater chances than ever, the men continued to dig. Soon a new obstacle presented itself:

> *When we arrived to the picket,* Zadock wrote, *we found it was placed upon a large stone. We then dug to the right, where we found another, which formed an angle with the first. Then, turning to the left, we also found a third.*[6]

The exhausted men emerged from their shift to report that the palisade seemed to be set on a foundation wall of large stones. It was almost as if the British had anticipated an attempt to dig under the compound wall. When the first stone was discovered, the man working at the tunnel face, by digging first left, then right, made a large enough space for more than one man, and working in pairs they came to realize the extent of the obstacle they faced. It might have been a continuous wall of rocks. They gathered in the barracks and listened gravely to the description of conditions at the end of the tunnel—"All which," Zadock recalled, "seemed to discourage my fellow-laborers, and led them entirely to give up the object."[7]

Zadock was not yet acquainted with the stones, and though the others might have been right to abandon the escape, he wanted to take the measure of the obstruction himself. With ingenuity and resolve they had managed to overcome what seemed like greater adversities than this. So he stripped, took up the knife and disappeared alone down the trap door under Hollister's bunk.

> *[B]eing in perfect health and in good spirits myself, I went in with a determination to remove one of these obstacles, if possible, before I returned. We had, by this time, made quite a large cavern near the pickets, which gave me considerable chance to work. After laboring during the space of two hours, I succeeded in removing one of the stones out of the way, and, to my great joy, found that the picket was hollow up a few inches above the ground, which emitted light into this before gloomy but now delightful place.*[8]

Looking up through the hollow log, Zadock could see the color of the sky and for the first time he could taste the freedom on the other side of the wall, but this was the time when the whole project was most vulnerable. The tunnel was close to the surface, and the hollow log would transmit the sound of digging clearly to any sentry walking past. He returned and informed his fellow prisoners of what he had done, which "occasioned transports of joy, raised the desponding, encouraged the faithless, confirmed the doubting, and put new vigor in every breast."[9]

News of this breakthrough would spread and possibly cause prisoners outside the inner circle to press for inclusion; and if that were met with rejection and resentment, the exposure of the entire scheme would become a real possibility. Abijah Hutchinson recalled that the men began to dig night and day, hoping to break out in a day or two.

> *[A]t 12 o'clock, they broke the turf beyond the pickets, and heard the guard distinctly cry out,* "All is well." *"That's the fact," said one of the company, "the dog speaks the truth now, if he never did before."*[10]

The sentry was only a few feet away on the inside of the fence.

> *[T]he guard at that moment stopped, as though some unusual noise had arrested his attention, and listened for some moments. But finding all silent, he started forth again on his solitary round.*[11]

Nearly given away by a muttered remark, the men came to the surface under cover of darkness just outside the wall; but come daylight, a sentry could easily discover the hole just by glancing out through the spaces in the upright logs. The tunnelers grabbed branches and brush to cover the hole as best they could, knowing it would not pass even a cursory inspection by daylight. Then they crawled back to the barracks, where a plan was hastily made to conceal the hole the following day. They would have to escape the following night before the tunnel was discovered, but in the meanwhile, the men decided they needed a plan to hide the hole in broad daylight.[12]

Simeon Belknap and Josiah Hollister were nominated to go to McDonell and say that the men wanted to harvest seeds from the vegetable gardens. They explained, Zadock wrote, that

> *[we] were forced to abandon all hopes of exchange that fall; Consequently we desired to secure all our garden seeds, that we might supply ourselves the ensuing year, should [we] remain on the island another season.*
>
> *Pleased that the prisoners were resolved to be submissive, he ordered one of the guard to see that no one absconded. Having cut and tied up in small bundles these vegetables, we proceeded to hang them up so as to fill the space between the pickets.*[13]

This covered gaps in the palisade so that the guards could not look out and see the tunnel opening. Slipping outside the wall they spread more underbrush over the escape hole, still miraculously undiscovered. No guards had patrolled the exterior perimeter of the stockade.

> *This we accomplished while our unsuspecting attendant was lounging about at a distance from us.*[14]

PART V
GONE

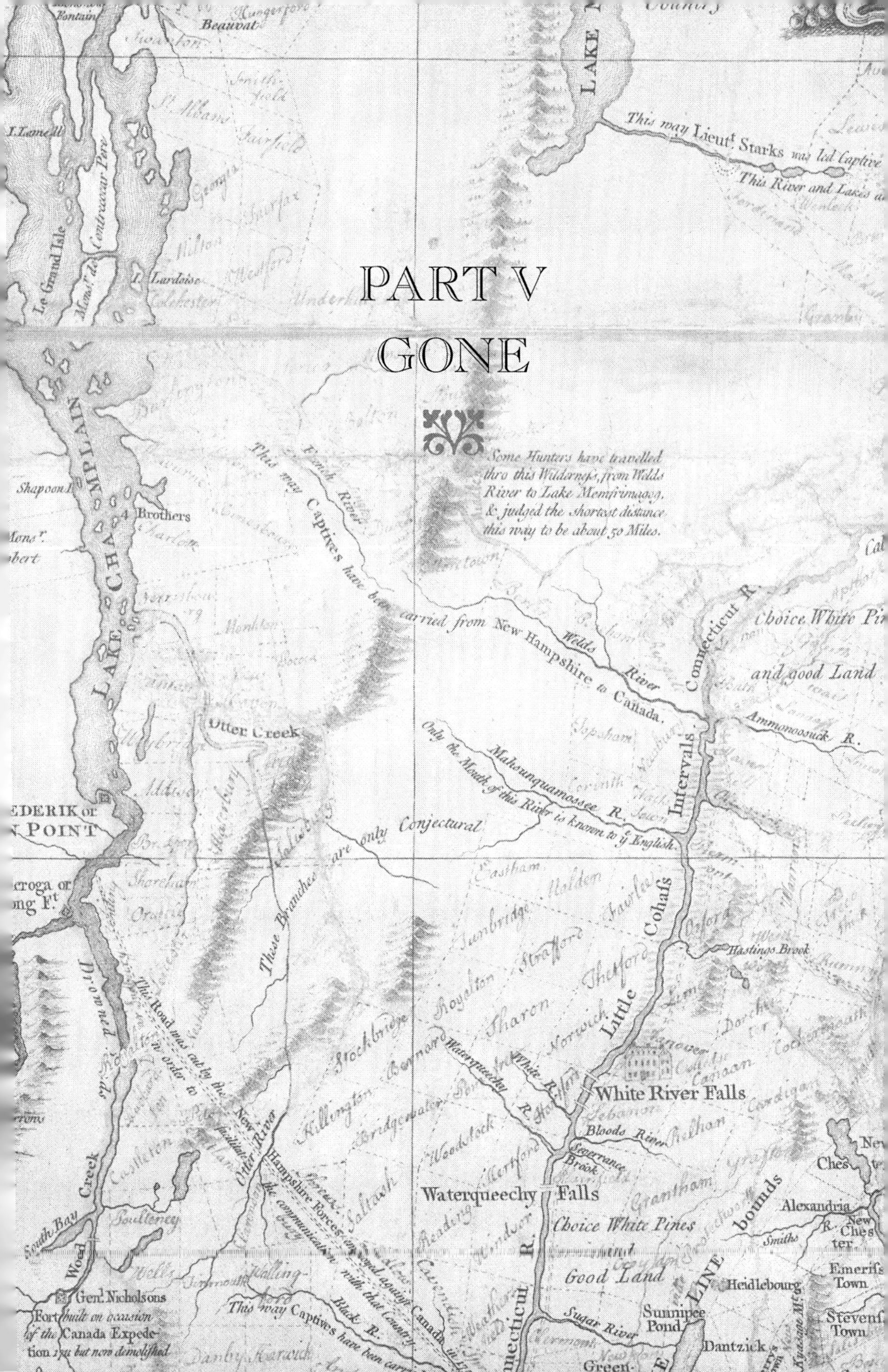

Beauvat
LAKE
This way Lieut! Starks was led Captive
This River and Lakes
Le Grand Isle
LAKE CHAMPLAIN
Shapoon I.
4 Brothers
Some Hunters have travelled thro this Wilderness, from Welds River to Lake Memfrimagog, & judged the shortest distance this way to be about 50 Miles.
This way Captives have been carried from New Hampshire to Canada.
Welds River
Connecticut R.
Choice White Pi
and good Land
Ammonoosuck R.
Otter Creek
Intervals
Mahounquamossee R.
Only the Mouth of this River is known to ye English.
These Branches are only Conjectural
Cohass
Hastings Brook
Little
White River Falls
Bloods River
Waterqueechy Falls
Choice White Pines
Good Land
Alexandria
Heidlebourg
Sunnipee Pond
Dantzick
Sugar River
Black R.
This way Captives have been carri
This Road was cut by the
New Hampshire Forces employed against Canada
Otter River
Wood Creek
South Bay
Genl. Nicholsons Fort built on occasion of the Canada Expedetion 1711 but now demolished

VERMONT

Some Hunters have travelled thro this Wilderness, from Welds River, to Lake Memfrimagog, & judged the shortest distance this way to be about 50 Miles.

NB. Connecticut River has been actually ...

Mons!
Leaperriere
Bolton
Worster
Lunenbourg
Shelburne
St George
This way Captives have been carried from New Hampshire to Canada.
French River
Waterford
Middlesex
Brothers
Charlotte
Hinesbourg
Danbury
Moretown
Berlin
LAKE CHAMPLAIN
Ferrisbourg
Hinesbourg
Barnet
Connecticut R.
Choice White Pines and good Land
Called
Peacham
Welds River
Ryegate
Lyman
Gunth
Loring
Mons! de
Pocock
Bath
Landaff
Franconia
Contracoeuse
Panton
New Heaven
Topsham
Ammonoosuck R.
Otter Creek
Weybridge
Middlebury
Only the Mouth of this River is known to y English.
Mahounquamosse R.
Newbury
Intervals
Haverhill
Lincoln
Addison
Corinth
Waitstown
Umpammonoosuck R.
Fairfield
RIK or
OINT
Waterbury
Salisbury
are only Conjectural
Bridport
Shoreham
These Branches
Eastham
Malden
Cohass
Piermont
Warren
Fairlee
Orwell
Stratford
Orford
Tunbridge
Thetford
Wentworth
Hastings Brook
Leister
Drowned Lands
Royalton
Little
Rumney
The Road which was cut by the New Hampshire Forces employed against Canada in 1759 to maintain the communication with that Country
Neshobe
Sharon
Lime
Dorchester
Cockermouth
Dunbar
Stockbridge
Norwich
Hanover
Bernard
Pomfret
White R.
Hartford
Dartmouth College
Canaan
Waterqueechy R.
Hubbardton
Pitsford
Killington
White River Falls
Cardigan
Plymouth
New
Otter River
Bridgewater
Woodstock
Lebanon
Bloods River
Relhan
Grafton
Rutland
Castleton
Hertford
Sunapee Brook
Plainfield
Grantham
New Chester
Shrewsbury
Clarendon
Waterqueechy Falls
Bay
Creek
Poultney
Saltash
Windsor
Choice White Pines
Protectworth
bounds
Alexandria
Reading
Corinth
and
Good Land
Smiths R.
New Chester
Wood
Wells
Cavendish
Weathersfield
Croydon
LINE
Heidlebourg
New Britain
Gen! Nicholsons
built on occasion
Canada Expedi...
... but now demolished
Tinmouth
Wallingford
This way Captives have been carried by the Indians.
Black R.
Connecticut R.
Sugar River
Sunapee Pond
Salisbury
Clermont
Newport
Dantzick
Kyasage Mt.
Perrys Town
Boscawen
Danby
Harwich
Green
CURVE
Pawlet
Flamstead
Unity
Rye Town
Little Sugar R.
Rupert
Dorset
Bromley
ward
Thomlinson
Rockingham
No.4
Ackworth
Lempster
No.8
New Concord
COUNTY
Charles Town
Contoocook R.
New Hopkinton
Winhall
Manchester
Sandgate
Saxtons R.
COUNTY OF CHESHIRE
Alstead
Marlow
Hillsborough
Henniker
Westminster
Wears Town
Mason
No.7
Sunderland
West River
Arlington
Townshend
Walpole
Limerick
Proprietors Lands reserved
Stratton
Pultney
Gilsum
Ashuelot R.
No.6
COUNTY OF HILLSBOROUGH
Piscataquog
New Boston
Shaftsbury
Glassenbury
New Fane
Dublin
Fulham
Westmoreland
Keene
Lyndeborough
Monadnock Mountains
Contoocook
Peterborough
Bennington
Woodford
Bratle
Chesterfield
Swansey
No.5.

CHAPTER 20

THE ESCAPE

"Adhesion to the raft"

SEPTEMBER 10, 1782. While Belknap and Hollister beguiled McDonell with feigned acquiescence and then lulled the guard assigned to watch them into boredom, Zadock and the others in the barracks were trying to assemble their gear without attracting attention. The men had decided to separate into small groups once off the island. Zadock was teamed with three others: Simeon Belknap, his Vermont neighbor; Fitch's assistant, William Clark of Virginia; and John Sprague of Ballston, New York. They twisted unraveled yarn from blankets into ropes. They filled small food bags with flour mixed with butter, salt pork, bread, parched corn, and black pepper. By an unexpected act of providence, the entire prison had been issued two weeks of food that day—usually they were issued food twice a week—so the food bags swelled.[1] As it was, they would have to escape with only the clothes on their backs and they would have to make a march of several hundred miles in their bare feet.

Men who had once scorned the tunnel as futile, who had neither helped nor made themselves ready for escape, now wanted to use the tunnel. They were casting about at the last minute for ropes, provisions, materials for rafts, and extra clothing. Zadock recalled that they were causing a stir:

> *[T]hey could not forbear collecting in small companies and whispering together, which raised suspicions in the minds of the guard. Under these apprehensions, McDonell ordered that, "If any prisoner should be found attempting to make his escape or be guilty of any misconduct..., he should not be spared alive."*[2]

McDonell and the rank-and-file guards knew the prisoners fairly well by then, and had learned to read the mood of the nearly 200 men. They all must have sensed that something was brewing and that no good would come of it. The guards who frequented John Fitch's workshop, relieving their numbing boredom, buying buttons, having watches repaired, and passing the time of day, may well have heard unguarded gossip. McDonell suspected an escape attempt or perhaps even an organized insurrection, against which his company of men might not have been able to prevail without reinforcement from the fort. The usual informers had apparently been silenced. Nighttime security was tight, as it had always been. No one was allowed outside, and there had been no escapes after curfew; so once the place was locked down, McDonell and the guards could feel more confident of containment.

> *At nine o'clock,* Josiah Hollister later wrote, *we were all ordered to go to bed, and at ten o'clock the Sergeant came round to every room and counted us to see if we were all there.* [3]

Hollister, whose bunk concealed the entrance to the tunnel, let a few minutes pass, then at a whispered signal rolled out of his bunk and lifted out the bottom, then the planks in the floor underneath. There had been handshakes and quiet fare-thee-wells earlier. Former neighbors and friends had told each other they'd meet on the other side, back home. They wondered who would get home first, who would get home at all.

The men were completely silent as they dropped through the trap door and entered the tunnel for the last time. They had pre-arranged the sequence: who was to go first, who second, who third, and where they would all rendezvous once on the outside. The men had decided that there must not be more than one man in the tunnel at a time. If there was a cave-in, only one would be lost. If a man was caught leaving the exit, the uproar would warn the others to abort. One man at time meant less noise as he left and moved to his rendezvous point. They allowed six or seven minutes for each man.[4]

> *When all was still,* Zadock wrote, *we tied our ropes to our packs and crawled, drawing our packs after us. I was preceded by six of my fellow-prisoners. The hole was nearly half filled with mud.* [5]

Zadock waited an interminable half hour for his turn and then descended. The darkness was absolute. The only sound was the thudding of his heart, his own labored breathing and the mud sucking at his hands and knees.

Just as Zadock entered, the man ahead was emerging beyond the picket. Back in the barracks, 12 more men waited in the dark. In all, 19 had chosen to escape that night. They remained in their bunks until summoned in turn, so that there would not be a crowd waiting at Hollister's bunk if a guard should burst in. Since all the doors were locked from the outside by the sentries after roll call, the men in the adjacent room dropped one by one through a trap door in their own floor into the crawl space.

Zadock moved through the tunnel and then sensed the enlarged cavern where, only hours earlier, he had managed to dislodge the big stone. The air here was cool and fresh. He scraped past the boulder that still half blocked the passage and then he scrambled for the opening.

> *The sentinel was walking directly across the hole just as I was about to crawl out, when he cried out, "All's well!" Thought I, "Be it so; continue the cry, if you please." My head at this time was not more than a yard from his feet. I crawled on, and was followed by more, who made a path in the grass which resembled that of a log drawn through the mud.* [6]

After the last man had disappeared down the hole, three were left in the room. One of them was Hollister, who later wrote:

> *Unfortunately for me I got sick in digging in the wet earth under ground, for it was quite muddy after the raine and having been so long sick before.*
>
> *They all advised me not to attempt to go. It was a greate mortification to me to give it up, but as my health was then I could not have stood it through the woods.* [7]

Like all the others, he had talked with the men who had escaped from Prison Island and the Provost in Montréal and were then recaptured, and he had a good idea of the strength and endurance the men would need to survive the rapids and then make it home through the wilderness. In his weakened condition he would slow the others down, forcing a decision to go slower or leave him behind. The others did not want to start their flight with a burden like that.

So Hollister and two others in the room who had decided not to go, Zarah Norton and James Burnett, had the place to themselves.[8] The silence that settled on the room was the silence of the sudden absence of people with whom these men had lived for two years. Hollister replaced the boards. The men turned in. There wasn't much to say now, so the three men were alone, sleepless with their thoughts of what retribution the morning might bring, and of the men easing along the shore of the island.

There had been a good deal of planning for this moment. The 19 men all knew what they would do as they left the tunnel. It being imperative that they all get off the island as quickly as possible, they had agreed ahead of time on the makeup of four groups of four and one of three—reduced in size, perhaps, by the absence of Josiah Hollister.[9] Each group had already gathered logs for rafts. As soon as Zadock was out, he and his team gathered and moved to a pre-arranged location. They moved as far as possible from the compound to the upstream end of the island, where the shore was littered with driftwood. Zadock wrote:

> *We rolled a large log into the river on the upper part of the north side of the island, on each side of which we placed another; then, putting sticks across both ends of them, underneath and on the upper side, opposite each other, we tied all of them together with our blanket ropes, [then] fastening our packs, which contained our provision, a large scalping knife, a pocket compass, a tinder box and fireworks.* [10]

Elsewhere on the shore, Abijah Hutchinson and two other Vermonters, John Hathaway and David Stone of Barnard, were fashioning their raft, as were others all along the shore—some using strips of blankets, some using the bark of the elm trees that grew all over the island. [11] There was a sliver of a moon that night, so the men laboring by the water were not likely to be seen. [12] Even so, if the guards had been a little more vigilant, if they had had a sentry patrolling the shore of the island as well as the inside perimeter of the picketed compound, the prisoners would probably never have planned such an ambitious escape.

Because they had been watching the current for months, they knew they would have to launch into the deep and furious channel along the north side of the island. The other side was shallow and treacherous, and if they did not fetch up on the rocks they could easily be swept into the backwater on the south side of the island where the boats landed. No, the best plan was to be swept away as far and as fast as possible. They sat each on a raft corner, Zadock wrote,

> *and set sail down the rapids.*
>
> *Death in its most frightful form now seemed to threaten us, and the foaming billows pointed us to a watery grave. Guided only by the current, sometimes floating over rocks, sometimes buried in the water, with little hope of again being carried out alive, we passed down the raging stream with the greatest rapidity imaginable, clinging to our logs, sensible that, under the guidance of divine Providence, our only ground of hope rested in our adhesion to the raft.* [13]

As Zadock swept downstream he glimpsed Hutchinson, Hathaway, and Stone clinging to their raft, kicking and stroking hard to break out of the main channel and reach the south shore. But the current carried the raft, spinning and bucking, out of sight. [14] Zadock had watched the current often enough to know there was no point in trying to resist it.

> *We passed down the river about nine miles. We landed on the north side of the river about two hours before day chilled with the cold and trembling with fear. Our bread had all washed to a jelly. None of our provision remained fit to carry*

> *with us except a little parched corn, which was in a small, wooden bottle, some salt pork, and our buttered flour, which we found to be water-proof. Our compass was also rendered useless.* [15]

The loss of the bread and the compass would prove to be a near-disastrous setback in the days to come. Like all the others they were soaked and had only the clothes they were wearing. Although shoeless, they had woolen stockings and coats made from blankets. Zadock did not mention their most precious possession: their fireworks. Of all the things they carried, this alone might mean the difference between life and death. The only way for them to make a fire was to have a large flake of flint, a roughened piece of steel, and a painstakingly prepared supply of tinder—some dry substance such as down, lint, goldenrod, or milkweed that would ignite when hit with a spark struck by the flint and steel. If any of these were lost, or if the tinder was wet, they could start no fire.

Of the other men, Zadock saw nothing. None fetched up where he and his companion did; for all he knew they were all drowned. It was still very dark, but now also very quiet along the wide, still body of water a few miles below the island. They dared not call out to the others. There was no time to lose. They had to find shelter and concealment before daybreak. They were in a populated area next to a road. A bone-chilling autumn rain set in.[16]

Where they came ashore they had no way to cross the wide lake to the south shore. Zadock could clearly see it would also be impossible to descend the river any farther, because at the narrow outlet of the lake ran a set of rapids every bit as dangerous as the ones they had just managed to survive. To descend farther than that would have put them closer to densely settled land, and worst of all, dangerously close to Kahnawake Village and Lt. Houghton. Their best chance to cross the river unseen, Zadock later wrote, was to go upstream:

> *We marched up the river till daybreak, when we discovered that we were near the fort opposite the island. We then turned north into the woods, which led us into a swamp, where we encamped under some old tree tops that had fallen together, about one mile from the fort, which formed no shelter from rain, but merely hid us from our expected pursuers. We plainly heard the report of the alarm guns on the morning of the 11th of September.*[17]

* * *

SEPTEMBER 11, 6:00 AM. Hollister, Norton, and Burnett, wakeful all night, were up early feeding the fire for their breakfast when they heard the latch lifted on the barracks door. If the sentry had looked in, nothing would have appeared immediately amiss in the gloom. Blankets hung up around the bunks concealed the absence of their occupants. Things were stirring in the adjacent room. Soon the camp would be humming with the news of the escape and the prisoners' pleasurable anticipation of its discovery. So Hollister just waited. The last man out had not bothered to hide the exit, as there was no chance the tunnel would be used again. And once the opening was found, it would be obvious that it originated from the nearest room—where Hollister, Norton, and Burnett were waiting.

> *The Corporal went out to his hooks and lines set in the river to catch fish,* Hollister's memoirs noted, *and finding where [the prisoners] had rolled down timbers to make floats, led to the discovery that some of the prisoners were gone. They went to viewing the pickets, and came to the hole where they went out.*
>
> *Sergeant Moss came into the room and asked if we were all that were left, there being only myself, Zerg Norton and John Bunnell* (probably Burnett or Bonette) *left in the room. I told him,*
>
> *"Yes."*
>
> *He said, "Are there any more gone? Oh! damn it, if you know you will not tell."*
>
> *We turned out to role call, and it happened that those that were gone were on the fore part of the role.*

The roll was called room by room, starting, as it always did, with the one at the end of the first row of barracks, which happened to be the tunnelers' quarters.

> *He began to call the role, laughed, and said: "By God, I believe they are half gone."*[18]

The sergeant already knew the first room was nearly emptied. Calling the roll for the next one, he realized the scale of the breakout.

> *Lieutenant [McDonell] turned about and looked very surly, and went into the block house. When he (Sergeant Moss) had finished calling the rolle he found that nineteen were gone. He then went into the block house and made his return to Lieutenant McDonell, who came into the room where I was and wanted to have the place shown him.*
>
> *By this time the room was full of prisoners and soldiers. He asked Sergeant Moss if all were gone out of the room, and was answered "Yes."*
>
> *"What, not one left?"*
>
> *"No, damn the one."*

A man named [John] Avery said: "Yes" pointing to me, "There is one."

He said to me, "Did you know they were going?"

I said, "Yes."

He turned to the Sergeant and said: "Take that gentleman and put him in irons."

The Sergeant said, "Oh, we have no crime against him, unless it was that he did not go when a dore was opened for him. It is their duty to get away if they can, and ours to keep them."[19]

Philosophical, tolerant, even mildly amused, Sergeant Moss probably knew Lieutenant McDonell well by now and found a way to defuse the situation before the volatile lieutenant lost his temper. In a case like this, the first thing to do would be to summon an officer from the fort. There had been some changes made. It was not Anderson who answered the alarm, but a new man, Captain Alexander McDonell. He was no relation to Lt. James McDonell, and in temperament could not have been more different.

The alarm gun being fired, Hollister recounted, *Captain McDonell, commander of the fort on the other side, came over and wanted to see the place they went out. I took up the floor and showed him the place.*

He said: "No, mon, they ne'er went oot there. If you will creep through there I will give you a half Joe."

I told him I did not like to be shut in.

"Ha! ha! ha! upon my soul it was well played. The guard have done their duty, and it was their (the prisoners') *duty to get away if they could. It is all right. Nobody to blame."*[20]

Not only was the captain unfazed by the escape, he could not conceal his amusement and even a sporting admiration for this audacious enterprise, though it hardly redounded to his credit as a warden. But he had reason to be lenient—he knew, as the prisoners did not, that the shooting war had been over for months, that both sides were warily standing down and that the gears of bureaucracy were slowly turning to send the prisoners home.

CHAPTER 21
ZADOCK AT LARGE

"Every wave dashing the water into our boat"

SEPTEMBER 11. Zadock and his mates, counting themselves lucky to be off the island free and still alive, had no idea that what they had just escaped from was a free ride home. The prospects of making the trip on foot were not promising. The weather had taken a turn for the worse and they had not moved from their first camp.

> *We remained under these tree tops three days and two nights,* wrote Zadock, *without going ten rods from the place, having nothing to eat but salt pork, parched corn, and our buttered flour, together with a few kernels of black pepper; for the want of which last I think we must have perished, as it rained with a mixture of snow every day and night sufficiently to keep us completely wet all the time.*[1]

News of the escape went quickly up the chain of command and General DeSpeth, commander of the Montréal military garrison, was not nearly so sanguine as Captain McDonell. He notified Haldimand immediately that patrols were combing the banks of the river and that four of the men had already been caught. He hoped "the rest will not save themselves at all."[2]

In fact, the recaptured group had never even reached the shore. After being swept down the rapids and breaking their paddle, perhaps trying to make for the south shore, this party had become trapped in a large, powerful eddy in the still water a few miles below the island.[3] When the alarm was sounded, sentries saw them immediately and sent out a boat to bring them ashore and hustle them back to the island to be shackled in close confinement.

The day following the breakout at Prison Island, DeSpeth wrote that seven officers living on parole in private Montréal residences had escaped, adding that the "savages" were at that point in pursuit.[4] Upon hearing this, Haldimand sent a dryly worded letter to General DeSpeth to the effect that the recent escapes, especially those from Prison Island, "must be owing to a remissness of duty, which you will please to inquire into."[5]

* * *

SEPTEMBER 14. It was a wonder that Zadock and his party had not been taken. They had been ashore three days and still found themselves within hailing distance of the fort. But they had deliberately waited, knowing that the hunt for them would be in full cry for a couple of days and then would die out. The British would have assumed that if the men were not caught soon, they would be far away, and local search would be called off. At that point the chances of escape might actually have been better. Zadock recalled:

> *On the morning of the 14th, benumbed and chilled with the cold, we traveled till we came in sight of a settlement. After nine o'clock at night we ventured a little nearer, when to our utter astonishment we heard the drum beat. We were near the fort. In passing we went through the commanding officer's garden, and I pulled up a hill of his potatoes and carried them along with me.*[6]

More immediate even than crossing the river, was the need to replenish the food supply so severely diminished in the rapids. It took only moments to raid the garden and in the dark the risk was worth taking, but they dared not linger to take more than a few potatoes.

Upstream of the fort the land quickly became less heavily settled, but there were a few regularly spaced farms. The forest was thick to the river's edge, the road was a rough muddy track no wider than an oxcart. Hard by the river there was an occasional clearing with a log hut, but the river was a well-traveled thoroughfare. Heavily laden fur-trade freight canoes carrying nine or ten men plied the river in both directions—sometimes only one a day, sometimes as many as four or five.[7] Zadock had been watching the traffic pass Prison Island all summer, and he was counting on being able to steal an unattended canoe to cross the lake.

The men followed the road along the St. Lawrence for about four miles, then came upon a boat at anchor near the shore. "I waded in toward it till I heard men in it snoring in their sleep," Zadock wrote, "when I quickly made my retreat."[8] There would be others.

Zadock had heard rumors that many French Canadian inhabitants were sympathetic to the rebel cause, and that they might take in fugitives such as himself and his mates. As hungry as they were, the four fugitives were not prepared to knock on doors, but they were not above chancing the theft of some food. When they saw the lights of a farm through the trees the fugitives emerged from the underbrush and crossed a clearing, believing that they were hidden by the dark. As they approached, their presence was somehow betrayed and a man in the house, suspecting they were up to no good, perhaps already having been visited by other escapees, shouted at them in French. Instead of taking flight, the four men took a calculated risk. Since they had already been discovered, they would rush into the barn, where they would surely be able to snatch some food before retreating.

> *We found one cow. As we were approaching towards her, two large dogs came at us with great rage, and, barking most furiously, appeared to be determined to bite us. The old Frenchman again came to the door and hailed us.*
>
> *Fearing that soldiers might be quartered there, we retreated as fast as we could, keeping an eye upon the dogs, and swinging our staves at them to keep them from biting us, while the old Frenchman was trying to set them on.*
>
> *The ground was descending as we retreated; and while we were all moving together very fast, having our eyes partially turned upon the dogs, we ran against a fence and threw down many lengths, which made such a rattling that it terrified the dogs and immediately put them upon their retreat.*[9]

As least as terrified as the dogs, Zadock and his mates took to their heels, getting as far as possible from the road and the buildings. The north shore of the river was settled for a few miles upstream of the fort, meaning there would be another chance for food, but also for discovery.

> *Trembling for our safety, we kept in the fields back of the street; while the dogs continued their barking. They succeeded in exciting all the dogs in the neighborhood to engage in the general alarm. They were at every house, and sometimes in great earnest, as we passed along the distance of several miles.*

Except for the one irate citizen, they had no further encounters as they hurried along the road, in spite of the dogs. They were now on the north shore, well upstream of the fort, and the river had widened into a lake four miles across. Zadock and the other escapees had to find food and cross this body of water before daybreak.

> *At length we came to a number of cattle in a field not far from the road, among which we found a two-year-old heifer, very tame and in good flesh.*

The favored moment had now arrived. We agreed that Belknap should go in search of a boat to convey us over the Lake St. Francis; that Sprague should stand with our scalping knife to defend against every foe; while Clark and myself should kill the heifer and procure a quantity of meat. By the help of a little salt I soon succeeded in catching the heifer; and, taking her by the horns and nose, I instantly flung her down, when Clark cut her throat with a large jackknife; and, not waiting for her to die or even spending time to skin her, we took off a gammon (hind quarter) *and left her bleeding.*

Belknap had now returned and informed us that he had found a boat, to which we immediately resorted, carrying with us our unskinned beef.

We set out upon the lake, steering for the south shore. A breeze arose from the north-west and drifted us ahead with great violence, every wave dashing the water into our boat.

The wind increased. The boat was fast filling in spite of all we could do. But we succeeded in landing just as our boat had filled with water.

Having fastened it to the shore we went into the woods, struck up a fire, skinned our beef and cut it into thin slices, which we partially roasted on sticks by the fire, and then lay down to sleep. This was the first time we had been to any fire since we left Prison Island.[10]

CHAPTER 22
HUTCHINSON

"A snake or a frog would have been a delicious morsel"

SEPTEMBER 11, EVENING. Abijah Hutchinson, John Hathaway, David Stone, and eight other men fetched up together on the north shore of the river, but in the dark and in the rapids they had lost track of Zadock and his party. Hutchinson's party knew nothing of their fate, nor of the other four trapped in a slowly revolving eddy in the middle of the river, doomed to recapture just after daybreak. This large group hurried under cover of darkness into the forest, where they hid for the entire day. That night they moved upstream and happened onto three canoes, in which they slipped away from the north shore. Once across the river, a mile wide here, they abandoned the canoes. As they had earlier planned to do, the 11 men split into groups and traveled separately.[1]

From here they had only one destination: Lake Champlain. To strike due south through the trackless heart of the Adirondack wilderness would have been suicidal. To try to skirt to the west of those mountains would have risked almost certain capture by Iroquois or loyalist scouting parties. The western shore of the lake was not especially safe either, but they could travel along it, staying concealed, until it narrowed at the landmark called Split Rock, and then they could cross to Vermont away from the British shipping that patrolled the lake.

SEPTEMBER 12 AND 13. Unlike the northern shore of the St. Lawrence, the side where they had landed was unsettled, so the several parties waited for daybreak and then set off at intervals. They headed southeast, hoping to reach Lake Champlain below the last British outpost on the western shore, at Point au Fer. There was another outpost, even farther south, called the Loyal Blockhouse, which stood at the north end of Grand Island. They would have to slip past it, staying of sight in the forest along the lakeshore.

For two days Hutchinson and his two companions, like all the others, walked across the flat, boggy country of the Chateauguay Plain, fording streams that flowed in meandering loops through dense forest. These streams did not run to Lake Champlain, but rather north into the St. Lawrence. The men could see no landmarks, and for these two days they could not even see the sun. It rained and occasionally snowed, and they were never dry. After the second day of travel, Stone was having trouble keeping up with Hutchinson and Hathaway. They helped him as much as they could but he weakened throughout the day. When they stopped for the night he was barely able to walk. They spent the night by a stream and in the morning Stone's condition had worsened. He told his two mates that he had become too ill and too weak to travel any farther, and insisted they go on without him.

It was a bleak choice, but it was one they must have rehearsed many times. It is safe to assume that before the breakout, this had been one of the many eventualities that the men discussed as a group: what to do with sick, injured, or disabled companions. Although each situation would be different, everyone had known at the outset that one of the choices that injury or illness might force on a small group of men would be abandonment—to sacrifice one that the others might live.[2]

In the end they did what they had in all probability agreed upon back at Prison Island: Stone was to stay behind. The other two gave him all the food they had left—about two pounds of meat—and at daybreak they set out, with no expectation of seeing him again.

SEPTEMBER 14–21. For two days Hutchinson and Hathaway traveled as quickly as they could. They were counting on being able to live off the land, and although they knew that there was probably a great deal that might sustain them in this forest, all they dared to eat were buds from basswood trees and the bark of the slippery elm. They scrutinized plants and mushrooms, and grubbed for roots, but they feared that unfamiliar plants were poisonous. They saw no creature, not even a snake or frog, although at the end of two days without any real food, Hutchinson wrote, "A snake or a frog would have been a delicious morsel fit for an epicure."[3]

They became so disoriented in the densely forested, featureless landscape that they found themselves going in circles. More than once they crossed their own path of a day or two earlier. As the crow flies, it was 50 miles from the St. Lawrence River to the northern end of Lake Champlain—not all that far—but seven days after leaving the river they were still making painfully slow progress through the bewilderingly flat, relentlessly soggy terrain. They were still without food, except for an occasional familiar edible wild plant.

There was ample water, but they were weak from hunger and the distance they were able to cover grew less and less each day. They saw not a single sign of human presence: no trails, no habitation, no man-made clearings, no campfires, no glimpse or sound of anyone, friend or foe.

And then, after seven days of this, with little warning the land dipped and they followed the slope toward a brightening beyond the dark, ancient spruce and hemlock forest, and they emerged on the inland ocean: the western shore of Lake Champlain.

CHAPTER 23

ZADOCK IN THE WOODS

"Fearing the face of man, suspicious of his design"

SEPTEMBER 14, MORNING. A day or two after Hutchinson and Hathaway were forced into abandoning David Stone, Zadock and his mates made it to the south shore of the St. Lawrence, where they left the stolen boat and cooked up the haunch of beef—their first decent meal in four days.

They were still uncomfortably close to the settlements, the fort, and patrols. They began to walk. Soon they were in the same dense forest that had nearly defeated Hutchinson's party. Among all the men who had escaped there was a wealth of first-hand familiarity with the frontier, both sides of Lake Champlain, and the lay of the land the escapees would traverse south of the St. Lawrence River. There were men on Prison Island who knew distances, compass bearings, landmarks, and drainages; the location of British outposts, old Indian trails, and hunting camps; the sites of ambushes and places of capture.

In addition to all the information that Zadock and his companions had absorbed back in the barracks, the two Vermonters knew that Pittsford, Vermont, was the northernmost rebel stronghold on the eastern shore of Lake Champlain. Once they reached the lake they would have to cross it as soon as possible and reach Vermont. The lakeshore was where they were most likely to be caught.

Zadock might well have heard, as the men planned their escape route and went over the known dangers, that agents of the British Secret Service ranged up and down the shores of the lake and would like nothing better than an encounter with the likes of Zadock and his mates. [1]

The men would also have known that the British navy was there in strength. It would have struck them as the height of irony, if they had been aware of it, that several southbound ships were at this moment transporting released prisoners, a few like themselves but most of them women and children.[2] If they were to see shipping going north it would be carrying fleeing loyalists.

But even before Zadock's party reached the lake, they would have to pass through country where the British were concentrating search efforts. Patrols from St. John's and from Isle aux Noix would be watching the network of roads that connected all the forward posts, and Houghton's scouts would be combing the forests between Prison Island and the lake. Houghton had sent them out more than once this year already and was likely to be doing it now.[3]

Zadock and his companions, preparing to leave their river campsite, knew they would have to move very fast and with purpose, so they elected a pathfinder.

> *Sep. 14*
>
> *Our companion, Mr. Clark, had been much accustomed to traveling in the woods, having been engaged in the business of surveying in the western part of the United States at the time he was taken by the Indians. We therefore chose him to be our leader through the wilderness and our pilot to a more favored country.*
>
> *We traveled all the first day over low, marshy land, timbered with cedar, but were unable to find any water to drink either in running brooks or by digging.*
>
> *Wishing to escape the vigilance of our expected pursuers, we traveled with great speed. The next day we found water in great plenty. We crossed many streams of such depth as to reach to our shoulders. Others we crossed by making a small raft sufficient to bear one of us with our baggage; while the other three stripped, and, hanging by one hand to the raft, swam by her side.*
>
> *Sep. 19*
>
> *After wandering in the wilderness, sometimes progressing, sometimes lounging in suspense, doubting which course to take, and waiting for the clouds to be dispelled, that the sun might appear, we arrived at Lake Champlain.*
>
> *During these days we saw no other human being, nor heard his voice, beheld his footsteps, or the works of his hand. We lived almost wholly on flesh, fearing the face of man, suspicious of his design, and dreading his approach.*[4]

The fugitives had no mishaps, and they even had a little food left. The only setback had been the loss of time when they were compelled to stop traveling because of heavy overcast. The sun was their only compass, since their instrument had been ruined in the rapids. The country had been flat, the forest trackless and full of obstacles: immense fallen trees, impenetrable thickets and bogs, and constant stream crossings. The sky had been so overcast on most days that Clark would at times advise stopping altogether until they could take a bearing on the sun. The land was so flat they could not orient by following the contours of a

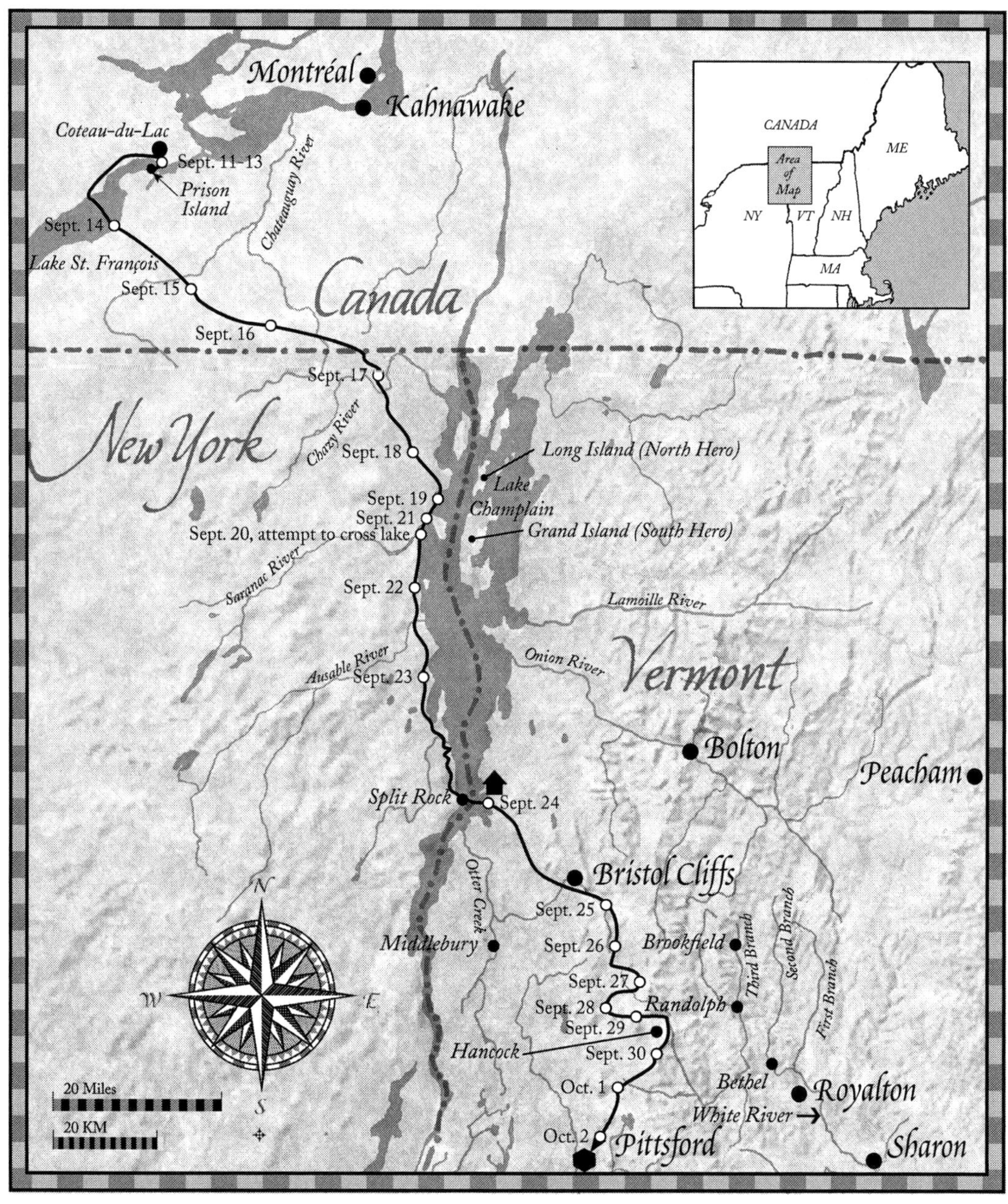

MAP 5. Zadock's Escape Route.

slope. They knew all too well how easy it would be to travel in circles, since they were weaving back and forth just to avoid the windfalls that blocked their path. It had taken them six days to reach the lake from the river, but, considering the obstacles and the fact that they were barefooted, they were moving well—an average of eight or nine miles a day. Walking in flat open country they might easily have covered 20 a day.

They came out of the forest on the shore of the lake not far north of the Saranac River. The lake was three to four miles wide here and the opposite shore must have seemed tantalizingly close. Zadock, Belknap, and Sprague had been here once before. A month short of two years ago, captured, hog-tied, and crammed into canoes and bateaux, they had been hurried north past this very shore, certain they would never return.

The shoreline that seemed so close was not, in fact, Vermont, but a pair of islands, Grand Isle and Isle Longue, that nearly touched each other. The southern tip of Isle Longue was Dutchman's Point. Just out of sight on the island was the strategically placed Loyal Blockhouse, residence of the head of the British Secret Service, an ex-Vermonter named Justus Sherwood.[5] Zadock and his mates had no idea it was there or how close they were to recapture. The traffic in shipping and couriers was heavy on the lake, and the Navy and the Secret Service did not trust anyone. They were under orders to detain and interrogate everyone they encountered.[6]

Sep. 20

Soon after we arrived at Lake Champlain we found a part of an old flat-bottomed boat, which we fitted up, for the purpose of conveying us across the lake, by lashing a log on each side with bark and withes.

At about sunset we went aboard and set sail to cross the lake. We had proceeded nearly half way across, when the wind arose against us and baffled all our exertions to proceed farther.

After laboring till about midnight without success, and fearing we should be taken by the British, we concluded to row back to the shore. A tempest arose, and the wind blew from various directions, shifting its course every few minutes. We labored with all our might till daybreak, having nothing to use for oars except sticks. We were now enabled to reach the shore, though several miles farther north.

Stupefied and chilled with the cold, we crept a few rods into the woods, built a fire, and laid down upon the ground.[7]

It was just as well that Zadock's party had been driven back, for they would have come ashore on one of the two islands, well within view of the Loyal Blockhouse, and they would have been in British custody in very short order. In fact, it was a wonder they had not been seen; the storm had blown them north toward another British outpost at Point au Fer on the western shore.

September 21

Having rested from the wearisome and fruitless labors of the night till nearly sunset the next day, we resolved to travel on the west side of the lake till we should come to a narrow place where we could cross. We resumed our march and traveled a few miles that night, then camped down and waited for the morning.

September 22

The next day we came to the River Saranac, which empties into Lake Champlain at a place now called Plattsburg, in the State of New York. We heard the noise of the British engaged in chopping a few rods up the river, while we crossed it between them and the lake, not far from its mouth.

Except for the abandoned boat that nearly had delivered them to the doorstep of the Loyal Blockhouse, this was the first sign that Zadock and his party had seen of people of any kind, British or otherwise. Whoever they were, they most likely had arrived in a boat and moored it not far upriver. The four fugitives had to make a decision: cross the river in broad daylight or wait for dark. None of the options were good, but what must have seemed most advisable was simply to keep moving. Zadock had no idea how many there were in the wood-cutting party, or how widely spread their sentinels were. There was great risk to crossing the river in broad daylight, but that was the fastest way out of the neighborhood, so they made the decision to slip into the water to the sound of the wood cutters' axes, and soon were out of earshot. They traveled a short distance on the other side and camped for the night in a small valley.[8]

* * *

When Abijah Hutchinson and John Hathaway lurched out of the forest onto the shore of the lake on September 21st, they were separated from Zadock and his party by at most a few miles, perhaps less. Having left all their food with Stone, and having found little to eat since then, the two were weak with hunger; when they reached the lake they did not have the strength to go any farther. At the water's edge, Hutchinson's barely recognizable reflection stared back at him. He had lost so much weight he could nearly circle his waist with his hands. While they were resting in hiding near the shore, Zadock and his companions passed them somewhere back from the shore, unseen and unheard.

But Hutchinson and Hathaway did see other people across the lake on the far shore, which they assumed to be the Vermont shore. The two men tried to signal for help by waving their coats and calling out, but to no avail. They could not attract the attention of the people on the far shore. Most likely they were looking at one of the islands separating them from the Vermont shore, and the people whose attention they so eagerly wanted to attract were in fact attached to one of the nearby the British outposts.

Then, quite unexpectedly, as Hutchinson and Hathaway rested and tried to gather strength and resolve, a British longboat heaved into view and it was all over. The tunnel, the river, the flight through the forest, leaving David Stone, starvation, despair—all this had led them in the end directly into the path of an enemy patrol traveling by boat along the shore of the lake. Hutchinson and Hathaway were too weak to hide, and indeed at this point they were all too willing to be recaptured, since the alternative appeared to be death by starvation. This might even have been the same wood-cutting detail that Zadock's party had slipped past on the Saranac River. The helmsman put the tiller over and the boat turned toward the shore, and rode up on the stones and gravel. After 11 days of freedom, Hutchinson and Hathaway were prisoners again.

They were prepared for the worst, but the British were unexpectedly kind. They fed, clothed, sheltered, and doctored the fugitives. They would have closely questioned the men about their escape, the route they took, whether or not they had help or collusion from Canadian inhabitants—and, of course, about David Stone. The two men could only make a rough guess as to his whereabouts, though they did not suppose he would be found alive. Hutchinson and Hathaway were then sent straight back to where they'd come from, and were duly listed once again in the British rolls as inmates of Prison Island.[9]

As the war was winding down each side had demanded a commitment from the other for humane treatment of prisoners and for their safe return. These guarantees included recaptured escapees. Thus, though they did not know it, Hutchinson and Hathaway were no worse off than they had been before escape. What lay in wait for them now was no more than a brief period of boredom on Prison Island, to be followed by a free ride home.

* * *

SEPTEMBER 23–24. Before the war, the western shore of Lake Champlain had contained hardly more than 20 isolated homesteads, each consisting of one or two houses. Now virtually all were deserted.[10] Some were used occasionally by landowners who dared to come periodically from safe homes farther south to harvest crops. While Zadock had seen no sign of people in the cedar swamps between the St. Lawrence and Lake Champlain, the western shore of the lake was quite different. There was a military road from Montréal to Crown Point that Zadock's party was careful to avoid, and there was the unmistakable swath left by the 7000 men of Burgoyne's Army who had passed this way five years before. The fugitives hugged the shoreline as they traveled, careful to avoid any settlement—abandoned or not—and careful as well to avoid exposed clearings or beaches.

From the Saranac River south the land was flat and marshy for about 12 miles, and they waded and swam creeks so often they were never able to dry. When they got to the wide mouth of the Ausable River, they had no choice but to swim, so into the water they went once again, pushing a log ahead of them which carried their dwindling food supply and fire-starting equipment.

It was just here, at the flat, marshy mouth of the Ausable River that two of this year's first fugitives from Prison Island had come to the end of their rope. In late April, only days after the ice on the St. Lawrence River went out, two unnamed men had launched themselves on logs into the frigid rapids at Prison Island. They were among those that Zadock knew had gone, and had given up for dead, so certain was he that no one could survive the rapids at that time of year. But in fact these men had survived not only the rapids, but also the flooded swamps to the south of the St. Lawrence. They had also managed to avoid Lieutenant Houghton's Kahnawake scouting parties who had been combing that patch of wilderness in late spring.[11] Like Zadock's party, the two men had made it to Lake Champlain and as far as the Ausable River, and there, like Hutchinson and Hathaway, they had collapsed, and "gave themselves up through hunger to one of the [British] vessels" on May 6, 1782.[12] They were brought back to St. John's by a ship returning from Crown Point with loyalist families fleeing to Canada.

Like most other Prison Island escapees later in the summer, these two had been taken to the more secure Provost in Montréal. There they could not mix with the escape-prone Prison Island population with whom they might well have shared invaluable knowledge about the way to the lake.

A few miles below the Ausable, Zadock and his party made camp for the night. They could feel the contour of the land to the west changing, steepening, forcing them closer to the water where the shoreline was rockier and they could be seen from the lake. But they could also see that the Vermont shore was closer, that the lake was narrowing, and that another ten miles to the south the two shorelines appeared nearly to touch.

In the morning they could see the great granite face of Split Rock Mountain. They hurried south along the shore, taking greater and greater chances as they crossed stony beaches and the mouths of creeks. Except for the sound of the woodcutters back on the Saranac River, they neither heard nor saw a soul.

> *We followed up the lake upon the western shore;* Zadock wrote, *crossed Duck Creek, River au Sable, Salmon River, and Gilliland's Creek; when we came to a place called Split Rock. We then went to work to build a raft, and while engaged, a little before sunset, espied a British armed vessel making towards us from the south. We went into the bushes and lay secreted from their view, though they were so visible to us that we could see their red coats, and even count the buttons upon them, while they sailed around at a small distance from us, apparently for amusement, and then returned again to the south, out of our sight, without discovering us.* [13]

The soldiers on the British vessel may just have been out for a pleasant evening turn, but they were out at just the hour and place they were most likely to catch escaped prisoners.[14] They were at Split Rock where the lake narrowed to less than a mile. Two peninsulas reached out toward each other, one from New York and one from Vermont. If anyone coming south on foot from Canada wanted to cross the lake safely on an improvised raft, this was where they would do it and they would be doing it at dusk, just as Zadock was. The arrival of the British patrol may have been more than happenstance.

The word had gone out from Montréal that there were 15 escaped prisoners heading south and that they would be seeking Lake Champlain, sneaking along the western shore and looking for a place to cross. The British patrol had no idea just how close the escapees had been. They did not know that four rebels had just been taking their measure, counting their brass buttons, and would slip across the lake as soon as they were out of sight. Which, Zadock reported, is exactly what they did:

> *September 24*
>
> *We then completed our raft at dark, set sail across the lake, and safely landed in a few hours in the State of Vermont. Being yet in a strange wilderness, we knew not which way to direct our course to reach inhabitants. Supposing ourselves to be between the mouth of Onion River and Otter Creek, we concluded to steer in a south-east direction, which we supposed would bring us to Pittsford Fort. We traveled into the woods a few rods and lay down for the night.* [15]

CHAPTER 24

VERMONT

"They wandered in the wilderness in a solitary way;
they found no city to dwell in"

SEPTEMBER 25, DAY 15 of the escape. Zadock was right about their landfall. They had landed on a long spit of land called Thompson's Point, less than three miles north of the mouth of Otter Creek and about 15 miles south of the Onion River. Pittsford was only 40 miles away but it was nearly due south, not southeast. Neither Zadock nor any of the others had been in this part of Vermont, and their grasp of the geography of the Champlain Valley and the west slope of the Green Mountains was weak.

What they probably did know, having heard it from other prisoners, was that Otter Creek led directly to Pittsford. It was well known that in 1778 the settlements of Otter Creek had been laid waste by British raiders who swept up the creek from the mouth, destroying every building they found. What Zadock may not have known is that the British were not yet done with Otter Creek. Just over a year ago, in April 1781 and then again in June, Mohawk and British raiding parties led by the swashbuckling loyalist ex-Vermonter Roger Stevens, had stormed up Otter Creek as far as Pittsford.[1] As recently as August of this year Stevens and other loyalists had been probing up Otter Creek as far as the destroyed settlement of Middlebury.[2] It was a fresh reminder to the inhabitants that British agents and scouting parties moved though the wilderness with just as much stealth and ease as did the rebels.[3] Even now, Stevens was actively moving in and out of Vermont via Otter Creek, plotting with his brother Abel, stirring pro-British sympathies in the state.[4]

So it was just as well that, instead of looking for Otter Creek, Zadock's party headed southeast toward the Green Mountains, away from the lake.

In the morning we resumed our march, and had not gone far before we came to an old log house, which had long been abandoned, and, by the long continuance of the war, had become greatly decayed.

We however found a few beans, which had probably been there a number of years, and were covered with mould. As our provision was mostly gone and we were extremely hungry, we took and parched them, as we would corn, by the fire, which gave some relish to the twigs, roots, and berries that had already, for some days, composed our principal food.

Our clothes were almost torn from our bodies by the bushes, twigs, and trees; and the blood from our naked feet witnessed the pains we suffered.

Parts of our stockings still remained about our feet; and, having a needle (but no thread) with us, we ravelled off the tops of them and sewed our tattered rags together as much as possible. [5]

It must have been reassuring to find this sign of human habitation so soon after coming ashore, even though it was a reminder of the war and how it had depopulated the Champlain Valley. There was a track, which had been cut by the Allens in 1772, connecting the Onion River settlements with Castleton, Vermont; but with the abandonment of those northern farms in 1778, the road had had little if any recent use. Zadock and his party must have unknowingly crossed this road, perhaps even where they had stumbled upon the deserted cabin, but that too would have led to Otter Creek and possible capture. [6]

The small party struck off with confidence away from the lake and into the Green Mountains. All that Zadock could be sure of, as he reconstructed this part of the journey in his narrative, was that the four men would walk through the townships of Bristol, Ripton, and Hancock, and that they would climb to the crest of the Green Mountains. Knowing this much, it's possible to reconstruct a probable route.

According to Zadock's narrative, they traveled southeast from their landfall on Thompson's Point. Moving across the gradually rising ground through dense forest they were headed toward the mountains. After a few miles, from the top of a low ridge, they would have had a full view of the west face of the Green Mountains and the first Vermont landmark in Zadock's narrative: the Bristol Cliffs, a sheer face of rock rising 500 feet straight up from the valley floor. There were passes to the north and south of this massif, both of them leading southeast into the mountains. They could hardly miss the immense gorge just to the north of the cliffs, and the New Haven River flowing from it. This pass would take them deeper and higher into the mountains. What was more, it would give them easy access to the summit of the Bristol Cliffs, from which they could see a great distance up and down the valley and out to the lake—one of the few places they would be able to get their bearings. Assuming they followed the New Haven River, they would have entered a broad valley, and, staying close to the ever-narrowing watercourse, their route would have angled southeast, climbing into a bowl.

> *September 26–29*
>
> *Our daily allowance of the food we brought with us from Prison Island was now reduced to about an inch square of salt pork and as much of our buttered flour as we could twice put upon the point of a large jack knife. We had eaten all our beef and parched corn.*
>
> *We dug roots of various kinds and ate them, together with birch and other twigs. Spikenard roots, which we roasted by the fire, comprised the greatest part of our subsistence.*[7] *We found several small frogs, which we killed and ate with great delight. But we could find only a few of them, though we searched diligently. Their meat tasted exceedingly sweet and delicious. We also found means to catch several small fish from a little rivulet which we crossed; but could not obtain more than two or three, although we spent much time and used every exertion in our power.*
>
> *Some time after we had dressed our fish and had advanced considerable distance, we espied a bear upon a tree a few rods ahead of us. We hastened to the foot of the tree, in view of killing her, as she descended, by stabbing her with our large scalping knife. But, on examination, we found the knife was left at the place of dressing the fish which frustrated our plan and blighted our hopes of obtaining any meat.*[8]

They could not find their way back to the brook where they had caught the fish. Everything would have looked the same in this dense forest, with its intersecting ravines and chaos of windfallen trees. It was only then that they realized how utterly lost they were. Even more disorienting was the fact that they were lost in a wilderness of no great size. Lake Champlain was a day or two westward; Pittsford was only a little farther southward. Even Royalton was about the same distance to the southeast, but the men could not be sure where the points of the compass lay.

They had not seen the sun for days, and without it they could not navigate. The weather that had pinned them down the night they got off Prison Island had plagued them more or less continuously since then, keeping them from navigating by the stars. In any case the leaf cover was still dense so the stars would have been largely obscured. Even if they could have seen them, they would not have dared to walk after dark for fear of injury or of missing a crucial landmark.

The Green Mountains rose steeply to the east, on their left. Hoping to find an easy route leading southeast, they would have followed the New Haven River higher and higher, through what is today the Breadloaf Wilderness in the township of Ripton. The men seem to have decided not to retreat out of this drainage but to climb as high as possible and then travel along the crest of the Green Mountains. The only way to get their bearings was to climb, even though it was costing them time and energy, both fading fast as their food ran out.

The view from high ground in the Green Mountains would have told them how short a distance they had actually come, only to find themselves so lost. From here they could get a better sense of the geography that had so bewildered them. The spine of the range ran north and south, just like the lake. But they could also see that there were confusing north-south ranges and occasional valleys in the blue distance which cut east and west. They got no glimpse of the friendly smoke from the hearths of Pittsford, somewhere off to the south. The only sign of human life of any kind would have been the faint, distant shapes on the lake: the ships of the British Navy.

There had been a fleet of British ships, manned by well over 200 men, standing off Crown Point since May. Their mission was to deal with the parade of people arriving under flags of truce from the New York and Vermont backcountry wanting to parley with British representatives: some to buy or sell food, and some with offers to serve as spies and informers.[9] The British trusted none of them and were determined to blockade and control all traffic on the lake and keep it from going farther north, detaining and sending suspicious individuals to Canada as prisoners.[10]

It was an impressive show of force, and Zadock and his party wanted to avoid it at all costs; but they were scarcely any better off where they were, disoriented and lost in the Green Mountains.

> *The barren mountains and rocky cliffs of Bristol, Ripton, and Hancock...We wandered from mountain to mountain and from valley to valley, keeping at a distance from the lake, lest we should fall into the hands of the British, who had command of the lake at that time.*[11]
>
> *Seeing no prospect of ever finding the habitations of friends, our companions, Clark and Sprague, like the lepers of old, said to one another, "Why sit we here until we die?" If we say we will pursue our journey, "we shall die; and if we sit still here, we die also." They therefore resolved to return to the lake if they could get there, and deliver themselves up into the hands of the British.*
>
> *They were both possessed of true courage, but they were wholly ignorant of the country east of Lake Champlain, and consequently had less to encourage them than*

Belknap and myself. They requested us to leave them to be food for wild beasts or a prey to an exasperated foe. [12]

If this had been the southern Appalachians or even the Adirondacks, Zadock might have been as discouraged as Clark and Sprague, but the two Vermonters knew that they did not have far to travel. Their real problem was not knowing what direction to take. Clark and Sprague saw the situation as hopeless, but did not suggest that the two Vermonters surrender with them, only that they part company while they still had energy to make it back to the lake and into the hands of the British. Even if friendly inhabitants were only three days' travel, they did not believe they had the will or the strength to continue, and the others would have to leave them.

Zadock said he did not believe that would be necessary and he made Clark, the nominal leader of the party, an offer he could hardly refuse: they would all continue together on the condition that Zadock take over as leader and guide. He sealed the agreement by offering most of his remaining food to Clark and Sprague.

They had been traveling in a part of the Green Mountains that was completely covered with dense forest. They had been walking for five days since leaving the lake, covering perhaps five or six miles a day. By this time they would have moved off the crest and were probably walking along the western slope not far from the present-day town of Goshen. Clark had no picture whatever of the range and its geography. Zadock's was far from perfect, but he knew that the mountain range ran north and south and that Pittsford lay on the west slope. By considering the geography lying ahead and how far they had already come, Zadock also realized that if they continued southeasterly, as they had been, they would veer ever farther away from Pittsford and deeper into the mountains. He knew they would now have to walk in a different direction, one that would take them toward the headwaters of drainages leading to Otter Creek and civilization. He was certain the problem had not been one so much of distance as of direction.

September 29

It being nearly night, we encamped till morning, when we concluded to change our course and steer nearly a south-southwesterly direction.

September 30

We traveled on moderately, fearful of the event, till about noon, when, being some rods forward of my companions, I was so fortunate as to come to a road.

Of this I notified my languishing companions, which occasioned transports of joy.

For we could say with David, that we had "wandered in the wilderness, in a solitary way, and found no city to dwell in. Hungry and thirsty, our souls fainted within us. Then we cried unto the Lord in our trouble, and he delivered us out of our distresses; and he led us forth by the right way, that we might go to a city of habitation."[13]

CHAPTER 25

FOUND

"Diametrically against our own ideas of the true point of compass"

September 30. After 20 days of wading through underbrush, crawling under blow-downs, trying to keep a straight heading, and hardly ever able to see more than a few feet ahead, Zadock had stumbled on a road that appeared before him as if from nowhere. He could have missed it by a few feet. He might have even missed other such roads by a few feet several times in recent days. The log cabin they had passed five days ago was abandoned; this road was apparently not. It would lead somewhere. They were no longer lost.

> *Animated with the prospect of soon finding inhabitants, we traveled on the road with joy and delight. We soon came in sight of an old horse, and an old mare with a sucking colt by her side in a valley some distance from the road. Soon [we] came to a stream but could not determine whether it was Otter Creek or only a branch of it. To follow the current of the creek itself would lead us directly to the lake, where we should be exposed to the British.* [1]

If the road meant they were no longer lost, it also meant they could be found by British or loyalist scouting parties. So it was understandable that Zadock and his companions became extremely cautious. They knew they had been moving obliquely, south-southwesterly toward the lake for a day. If the road led them to Otter Creek, it could also lead them back into the hands of the British.

So, taking no chances,

> *We however thought it most prudent to follow down the stream, and soon came to its mouth, and still were left in doubt whether the stream into which the first we discovered emptied itself was Otter Creek or some other branch.*

As it began to draw near sunset, and seeing no prospect of finding inhabitants that night, we resolved to return to the place where we came to the first stream, having there found the walls of an old log house. Clark and myself went and procured the horses and colt; while Belknap and Sprague struck up a fire and built a camp.

Having returned with the horses and confined them in the old log house, we killed and dressed the colt and roasted some of the meat upon sticks by the fire and ate it. I never ate any meat of so delicious a flavor, although without bread, salt, or sauce of any kind.

October 1—The next morning we started with our old horse and coltless mare, and traveled till after the middle of the day, when we came to the place we passed about noon the day preceding. We were confident it was the same place, by finding some spikenard roots which we had thrown away soon after we found the road.

Knowing not whether to turn to the right hand or to the left, having obtained a new supply of meat, and as the sun had been invisible to us for several days, we concluded to tarry there through the day and encamp for the night, hoping the sun would rise clear the next morning, which would enable us the better to determine what course to take.

While we were patrolling about the fields, which appeared to have been unoccupied and but partially cultivated during the long war, we found a large yard of turnips.

We then prepared our camp, built a fire, and, having procured some turnips, kept continually roasting them successively during the night, first sleeping a little and then eating.[2]

Zadock and his party had finally found the way out of the mountains. The road they had happened upon ran beside not Otter Creek, but probably Furnace Brook, Little Brook, or Sugar Hollow Brook, which flowed south out of the Green Mountains into Otter Creek at the village of Pittsford. They could now navigate with certainty.

October 2—In the morning the sky was clear, and the sun rose. Feeling much refreshed and strengthened, we took our horses and directed our course according to the sun, diametrically against our own ideas of the true point of compass.

We had not proceeded far when we came to three other horses, which we took, leaving the old mare for the benefit of the owner.

After traveling till about noon we came to a man chopping in the woods. Seeing us all on horseback, with bark bridles and no saddles, having on coats made of

Indian blankets, which were all in rags, with beards an inch long, and each one of us armed with a cudgel, the woodcutter stood with his axe raised above his shoulder, dreading our approach.

We informed him of our condition. Finding we were not his enemies, he invited us to go with him and he would lead us to Pittsford Fort, which was only about one mile distant, where we should be made welcome to every thing necessary for our comfort.

We soon arrived at the fort. It was now about one o'clock in the afternoon. We were received with the greatest marks of sympathy and commiseration.[3]

* * *

And quite suddenly it was all over.

Only three days earlier, the four men had been trapped in a wilderness with no apparent way out, considering the option of surrendering to a British patrol to keep from starving. The fort had been hardly farther than the next valley; they just had no idea how close they were. For Zadock and his mates this must have seemed like the bosom of civilization, but it was hardly that. Pittsford was the very edge of the northern frontier, and the settlement had had its share of attacks during the course of the war—one within the last month—and the place was in a more or less constant state of alert.

Commanding a rise of ground just east of a ford on the Otter Creek where a well-traveled road came in from the Connecticut River, Fort Vengeance was a stout stockade enclosing an acre of ground. It had been built just two years earlier at the time of the Royalton Raid, and was constructed of straight hardwood logs, 22 feet long, their ends sharpened, set in a deep ditch to form a palisade. On each corner was a flanking projection; there were loopholes for muskets in all the walls, and within the enclosure were storehouses and barracks. The houses of the townspeople were scattered along the creek bottom. They worked in their fields heavily armed, and whenever there was an alarm of any kind, they all spent the night inside the fort.[4]

Over the last few years, houses had been burned, people had been killed and captured. The last attack of any consequence had been just over a year ago when a war party of Kahnawakes had struck but then had been driven off by a company of militia.[5] Because there was no inhabited village farther north on this side of Vermont, Pittsford had seen more than its share of refugees moving south after having abandoned their land and means of subsistence. This driving in of the frontier was the purpose behind the British backcountry raids of recent years. It had placed great strain on the ability of outpost settlements to support themselves, and the situation had become especially severe this year. Until recently, there had been so little rain that Lake Champlain was at its lowest level in memory; the hay and grain crop was half what it usually was, and the prospect of food shortages loomed[6] So when the four half-starved, half-naked apparitions appeared on the doorsteps of Captain Ebenezer Allen's Fort Vengeance they were, among other things, four more mouths to feed in a place that had been hard pressed just to look after its own for many years. What began as a warm welcome by the villagers turned decidedly cooler when Zadock arrived at the fort. "I could not forbear to notice that cold indifference, common in those familiar with scenes of wretchedness, manifested by the commander of the fort on our arrival at that place," he wrote.[7]

Zadock and his party were not the first desperate arrivals from Canada. In previous years, other escaped prisoners had reached Pittsford from time to time.[8] And Zadock's party was not even the first one this year. As they soon found out, eight of their mates from Prison Island had come this way two months earlier. On June 9, before the stockade around the prison compound had gone up, a party of three, James Butterfield, George Ransom, and John Brown, escaped and made it to Castleton, Vermont, the next town south of Pittsford.[9] Four days later, five more men had slipped away from Prison Island, ridden a log raft through the rapids, and followed virtually the same route as Zadock and his mates, arriving at Pittsford in early August.[10]

During 1782, at least 43 men escaped from British prisons in Canada.[11] From Montréal, the most commonly used escape route led to the upper Connecticut Valley and Newbury. Escapees were sometimes recaptured by British or Indian patrols in northern Vermont, but more often than not they made it to Newbury and, without exception, they were warmly greeted, well fed, supplied with clothing, shoes, money, and other necessities before going on their way down the Connecticut River Valley to Massachusetts and from there to homes as distant as Virginia.[12]

Twenty-one men had escaped from Prison Island without being recaptured and those who had survived would almost certainly have followed the same route that Zadock's party had—across the St. Lawrence to Lake Champlain and then down either the western or eastern shores. Pittsford was the logical first stop on the eastern shore, but if escapees who had come before helped themselves to livestock, it had not in the least embittered the locals whom Zadock encountered.

> *Not long after we arrived at the fort the owners of the horses came up, carrying their saddles upon their backs. They had been out for the purpose of surveying land, and had turned out their horses to feed. After hearing a short account of our*

sufferings and being made acquainted with our deplorable condition, they readily replied that they were only sorry we had not been so fortunate as to find their saddles likewise.[13]

The surveyors' gallant good humor—once they realized their horses had not been lost to another attack—eclipsed the dour reception by Ebenezer Allen, the commander of the fort. The four men began to feel something they had not experienced for two years: that they were among friends—and what was more, among optimists who were out surveying land and thinking of an expanding future, new people, and new farms.

After receiving the garrison's help, Zadock and his companions were advised that a British attack was expected, and that they ought to continue on with their travels that night.[14]

Captain Allen was absorbed in preparations for action, and the arrival of these four prodigals was becoming a distraction. Both the British and the Vermonters had been receiving a steady stream of intelligence and each side thought the other was about to attack, even though the war was essentially over and Haldimand had received orders to initiate no further offensives. American and British representatives were in fact deep in negotiations in Paris for and end to hostilities, but news from that quarter was both stale and vague on the frontier. In spite of the negotiations, both sides in the northern back country were prepared for the worst: a breakdown of the talks or a betrayal of the agreement they might reach.

Besides the British fleet off Crown Point, there had been a massive buildup of British forces at the outposts of St. John's, Isle aux Noix, Point au Fer, and the Loyal Blockhouse. They were working day and night to raise fortifications and were laying in provisions for thousands of troops, primarily for defensive purposes.[15] An American spy had arrived in Newbury on September 19 with the news that 2,000 troops had just embarked on ships at St. John's and that there were three to four thousand men at Isle aux Noix. British agents and loyalist scouting parties were still taking captives in northern Vermont and compelling residents in isolated communities to swear allegiance to the king. The spy reported that he supposed they planned to invade Vermont, and General Bayley immediately wrote Washington a letter to that effect.[16] Washington was, himself, reconsidering an invasion of Canada.[17]

Furthermore, there were persuasive rumors in New Jersey and New York City, as the Albany newspaper reported, that an invasion from Canada was imminent and that militias were ordered to hold themselves ready. Vermont was concerned with the immediate threat to its own territorial integrity, while New Yorkers saw the invasion of Vermont from Canada as a diversion to distract rebel attention from the movements of British forces around New York City.[18] Whatever the reason, rumors were spreading and the entire frontier was on alert. Despite the defeat of Cornwallis a year ago and wholesale release of prisoners by the British, people here saw no sign of a British stand-down; in fact quite the opposite seemed to be the case. Adding to the uncertainty, word of the basic agreement on terms in the Treaty of Paris would not arrive in Vermont for another month.

Watching the preparations for an impending British attack and heeding the harried fort commander's advice to remove well behind the frontier for safety, it was reasonable for Zadock to think that they had escaped in the nick of time—that there was, in fact, no end in sight to the war. Zadock still had reason to believe that the guards back at Prison Island had been feeding the prisoners lies about release just to keep the place quiet. So the same afternoon they arrived in Pittsford, the four barefoot men added ten more muddy miles to their travels. Two roads led south from Pittsford: one crossed the Green Mountains to the lower Connecticut Valley, and the other, the one they took, stayed west of the mountains.[19] They followed it to the next settlement, where they knocked on doors until they found someone who would give them shelter for the night.

> *We proceeded on towards Rutland several miles, when we obtained lodgings in the house of a "poor widow." Instead of making our bed upon the cold ground, with our clothes wet and our bodies benumbed, we could now enjoy sweet repose by the fireside, surrounded with friends. Instead of feeding upon frogs, roots, twigs, and bark, we could now taste the fruits of labor and industry. Instead of wandering through a lonely wilderness, we could now travel through a country of civilization free from enemies.*[20]

While under the roof of the good widow of Rutland, Zadock and his mates overate so prodigiously that their food "lay like lead in our stomachs, and caused us the most agonizing distress for some hours."[21]

In the morning, appetites under control, the men looked at one another, each wondering if he looked as wretched as the others. Their appearance was such that wherever they went, they would have to begin by explaining who they were and where they had come from. Once people heard their story, if they believed it, the initial fright would wear off; but at first encounter they looked dangerous. People recoiled at their hollow eyes, stained teeth, beards and tangled hair, the filthy, torn blanket coats alive with lice, the broken fingernails, their bruised, scabbed calves, their shoeless feet, and their overpowering reek.

The good widow of Rutland gave what she could, but all the same, she may well have been relieved to see Zadock and his mates leave. It was well known that escaped prisoners, be they ever so zealous in the cause, were not above a bit of larceny.[22]

The men continued south on the road, passing the occasional log cabin in a clearing cut out of the otherwise unbroken hardwood forest. There were sparse stands of parched-looking wheat and corn growing around the great, leafless maple, ash, and beech trees. People were bringing in the harvest, as they had been two years earlier when the raiders struck Royalton.

As the four men walked the road, people stopped their work to stare and offer an occasional greeting. The children just stared. In fact the men did not look a great deal worse off than some of the inhabitants they passed. The four men became accustomed to explaining who they were, for toward the end of every day of walking they had to look for a house where they could find some shelter and a meal. It was the custom for travelers on such roads to pay for such conveniences, but these men had not a penny among themselves to offer. Even though the families could hardly afford to be so generous, they would never turn away an honest stranger in need. Most dwellings were small one-room cabins. Some had a sleeping loft. If not, the whole family might sleep together on a straw or corn-husk mattress.[23] The four guests took the floor. Their feet were still shoeless and sore, albeit tough as leather, so the men did not hurry. It would have taken them several days to travel the 30 miles from Rutland to Manchester, and the 20 miles from there to Bennington.

Bennington was the most substantial town they had seen yet. One of the oldest Vermont settlements, it had churches, fine dwellings, buildings, taverns, and, most important of all for the four men, the potential for them to improve their circumstances. The foursome certainly constituted one of Bennington's most singular recent arrivals and the men attracted offers of employment and generosity from the townspeople. Here the fugitives found paying work, rested up, ate all they could, gathered strength, bought clothes and shoes. With winter coming on, they intended to stay only until they had the resources for the rest of their journeys.

Bennington was a fork in the road for the four men. Zadock and Simeon Belknap, the two Vermonters, were bound for their family homes in Ellington, Connecticut. William Clarke, the Virginian, and John Sprague, the New Yorker, were likewise homeward bound and would head west and south from Bennington.

Zadock was, understandably, moved by their separation:

> *We had acquired that affection for each other which will remain, I trust, till death. Having suffered many hardships and endured many trials together, having been rescued from many dangers and delivered out of many troubles, sharing equally in hunger, pains, and distress, as well as in the joys resulting from our deliverance, we now reluctantly parted, affectionately taking our leave, perhaps never again to see each other.*[24]

From Bennington, Zadock and Simeon Belknap set out, traveling much as they had since Pittsford, going south a few miles to Fort Massachusetts, then turning east across the Green Mountains on the road to Fort Dummer on the Connecticut River. At this point Zadock and Belknap completed a circle. Some two-and-a-half years earlier, both men had passed this very place as they headed north for a summer of work on new land. From here Zadock and Belknap followed the familiar route south, continuing to live off the generosity of the people along the way. From Fort Dummer to Ellington it was nearly 80 miles, and the two men, now fed, clothed, decently shod, and on a decent road, were strong enough to cover as much as 20 miles a day. They arrived on October 17th to similarly stunned households, two years to the day since their capture.

> *Our fathers, seeing us while yet a great way off, ran and fell upon our necks and kissed us.*
>
> *Behold now a father. Hear him say, "This my son was dead, and is alive again; he was lost, and is found."*
>
> *See "the best robe" cast around him, with "the ring upon his hand and the shoes upon his feet." See brothers and sisters surrounding, embracing their once lost but now living brother.* [25]

CHAPTER 26

BACK AT PRISON ISLAND

"If you breed no more riots"

On the very day that Zadock's prodigal return and resurrection was making his family whole, Josiah Hollister, Abijah Hutchinson, John Hathaway, and some 180 prisoners awoke on Prison Island to the news that they were going home. Hollister remembered that a few days earlier, George Lawe, the commissary of prisoners, had made a special trip to Prison Island to announce, "If you breed no more riots, upon my word of honor you shall all be released." [1]

On the 16th of October, Lawe returned and was as good as his word. He arrived with orders from Haldimand to make "arrangements of all of the prisoners which will relieve...the [King's] service of much trouble." [2] The British were only too relieved to be seeing the last of these unruly prisoners. The men leaving Prison Island would be joining 162 others on ships bound for American ports. [3]

When Lawe left the island the entire guard went with him, leaving the men on the island free to do as they pleased. They immediately set about baking bread and cakes from stockpiled flour, working well into the night. Riotous celebrations in the barracks kept everyone up until dawn. [4] There appeared to be only one man not entirely ready to take his leave.

John Fitch simply had too many possessions that he wanted to take with him; and as he packed a cedar chest with clothes, money, and tools, the departing guards made merry with him, calling him their own Robinson Crusoe, so reluctant was he to abandon his wealth when rescued from his desert island.

The following morning all were removed, Fitch included, given new clothes at the fort, and sent on their way home. Owing to the lateness of the season, all the ships had been removed from Lake Champlain, so the prisoners to be released were marched to Montréal, where they caught a boat for Québec and outbound shipping. The ships left Canada, their captains under strict warning that they were answerable for the humane treatment of the prisoners, who were to be fed the same provisions as the British troops going with them.[5]

When Abijah Hutchinson and Josiah Hollister were landed at Boston harbor, once again among friends and on American soil, they may well have wondered at first why they had bothered to come home at all.

> *The fifteenth day after we left Québeck we got into Boston harbor,* Hollister wrote. *It being Thanksgiving day, Governor Hancock would not attend to receipting the prisoners, and we very impatiently were obliged to stay on board two nights. After we came on shore we expected to draw some provisions, but Governor Hancock would allow none to those who were taken on their farms. So I set out to find my family and friends, without money or provisions.*[6]

The British return of 228 prisoners that included Hutchinson and Hollister listed their place of capture and made it clear who was "taken in arms" and who "on their farms."[7] It was the custom to deliver such a return with the prisoners upon release, so the authorities receiving them apparently separated the prisoners into two groups: those "taken in arms" to be fed; and those "taken on farms" to go hungry.

Considering Washington's adamant opposition to the British practice of taking civilian prisoners and the Continental Congress's efforts to meet the needs of civilians in captivity "whose welfare was a matter of moment," it is difficult to understand Hancock's welcome.[8] It is conceivable that he was discriminating against Vermonters, but there was no indication of that. In any case, Governor Hancock, first signer of the Declaration of Independence, President of the Continental Congress, and with a reputation for arrogance, was not about to bestow any generosity on men who had been taken as non-combatants—no matter how else they may have served in the American military enterprise before capture.[9]

* * *

SPRING 1783. Zadock spent the winter in Connecticut and the news of the prisoner release spread across New England by word of mouth and in newspapers. News of the other escapees was elusive: who had been caught, who got away, and who was never seen or heard from again. As for himself, while at his father's house Zadock relished the fortuitous outcome of his defiant enterprise:

> *Notwithstanding the prisoners on the island were set at liberty shortly after our escape, and although our sufferings in the wilderness were exceedingly great, yet I never found cause to lament that I improved the opportunity to free myself.*[10]

The war was over, Zadock had cheated death, and the imperatives that had drawn him north to Vermont three years earlier were as pressing as they had been then. There was even less good farm land in Connecticut, and the competition for homesteads in Vermont would only intensify now that there were thousands of veterans being mustered out of the Continental Army with promises of land in exchange for service. Zadock had had no word from Randolph on the status of his property, but his father, still in Connecticut and determined not to lose possession of the land, had been paying the required charter fee during his captivity.[11] Zadock wanted to go back and begin again, and in the summer of 1783 he left Connecticut and doggedly returned to the site of his capture. Covering 20 miles a day, he was at the charred timbers of his cabin in six days.

> *As the war had now terminated, my return to Randolph would not be attended with the danger of being again made captive by the Indians; which induced me, the spring following, to go to that place and resume my settlement. On my arrival there I found my house was demolished, which recalled to mind the confusion and horror of that dreadful morning.*
>
> *I went to work and erected a house upon the same spot. The grass seed which the Indians had scattered for some distance from the house had taken root, stocked the ground, and remained for many years a memento of that woful event.*[12]

VERMONT

Some Hunters have travelled thro this Wilderness, from Welds River, to Lake Memfrimagog, & judged the shortest distance this way to be about 50 Miles.

Nº Connecticut River has been actua

Mons.
Leaperriere
Shelburne
Sᵗ George
This way Captives have been carried from New Hampshire to Canada.
French River
Bolton
Worster
Waterford
Middle Sex
Durbury
Moretown
Berlin
Eunen bourg
Brothers
Charlotte
Hinesbourg
Hinesbourg
LAKE CHAMPLAIN
Ferris bourg
Mons. de
Pocock
Contracoeuse
Panton
New Heaven
Otter Creek
Weybridge
Middle bury
Addison
Water bury
Salisbury
RIK or
OINT
Bridport
Shoreham
Orwell
Leister
Neshobe
Dunbar
Hubbard ton
Pittford
Castleton
Rutland
Poultney
Clarendon
Wells
Gen. Nicholsons
built on occasion
Canada Expede
but now demolished
Wood Creek
Bay
Drowned Lands
The Road was cut by the New Hampshire Forces employed against Canada in 1759 to facilitate the communication with that County
These Branches are only Conjectural
Otter River
Stock bridge
Bernard
Killing ton
Bridge water
Woodstock
Shrews bury
Saltash
Reading
Windsor
Cavendish
Weath ers field
Tinmouth
Wallingford
This way Captives have been carried by the Indians
Black R.
Danby
Harwich
Pawlet
Flamstead
Rupert
Dorset
Brumley
Thomlinson
Rockingham
Sandgate
Manchester
Winhall
Sunderland
West River
Arlington
Stratton
Shaftsbury
Glaffenbury
New Fane
Townshend
Pultney
Fulham
Bennington
Woodford
Bratle
Peacham
Barnet
Ryegate
Welds River
Topsham
Newbury
Only the Mouth of this River is known to ye English.
Mahounquamosse R.
Corinth
Waits town
Intervals
Eastham
Malden
Fairlee
Stratford
Tunbridge
Thetford
Cohass
Royalton
Sharon
Norwich
Little
Pomfret
White R.
Hartford
Waterqueechy R.
Hertford
Waterqueechy Falls
Connecticut R.
Choice White Pines
and good Land
Lyman
Gunth
Loring
Bath
Landaff
Francon
Ammonoosuck R.
Haverhill
Lincoln
Umpammonoosuck R.
Fairfield
Pierment
Warren
Orford
Wentworth
Hastings Brook
Rumney
Lime
Dorchester
Cockermouth
Hanover
Dartmouth College
Canaan
White River Falls
Cardigan
New Plymouth
Lebanon
Bloods River
Relhan
Grafton
Severance Brook
Plainfield
Grantham
New Chester
Alexandria
Choice White Pines and Good Land
Protectworth
bounds
Smiths R.
New Chester
Corinth
Croydon
LINE
Heidlebourg
New Britain
Sunnipee Pond
Sugar River
Salisbury
Clermont
Newport
Green
Dantzick
Perrys Town
Kyasage Mᵗ
Boscawen
Unity
CURVE
Rye Town
Little Sugar R.
Lempster
Nº 8
Nº 4
Ackworth
Charles Town
New Concord
COUNTY
Hills borough
Hencker
New Hopkin
Contoocook R.
Saxtons R.
Westminster
COUNTY OF CHESHIRE
Alstead
Marlow
Nº 7
Walpole
Limerick
Mason
Wears Town
COUNTY OF HILLSBOROUGH
Proprietors Lands reserved
Gilsum
Ashuelot R.
Nº 6
Dublin
New Boston
Westmoreland
Keene
Peterborough
Lyndeborough
Monadnock Mountains
Contoocook R.
Chesterfield
Swansey
Nº 5

PART VI
AFTER THE WAR

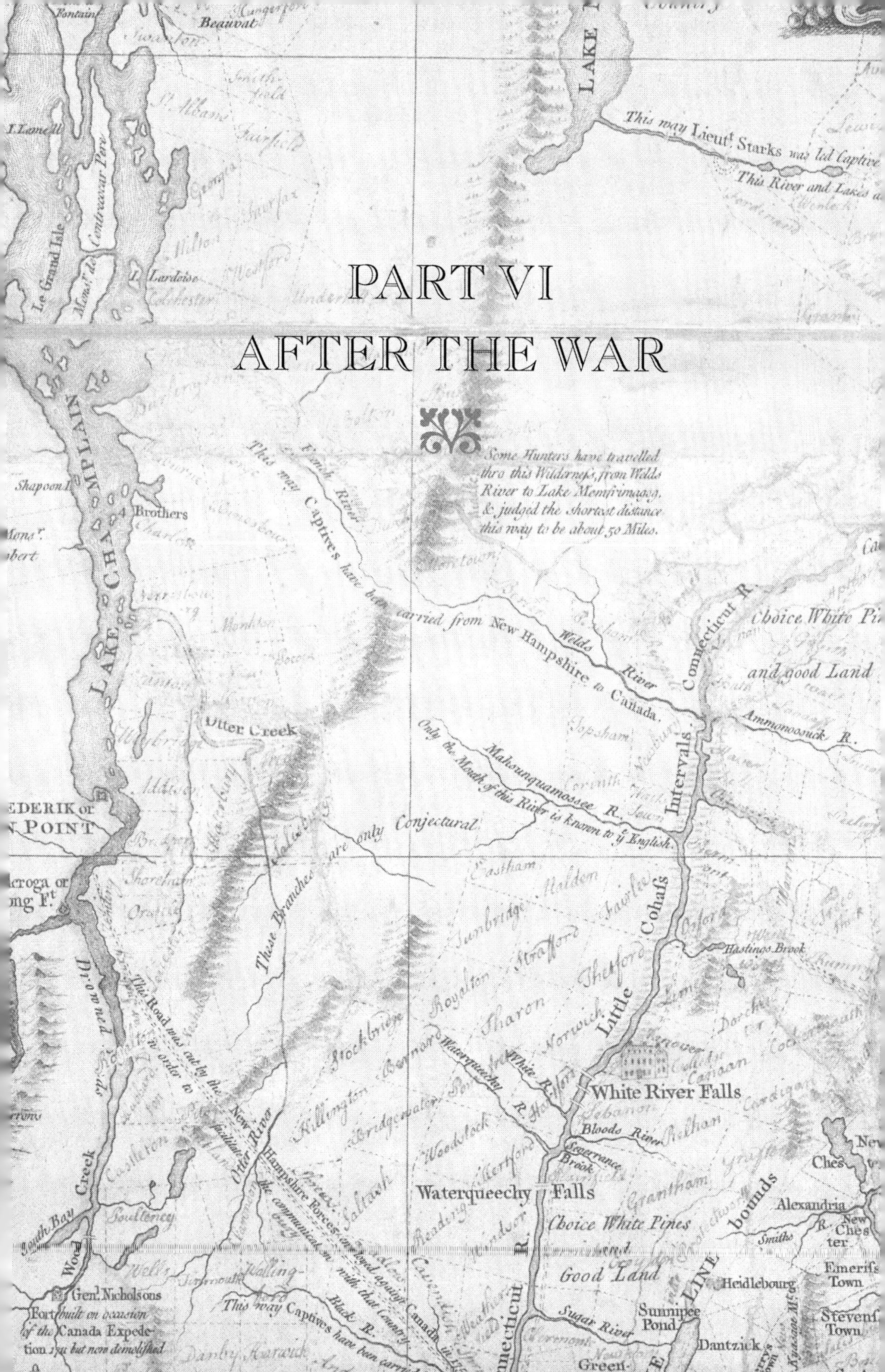

VERMONT

Some Hunters have travelled thro this Wilderness, from Welds River, to Lake Memfrimagog, & judged the shortest distance this way to be about 50 Miles.

NB. Connecticut River has been actually

Lunenbourg

LAKE CHAMPLAIN

Leaperriere
Shelburne
St George
Bolton
Worster
Waterford
Middlesex
Durbury
Moretown
Berlin
French River
Brothers
Charlotte
Hinesbourg
Ferrisbourg
Mons. de
Pocock
Contracocuese
Panton
New Heaven
Otter Creek
Weybridge
Middlebury
Addison
Waterbury
Salisbury
Bridport
Shoreham
Orwell
Leister
Neshobe
Dunbar
Hubbardton
Pittsford
Rutland
Castleton
Clarendon
Otter River
Poultney
Wells
Tinmouth
Wallingford
Wood Creek
Bay
Drowned Lands

Captives have been carried from New Hampshire to Canada

These Branches are only Conjectural

The Road was cut by the New Hampshire Forces employed against Canada in 1759 the communication with that country

Genl. Nicholsons built on occasion Canada Expedn but now demolished

This way Captives have been carried by the Indians

Black R.
Danby
Harwich
Pawlet
Rupert
Dorcet
Brumley
Sandgate
Manchester
Winhall
Sunderland
Arlington
West River
Stratton
Shaftsbury
Glassenbury
New Fane
Bennington
Woodford
Bratle
Chesterfield
Fulham
Pultney
Townshend
Westminster
Saxtons R.
Thomlinson
Rockingham
Plamstead
Cavendish
Weathersfield
Windsor
Reading
Saltash
Shrewsbury
Killington
Bridgewater
Woodstock
Hertford
Stockbridge
Barnard
Pomfret
Waterqueechy R.
White R.
Hartford
Royalton
Sharon
Norwich
Tunbridge
Stratford
Thetford
Eastham
Malden
Fairlee
Little Cohass
Intervals
Corinth
Watstown
Mahounquamosse R.
Only the Mouth of this River is known to ye English
Topsham
Newbury
Peacham
Ryegate
Welds River
Barnet
Connecticut R.

Choice White Pines and good Land
Lyman
Bath
Landaff
Ammonoosuck R.
Franconia
Loring
Lincoln
Haverhill
Umpammonoosuck R.
Fairfield
Piermont
Warren
Orford
Wentworth
Hastings Brook
Rumney
Lime
Dorchester
Cockermouth
Hanover
Dartmouth College
Canaan
White River Falls
Cardigan
New Plymouth
Lebanon
Bloods River
Relhan
Grafton
Severance Brook
Plainfield
Grantham
Waterqueechy Falls
New Chester
Alexandria

Choice White Pines and Good Land
Corinth
Protectworth
Smiths R.
New Britain
Heidlebourg
Croydon
Sugar River
Sunnipee Pond
Salisbury
Kyasage Mt.
Dantzick
Perry's Town
Boscawen
Newport
Green
Clermont
Unity
Little Sugar R.
Lempster
Ackworth
No. 4
Charles Town
Rye Town
No. 8
New Concord
Hillsborough
Contoocook R.
New Hopkinton
Henniker
Alstead
Walpole
Marlow
No. 7
Limerick
Gilsum
Mason
Wears Town
Proprietors Lands reserv'd
New Boston
Ashuelot R.
No. 6
Dublin
Westmoreland
Keene
Swansey
No. 5
Peterborough
Lyndeborough

CONNECTICUT R.

LINE

CURVE

COUNTY OF CHESHIRE

COUNTY OF HILLSBOROUGH

CHAPTER 27

THE CAPTIVES

In July 1783 the last of the prisoners held in Canada arrived at Ticonderoga by boat from St. John's: 196 men, women, and children, some in captivity since 1775, others captured as recently as May in northern Vermont. Among them, returning to his Vermont home, was none other than David Stone—to the astonishment of his neighbors and especially his fellow prisoner and Prison Island escapee, Abijah Hutchinson.[1] Stone had fallen into British hands after Hutchinson and Hathaway had left him in the swamps of the Chateauguay Plain. Either he had regained his strength and made it back to the river to give himself up, or a British or Indian patrol found him. The written record does not say.

Zadock never again heard from William Clark or John Sprague. The latter found his way back to Ballstown, New York, only 40 miles from Bennington, an easy two- or three-day walk. He married an Irish girl by the name of Polly Kennedy and they settled first in Milton, New York, south of Poughkeepsie on the Hudson River, then in Pompey, south of Syracuse. In 1810, Sprague went to sea as a supercargo on a ship bound for Jamaica and, presumably lost at sea, was never heard from again by his family.[2]

Where William Clark went from Bennington is a mystery. There is a William Clark listed on the 1790 census in Ballstown, as is John Sprague, but that Clark does not reappear and there is no telling if this is the same man as the Prison Island captive. American census and pension records of the period are full of William Clarks; if one of them is ours, there is no way to be sure.

Zadock Steele's escape from Prison Island was his finest hour. He could easily have been killed in escaping, as some certainly were, or he could have been ignominiously recaptured, as even more were. But he survived. He said he had no regrets about taking what turned out to be an unnecessary risk. He was one of many who did not trust the British, and took deep satisfaction in escape as an act of defiance.

Zadock remembered, after returning and rebuilding in Vermont, how his father had arrived from Connecticut and over the years "spent many a winter's evening in rehearsing the mournful tale of my captivity and sufferings" for the rest of the family and assembled neighbors.[3]

Whatever he may have told his father and the rest of the family, no reflection by Zadock on the mystery of his extra year of imprisonment is in his narrative. Nor do British military archives indicate why, of all the Royalton captives, only Zadock and four others remained in captivity for an additional year while the rest were released on parole in the fall of 1781.

Zadock's narrative makes no mention of the early release of his Royalton and Randolph mates either, saying only that in October 1781 all the captives in the Provost were moved to Prison Island—which was not the case. He wrote not a word of outrage at the unfairness of his lot. He remembered other injustices so vividly; why not this one? Had he forgotten in the long lapse of time? Was he holding something back?

Whatever reticence or forgetfulness he may have had on this score, he minced no words in his opinions of his captors. He began his captivity with the Mohawks and Abenakis of the Royalton war party with the standard preconceptions about Indian savagery. "Who would not shudder," he wrote, "at the idea of being compelled to take up their abode with a herd of tawny savages?"[4]

While he was not surprised by their ferocity during the attack, like the vast majority of New England captives of the previous hundred years or more he began to see what he least expected once the war party came home to Kahnawake.[5] As he remembered:

> *Scarce can that man be found in this enlightened country who would treat his enemy with as much tenderness and compassion as I was treated by the savage tribe.*[6]

The theme that runs throughout his account of Indian captivity is consistent: He found the Mohawks of Kahnawake capable of more humanity, generosity, and decency than he was ever led to hope for. The symbolic process of adoption changed his status to one of accepted member of a family and of the tribe—a standing rarely if ever accorded to an Indian captured by New England colonists.[7] This unexpected status notwithstanding, Zadock, like his fellow Royalton captives and the vast majority of New England captives, chose to be turned over to the British, keepers of a more familiar culture. As much as Zadock came to revile the British and his treatment at their hands, he never says he would have preferred life at Kahnawake. Voluntary, even temporary transculturation was rarely noted in Revolutionary War prisoner narratives, though not unheard of.[8]

Not only did Zadock see decency in the Indians, he lifted some of the blame for the Royalton Raid from them, writing:

> *And I think the destruction of Royalton and all its evil consequences may with less propriety be attributed to the brutal malevolence of the savage tribe than to the ignoble treachery and despicable fanaticism of certain individuals of our own nation.*[9]

Most probably, by "nation" he meant race, though there is in his narrative an assertion (inconclusive and unsubstantiated by British documents) that there were "Tories," meaning loyalists, among the Royalton raiders. In any case Zadock's bitterest memories are of Prison Island and the "condition while in the hands of the British and under the domineering power of a company of refugees and Tories."[10]

This is another reminder that this was a civil war, a term in common use at the time.[11] Whatever Zadock and the other prisoners in Canada may have thought of loyalists before capture, their experience hardened them toward the men who took up arms against former neighbors and countrymen on behalf of the king.

Yet despite the cruel martinets like James McAlpin and James McDonnell, it cannot be forgotten that there was also William Jones, the Provost Marshal of Montréal, who was remembered by many prisoners for acts of kindness.[12] British doctors were nearly always remembered for their magnanimity and compassion—especially the good Surgeon's Mate James Connor.

There were also the even-handed Ensign Joseph Anderson, who succeeded McAlpin on Prison Island; the two level-headed sergeants, Moss and Perrigo, who saved the life of more than one prisoner (not to mention the careers of their superior officers); and the sporting Captain Alexander McDonell, who admired the pluck of the tunnelers the day after their escape. Finally, of course, there was Lt. Richard Houghton, who, though a battle-hardened, relentless professional soldier, should not be forgotten as the man who acceded to Hannah Handy's wishes, overruled the Mohawk and Abenaki warriors, and released nine terrified and very possibly doomed young boys.

These two people were at the center of the most dramatic and by far the most famous moment of the raid. Aside from the collective memory of her family and the village and contemporaneous newspaper articles about her, Hannah's story was not widely publicized until it was told by Zadock Steele. He was clearly impressed with her and made a point of stating that her account was confirmed by "several gentlemen, now living, who were eyewitnesses." Inexplicably, her husband Robert vanishes from the historical record within a year of the raid.

There is no mention of his death or disappearance, only that there is an oral tradition that he was never seen after the day of the raid. He was, in fact, on hand for at least a few months, as he was named as a petitioner on February 2, 1781, when the town of Royalton applied to the state for relief of annual charter fees. Not long after that he deeded a plot of land.[13] In any case by 1787, Hannah was a single woman, though not listed as a widow, and a guardian had been appointed for her son, Michael. She then married a Sharon man named Gideon Mosher, whom she also outlived; and then she moved to Hoosick Falls, New York, to live with her married daughter Lucretia. Neither the date of her death nor the location of her grave is known, though she was vividly remembered by her grandchildren, to whom she was the charismatic, blue-eyed "Granny Mosher."

Houghton's regiment, the 53rd, stayed in Canada until 1789, when it was posted back to England. By then Houghton had been promoted to captain and presumably went to England with his regiment; but following his departure from the regiment in 1793, he drops from sight. There are two tantalizing pieces of folklore that could not be confirmed and must be discounted, but they are worth noting as items of oral history that have persisted in the social memory of the town. In a 1906 edition of *The Burning of Royalton* there are two stories. One is about two Royalton residents who went to Canada in 1857 and encountered a Mrs. Reid, who was at the time living north of Montréal in L'Assomption with her elderly father, thought to be none other than Richard Houghton.[14] In a related story a Royalton man fell in love with a Canadian girl who, it was said, was the granddaughter of Lt. Houghton. She could not, she said, in good conscience come to live in the town her grandfather had destroyed. A thorough search of Canadian records for Houghton and for a Mrs. Reid of L'Assomption, however, has drawn a blank and must remain a piece of unlikely local tradition.

CHAPTER 28

THE LAND — INDIANS AND SETTLERS

After the war was over, Abenakis began to reoccupy their traditional hunting territories in northern Vermont, and word went out in March 1783 that they would capture any hunters they found trespassing there. In fact, the last prisoner to be listed on a Canadian-British return was Jonathan Perney, taken captive in the heart of Abenaki territory in May 1783 at Lake Memphremagog.[1]

Abenakis on both sides of the border had spent the war in neutral isolation if they could, taking sides only when they had no choice or when it suited their own purposes. The last refuge of the Abenaki in Vermont was in the region known as the Northeast Kingdom, otherwise virtually unpopulated, where scattered bands lived well into the 1790s.[2] But expansionist Vermonters, especially Ethan Allen and his brothers, saw all Indians as rootless nomads and perennial raiders from Canada, and therefore with no rights to land south of the border.

Nothing could have been further from the truth, of course, but that did not stop the Allens from moving back to their "empire" on the Onion River, where they began to push from their land the few Abenakis who remained.[3] Before the war Allen had sung quite a different tune, reportedly telling the Abenaki:

> *I always love Indians. I want your warriors to join with me and my warriors like brothers...if you will I will give you money, blankits, tomehawks, knives and paint...If you do not fight on either side still we will be friends and brothers and you may come and hunt in our woods and pass through our country.*[4]

North of the border, things were only marginally better. The Abenaki village of St. Francis was on land that had been granted by the Catholic church, so it was reasonably secure. But elsewhere, loyalists from New York and New England forced to flee to Canada began to seize land in long-established Abenaki settlements along the border while the British government looked the other way.[5]

For the Six Nations life would never be the same. The once-powerful confederacy was irreversibly fractured by the intramural divisions of the Revolution (a process already underway before the war). Most of them had sided with the British and as a result lost vast tracts of land to massive expropriations in New York State. Joseph Brant denounced the British for not making demands on the Americans for the restoration of Iroquois land during the negotiations for the Treaty of Paris. He wanted to continue to make war on the rebels, though he could no longer do so without British help. He wrote, "We think the rebels will ruin us at last if we go on as we do one year after another... doing nothing... So we are as it were between two hells."[6] Following much bitter dispute and complex negotiations, Brant and most of the loyalist Iroquois were granted land in southern Ontario.[7]

While the Abenakis retreated northward, Vermont was filling up with new and returning settlers. The Vermont to which Zadock, Stone, Hutchinson, and all the other captives and veterans returned was in many ways no different from the one they had left, though it would soon change rapidly. Except for the fact that they were now safe from attack and capture, there was much political uncertainty. Though the United States had won its independence, the new nation's biggest unsolved task was unifying and governing itself. Vermont's was no different. It had declared its independence, too, but it was still divided into bitterly rival factions and had yet to resolve its relationship with the United States, Canada, and Great Britain.

Daily life was a round of back-breaking labor for men and women, and women faced the added ordeal of bearing children at the rate of one every two years for as long as fertility lasted.[8] Zadock married Hannah Shurtlieff of Ellington in 1787, and in due course from 1787 to 1807, she gave birth to seven sons and three daughters. When the children were not in school, their life, like those of other American yeoman farmers and their children, was devoted to bringing productive order to the landscape. It was not always a pretty picture.

One traveler in the state wrote:

> *Most of the country is still unsubdued by the plough. Innumerable stumps, the remains of the pristine forest, deform the fields—pines and other trees girdled, dry and blasted by summer's heat and winter's cold—scorched and blackened by fire or piled in confusion on fields cleared half by the axe, and half by burning. Numerous*

> *log houses of a rude construction—all these and many other objects indicate a country in some parts at least imperfectly subdued by man.*[9]

Once the land was cleared, the settlers still had to contend with periodic crop-devouring insect scourges, outbreaks of cholera, smallpox and dysentery, brutal winters, and short growing seasons.[10] In spite of all this, the population nearly tripled between 1780 and 1791, when, according to the census, over one half of Vermonters were under 16 years old.[11]

Then, in the early 19th century, a great exodus began. Vermont might have had better farmland than the rest of New England, but even better land was opening up. The promise that drew the first settlers north from Connecticut would now draw their descendants away from Vermont. Deforestation would lead to erosion and loss of soil and by the middle of the 19th century, 42 percent of the people born in Vermont were living elsewhere, on rich agricultural land to the west and in Canada.

Zadock's family was typical. Of his ten children, six of his sons emigrated. Three went to New York State; one to New York and then to Ohio; and two accompanied Zadock when he himself left Vermont with his wife within a few years of his 1817 purchase of his property in Stanstead, Québec.[12]

It is an ironic twist that when Zadock made a move to what he saw as a better place to live than Vermont, it was to Canada, where he had so often come close to death as a prisoner of the British. He settled comfortably in the border town of Stanstead, which had been founded in the 1790s by a Tory from Newbury.[13] Zadock was one of many hundreds of Vermonters, loyalist and rebel alike, who moved to Canada soon after the Revolution. He lived there until his death in 1845—27 years, nearly as long as he had lived in Vermont—farming the rich, bottomless black earth of the St. Lawrence River Valley, so different from the hills of Vermont. Among his nearest neighbors, in addition to the smugglers and outlaws that frequented the border, were certain to have been passing bands of Abenaki hunters and more than a few loyalists. There were maybe even one or two from the King's Royal Regiment of New York, who had pulled guard duty at Prison Island in 1781 and 1782.

CHAPTER 29

LOYALISTS

Loyalist numbers can only be estimated, but they might have comprised as much as 20 percent of the population of the colonies before the Declaration of Independence.[1] They came from all walks of life and from all quarters of the American colonies. Once the revolution got underway, deep and bitter divisions opened up between revolutionaries and those who opposed rebellion or who were simply neutral.

Although George Washington was opposed to gratuitous persecution of peaceful loyalists, he came down hard on active ones. He wrote to Governor Trumbull of Connecticut:

> *Why should persons who are preying upon the vitals of their country be suffered to stalk at large, while we know they will do us every mischief in their power? Would it not be prudence to seize of those Tories who have been, are, and that we know will be active against us?*[2]

As a result of such animosity, it is estimated that 100,000 loyalists fled the United States—about 4 percent of the entire population—but that figure conceals the far greater number of people who stayed and were forced to hide their true loyalty. The vast majority who fled were never able to return to their homes, though if some managed to, they were often forced to take an oath of allegiance to the United States.[3] Some went back to England, some to the British West Indies or east Florida, but most went to Canada. There they settled in great numbers in the St. Lawrence Valley, north of Lake Ontario, Nova Scotia, New Brunswick, and in border settlements known as the "Eastern Townships of Québec."[4]

Although there appear to have been no loyalists in Royalton, they were scattered elsewhere throughout Vermont, with high concentrations in certain areas. Loyalists were severely dealt with in Connecticut Valley towns, such as Hartland and Windsor, through public humiliation, flogging, confinement, and property loss.[5] Those in Strafford, Thetford, Sharon, and Norwich, near Royalton, appear to have been more or less tolerated, though some lost their land.[6] Newbury, Vermont, was home to what seems to have been a disproportionate number of active loyalists.[7] In mid-1782 roving bands of loyalists were forcing frontier settlers north of Newbury to swear allegiance to the king. There were so many dedicated Tories in Newbury—perhaps 20 or 30—that in June 1782, some people were briefly (though unnecessarily) worried that the Tories would enter the town in force and raise the Union Jack.[8]

Of the 158 loyalist estates seized by Vermont, virtually none were recovered by their original owners, nearly all of whom fled to Canada during the war. Many joined the Queen's Loyal Rangers.[9] Canadian records show that most of them petitioned the British Government for some reimbursement of their losses as a recognition from the king for the cost of their loyalty.[10]

John Peters, an arch Newbury Tory and a founding member of the Queen's Loyal Rangers, never returned to Newbury, though his equally loyalist son did. The younger Peters settled down and lived out his life there, holding a variety of elective offices. Loyalists such as John Taplin, Levi Sylvester, and Abel Davis remained in the Newbury area, but Taplin's son Johnson moved north in the 1790s to found what was to become Zadock Steele's new home, Stanstead. Roger Stevens, who led raids against his neighbors in Pittsford, was one of the few to come home and pick up his life, even though his sympathies were well-known and his property had been confiscated; he, too, eventually moved to Canada in the 1790s.[11]

Because Vermont remained non-aligned and levied no taxes to pay for war costs, it was attractive to loyalists from other states, not only because of its tax policy but also because of the distant, ever-alive possibility of reunion between Vermont and Great Britain.[12] Failing that, Vermont was the quickest route from the United States to major settlements in British Canada. If a fleeing loyalist family could make it to the shores of Lake Champlain, it stood a good chance of hailing a British ship for transport to Québec.[13]

As the war came to a close and Vermont's government looked ahead, the Ethan Allen faction was actively encouraging loyalists to settle there so as to support his relentless effort to build political and commercial ties to Canada and Great Britain.[14] Although Frederick Haldimand never really trusted Ethan Allen, Vermont remained a wild card at the end of the war, possibly one the United States could be persuaded to part with.[15]

CHAPTER 30

THE FOURTEENTH STATE

"I suppose the independence of the United States is so established that the gales of hell cannot prevail against them."

Jacob Bayley[1] to George Washington

"I would give my whole fortune to know what would be the fate of america."

Ira Allen[2]

NEWBURY'S JACOB BAYLEY, flush with the American victory over Great Britain, was more confident than he had any right to be when he wrote this to Washington in 1783. Ira Allen's vivid rhetoric was closer to the mark, for the fledgling United States were anything but "established," and the status of the Vermont to which Zadock returned in the spring of 1783 was even less so. Although most of the terms of a peace treaty between the United States and Great Britain had been settled in late 1782, they had not been formalized and were the subject of rumors. All that was clear was that Vermont was not to be the 14th state.

In fact, as of 1782 Vermont was no longer as eager for statehood as it once had been: there was the issue of war costs, for which an influential minority of still-resident loyalists opposed paying; and many Vermonters thought the Congress too ineffectual to manage the affairs of the sprawling new nation.[3] Although there was some support among the states for admitting Vermont, there was still opposition from New York as well as large southern states. They were convinced that recognition of Vermont's secession from New York would set a dangerous precedent for dissident regional populations that might want to partition existing states and found new ones. Nor did southern states want to see the balance of power in the Continental Congress affected by the addition of another northern state. In the spring of 1782, the "Vermont Problem" had been one of the most hotly debated topics in the Continental Congress. Arthur Lee of Virginia declared, perhaps somewhat hyperbolically, that if Vermont were admitted it "would destroy the confederacy." [4] Washington considered Vermont a loose geopolitical cannon. He was eager to be able to count on its resources and manpower and was worried about losing Vermont to the British. Within eight months of the October 1780 raids on Vermont and New York State, Washington proposed sending the continental officer General Stark to Vermont to command a force of locally conscripted militia to defend the northern frontiers. [5] He was impatient with the Continental Congress for its bickering over Vermont's status, wishing to see it granted statehood. [6] But he was equally impatient with Vermont for trying to claim territory beyond its traditional boundaries and argued to Chittenden that, if greedy, it would lose its case before the Continental Congress. [7]

While the delegates in the Continental Congress were arguing about Vermont, Frederick Haldimand grew impatient with the lack of resolution to his negotiations with the government of Vermont. He had also heard rumors that the Continental Congress might order an invasion of Vermont in order to bring an end to the disruption it was causing—an approach that Washington considered and rejected. [8] Throughout 1782, London pressed Haldimand to annex Vermont, on the grounds that it was "of the greatest importance," and he must "spare no expense." He was ordered "to appear on the border of Vermont with a large force to make them" rejoin Great Britain if they did not commit soon. [9] Increasingly frustrated by Vermont's lack of commitment, Haldimand declared in a letter to General Clinton that "only force will work on Vermont; we must lay waste their country if they do not come over." [10] Convinced Chittenden was playing for time (as was Washington), Haldimand was moving closer to forming a plan for invading Vermont so as to annex it to Canada by force, and was massing troops at border posts. But at the last moment, in August 1782, his hand was stayed by a general agreement on terms for peace between Great Britain and American delegates meeting in Paris. [11]

Although it was widely known in Vermont that a treaty between the United States and Great Britain was taking shape, some of the details remained in doubt in early 1783. Loyalists like Justus Sherwood thought they had in fact broken down over a disagreement on the fate of Vermont. [12] Jacob Bayley had heard rumors himself, and expressed concern in a letter to Washington, writing, "I have heard Vermont is not to be included, and there is word that the people will benefit if under British control as they will be clear of the charge of the war...can't we settle with Britain?" [13]

One of the knotty problems that had arisen during the peace talks was the question of boundaries. John Adams, Benjamin Franklin, and John Jay were the American negotiators, and if Franklin had had his way, all of Canada would have been among the spoils of war. The British negotiator, Richard Oswald, who had granted many favorable terms, said the king would not cede Canada. Haldimand, in turn, had sent word that British demands for territory should include Vermont, which was now becoming a pawn in the intricate negotiations. They compromised: the United States could have Vermont but not Canada, and the boundary was drawn where it has remained ever since, along the 45th parallel, defining the northern borders of New Hampshire, Vermont, and New York.[14]

In the years to come, support for joining the United States gained traction in Vermont and elsewhere. Powerful New Yorkers like Alexander Hamilton and his father-in-law, Philip Schuyler, were beginning to see that continued friction between New York and Vermont was pointless and that there were real dangers to having an independent Vermont that still might be tempted into an alliance with Canada. After all, Lake Champlain and the St. Lawrence River constituted the Green Mountain Republic's principal commercial export route. Southern states began to come around as well, and in 1791 an agreement was reached in Congress to admit Vermont as the 14th state and to balance it with the creation of a new southern state, Kentucky. Vermont had been an independent republic for 14 years.

* * *

This put an end to all of the schemes for union with Great Britain and began the decline of the power of the Allen family, which had lost its most illustrious member when Ethan died in 1789. In spite of the 1783 peace treaty, the Allens had tried to continue secret talks with Great Britain, and had some limited success in securing commercial agreements. These eventually collapsed and relations soured, and in a desperate power play in 1794, Ira and his brother Levi conceived a scheme whereby they and a group of conspirators would forge an allegiance with Revolutionary France to seize Canada from the British. The reckless plan foundered utterly and with it the Allen family's ability to influence the course of events in Vermont.[15]

CHAPTER 31

EPILOGUE

Zadock Steele was one of some two-and-a-half million Americans who returned from the war to pick up their lives and collectively continue with the unfolding of the "fate of America," as Ira Allen had put it. Zadock's story, one man's experience in the final years of the Revolution in a backwater to the conflict as a whole, is both singular and universal.

What seems at first glance no more than one individual's compelling story is a window on a much wider picture. It reveals the strategic importance of a second front in the Revolution; the role of indigenous peoples and how crucial the outcome of the war would be to all of the tribes east of the Mississippi; an often hidden population of loyalists and spies; it reveals the degree to which a vast number of Americans played only a minor role in the war—some of them going to places like Vermont and Kentucky, in part to avoid serving in the war or paying for it once it was over; the degree to which the war swept up non-combatants; and, in the uncertain status of Vermont, it reveals what a fragile union the early United States truly was. It reveals, in the friction between New York and Vermont, and among the various cultures at Prison Island, that the durable regional characters and folk-ways that were established so early in colonial America and have remained in many ways constant since then, were arguably more stable than (and in competition with) a sense of nationhood at the close of the Revolutionary War. And, of course, it reveals the preoccupation of the veterans of the Revolution with establishing a record of their accomplishments and sacrifices and the readiness of the public to preserve and absorb these raw materials of national identity. From this point of view, by the time Zadock wrote his story, the line between the identity of the Republic of Vermont and the United States was blurred in the public memory.

It is safe to say that in most peoples' minds, Revolutionary Vermont is now conflated with the 13 original states. Its ambiguous status often comes as a surprise. An unfolding of the events in Vermont before, during and after the Revolution reveals that this small and sparsely populated republic was a microcosm of the greater Revolutionary drama.

Like the original persecuted and dissatisfied English colonists, many people moved to pre-Revolutionary Vermont out of dissatisfaction with religious or governmental practices they had found elsewhere in the colonies. These migrants were far from uniform in their dislikes and aspirations, and they brought their fractiousness with them. The Green Mountains, from which the state took its name, formed anything but a unifying geographical feature, and the range tended to magnify the differences between the people in the widely separated population centers of the state. Those in the north and the south and on the west and east sides of the mountains had little in common with each other politically, culturally, or commercially, and these divisions were only aggravated by the extreme difficulty of transmontane communication and travel.

Competing power centers in the Champlain Valley and the Connecticut River Valley were able to come together in 1777 around the cause of rebellion against Great Britain and eventually on the issue of independence from New York and New Hampshire. But as the Revolution wore on, distrust and friction built. General Jacob Bayley and others in the upper Connecticut River Valley were tied closely to Washington and the Continental Congress and looked to them for military support as well as for taking the initiative in another invasion of Canada—more pressing to them than the status of Vermont. On the other hand, when the Allens and other members of the "Bennington Party," Vermont's ruling faction, saw that the Continental Congress was not going to recognize Vermont's independence, they began to look to the British in Canada for a solution to Vermont's problems.

Thus the stage was set for the events that eventually led to the Royalton Raid. Threads of the narrative to come were drawing together in early 1780. The British saw both a problem and an opportunity in Vermont's predicament, as did the deadlocked Continental Congress. Vermont was caught in the middle between these two forces and at the same time pulled in different directions internally. In the Upper Valley, Bayley was pleading with Washington for more troops and for an invasion force—an eventuality the British wanted most to prevent. In the Champlain Valley, Ethan Allen, Chittenden, and others were edging toward an agreement with the British that might leave at least a part of Vermont *hors de combat.* The people of Royalton and Zadock Steele in particular had no idea of the geopolitical forces bearing down upon them. They knew the war was far from over in 1780 and that the northern frontier was particularly dangerous, but for these people, there had been warfare in every preceding generation for over one hundred years. For them, the prize of virgin land was worth the risk.

This story does not end on a triumphalist note with victory and the Founding Fathers. In Vermont, the Treaty of Paris did not mean, at least right away, what it meant to the 13 states. In some ways it left open possibilities for more conflict rather than an end to it. To a certain extent the British still coveted Vermont at the end of the war—as did New York and New Hampshire to varying degrees. Vermont itself was riven by factionalism.

So the story ends on the northern frontier where it began, a place where the land was colonized after being "widowed" by the forced departure of native people who had thought they might one day return to it should the British prevail. Like so many other Vermonters, Zadock followed the advancing frontier (and the Abenaki withdrawal) northward, moving from Randolph to Brookfield and finally to Canada. As a member of the Revolutionary generation, Zadock's most persuasive legacy, as much as his compelling narrative, was the trajectory of his children—prosperous, accomplished, educated, widely dispersed—who had listened to his stories in those long winter evenings and who felt compelled to see that they would not be forgotten.

ACKNOWLEDGMENTS

BECAUSE I AM NOT a trained historian, the list of people and institutions without which this book would never have come to be is large; and, as is so often the case, forms a community that has never entirely convened, but which in one sense comes together on these pages.

For early and prolonged support I am grateful to my old friend and agent, Ike Williams, who can take credit for, among other things, coming up with the book's main title. Tom Powers, who was interested in the subject long before I was, welcomed me to the field and has been a source of encouragement ever since. Gavin Watt's deep knowledge of military lore and the history of the period was invaluable as has that of other scholars and researchers: Pauline Maier, Mike Barbieri, Hector Besmer, Andre Fortin, and Raymond Dumais. John Dumville opened up the entire archive of the Royalton Historical Society and introduced me to Wes and Mim Herwig, who have researched and written widely on the Royalton Raid and the descendants of the families of the Revolutionary generation.

I am especially grateful to the relentless and productive research of Katherine Stebbins-McCaffery, James Fichter, David Naumec, and Krista Ainsworth.

To those who were willing to labor through long and flawed early versions of the manuscript, offering encouragement where they saw virtue, painful advice where they saw trouble, I am especially grateful: David McCullough, John Demos, Colin Calloway, Phil Pochoda, Don Metz, Rita Guastella, and Kevin Graffagnino.

Of course an enterprise like this depends utterly on libraries and archives and my debt of gratitude is immeasurable to: The Public Archives of Canada and especially Patricia Kennedy; the Baker-Berry Library and the Rauner Rare Book Library of Dartmouth College; the New England Historical Genealogical Society; the Boston Public Library; Harvard's Widener and Houghton Rare Book Libraries; the Kahnawake Cultural Center; the New Hampshire Historical

Society; the Vermont State Archives; the Coteau-du-Lac Historic Site; McGill University's McCord Museum; the Stanstead Historical Society; the Libraries of the University of Vermont.

I am especially grateful to the Vermont Historical Society, not only for their excellent collections of documents and for assistance with research, but especially for its support, encouragement, and enthusiasm for bringing this book into print. I want to thank Alan Berolzheimer for his faith in this project and for his tireless work in shaping and refining it. I want to thank Rob Gurwitt for his clear-headed reading of the manuscript and for his expert and painstaking copyediting.

To Jennifer Kafka-Smith and Kenneth Anderson and other descendants of Zadock Steele, I am especially grateful for their willingness to trust a total stranger and for sharing family archives and the family network. I hope they feel this book does justice to a remarkable ancestor.

Above all, to Margot, who was there from the beginning.

BIBLIOGRAPHY

Manuscript Sources

U.S. National Archives (USNA)

Census Records.
George Washington Papers at the Library of Congress (GWPLC).
Revolutionary War Pension Applications.

Public Archives of Canada, Ottawa (PAC)

Claus Family Papers.
Fraser Family Papers.
Moses Hazen Papers.
William Humphrey Journal.
John Polley Journal, 1775.
William Twiss Journal, May 1, 1779-July 31, 1781.

National Archives of Great Britain (NAGB)

Audit Office Records.
The British Army: Officers' Records.
Colonial Office Records.
Sir Frederick Haldimand, Unpublished Papers and Correspondence, 1758-1784. Microfilm, based on Catalogue of Additional Manuscripts (HP).
War Office Records.

Vermont State Archives, Montpelier (VSA)

Rolls of the Soldiers in the Revolutionary War, 1775-1783, Manuscript Collection, State of Vermont.
Stevens Collection Microfilm – Correspondence.

Index to the Papers of the Surveyors-General, State Papers of Vermont, Vol. 1. Montpelier, 1918.

Journals and Proceedings of the General Assembly. 1778-1781, State Papers of Vermont, Vol. III. Bellows Falls: Aaron Grout, Secretary of State, 1924.

Records of the Governor and Council of the State of Vermont, Vol. II. Montpelier: E.P. Walton, editor and publisher, 1874.

Sequestrations, Confiscations and Sale of Estates, State Papers of Vermont. ed. Mary Greene Nye, 1941.

Survey Books of Ira Allen.

New Hampshire State Papers, comp. and ed., Isaac W. Hammond, librarian, New Hampshire Historical Society. Manchester, N.H.: John B. Clarke, Printer, 1887, (Vol. XVII), Vol. 3.

Kahnawake Reserve

St. Francis-Xavier Mission du Sault St. Louis at Kahnawake: Philips Family Documents.

Archives of the City of Montréal

Province de Québec, District de Montréal (1764-1791), Cour Des Plaidoyers Communs–Civils. (For material relating to the captivity of George Avery.)

Coteau-du-Lac National Historic Site

Parks Canada, Manuscript Report Series #186, Department of Indian and Northern Affairs, 1977.

McCord Museum, McGill University, Montréal.

Captain Archibald McDonnell's Orderly Book. Terre Bonne, December 25, 1882; 1 Battalion KRRNY.

Brigadier General Hope, General Orders Book, Québec, 1786-1789 (Barrack Master's Book).

Documents of the American Revolution, 1770-1782: Colonial Office, ed. K.G. Davies. Shannon: Irish University Press, 1972-1981.

Documents Relating to the Colonial History of the State of New York. Vol. X, ed. Berthold Fernow. Albany: State Archives, 1887.

Ethan Allen and His Kin: Correspondence 1772–1819, ed. John J. Duffy, et al. Vol. I. Hanover: University Press of New England, 1998.

A History of the Organization, Development and Services of the Military and Naval Forces of Canada. 3 vols. Edited by the Historical Section of the General Staff. Ottawa, 1919-1920.

Papers of Sir William Johnson. Division of Archives and History. Albany: The University of the State of New York, 1921-65.

"Personnel and Garrisons at Coteau Du Lac 1779-1858," Karen Price. Parks Canada, Department of Indian and Northern Affairs, 1969.

Records of the Revolutionary War, ed. W.T.R. Saffell. Philadelphia: G.G. Evans, 1860.

Wheelock Papers. Manuscript Collection, Rauner Library, Dartmouth College, Hanover, N.H.

Personal Papers Collections

Wesley and Miriam Herwig Private Collection, Randolph, Vermont.

Papers relating to Pember Family History.

Massachusetts Historical Society (MHS)

Richard Frothingham Papers, 1683-1865.
John Kettell Diary, May 17-October, 1775.

New Hampshire Historical Society (NHHS)

Timothy Bedel Papers, 1763-1787.
Unpublished Papers of Jonathan Chase.

Royalton (Vermont) Historical Society (RHS)

Evelyn Lovejoy Papers.

Vermont Historical Society (VHS)

The Writings of Daniel Clark.
John Charles Huden Papers.
Johnson Family Papers.

Personal Narratives, Diaries, Papers, Genealogies

Allen, Ethan. *Ethan Allen's Narrative of the Capture of Ticonderoga, His Captivity and Treatment by the British. Written by Himself.* First edition, Philadelphia, 1779.

Anburey, Thomas. *With Burgoyne from Quebec.* ed. Sydney Jackman. Toronto: Macmillan of Canada, 1963.

Anderson, Isaac. *Diary of Isaac Anderson.* Unpublished, from collection of Cincinnati Historical Society.

Avery, George. "Narrative," in Evelyn Lovejoy, *History of Royalton, Vermont, with Family Genealogies, 1769-1911.* Burlington, Vt.: Free Press Printing Company, 1911.

Blackmer, Joel. "Narrative," in Lovejoy, *History of Royalton.*

Carpenter, Jonathan. *Jonathan Carpenter's Journal,* ed. Miriam and Wes Herwig. Randolph Center, Vt.: Greenhill Books, 1994.

Castiglioni, Luigi. *Luigi Castiglioni's Viaggio: Travels in the United States of North America, 1785-1787,* ed. and trans., Antonio Pace. Syracuse: Syracuse University Press, 1983.

Cometti, Elizabeth, ed. *The American Journals of Lt. John Enys.* Syracuse: Syracuse University Press, 1976.

Cruikshank, Ernest, and Gavin Watt. *The History and Muster Roll of the King's Royal Regiment of New York.* Campbellville, Ont.: Global Heritage Press, 2006.

Echevarria, Durand. *The Iroquois Visit Rochambeau at Newport in 1780.* In *The Unpublished Journal of the Comte de Charlus. Rhode Island History* 2(1952): 73.

Elkins, Jonathan. "Memoir Of Jonathan Elkins," in *The Upper Connecticut River,* Vol. 1. Montpelier: Vermont Historical Society, 1943.

Fisher, Mathias. *Narrative.* Pension Application, U.S. National Archives. Series: M805 Roll: 322, Image: 488, File: S22239.

Fitch, Asa. *Asa Fitch Papers, Oral Histories of the Mohawk Valley.* Fort Campbell, Ky.: The Sleeper Co., 1997.

Gould, Jay. "Freegift Patchin Narrative," in *History of Delaware County and Border Wars of New York.* Roxbury, N.Y.: Keeny & Gould, 1856.

Hadfield, Joseph. *An Englishman in America, Joseph Hadfield's Diary, 1785.* Toronto: The Hunter-Rose Co.,1933.

Hollister, Josiah. *A Journal of Josiah Hollister, a Soldier of the American Revolution and a Prisoner of War in Canada.* 1815. Republished 1928 by Romanzo Norton Bunn, Historian of the Illinois Society, Sons of the Revolution.

Hutchinson, K.M. *Memoir Of Abijah Hutchinson, a Soldier Of The Revolution.* William Alling, Printer, 1843.

Johnson, Thomas. "Journal of Thomas Johnson While a Captive," in Frederic P. Wells, *History of Newbury, Vermont, from the Discovery of the Coos Country to Present Time.* St. Johnsbury, Vt.: The Caledonian Company, 1902.

Johnson, Warren. "Warren Johnson's Journal," *in Papers of Sir William Johnson.* Division of Archives and History. Albany: The University of the State of New York, 1921-65., Vol. 13.

Kendall, Thomas. *Diary Of Thomas Kendall, A Missionary to the Caughnawaga from Dartmouth in 1773.* Rauner/Dartmouth Manuscript Collection.

Long, John. *Voyages and Travels of an Indian Interpreter and Trader. April 10, 1768-Spring, 1782.* London: Printed for the author, and sold by Robson [etc.], 1791.

Lorimier, Claude. *At War with the Americans, the Journal of Claude de Lorimier.* Victoria, B.C.: Press Porcépic.

Monroe, William Newton. *Richard Newton of Sudbury, Massachusetts. Also an Account of the Indian Raid in Barnard, Vermont.* Woonsocket, R.I., 1912.

Parkhurst, Benjamin. *Life of Benjamin Parkhurst.* Unpublished manuscript., Lovejoy Papers, South Royalton (Vt.) Library.

Pember, Karl, and Jay Reade. *Pember Family History.* Woodstock, Vt.: The Spear Press. 1916. Complete booklet in Archives, State Library, Montpelier.

Perkins, Nathan. *A Narrative of a Tour Through the State of Vermont from April 27 to June 12, 1789, by the Rev. Nathan Perkins.* Woodstock, Vt.: The Yankee Bookshop, 1937.

Phoenix, Stephen Whitney. *The Whitney Family of Connecticut.* New York: Priv. Print. [Bradford Press], 1878.

Priest, Josiah. *Life and Adventures of Isaac Hubbell.* Albany, N.Y.: J. Munsell, 1841; New York: Garland Publishing, 1977.

Rix, Garner. "Garner Rix Narrative," in Lovejoy, *History of Royalton.*

Roberts, Lemuel. *The Memoirs of Captain Lemuel Roberts, 1809.* New York: Arno Press, 1969.

Rogers, Horatio, ed. *Hadden's Journal and Orderly Books.* Albany, N.Y., 1884.

Rogerson, Col. W., *Historical Records of the 53rd Regiment* (personnel). London: Simpkin, Marshall, Hamilton, Kent, & Co., 1891.

Scudder, William. *The Journal of William Scudder*, 1794. New York: Garland Publishing, 1977.

Segar, Nathaniel. *A Brief Narrative of the Captivity and Sufferings of Lt. Nathaniel Segar.* Paris, Me.: Printed at the Observer Office, and published at the Oxford Bookstore, 1825.

Smith, James. *Scoouwa: James Smith's Captivity Narrative.* Columbus: Ohio Historical Society, 1978.

Sprague, Dr. Warren Vincent. *Sprague Families in America.* Rutland, Vt.: The Tuttle Company, 1913.

Steele, Zadock, *The Indian Captive; Or a Narrative of the Captivity and Sufferings of Zadock Steele, Related by Himself.* Published by the author, E.P. Walton, printer, Montpelier, Vt., 1818.

Talman, James John, *Loyalist Narratives from Upper Canada,* 1904 edition. Toronto: The Champlain Society, 1946.

Vaughan, Alden T., *Narratives of North American Captivity: A Selective Bibliography.* New York: Garland Publishing, 1983.

Walton, William, ed. *The Narrative of the Captivity of Benjamin Gilbert and his Family.* New York: Garland Publishing, 1975.

Webster, Isaac. *The Narrative of the Captivity of Isaac Webster.* New York: Garland Publishing, 1978.

Wheelock, Eleazar. *A Continuation of the Narrative of the Indian Charity School, Begun in Lebanon, in Connecticut.* Hartford, Ct.: 1773.

Williams, John. *The Redeemed Captive Returning to Zion.* Bedford, Mass.: Applewood Books, 1993.

Versions of the Zadock Steele Narrative and Burning of Royalton, in order of publication date.

Steele, Zadock. *The Indian Captive; or A Narrative of the Captivity and Sufferings of Zadock Steele, Related by Himself.* Published by the author. E.P. Walton, printer, Montpelier, Vt., 1818.

Indian Narratives. Claremont, N.H.: Tracy and Brothers, 1854.

Chase, Francis. *Gathered Sketches from the Early History of New Hampshire and Vermont.* N.H.: Tracy, Kenney & Co., 1856.

Dunklee, Iva. *Burning of Royalton.* Boston: G.H. Ellis Co., 1906.

The Indian Captive, or A Narrative of the Captivity and Sufferings of Zadock Steele, Related by Himself. Springfield, Ma,: The H.R. Huntting Company, 1908.

Lovejoy, Evelyn. *History of Royalton Vermont, with Family Genealogies, 1769-1911.* Burlington, Vt.: Free Press Printing Company, 1911.

French, Mary Billings. *Indian Captive*. Woodstock, Vt.: The Elm Tree Press, 1934.

The Indian Captive; or A Narrative of the Captivity and Sufferings of Zadock Steele, Related by Himself. Reprint of the 1908 edition. [New York]: B. Blom [1971].

The Indian Captive; or A Narrative of the Captivity and Sufferings of Zadock Steele, Related by Himself. New York: Garland Publishing, 1977.

Calloway, Colin. *North Country Captives: Selected Narratives of Indian Captivity from Vermont and New Hampshire.* Hanover: University Press of New England, 1992.

The Indian Captive, or A Narrative of the Captivity and Sufferings of Zadock Steele, Related by Himself. Reprint of the 1908 edition. Kessinger Publishing LLC, 2009.

Newspapers

1781 Depositions by John Edgar and David Abeel about Vermont Secession to Canada, Printed by John Holt, Poughkeepsie, New York.

American Journal and General Advertiser, Boston, 1780.

American Journal Extraordinary, Providence, R.I., November 13, 1780.

Andover Review for May 1889, from the *Montreal Star* of June 1889.

Boston Gazette and Country Journal, November 20, 1780.

Connecticut Courant and Weekly Intelligencer, August 19, 1780.

Connecticut Gazette & The Universal Intelligencer.

Connecticut Journal, November 30, 1780.

Continental Journal and Weekly Advertiser, March 22, 1781.

New York Gazetteer or the Northern Intelligencer, October 21, 1782.

Norwich (Ct.) *Packet,* November 14, 1780.

Providence (R.I.) *Gazette,* November 29, 1780.

Québec Gazette, 1779-1781.

The Vermont Gazette, or, Freemen's Depository Weekly, June 5, 1783-May 31, 1784.

The Vermont Journal and the Universal Advertiser, August 7, 1783-March 13, 1792.

State, Town Histories

Benton, Nathaniel. *History of Herkimer County.* Albany, N.Y.: J. Munsell, 1856.

Brookfield: Incidents Attending the First Settlement, and General History Previous to the Town Organization in March 1785. Brookfield Historical Society, 1987.

Carpenter, W. H., and T. S. Arthur. *History of Vermont*. Philadelphia: Lippincott, Grambo, 1853.

Caverly, A.M., *History of The Town of Pittsford, Vt.* Rutland: Tuttle & Co., 1872.

Chase, Francis, ed.. *Gathered Sketches from the Early History of New Hampshire and Vermont.* Claremont, N.H.: Tracy, Kenney & Co., 1856.

Chase, Frederic, *A History of Dartmouth College and the Town of Hanover, New Hampshire.* Brattleboro: The Vermont Printing Company, 1928.

Dorrough, Richard, and Heritage Hunters of Saratoga County. *Daniel McAlpin, Loyalist.* Saratoga NYGenWeb, Project Saratoga County, New York, 2002.

Duerden, Timothy. *A History of Delaware County, New York: A Catskill Land and its People, 1797-2007.* Fleischmanns, N.Y.: Purple Mountain Press, 2007.

Hurd, Duane Hamilton. *History of Clinton and Franklin Counties, New York*. Philadelphia: J. W. Lewis & Co., 1880.

Johnston, Henry P. *Record of Connecticut Men of the Military and Naval Service During the Revolutionary War.* Hartford 1886.

Lovejoy, Evelyn. *History of Royalton, Vermont, with Family Genealogies, 1769-1911.* Burlington, Vt.: Free Press Printing Company, 1911.

Oread Literary Club. *History of the Town of Johnson, Vermont.* 1907.

Powers, Grant. *Historical Sketches of the Discovery, Settlement, and Progress of Events in the Coos Country and Vicinity, Principally Included Between the Years 1754 and 1785.* Haverhill, N.H.: Henry Merrill, 1880.

Rann, William S. *History of Chittenden County.* Syracuse, N.Y.: D. Mason & Co., 1886.

Rockwell, Rev. Charles. *The Catskill Mountains and the Region Around.* New York: Taintor Brothers & Co., 1867.

Roscoe, William E. *History of Schoharie County.* Syracuse, N.Y.: D. Mason & Co., 1882.

Simms, Jeptha. *Frontiersmen of New York.* Albany: Geo. C. Riggs, 1883.

Thompson, Zadock. *A Gazetteer of the State of Vermont.* Montpelier: E.P. Walton, Printer, 1824.

Waldo, Loren P. *The Early History of Tolland, Connecticut.* Hartford: Press of Case, Lockwood & Company, 1861.

Wells, Frederic P., *History of Newbury, Vermont, from the Discovery of the Coos Country to Present Time.* St. Johnsbury, Vt.: The Caledonian Company, 1902.

Williams, Wendell Wales. *History of Rochester.* Montpelier, Vt.: E. Ballou, Printer, 1869.

General Reference

Dictionary of Canadian Biography Online.

Boatner, Mark, M. III, *Encyclopedia of the American Revolution.* Mechanicsburgh, Pa.: Stackpole Books, 1994.

Ph.D., Masters Theses

Blanchard, David Scott. "Patterns of Tradition and Change: The Re-creation of Iroquois Culture at Kahnawake," Ph.D. diss., University of Chicago, 1982.

Dendy, John Oliver. "Frederick Haldimand and the Defence of Canada, 1778-1784." Ph.D. diss., Duke University, 1972.

Denn, Robert John. "Prison Narratives of the American Revolution," Ph. D. diss., Michigan State University, 1980.

Dixon, Martha W. "Divided Authority: The American Management of Prisoners of War in the Revolutionary War, 1775-1783," Ph.D. diss., University of Utah, 1977.

Green, Gretchen. "A New People in an Age of War: The Kahnawake Iroquois, 1667-1760," Ph.D. diss., College of William and Mary, 1991.

Knepper, George. "The Convention Army, 1777-1783," Ph.D. Diss., University of Michigan, 1954.

Ostola, Larry. "The 7 Nations of Canada and the American Revolution," Masters thesis, University of Montréal, 1989.

Stevens, Paul L. "His Majesty's Savage Allies," Ph.D. diss., State University of New York-Buffalo, 1984.

Taplin, Winn L., Jr. "The Vermont Problem in the Continental Congress and in Interstate Relations, 1776-1787," Ph.D. diss., University of Michigan, 1955.

Articles, Papers

Bryce, P. H. "The Quinté Loyalists of 1784," *Ontario Historical Society Papers and Records*, 27(1931): 5-14; on "Major Daniel McAlpine, a Retired Officer of the 60th Regiment."

Burns, Brian. "Carleton in the Valley, or the Year of the Burning," *Fort Ticonderoga Bulletin* 13(1980): 398-411.

Calloway, Colin. "Algonkians in the American Revolution," in Peter Benes, ed., *Algonkians of New England: Past and Present* (Dublin Seminar For New England Folklife, Boston: Boston University, 1991), 57.

———. "Sentinels of Revolution: Bedel's New Hampshire Rangers and the Abenaki Indians on the Upper Connecticut," *Historical New Hampshire* 45(1990): 271-295.

———. "An Uncertain Destiny: Indian Captivities on the Upper Connecticut River Valley," *American Studies* 17(1983): 189-210.

Duncan, Kelvin. *Spruce Beer History*, http://www.agingincanada.ca/trivia.htm.

Everest, Allan. "Early Roads and Taverns in the Champlain Valley," *Vermont History* 37 (Autumn 1969).

Gerlach, Don. "The British Invasion of 1780 and a Character Debased Beyond Description," *Fort Ticonderoga Bulletin* 14(Summer 1984): 311-321.

Gordon, James. "Reminiscences of James Gordon," *Proceedings of the New York Historical Association*, 24 (*New York History* 17 [1936]).

Graymont, Barbara. "Six Nations in the Revolutionary War," 1976 Conference Proceedings, Sponsored by the Arthur C. Parker Fund for Iroquois Research.

Herwig, Wes. "The Royalton Raid," *Vermont Life* (Autumn 1964).

Hough, Franklin B, ed. *The Northern Invasion of October 1780: A Series of Papers Relating to the Expeditions from Canada under Sir John Johnson and Others against the Frontiers of New York*. New York: Bradford Club, 1866.

Kaplan, Roger. "The Hidden War: British Intelligence Operations During the American Revolution," *William and Mary Quarterly* 47(January 1990): 115-138.

Kelly, Eric P. "The Dartmouth Indians," *Dartmouth Alumni Magazine* 22(December 1929).

Lampee, Thomas. "The Mississquoi Loyalists," *Proceedings of the Vermont Historical Society* 6(1938): 80-140.

Metcalfe, Simon. "Little Book," *Fort Ticonderoga Bulletin* 18(Winter 1988).

Millard, James P. "War in the Northern Department: The British Campaign of 1777," http://www.historiclakes.org/Timelines/timeline4b.html

Morris, George F. "Major Benjamin Whitcomb: Ranger and Partisan Leader in the Revolution," *New Hampshire Historical Society Proceedings*, 4(June 1903): 299-320. Reprinted in *Historical New Hampshire*, 11(October 1955): 1-20.

Pemberton, Ian C. "The British Secret Service in the Champlain Valley During the Haldimand Negotiations, 1780-1783," *Vermont History* 44(1976): 129-140.

Pershing, Edgar J. "Lost Battalion of the Revolutionary War," *Pennsylvania Quarterly* 16(1928): 44-51.
Richardson, Leon B., "The Dartmouth Indians, 1800-1893," *Dartmouth Alumni Magazine* 23(June 1930).
Sherwood, Justus. "Journal," *Vermont History* 24(April 1956): 101-109.
Smith, Donald. "Green Mountain Insurgency: Transformation of New York's Forty-Year Land War," *Vermont History* 64(Fall 1996): 197-231.
Smith, Robinson V. "New Hampshire Remembers the Indians," *Historical New Hampshire* 8(1952): 36.
Sosin, Jack. "The Use of Indians in the War of the American Revolution: A Reassessment of Responsibility," *Canadian Historical Review* 46(June 1965): 101-121.
Steele, Ian K. "Surrendering Rites: Prisoners on Colonial North American Frontiers," in *Hanoverian Britain and Empire: Essays in Memory of Philip Lawson* (Woodbridge, Suffolk, U.K: The Boydell Press, 1998).
Underwood, Wynn. "Indian and Tory Raids on the Otter Valley, 1777-1782," *Vermont Quarterly* 15(October 1947): 195-221.
Vaughan, Alden T., and Daniel Richter. "Crossing the Cultural Divide: Indians and New Englanders, 1605-1763," *Proceedings of the American Antiquarian Society* 90(October 1980): 23-99.

Secondary

Allen, Robert. *His Majesty's Indian Allies.* Toronto: Dundurn Press, 1992.
Axtell, James. *The European and the Indian: Essays in the Ethnohistory of Colonial North America.* Oxford, New York: Oxford University Press, 1981.
Baker, C. Alice. *True Stories of New England Captives Carried to Canada During the Old French and Indian Wars.* New York: Garland Publishing, 1976.
Bellesiles, Michael. *Revolutionary Outlaws: Ethan Allen and the Struggle for Independence on the Early American Frontier.* Charlottesville: University Press of Virginia, 1993.
Bellico, Russell P. *Sails and Steam in the Mountains: A Maritime and Military History of Lake George and Lake Champlain.* Fleischmanns, N.Y.: Purple Mountain Press, 2001.
Bowman, Larry. *Captive Americans: Prisoners During the American Revolution.* Athens: Ohio University Press, 1976.
Calloway, Colin. *The American Revolution In Indian Country.* Cambridge, New York: Cambridge University Press, 1995.

———. *North Country Captives: Selected Narratives of Indian Captivity from Vermont and New Hampshire*. Hanover, N.H.: University Press of New England, 1992.

———, ed., *Dawnland Encounters: Indians and Europeans in Northern New England*. Hanover, N.H.: University Press of New England, 1991.

———. *The Western Abenakis of Vermont, 1600–1800*. Norman: University of Oklahoma Press, 1990.

Demos, John. *The Unredeemed Captive*. New York: Knopf, 1994.

Derounian-Stodola, Kathryn Zabelle, and James A. Levernier. *The Indian Captivity Narrative, 1550-1900*. New York: Twayne's U.S. Authors Series 622, 1993.

Devine, E.J. *Historic Caughnawaga*. Montréal: The Messenger Press, 1922.

Dexter, Franklin Bowditch. *Biographical Sketches of the Graduates of Yale College*. New York: Henry Holt and Company, 1885.

Dodge, Bertha S. *Vermont By Choice*. Shelburne, Vt.: New England Press, 1987.

Fenton, William N. *The Great Law and the Longhouse*. Norman: University of Oklahoma Press, 1998.

Ferling, John E. *Almost a Miracle: The American Victory in the War of Independence*. Oxford and New York: Oxford University Press, 2007.

Fischer, David Hackett. *Washington's Crossing*. Oxford and New York: Oxford University Press, 2004.

———. *Albion's Seed: Four British Folkways in America*. New York: Oxford University Press, 1989.

Fitch, John. *The Autobiography of John Fitch*, ed. Frank Prager. Philadelphia: American Philosophical Society, 1976.

Foster, William Henry. *Captor's Narrative: Catholic Woman and their Puritan Men on the Early American Frontier*. Ithaca: Cornell University Press, 2003.

Fraser, Jay. *Skulking for the King: A Loyalist Plot*. Erin, Ont.: Boston Mills Press, 1985.

Fryer, Mary Beacock. *King's Men: Soldier Founders of Ontario*. Toronto: Dundurn Press, 1980.

———, and William A. Smy. *Rolls of the Provincial Loyalist Corps, Canadian Command, American Revolutionary Period*. Toronto: Dundurn Press, 1981.

Gill, Charles Ignace. *Notes Historiques sur L'origine de la Famille Gill de Saint-François du Lac et Saint-Thomas de Pierreville, et Historie de Ma Propre Famille*. Montréal: E. Senécal & fils, 1887.

Graffagnino, J. Kevin. *The Shaping of Vermont: From the Wilderness to the Centennial, 1749-1877*. Rutland: Vermont Heritage Press; Bennington: Bennington Museum, 1983.

Graymont, Barbara. *The Iroquois in the American Revolution*. Syracuse: University of Syracuse Press, 1972.

Haefeli, Evan, and Kevin Sweeney, *Captors and Captives: The 1704 French and Indian Raid on Deerfield*. Amherst: University of Massachusetts Press, 2003.

Hall, Benjamin. *History of Eastern Vermont*. Albany, N.Y.: J. Munsell, 1865.

Hill, Ralph N. *Lake Champlain: Key to Liberty*. Taftsville, Vt.: Countryman Press, 1977.

Lanctot, Gustave. *Canada and the American Revolution, 1774-1783*. Toronto: George G. Harap & Co., 1967.

Lepore, Jill. *The Name of War: King Philip's War and the Origins of American Identity*. New York: Knopf, 1998.

Maier, Pauline. *American Scripture: Making the Declaration of Independence*. New York: Knopf, 1997.

———. *From Resistance to Revolution: Colonial Radicals and the Development of American Opposition to Great Britain, 1765-1776*. New York: Knopf, 1974.

Mathews, Hazel. *Frontier Spies: The British Secret Service, Northern Department, During the Revolutionary War*. Fort Myers, Fl.: Ace Press, 1971.

McCallum, James D. *Eleazar Wheelock, Founder of Dartmouth*. Hanover, N.H.: Dartmouth College Publications, 1939.

Meeks, Harold A. *Time and Change in Vermont: A Human Geography*. Chester, Ct.: Globe Pequot Press, 1986.

Metzger, Charles H. *The Prisoner in the American Revolution*. Chicago: Loyola University Press, 1971.

Montréal Branch of the United Empire Loyalist Association of Canada. *The Loyalists of Québec*. Belleville, Ont.: Mica Publishing, 1992, 1984.

Pringle, J. F. *An Index of Names in Lunenburgh: or, the Old Eastern District*, comp. Lyall Manson. Cornwall, Ont.: Stormont, Dundas and Glengarry Historical Society, 1975.

Raphael, Ray. *A People's History of the American Revolution*. New York: The New Press, 2001.

Russell, Howard S. *A Long Deep Furrow: Three Centuries of Farming in New England*. Hanover, N.H.: University Press of New England, 1976.

Sherman, Michael, ed. *A More Perfect Union: Vermont Becomes A State, 1777-1816.* Montpelier: Vermont Historical Society, Vermont Statehood Bicentennial Commission, 1991.

———, Gene Sessions, and P. Jeffrey Potash. *Freedom and Unity: A History Of Vermont.* Barre: Vermont Historical Society, 2004.

Sloan, William, MD. *Praxis Medica, The Practice of Physick.* London: 1716.

Sosin, Jack. *The Revolutionary Frontier, 1763-1783.* New York: Holt, Rinehart and Winston, 1967.

Stillwell, Lewis D. *Migrations From Vermont.* Montpelier: Vermont Historical Society, 1948.

Stone, William L. *Life of Joseph Brant-Thayendanegea.* Albany, N.Y.: J. Munsell, 1865.

Sturtevant, William C., general ed. *Handbook of North American Indians,* Vol. 15. Washington, D.C.: Smithsonian Institution, 1978.

Taylor, Alan. *The Divided Ground: Indians, Settlers and the Northern Borderland of the American Revolution.* New York: Knopf, 2006.

———. *American Colonies.* New York: Viking, 2001.

Tufts, Henry. *The Autobiography of a Criminal.* New York: Duffield and Company, 1930.

Washington, Ida, and Paul A. Washington. *Carleton's Raid.* Canaan, N. H.: Phoenix Publishing, 1977.

Watt, Gavin. *Burning of the Valleys.* Toronto: Dundurn Press, 1997.

Wessels, Tom. *Reading the Forested Landscape: A Natural History of New England.* Woodstock, Vt.: Countryman Press, 1999.

Westcott, Thompson. *The Life of John Fitch, the Inventor of the Steamboat.* Philadelphia: J. B. Lippincott & Co., 1878.

Williams, Eleazer, and Franklin Hough. *Life of Te-ho-ra-gwa-ne-gen (Thomas Williams).* Albany, N.Y.: J. Munsell, 1859.

Williamson, Chilton. *Vermont in Quandary: 1763-1825.* Montpelier: Vermont Historical Society, 1949.

Woodward, Florence M. *The Town Proprietors in Vermont: The New England Town Proprietorships in Decline.* New York: Columbia University Press, 1936.

CAST OF CHARACTERS, PEOPLE CITED IN NOTES

Allbright, Jonathan	American captive, Prison Island
Allen, Capt. Ebenezer	Commander of Fort Vengeance, Pittsford, Vermont
Allen, Ethan	War hero, major figure in Vermont politics
Allen, Ira	Major figure in Vermont politics
Anderson, Capt. Joseph	Commander of Coteau-du-Lac
Anderson, Ens. Joseph	Nephew of Joseph Anderson, one of the officers on Prison Island
Avery, John	American captive, Prison Island
Avery, George	Captured in Royalton Raid
Bayley, Gen. Jacob	Vermont militia officer, influential Newbury figure
Bedel, Col. Timothy	Continental officer at Haverhill, Newbury
Belknap, Simeon	Captured in Royalton Raid
Bonette, Joseph	American captive, Prison Island
Brannan, Abraham	American captive, Prison Island
Brown, John	American captive, Prison Island

Burnett, James	American captive, Prison Island
Butterfield, James	American captive, Prison Island
Button, Peter	Killed in Royalton Raid
Campbell, Lt. Col. John	Commandant of Indian Affairs of Québec Province
Carleton, Maj. Christopher	British regular army officer
Carswell, David	American captive, Prison Island
Charley (Grandison)	American captive, Prison Island
Chambers, Com. William	Commander of British fleet on Lake Champlain
Chase, Gen. Jonathan	Influential figure in the Upper Valley, Cornish, New Hampshire
Chittenden, Gov. Thomas	Governor of Vermont
Clark, William	American captive, Prison Island, escaped with Zadock Steele
Claus, Lt. Col. Daniel	Officer of Canada Indian Department
Clinton, Gov. George	Governor of New York
Clinton, Gen. Henry	British officer
Connor, James	British surgeon's mate in Canadian prisons
Cornwallis, Gen. Charles	Commander of British forces defeated at Yorktown, October, 1781
Crofts, Lt. Wills	Officer of Canada Indian Department at St. Francis (Odanak)
DeSpeth, Brig. Gen. Friedrich Wilhelm	Commander of the Montréal military garrison
Dow, Moses	Member of New Hampshire state government

Dundas, Col.	British officer involved in prisoner exchanges
Fitch, John	American captive, Prison Island
Fraser, Capt. Wm.	Loyalist officer from New York
Germain, Lord George	Secretary of State for the American Colonies
Gibbs, Giles	Killed in the Royalton Raid
Gilbert, Nathaniel	Captured in the Royalton Raid
Gray, Maj. James	Officer in the King's Royal Regiment of New York (KRRNY)
Haldimand, Gen. Frederick	British Commander-in-Chief, Northern Department, Governor General of Canada
Hamilton, Richard	Grenadier of the British 21st Regiment, guide of Royalton Raid
Handy, Hannah	Heroine of Royalton Raid
Hathaway, John	American captive, Prison Island, escaped with Zadock Steele
Havens, Daniel	Son of Robert Havens
Havens, Lorenza	Daughter of Robert Havens
Havens, Robert	Royalton's first settler
Hopkins, Robert	American captive, Prison Island
Hollister, Josiah	American captive, Prison Island
Houghton, Lt. Richard	British commander of Royalton Raid
Hutchinson, Abijah	Captured in Royalton Raid, escaped from Prison Island
Hutchinson, John	Captured in Royalton Raid
Jessup, Lt. Col. Ebenezer	Officer in the KRRNY

Jessup, Maj. Edward	Officer in the King's Loyal Americans Regiment
Johnson, Sir Guy	Loyalist officer, Canada Indian Department
Johnson, Lt. Col. John	Commander of the KRRNY
Johnson, Col. Thomas	American officer captured at Peacham, Vermont
Jones, William	Provost Marshal of Montréal
Kendall, Thomas	Missionary from Dartmouth to Kahnawake
Kneeland, Edward	Captured in the Royalton Raid
Kneeland, Joseph	Killed in the Royalton Raid
Knieskern, William	American captive, Prison Island
Langan, Lt. Patrick	Loyalist officer, KRRNY
Lawe, George	Commissary of Prisoners, Montréal
le Maistre, Capt. Francis	Officer of British 8th Regiment
Lyons, Lt. Robert	American captive, Prison Island
MacLean, Brig. Gen. Allan	Officer of the British 84th Regiment, Commander of Montréal military garrison
Marsh, Joseph	Political leader in Hanover, New Hampshire
Marsh, Wm.	British Secret Service agent
Mathews, Capt. Robert	Frederick Haldimand's secretary
McAllen	British officer involved in prisoner exchanges
McAlpin, Ens. James	British officer on Prison Island
McCullough, James	American captive, Prison Island

McDonell, Capt. Alexander	British officer in command at Coteau-du-Lac
McDonell, Lt. James	British officer on Prison Island
McKee, Alex	British officer in the Canada Indian Department
McMullen, James	American captive, Prison Island
McNutt, Alexander	American captive, Prison Island
Monsell, Capt. William	Officer of the British 29th Regiment
Morey, Israel	New Hampshire legislator, public figure
Moss, Sgt. Samuel	British non-com, Prison Island
Murray, Richard	Commissary of Prisoners
Nairne, Maj. John	Captain, Royal Highland Regiment
Norton, Zarah	American captive, Prison Island
Parkerson, Joseph	American captive, Prison Island
Parkhurst, Phineas	Royalton resident, wounded in raid
Parks, John	American captive, Prison Island
Patterson, Benjamin	Loyalist in British Secret Service
Pember, Thomas	Killed in Royalton Raid
Perrigo, Sgt. James	British non-com, Prison Island
Peters, John	Loyalist in British Secret Service
Philips, Talbot	Son of Sanorese, Kahnawake student at Dartmouth
Powell, Brig. Gen. Henry Watson	British Lake Champlain District commander
Powell, Jeremiah	President of the Council of Massachusetts Bay
Prentice, Lt. John	British officer on Prison Island

Pritchard, Azariah	Loyalist in British Secret Service
Ransom, George	American captive, Prison Island, escaped
Riedesel, Baron Friedrich Adolphus	Commander of German troops under contract to British King
Rix, Garner	Captured in the Royalton Raid
Safford, Capt. Jesse	Militia officer at Bethel, Vermont
Sammons, Fred	American captive, Prison Island, escaped
Schmid, Capt. Luc	French Canadians' militia
Sanorese (Philips)	Captive adopted into Kahnawake tribe
Schuyler, Gen. Philip	American officer, New York
Segar, Nathaniel	American captive, Prison Island
Sherwood, Justus	Head, British Secret Service
Simpson, John	American captive, Montréal Provost
Smyth, George	Loyalist in British Secret Service
Sprague, John	American captive, Prison Island, escaped with Zadock Steele
Stacey, John	Captive adopted into Kahnawake tribe
Stevens, Elias	Prominent Royalton citizen and one of Zadock Steele's prime informants
Stevens, Roger	Loyalist spy
St. Leger, Brig. Gen. Barry	British 34th Regiment
Stone, David	American captive, Prison Island, escaped
Stuart, John	Loyalist in British Secret Service

Twiss, Capt. William	Chief Engineer under Frederick Haldimand
Valentine, Stephen	American captive, Prison Island
Waller, David	Captured in Royalton Raid
Weare, Meshach	President of New Hampshire Council
Webster, Alexander	Commander of a militia regiment in Charlotte County, N.Y.
Wentworth, Benning	Governor of New Hampshire
Williams, Eunice	Captured in 1704 Deerfield Raid
Williams, Thomas	Also *Tehoragwanegen,* grandson of Eunice Williams
Wheelock, Eleazar	Founder of Dartmouth College
Whitcomb, Benjamin	American officer at Newbury, Vermont
Woodward, Beza	Representative of the people of the Upper Valley to the Vermont General Assembly

END NOTES

Abbreviations used in End Notes

GWPLC	George Washington Papers at the Library of Congress
HP	Haldimand Papers
KRRNY	King's Royal Regiment of New York
NHHS	New Hampshire Historical Society, Concord
PAC	Public Archives of Canada, Montréal
USNA	United States National Archives
VHS	Vermont Historical Society, Barre
VSA	Vermont State Archives, Montpelier

PREFACE

1 George Avery's narrative appears on p. 151 of *History of Royalton, Vermont*; also in Colin Calloway, *North Country Captives: Selected Narratives of Indian Captivity from Vermont and New Hampshire* (Hanover, N.H.: University Press of New England, 1992), 150; K.M. Hutchinson, *Memoir of Abijah Hutchinson, A Soldier of the Revolution* (William Alling, Printer, 1843).

2 Josiah Hollister, *A Journal of Josiah Hollister, A Soldier of the American Revolution and a Prisoner of War in Canada* (Romanzo Norton Bunn, 1928).

3 John Fitch, *The Autobiography of John Fitch*, ed. Frank Prager (American Philosophical Society, 1976); Thompson Westcott, *The Life of John Fitch: The Inventor of the Steamboat* (Philadelphia: J.B. Lippincott & Co., 1878).

4 Nathaniel Segar, *A Brief Narrative of the Captivity and Sufferings of Lt. Nathaniel Segar* (Paris, Me.: Printed at the Observer Office, and published at the Oxford Bookstore, 1825).

5 Ethan Allen, *Ethan Allen's Narrative of the Capture of Ticonderoga, his Captivity and Treatment by the British, Written by Himself* (Philadelphia, 1779).

6 Zadock Steele, *The Indian Captive; Or a Narrative of the Captivity and Sufferings of Zadock Steele, Related by Himself* (Montpelier, Vt.: 1815), 1, 44.

7 Zadock Steele Pension Application CT, VT s14571, roll # 2278, frame #1017–1085, 1820/7/4; Horace Steele to J.H. Eaton, Secretary of War, with Zadock Steele Pension Application, 1829/9/16; Zadock Steele testimony, 1832/08/15 Pension Application, all in USNA.

8 Congress enacted legislation on May 1, 1820 (3 Stat. 569). The new law required every pensioner receiving payments under the 1818 act, and every would-be pensioner, to submit a certified schedule of his estate and income to the Secretary of War. The Secretary was authorized to remove from the pension list the names of those persons who, in his opinion, were not in need of assistance. Within a few years the total of Revolutionary War service pensioners was reduced by several thousand.

9 Zadock Steele testimony 1833/11/5, Pension Application, USNA. CT, VT s14571, roll # 2278, frame #1017-1085.

10 Zadock Steele Pension Application 1820/7/4, USNA.

11 Robert John Denn, "Prison Narratives of the American Revolution" (PhD. diss., Michigan State University, 1980), 3, 121, 124.

12 Kathryn Zabelle Derounian-Stodola and James A. Levernier. *The Indian Captivity Narrative 1550–1900*. New York: Twayne's U.S. Authors Series 622, 1993.

13 There are a number of passages quoting Edward Young, an 18th-century British poet and the author of the widely known and immensely popular epic poem, "Night Thoughts."

14 The original in 1818, published by the author. *Indian Narratives* (Tracy and Brothers, Claremont, N.H.: 1854); Francis Chase, *Gathered Sketches from the Early History of New Hampshire and Vermont* (N.H.: Tracy, Kenney & Co., 1856); Iva Dunklee, *Burning of Royalton* (Boston: G.H. Ellis Co., printers, 1906); *Narrative,* republished 1908; Evelyn Lovejoy, *History of Royalton Vermont, With Family Genealogies, 1769–1911* (Burlington, Vt.: Free Press Printing Company, 1911); Mary Billings French, *Indian Captive* (Woodstock, Vt.: The Elm Tree Press, 1934); Colin Calloway, *North Country Captives* (Hanover, N.H.: University Press of New England, 1992); *Narrative,* republished 1971, 1977, 2009 (see bibliography).

PROLOGUE: BEFORE THE RAID

1 Jacob Bayley to George Washington, Jul. 15, Aug. 31, Sep. 7, Oct. 28, 1780, GWPLC.

2 For discussion of loyalists in the Northeast, see *The Loyalists of Québec,* 1989, Montréal Branch of the United Empire Loyalist Association of Canada;

Mary B. Fryer, *King's Men: Soldier Founders of Ontario* (Toronto: Dundurn Press, 1980); Hazel Mathews, *Frontier Spies: The British Secret Service, Northern Department, During the Revolutionary War* (Fort Myers, Fl.: Printed by Ace Press, 1971); P.H. Bryce, *The Quinté Loyalists of 1784* (Toronto: Ontario Historical Society, 1931); Mary Greene Nye, *Sequestrations, Confiscations and Sale of Estates* (State Papers of Vermont, State of Vermont, 1941); Thomas Lampee, "The Mississquoi Loyalists" (Proceedings of the Vermont Historical Society, June 1938); *Tyranny and Toryism Exposed*: *Two Sermons by Peter Powers at Newbury, Sep. 10, 1780* (Westminster: Spooner and Green, 1781); Jay Fraser, *Skulking for the King, A Loyalist Plot* (Erin, Ont.: Boston Mills Press, 1985).

3 Steele, *Narrative*, 1.

4 Ibid., 46.

5 Zadock Steele's Pension Applications, USNA. CT, VT File # s14571, roll # 2278, frame #1017-1085. 1776 Connecticut Line; 1777, 1778 Connecticut Militia.

6 Charles Royster, *A Revolutionary People at War: The Continental Army and American Character, 1775–1783* (Chicago: Loyola University Press, 1979), 127–128, 131; Denn, *Prison Narratives*, 40.

7 Zadock Steele's Pension Applications; "Family of Zadock Steele" in Benjamin Hubbard, *Forests and Clearings: The History of Stanstead County, Province of Québec* (Lovell Printing and Publishing, 1874), republished in: *Stanstead Historical Society Red Journal 1973*, 5: 216–217; Death of Aaron: Steele, *Narrative*, 1.

8 Ida Washington and Paul Washington, *Carleton's Raid* (Canaan, N.H.: Phoenix Publishing, 1977), 21; Colin Calloway, The *Western Abenakis of Vermont, 1600-1800: War, Migration, and the Survival of an Indian People* (Norman: University of Oklahoma Press 1990), 160, 161; Evan Haefeli and Kevin Sweeney, *Captors and Captives: The 1704 French and Indian Raid On Deerfield* (Amherst: University of Massachusetts Press, 2003), 268–69

9 Royster, *Revolutionary People at War*, 268.

10 Jack Sosin, *The Revolutionary Frontier, 1763–1783* (New York: Holt, Rinehart and Winston, 1967), 46; Lewis D. Stillwell, *Migrations from Vermont* (Montpelier: Vermont Historical Society, 1948), 90, 95.

11 Franklin B. Dexter, *Biographical Sketches of the Graduates of Yale College* (New York: Henry Holt and Company, 1885), 196; Loren P. Waldo, "An Address Delivered Before the Tolland County Historical Society" (1861), 28–36.

12 Peace negotiations had been under way since 1780, but following the British defeat at Yorktown, Virginia, in October, 1781, there were virtually no more

major engagements. The commissioners were Americans Benjamin Franklin, John Adams, and John Jay, and their British counterparts Richard Oswald and Henry Strachey. By September 1782, the terms of what was to be known as the Peace Treaty of 1783 were agreed upon by the commissioners in Paris. Mark M. Boatner, *Encyclopedia of the American Revolution* (Mechanicsburg, Pa.: Stackpole Books, 1994), 848.

13 Alan Taylor, *The Divided Ground: Indians, Settlers and the Northern Borderland of the American Revolution* (New York: Alfred A. Knopf, 2006), 3; Calloway, *Western Abenakis of Vermont*, 22.

14 Pauline Maier, *American Scripture: Making the Declaration of Independence* (New York: Alfred A. Knopf, 1997), 40.

15 Royster, *Revolutionary People at War*, 116.

16 John O. Dendy, "Frederick Haldimand and the Defence of Canada, 1778–1784" (PhD. diss., Duke University, 1972), 13, 35–43.

17 Jack Sosin, "The Use of Indians in the War of the American Revolution," *William and Mary Quarterly*, vol. XLVI, No. 2, June 1965; Bunker Hill: John Kettell Diary 17 May–October 1775, Richard Frothingham Papers 1683–1865, Massachusetts Historical Society.

18 Colin Calloway, "Algonkians in the American Revolution," in Peter Benes, ed., *Algonkians of New England: Past and Present* (Dublin Seminar For New England Folklife, Boston: Boston University,1991), 57.

19 Ibid., 58.

20 Jay Fraser, *Skulking for the King: A Loyalist Plot* (Erin, Ont.: Boston Mills Press, 1985), 15; quoting Little Abraham, May 22, 1775, *Minutes of the Albany Committee of Correspondence, 1775–1778.* 2 vols., (Albany: University of the State of New York, 1923-25).

21 Calloway, *Western Abenakis of Vermont*, 205, quoting letter from Henry Young Brown, 1775/05/16 that appears in Peter Force, ed., *American Archives*, 4th ser., 2:621.

22 Robert Allen, *His Majesty's Indian Allies* (Toronto: Dundurn Press, 1992), 49; Larry Ostola, "The Seven Nations of Canada and the American Revolution" (Masters Thesis, University of Montréal, 1989), 43, quoting Joseph Brant.

23 Barbara Graymont, *The Iroquois in the American Revolution* (Syracuse, N.Y.: University of Syracuse Press, 1972), 70–71, 103.

24 Ostola, "The Seven Nations and the American Revolution," 30.

25 E.J. Devine, S.J., *Historic Caughnawaga* (Montréal: Messenger Press, 1922), 41.

26 William C. Sturtevant, genl. ed., *Handbook of North American Indians*, vol. 15 (Washington: Smithsonian Institution, 1978), 469.

27 1778, Col. Bedel's Account of Northern Posts, Summary of Dealings With Indians, VSA; Stevens Collection Microfilm—Bedel claims 400 warriors; Joseph Hadfield, *An Englishman in America, Joseph Hadfield's Diary 1785* (Toronto: The Hunter-Rose Co., 1933), 49—Hadfield estimates a total of 1,000 in 1785; Gretchen Green, "A New People in an Age of War: The Kahnawake Iroquois 1667–1760" (PhD. diss., College of William and Mary, 1991), 285; Ostola claims a population of 700 in 1774 with 175–200 males; Green claims a population of 1,000 in the 1750s—soon to decrease with war and disease.

28 Haefeli and Sweeney, *Captors and Captives,* 14; Calloway, *Western Abenakis of Vermont,* 19.

29 Calloway, *Western Abenakis of Vermont*, 35, quoting Francis Jennings, *The Invasion of America: Indians, Colonialism, and the Cant of Conquest* (Chapel Hill: University of North Carolina Press, 1975).

30 Taylor, *Divided Ground*, 6.

31 Ostola, "The Seven Nations and the American Revolution," 62–70; Allen, *His Majesty's Indian Allies*, 54.

32 Winn L. Taplin, "The Vermont Problem in the Continental Congress and in Interstate Relations" (PhD. diss., University of Michigan, 1955), 9.

33 Stillwell, *Migrations from Vermont*, 79.

34 Michael Sherman, ed., *A More Perfect Union: Vermont Becomes A State, 1777–1816* (Montpelier: Vermont Historical Society, Vermont Statehood Bicentennial Commission, 1991), 4–7.

35 Washington and Washington, *Carleton's Raid*, 7, quoting Jean N. McIlwraith, *Sir Frederick Haldimand* (London: Oxford University Press, 1926), 208–210.

36 Frontier Line: 1778/4/3, Governor and Council of Vermont, from Wynn Underwood, "Indian and Tory Raids on the Otter Valley 1777–1782," *Vermont Quarterly* 15, no. 4, (1947): 204; Lovejoy, *History of Royalto*n, 105.

37 See a series of 1779 letters from Col. Timothy Bedel to various Continental Army officers, New Hampshire Historical Society: Bedel Papers: folder 3; Washington and Washington, *Carleton's Raid*, 10; Gustave Lanctot, *Canada and the American Revolution, 1774–1783* (Toronto: George G. Harap & Co., 1967), 182; Paul L. Stevens, "His Majesty's Savage Allies" (PhD. diss., State University of New York at Buffalo, 1984), 649; Bedel to Horatio Gates, 1779/01/13, Haverhill, New Hampshire Historical Society: Bedel Papers: folder 3.

38 Timothy Bedel to Gen. Clinton, Jan. 6, 1779, New Hampshire Historical Society, Bedel Papers: folder 3.

39 Bedel to Horatio Gates, Mar. 3, 1779, ibid.; Calloway, *Western Abenakis of Vermont*, 216.
40 Bedel to Bayley, Jan. 6, 1779, New Hampshire Historical Society: Bedel Papers: folder 3.
41 Taplin, "The Vermont Problem," 160.
42 Bayley to Washington, Jun. 3, Aug. 24, 1780, GWPLC.
43 Washington to Meshach Weare, Jul. 22, 1780, GWPLC.
44 Referring to resolves of Congress of Oct. 3 and 21, 1780, Washington to Benjamin Whitcomb, Jan. 1, 1781, GWPLC.
45 Washington to Bayley, Mar. 15, 1780, GWPLC.
46 Bayley to Washington, Aug. 24, 1780; Beza Woodward to Washington, Aug. 31, 1780, GWPLC.
47 Haldimand to Powell, 1780/09/17, HP 21,795, reel 63, p. 200; See Gavin Watt, *The Burning of the Valleys* (Toronto: Dundurn Press, 1997), 259, for a full discussion of the military rationale and effectiveness of this campaign.
48 Justus Sherwood to Powell, 1780/08/24, HP 21,741, reel 92, p. 114.
49 Maj. Carleton to Haldimand, 1779/11/14, HP 21,792, reel 61, p. 26; Fryer, *King's Men*, 1980.
50 These two men were probably John Gibson and Abner Barlow, who were in fact captured by the raiding party.
51 This could have been either a militia or continental officer: Militia Col. Thomas Johnson, (Continental), Major Ben Whitcomb or, most likely, (Continental) Col. Timothy Bedel.
52 Bayley to Washington, Newbury, Oct. 28, 1780, GWPLC.

PART I: THE RAID

1. ZADOCK

1 Bertha S. Dodge, *Vermont by Choice* (Shelburne, Vt.: New England Press, 1987).
2 Durkee Letter from William Rix to Charles Callison; Zebulon Lyon Genealogy; Lovejoy Papers in Royalton Historical Society.
3 Donald Smith, "Green Mountain Insurgency: Transformation of New York's Forty-Year Land War," *Vermont History* 64 (Fall 1996): 213; Stillwell, *Migrations from Vermont*, 71.
4 "Life of Benjamin Parkhurst," Lovejoy Papers, Ben Parkhurst folder.
5 Bayley to Washington, Oct. 25, 1780, GWPLC.

6 The route is reconstructed by examining topographical maps and by backtracking from the approximate site of the Zadock Steele cabin along the most likely route he would have followed: a streambed leading down to the Second Branch.
7 "Pember Family History," 88, 89, in Wesley and Miriam Herwig Private Collection.
8 K.M. Hutchinson, *Memoir of Abijah Hutchinson, A Soldier of the Revolution* (William Alling, Printer, 1843; reprint 1977, Garland Publishing), 9.
9 Washington and Washington, *Carleton's Raid*; Underwood, "Indian and Tory Raids."
10 In reference to the planned attack on Vermont, the British cite intelligence from Bennington that Vermonters are prepared for an attack; Haldimand to Gen. Powell, HP 21,796, reel 63, pp. 208–209; A.M. Caverly, *History of the Town of Pittsford, Vt.* (Rutland: Tuttle & Co., 1872), 164. Troops of the Continental Army had been withdrawn from Vermont this year, so it was vulnerable and could count only on its own militia for defense.
11 Jonathan Carpenter, *Jonathan Carpenter's Journal*, ed. Miriam and Wes Herwig (Randolph Center, Vt.: Greenhill Books, 1994), 76; Daniel Havens Pension Application, M805, roll 409, image 576, file S19324, USNA.
12 Petition of Zadock Steele, October 13, 1794, VSA; Manuscript Collection.
13 George Avery Pension Application, W. 23477 Blwt. 26129-160-55, USNA.
14 Lovejoy, *History of Royalton*, George Avery Narrative, 151.
15 Ibid.

2. ATTACK

1 Steele, *Narrative*, 53.
2 Lovejoy, *History of Royalton*, 63.
3 Ibid., 146.
4 Ibid., 121.
5 Edward Kneeland's statement, "The Destruction of Royalton, Oct. 16, 1780," Papers of General Jonathan Chase, New Hampshire Historical Society.
6 Description of scalping from: Josiah Priest, *Life and Adventures of Isaac Hubbell* (Albany: J. Munsell, 1841; reprint, Garland Publishing, 1977), 28.
7 Lt. Crofts says that Houghton's health is not good; Houghton had recently been disabled by a splinter of wood piercing his foot, Lt. Wills Crofts to Haldimand, 1780/10/07, HP 21,777, reel 53, p. 248; Campbell to Haldimand and Mathews, 1780/05/25, HP 21,772, reel 49, p. 205.

8 Campbell to Haldimand and Mathews, 1780/05/25, HP 21,772, p. 205; Lt. Wills Crofts to Haldimand, 1780/10/07, p. 248.

9 1783 Memorial of Lieutenant Richard Houghton to His Excellency Frederick Haldimand, *History of Royalton*, 142–143.

10 Col. W. Rogerson, *Historical Records of the 53rd (Shropshire) Regiment* (London: Simpkin, Marshall, Hamilton, Kent, & Co., 1891); Elizabeth Cometti, ed., *The American Journals of Lt. John Enys* (Syracuse: Syracuse University Press, 1976), 23; Memorial of Houghton to Haldimand, Nov. 1782, Lovejoy, *History of Royalton,* 142–143; Campbell to Haldimand, 1779/12/06, HP 21,772, reel 49, p. 178.

11 Campbell to Haldimand, 1780/01/01, HP 21,772, reel 49, p. 180.

12 On Indian dress, see James Smith, *Scoouwa: James Smith's Captivity Narrative* (Columbus: Ohio Historical Society, 1978), 28; Richard Hadden, *Hadden's Journal and Orderly Books*, Horatio Rogers, ed. (Albany: J. Munsell's Sons, 1884), 13; Hadfield, *An Englishman in America*, 62. On "Canadian" dress, see Thomas Anburey, *With Burgoyne from Québec*, ed. Sydney Jackman (Toronto: Macmillan of Canada, 1963), 157; Mathews, *Frontier Spies*, 79.

13 Lovejoy, *History of Royalton,* 119*;* Steele, *Narrative*, 7; British Secret Service Intelligence Report, St. John's, probably Jun. 20, 1779, HP 21,841, p. 135.

14 Steele, *Narrative*, 7.

15 Lovejoy, *History of Royalton*, 146.

16 The British encouraged "humane" behavior among their Indian allies, making it clear that such conduct would "ensure them the King's favor and protection." Mathews to Campbell, 1780/10/23, HP 21,773, reel 50, pp. 163b–165; Haldimand to Campbell, 1780/09/21, ibid., pp. 153b–154; Haldimand to John Johnson, 1780/05/01, HP 21,819, reel 80; Alexander Fraser to Houghton, 1779/05/27, HP 21,780, reel 54, p. 26.

17 Graymont, *Iroquois in the American Revolution,* 21, 232, referring to HP 21,760, p. 92; 21,779, p. 150; 21,774, p. 115.

18 Houghton to Mathews, 1779/06/10, HP 21,841, reel 92, p. 128; Houghton to Gen. de Riedesel, 1782/03/31, HP 21,734, reel 31, p. 317; Houghton to Campbell, 1779/06/19, HP 21,841, reel 92, p. 132.

19 Daniel Claus to Haldimand, 1780/05/15, PAC vol. 25, Claus Family Papers, Roll C1485: p. 199.

20 James Axtell, *The European and the Indian, Essays In the Ethnohistory of Colonial North America* (Oxford: Oxford University Press, 1981), 181; Taylor, *Divided Ground,* 21.

21 Taylor, *Divided Ground*, 21; Axtell, *European and the Indian,* 181; Robert Allen, *The British Indian Department and the Frontier North America, 1775–*

1830, Cat. No. R61-2-1-14, Canadian Historical Sites, No. 14 (Canadian Government Publications Centre, December 1975), 26; Captain Crawford was burned at the stake by Shawnees in 1782 in the Ohio Valley in revenge for the slaughter of 90 peaceful Indians; Isaac Hubbell's narrative describes the burning of an unidentified victim at the stake by unidentified Indians in 1776 "near the headwaters of the Hudson River, *Life and Adventures of Isaac Hubbell*, 11.

22 Lovejoy, *History of Royalton*, 129, 147.

23 Graymont, *Iroquois in the American Revolution*, 183–191.

24 Lovejoy, *History of Royalton*, 124.

25 Ibid., 128; Parkhurst Statement, George Avery Pension Application VT, NH, W. 23477 BLWt. 26129-160-55, frame start: 752, USNA.

26 John Goodrich, *Rolls of the Soldiers in the Revolutionary War 1775–1783*, VSA, Montpelier, 792.

27 Ibid.

28 Lovejoy, *History of Royalton*, 151.

3. HANNAH

1 Lovejoy, *History of Royalton*, 132: direct quote from Hannah. The ensuing scene is reconstructed from a variety of sources: Zadock Steele's 1815 interview with Hannah; oral history provided by the descendants of Hannah; the Abijah Hutchinson and Garner Rix narratives; and contemporaneous newspaper articles in: *Providence* (R.I.) *Gazette and Country Journal,* Nov. 11, 1780; *Norwich* (Ct.) *Packet and Weekly Advertiser*, Nov. 14, 1780.

2 Lovejoy, unpublished typescript, "The Burning of Royalto*n*," Lovejoy Papers, Hannah Hendee folder. The memory of the old Indian was held, as of 1911, by the descendants of Hannah's daughter, Lucretia.

3 Lovejoy, *History of Royalton*, 131. This is a quote from an interview with Hannah in 1818 and appears in Zadock Steele's *Narrative.*

4 These were probably the French Canadians. But, although there is no official record, it is not out of the question that some loyalists were attached to the raid. Oral history mentions that there were "Tories" in the raiding party.

5 Lovejoy, *History of Royalton*: 132. A direct quote from Hannah.

6 Ibid., 207.

7 Peters to Haldimand, 1778/08/11, describing how Houghton coerced an Indian war party into action during an attack on the Onion River

settlements when they did not want to proceed, HP 21,876, reel 110, p. 4; Carleton to Haldimand, 1778/11/28, HP 21,792, reel 61.

8 For a thorough discussion of the practice of taking captives and transculturation, see Axtell, *European and the Indian,* ch. 7; Haefeli and Sweeney, *Captors and Captives*; William H. Foster, *Captor's Narrative: Catholic Women and their Puritan Men on the Early American Frontier* (Ithaca, N.Y.: Cornell University Press, 2003).

9 Alden Vaughan and Daniel Richter, "Crossing the Cultural Divide: Indians and New Englanders, 1605–1763," *Proceedings of the American Antiquarian Society* 90(October 1980): 75–78.

10 Haldimand to Daniel Claus, 1780/05/04, HP 21,774, reel 51, p. 116.

11 Early draft of "The Burning of Royalton," Handy folder, section D, Lovejoy Papers, South Royalton Library.

12 Eleazer Williams and Franklin Hough, *Life of Te-ho-ra-gwa-ne-gen (Thomas Williams)* (Albany, N.Y.: J. Munsell, 1859).

13 Garner Rix narrative, Elias Stevens folder, Lovejoy papers, Royalton Historical Society.

4. GOING NORTH

1 Houghton to Haldimand, 1780/10/26, HP 21,772, reel 50, p. 249. There was no fort at Royalton, though Hamilton might have thought there was; his information was out of date. The Royalton fort had been dismantled and moved to Bethel in September in response to the small-scale raids of August and September on Barnard and Bethel. The company of militia at Royalton and its commander, Jesse Safford, had also gone to Bethel.

2 Houghton's report to General Haldimand, 1780/10/26.

3 Lovejoy, *History of Royalton*, 151, George Avery Narrative. Avery overestimates the size of the war party, which was actually 265 (Campbell to Haldimand and Mathews, 1780/10/05, HP 21,772, reel 49, p. 49). There were at least 30 captives on the night of the 16th. Avery was probably only aware of the 25 or 26 from Royalton. Five more were captured as the war party went through Randolph, but they were so spread out that Avery apparently did not know about them. By the time Houghton returned to Canada he had 32 captives.

4 Lovejoy, *History of Royalton*, George Avery Narrative, 151.

5 David Waller Pension Application, roll 2481, frames 0331-0349, VT S14.793, USNA.

6 Lovejoy, *History of Royalton*, George Avery Narrative, 151.

7 Philips and two other Dartmouth parents came to Hanover in 1772. Eleazar Wheelock, *A Continuation of the Narrative of the Indian Charity School, Begun in Lebanon, in Connecticut.* (Hartford: 1773).
8 There are several variant spellings. This is used by Stevens, "His Majesty's Savage Allies."
9 Berthold Fernow, ed., *Documents Relating to New York Colonial History,* vol. X (Albany: State Archives, 1887), 212, 214.
10 Stevens, "His Majesty's Savage Allies," 89.
11 Philips and his son mentioned in a letter to Mr. John Stacey at Kahnawake from Eleazar Wheelock, Jul. 3, 1775; Rauner/Dartmouth Manuscript Collection; Eric P. Kelly, "The Dartmouth Indians," *Dartmouth Alumni Magazine* 22 (December 1929): 123.
12 Axtell, *European and the Indian,* "Wheelock's Little Red School," 102.
13 Ibid., 9.
14 Ibid., 100, referring to James Dow McCallum, *The Letters of Eleazar Wheelock's Indians*, 287–288.
15 Ibid., 106; referring to *Continuation of the Narrative*, 11, 14.
16 Letter from John Wheelock to New Hampshire Delegate to Continental Congress, Jun. 2, 1780; Rauner/Dartmouth Manuscript Collection.
17 Wheelock to Benning Wentworth, 1774, in James Dow McCallum, *Eleazar Wheelock, Founder of Dartmouth* (Hanover, N.H.: Dartmouth College Publications, 1939), 198; Ibid., 202; Letter from John Wheelock to New Hampshire Delegate to Continental Congress, Jun. 2, 1780, Rauner/Dartmouth Manuscript Collection, #780352.
18 Haefeli and Sweeney, *Captors and Captives*, 250–264.
19 Lovejoy Papers, Royalton Historical Society, Kneeland folder. There is a family tradition that, at 56, Edward Kneeland, Sr. was weakened by illness and hard work; "The Destruction of Royalton, Oct. 16, 1780," Unpublished Papers of Jonathan Chase, NHHS: Statement of Edward Kneeland that he "interceded with Capt. Philips to be released."
20 In this Houghton might have been encouraged by Eunice Williams's grandson, Thomas. He claimed that he interceded on behalf of an old man and saved his life. Williams and Hough, *Life of Te-ho-ra-gwa-ne-gen*, 32.
21 This reconstruction of events is based largely on a written statement made by Edward Kneeland, "The Destruction of Royalton, Oct. 16, 1780," Unpublished Papers of Jonathan Chase, NHHS. See appendix for full text.
22 Herwig, ed., *Jonathan Carpenter's Journal*, 78.
23 Elias Stevens eyewitness account, Pension Application, roll 2284, frames 0157-0208 Conn. W.9314, BLWt. 6022-160-55, USNA; Lovejoy, *History of*

Royalton, 168. See also Zadock Thompson, *A Gazetteer of the State of Vermont* (Montpelier: E.P. Walton, 1824), 70, for this sequence of events. It varies in some ways from the Lovejoy version and is more detailed than the Avery and Steele versions, but also makes more sense. None of the details are attributed though, so it is hard to know what really happened.

24 Houghton to Haldimand, 1780/10/26, HP 21,772, reel 50, p. 249.

25 Lovejoy, *History of Royalton*, George Avery Narrative, 151.

26 The Zadock Steele and Hutchinson narratives, as well as contemporaneous newspaper accounts and Vermont state and town histories, all agree that a message of warning not to pursue was delivered; contemporaneous account: "Daniel Clark Diary," Daniel Clark folder, Document Box 37, VHS.

27 The contents of the Philips letter and whether it was ever delivered are unknown. Kneeland, "The Destruction of Royalton, Oct. 16, 1780," Unpublished Papers of Jonathan Chase, NHHS.

28 Houghton to Haldimand, 1780/10/26, HP 21,772, reel 50, p. 249.

29 VSA; in *Rolls of the Soldiers in the Revolutionary War, 1775–1783*, there is a bill from Dr. Laban Gates for removing the ball from Phineas Parkhurst's abdomen and for attending to Tilden, who was "hurt in night attack on Indian camp at Brookfield."

30 Steele, *Narrative*, 11.

31 *An Account of the Persons Killed at Royalton by the Indians Ye 16th October, 1780*, taken from Mr. Edward Kneeland, 164, Jonathan Chase Papers, NHHS.

32 Samuel Pember biography in *Pember Family History*.

33 Houghton's report claims four scalps. After those of Pember and Button in Royalton, the only two other possibilities are Kneeland and Gibbs. Gibbs is described in the Royalton history as having been found with a tomahawk buried in his head. Lovejoy Papers, Royalton Historical Society, Kneeland folder: A family tradition that Joseph was killed for insisting on clothes for his brother.

34 Houghton to Haldimand. 1780/10/16/; HP 21,772, reel 50, p. 249.

35 Lovejoy, *History of Royalton*, 146.

36 Herwig, ed., *Jonathan Carpenter's Journal*, 79.

5. ZADOCK TAKEN

1 Benjamin Parkhurst Pension Application, roll 1876, frame 301, VT S19421, USNA.

2 All of Zadock Steele's statements emphasize his membership in the local militia and service in the line of duty at the time of his capture. Confirming

a military record in narratives, statements, petitions, and pension applications was of the utmost importance for anyone seeking veteran's or widow's pensions under the various Pension Acts passed by Congress following the Revolution.

3 Steele, *Narrative*, 53.
4 Ibid., 51.
5 Ibid., 53.
6 William S. Rann, *History of Chittenden County* (Syracuse: D. Mason & Co., 1886), 623; *History of the Town of Johnson, Vermont 1784–1907* (Burlington: Free Press Printing Co., 1907), 5.
7 Steele, *Narrative*, 53.
8 Zadock Steele Pension Application, roll 2278, frames 1017, 1085, VT S14571, USNA.
9 Caverly, *History of the Town of Pittsford*, 170–174.
10 Steele, *Narrative*, 54.
11 Ibid.

PART II: ANOTHER WORLD

6. CAPTIVITY

1 The others were Experience Davis, John Parks, Timothy Miles, and William Evans.
2 Steele, *Narrative*, 56.
3 Watt, *The Burning of the Valleys*, 145; Haefeli and Sweeney, *Captors and Captives*, 127, 130, 135, 141.
4 Haefeli and Sweeney, *Captors and Captives*, 3, 127. However, Colin Calloway, ed., *Dawnland Encounters: Indians and Europeans in Northern New England* (Hanover, N.H.: University Press of New England, 1991), 222, states that Abenakis rarely tortured captives, as does Foster, *Captor's Narrative*, 7. On Jesuit influence opposing torture, see Anna Dill Gamble, "Col. James Smith and the Caughnawaga Indians," *Records of the American Catholic Historical Society of Philadelphia* (1938): 9; Haefeli and Sweeney, *Captors and Captives*, 134.
5 Haefeli and Sweeney, ibid., 3, 100.
6 Ibid., 125, 130.
7 Ibid., 2, 71.
8 Ibid., 135.
9 Ibid. 119, 127.

10 Colin Calloway, "An Uncertain Destiny," *Journal of American Studies* 17(1983): 189; Derounian-Stodola and Levernier, *Indian Captivity Narrative*, 1–21.

11 Haefeli and Sweeney, *Captors and Captives,* 152, 155, 161; Vaughan and Richter, "Crossing the Cultural Divide," 85.

12 The Rev. John Williams, *The Redeemed Captive Returning to Zion* (reprint, Bedford, Mass.: Applewood Books, 1993).

13 Loren P. Waldo, *The Early History of Tolland, Connecticut* (Hartford: Press of Case, Lockwood & Company, 1861), 28–36.

14 Alden T. Vaughan, *Narratives of North American Captivity, A Selective Bibliography* (New York: Garland Publishing, 1983), xv.

15 Lovejoy, *History of Royalton*, 150.

16 Calloway, "Uncertain Destiny," 198; Haefeli and Sweeney, *Captors and Captives*, 132.

17 Steele, *Narrative*, 56.

18 Lovejoy, *History of Royalton*, 179.

19 Isaac Webster, *A Narrative of the Captivity of Isaac Webster* (New York: Garland Publishing, 1978).

20 David Waller Pension Application, roll 2481, frames 0331-0349, VT S14.793, USNA.

21 Calloway, "Uncertain Destiny," 195.

22 Foster, *Captor's Narrative,* 1–20.

23 D. Peter MacLeod, Catholicism, Alliances, and Amerindian Evangelists During the Seven Years War (Paper read at Université de Québec à Montréal, June 9, 1995, Canadian Catholic Historical Association, see *Historical Studies*, 62(1996): 63-72; Calloway, ed., *Dawnland Encounters*, 16; John Long, *Voyages and Travels of An Indian Interpreter and Trader. April 10, 1768–Spring, 1782* (London: 1791).

24 Haefeli and Sweeney, *Captors and Captives*, 69.

25 Abijah Hutchinson Pension Application, Connecticut Line (Continental), S.13491, reel 1384, start frame 1, USNA; Hutchinson, *Memoir of Abijah Hutchinson*, 9.

26 This is reconstructed from the detailed description in *Memoir of Abijah Hutchinson,* 14. See also Kelly, "The Dartmouth Indians." The presence of Hutchinson's friend adds one more strand to the connections between the makeup of the war party and Dartmouth. Hutchinson, born in 1756, apprenticed 1772, enlisted in 1775, so he might have known Indian boys at Moors between 1764 and 1770, when the school moved to Hanover. There were these possibilities: Paulus, Mohawk enrolled Sep. 28, 1766; Cornelius,

Peter, Oneyadas enrolled Sep. 24, 1767; James Simons, Oneyadas, enrolled Oct. 14, 1767; Apolles, Mohawk, enrolled Oct. 29, 1767; Oneidas are less likely to have been on this war party because they were generally pro-rebel. Paulus or Paul, also called Ograshuskon, is mentioned in a Jun. 17, 1780 letter from Daniel Claus to John Johnson as providing help in translating a prayer book. PAC, vol. 25, Claus Family Papers, roll C1485, p. 219–221. Subsequent discussion on Sep. 9, 2009, with Professor Colin Calloway confirms Paul as the most likely candidate.

27 Steele, *Narrative*, 57.

28 Haefeli and Sweeney, *Captors and Captives*, 14, 21, 195; Smith, *James Smith's Captivity Narrativ*e, 60–79; Joseph Havens Pension Application, reel 1225, # R4757, start frame 428, USNA.

29 Jan Albers, *Hands on the Land* (Cambridge, Ma.: MIT Press, 2000), 42–43.

30 Wolves are mentioned by early writers and diarists: Jonathan Carpenter, *Journal*, 90; Lovejoy, *History of Royalton*, 4; Lemuel Roberts, *The Memoirs of Captain Lemuel Roberts* (1809; reprint, New York: Arno Press, 1969), 91; Wendall Wales Williams, *History of Rochester* (Montpelier: E. Ballou, Printer, 1869), 16; Stillwell, *Migrations from Vermont*, 72; Hubbard, *Forests and Clearings*, 3.

31 Fryer, *King's Men*, 125–133.

32 Ibid., 137; John Peters to Haldimand, 1778/10/24, HP 21,732, reel 29, p. 98.

7. THE LAKE

1 Capt. Chambers Journals, Returns, HP 21,802, p. 268.

2 William Monsell to Haldimand, 1780/10/22, HP 21,793, p. 338; Watt gives number of Indians under Lt. Johnson as 108 in *Burning of the Valleys*, 96.

3 Hutchinson, *Memoir of Abijah Hutchinson*, 14.

4 Haldimand to Claus, 1780/06/05, 21,774, p. 116.

5 Monsell to Mathews, 1780/10/22, HP 21,793, reel 61, p. 338.

6 Houghton to Haldimand, 1780/10/26, HP 21,772, reel 50, p. 249.

7 Number of families: petition by the inhabitants of Royalton, Vermont, manuscript collection, MsVtSP vol. 17, 36, VSA.

8 Houghton to Haldimand, 1780/10/26, HP 21,772, reel 50, p. 249

9 Haldimand to Germaine, Oct. 25, 1780, from the *London Gazette*, Jan. 6, 1781.

10 Lovejoy, *History of Royalton*, 154.

11 Thomas Kendall, "Diary of Thomas Kendall, A Missionary to the Caughnawaga from Dartmouth in 1773," Rauner/Dartmouth Manuscript Collection.

12 Claus to Johnson, Aug. 3, 1771, Papers of Sir William Johnson, vol. VIII, 209.
13 Letter to Mr. John Stacey at Caughnawaga from Eleazar Wheelock; for a description of visits by Stacey and Philips, see Wheelock, *A Continuation of the Narrative of the Indian Charity School.*
14 Kelly, "The Dartmouth Indians," 122.
15 Lovejoy, *History of Royalton*, 194.
16 Col. Timothy Bedel, "Account of Northern Posts, Summary of Dealings With Indians," Stevens Collection Microfilm—Correspondence, 1st Item, 1778, VSA; on the 108 Canada Indians under Lt. Johnson to New York see Watt, *Burning of the Valleys*, 96.
17 Smith, *James Smith's Captivity Narrative*, 21; Hubbell, *Life and Adventures of Isaac Hubbell*, 30; Rev. Charles Rockwell, *The Catskill Mountains and the Region Around* (New York: Taintor Brothers & Co., 1867), see ch. 6, "Suffering and Escapes of Prisoners—Ravages of Tories and Indians."
18 William Scudder, *The Journal of William Scudder, 1794* (New York: Garland Publishing, 1977), 46.

8. KAHNAWAKE

1 Green, "New People in an Age of War," 212, 287–289; *Journal of Warren Johnson* (William's brother) 1760–1761, William Johnson Papers, vol. 13, 194; Father Joseph François Lafitau, *Customs of the American Indians Compared With the Customs of Primitive Times*, trans. Elizabeth Moore and William Fenton (Toronto: The Champlain Society, 1977), 16–71; Scudder, *Journal of William Scudder*, 54; Calloway, ed., *Dawnland Encounters*, 248; Luigi Castiglioni, *Luigi Castiglioni's Viaggio: Travels in the United States of North America 1785–1787*, Antonio Pace, ed. and trans. (Syracuse, N.Y., Syracuse University Press, 1983), 249.
2 Green, "New People in an Age of War"; Moore and Fenton, *Customs of the American Indians,* 284.
3 Colin Calloway, *The American Revolution in Indian Country* (Cambridge: Cambridge University Press, 1995), 35, 70, 72, 80; Claus to Haldimand, 1778/11/19, HP 21,774, reel 51, p. 13; Stevens, "His Majesty's Savage Allies, ch. 10; Ostola, "The Seven Nations of Canada and the American Revolution," 131–132.
4 Père Joseph Huguet to Campbell, 1780/10/18, HP 21,772, reel 50, p. 239; Devine, *Historic Caughnawaga*, 304–308.
5 Campbell to Haldimand and Mathews, 1780/10/16, HP 21,771, reel 49, p. 237; Mathews to Claus, 1780/10/19, HP 21,774, p. 148; Campbell to

Mathews, 1781/05/28, HP 21,773, p. 40; Claus to Mathews, 21,774, reel 51, p. 150; Lanctot, *Canada and the American Revolution,* 194; Haldimand to Campbell 1780/10/19, HP 21,773, reel 50, p. 161.

6 Houghton to Campbell, 1781/05/26, HP 21,773, reel 50, p. 36; Calloway, *American Revolution in Indian Country*, citing unpublished Journal of the Compte de Charlus, *Rhode Island History* 11 (1952), 73–81; Lanctot, *Canada and the American Revolution*, 194, fn. 21, p. 312; Haldimand to Germain, Oct. 25, 1780, from the *London Gazette*, Jan. 6, 1781.

7 Devine, *Historic Caughnawaga*, 308; *Loyalists of Québec*, 23.

8 Calloway, *American Revolution in Indian Country*, 35; Ostola, "The Seven Nations of Canada and the American Revolution," 131.

9 David Blanchard, "Patterns of Tradition and Change: The Re-creation of Iroquois Culture at Kahnawake" (PhD. diss., University of Chicago, 1982), 190.

10 Steele, *Narrative*, 63.

11 Captured in 1747 at the age of 14, Philips had been given the chance to return home in 1750, at the close of King George's War (The Third Intercolonial War, 1744–1748).

12 Records of St. Francis Xavier church at Kahnawake; *Documents Relating to New York Colonial History*, vol. X, 212–214; Devine, *Historic Caughnawaga,* 244; Stevens, "His Majesty's Savage Allies," 89.

13 Steele, *Narrative*, 63.

14 Haldimand to Claus, 1780/05/05, HP 21,774, reel 51, p. 116.

15 Steele, *Narrative*, 64.

16 Devine, *Historic Caughnawaga,* 244; Benjamin Peart and Thomas Peart's Narrative in *The Narrative of the Captivity of Benjamin Gilbert and His Family,* ed. William Walton (New York: Garland Publishing, 1975); Hubbell, *Life and Adventures of Isaac Hubbell*, 31.

17 Axtell, *European and the Indian,* 182–187; Smith, *James Smith's Captivity Narrative*, 28.

18 Lovejoy, *History of Royalton*, 154.

19 Graymont, *Iroquois in the American Revolution*, 232; Calloway, "Uncertain Destiny," 194.

20 Smith, *James Smith's Captivity Narrative*, 28; Axtell, *European and the Indian*, 190.

21 Vaughan and Richter, "Crossing the Cultural Divide," 88–89.

22 Foster, *Captor's Narrative,* 10.

23 HP 21,772, reel 49, p. 49: State of pay due to the Officers, Interpreters and Others in the Indian Dept. from Jul. 1 1778 to 24th Dec. 1778.

24 Haldimand to Claus, 1780/05/04, HP 21,774, reel 51, p. 116.
25 Robert Mathews to George Lawe, 1780/12/04, HP, MS 21,843, reel 93, p. 124.
26 Lovejoy Papers, Royalton Historical Society, *White River Herald*, March 19, 1908; Roll of the 2nd Battalion of the King's Royal Regiment of New York, from J.F. Pringle, *Lunenburgh, or the Old Eastern District* (Cornwall, Ont.: Standard Print House, 1890), 369, Appendix B; Gavin Watt letter, Mar. 2, 2004; David Waller's pension application claims that both Gilbert and Edward Kneeland enlisted: roll 2481, frames 0331-0349, VT S14.793, USNA.
27 Steele, *Narrative*, 64.
28 Ibid., 65.
29 Ibid.
30 Ibid., 66.
31 Scudder, *Journal of William Scudder*; Roberts, *Memoirs of Captain Lemuel Roberts*; James Gordon, *Reminiscences of James Gordon*, Proceedings of the New York Historical Association, vol. XXIV, *New York History* 23(1936); "Journal of Thomas Johnson While A Captive," in Frederick P. Wells, *History of Newbury, Vermont* (St. Johnsbury: The Caledonian Company, 1902).
32 Return of Prisoners in and around Montréal, 1780/10/30, HP 21,843, reel 93, p. 109.
33 A unit of money worth about eight dollars at the time.
34 Steele, *Narrative*, 66.

9. WRONG RAID, WRONG PLACE, WRONG TIME

1 Haldimand to Barry St. Leger, 1780/12/31, HP 21,795, reel 63, p. 262.
2 Lanctot, *Canada and the American Revolution,* 191–194, quoting "Writings of Washington," Washington to Lafayette, May 19, 1780.
3 Marsh to Mathews, 1780/10/10, HP 21,821, reel 81, p. 142.
4 Germain to Haldimand, Mar. 17, 1780, *Documents of the American Revolution, 1770–1782, Colonial Office* (No 23, XV, p. 60); Chilton Williamson, *Vermont in Quandary* (Montpelier: Vermont Historical Society, 1949), 95.
5 Arnold to Germain, Oct. 28, 1780, LXXXV, p. 211, *Documents of the American Revolution 1770–1782, Colonial Office.*
6 Chittenden to Haldimand, 1780/09/27, HP 21,835, reel 88, p. 27.
7 Haldimand to Chittenden, Oct. 22, 1780, GWPLC.
8 *Records of Governor and Council of the State of Vermont*, vol. II, Nov. 2, 1780, p. 50; Ira Allen and Joseph Fay were to become the representatives following Ethan Allen's initial contact with Sherwood.

9 Sherwood to Henry Watson Powell, 1780/08/24, HP 21,741, reel 92, p. 114; Sherwood to Powell, 1780/08/12, HP 21,841, p. 105; Sherwood to Hawkins, 1780/08/24, HP 21,842, reel 92, p. 116.
10 Washington to Allen, Aug. 30, 1780, GWPLC; Washington to James Clinton, Jul. 9, 1781, GWPLC.
11 See Ethan Allen, *Narrative of the Capture of Ticonderoga.*
12 Mathews to Campbell 1780/10/09, HP 21,773, reel 50, p. 157; Campbell to Haldimand and Mathews, 1780/10/05, HP 21,772, reel 49, p. 223.
13 *State Papers of Vermont,* vol. III*: Journals and Proceedings of the General Assembly 1778–1781,* Oct. 21, 1780, p. 139; *Records of Governor and Council of the State of Vermont,* vol. II, Oct. 26, 1780, p. 46.
14 *State Papers of Vermont*, vol. III: *Journals and Proceedings of the General Assembly, 1778–1781*, Oct. 26, 1780, p. 140. The letters referred to here have not survived, but it is reasonable to assume that they cite the Royalton Raid since this was the only incursion on Vermont soil of the British offensive; war footing, See *Records of Governor and Council of the State of Vermont,* vol. II, 61.
15 Mathews to Houghton, 10/30/1780, HP 21,773, reel 50, pp. 163b–165.
16 Mathews to Campbell, 11/9/1780, ibid.
17 Bayley to Washington, 1780/09/07; Beza Woodward to Washington, 1780/08/31; Newbury Committee to Washington, Dec. 8, 1780, GWPLC.
18 Report of Nathan Noyes, 1779/03/04, HP 21,741, reel 92, p. 5; Wills Crofts to Haldimand, 1779/06/11, HP 21,841, reel 92, p. 130; Report from St John's, 1779/06/20, ibid., p. 135; Col. Jones on the Connecticut River, 1779/09/18, ibid., p. 173; Haldimand to Luc Schmid, 1780/10/17, HP 21,777, reel 53, p. 254.
19 Carleton to Haldimand, 11/1/1779, HP 21,792, reel 61, p. 26.
20 The first of many: Haldimand to Powell, 1780/09/17, 21,795, reel 63, p. 200.
21 Haldimand to Campbell, 1780/09/21, HP 21,773, reel 50, pp. 153b–154.
22 Haldimand to Powell, 1780/09/17, HP 21,795, reel 63, p. 200. On Indians coming from St. Francis, see Wills Crofts to Haldimand, 1780/08/10, 21,777, reel 53, p. 226, 228; Intelligence Report, St. John's, 1780/09/23, HP 21,741, reel 92, p. 130.
23 Intelligence Report from St. John's, ibid.
24 Fort Hunter Mohawks were refugees from Fort Hunter, New York, one of the villages of the Six Nations Confederacy driven north by rebels to safety and temporary quarters at Lachine, near Montréal. Watt has a count of 971 in *Burning of the Valleys,* 96.
25 Cometti, ed., *American Journals of Lt. John Enys*, 35.
26 Powell to Haldimand 1780/09/30, HP 21,793, reel 61, p. 304.

27 Carleton to Haldimand, 1780/11/24, quoting from: Brian Burns, "Carleton in the Valley, or The Year of the Burning," *Fort Ticonderoga Bulletin*, vol. 13, no. 6 (Fall 1980): 407.
28 Powell to Haldimand 1780/09/30, HP 21,793, reel 61, p. 304.
29 Campbell to Haldimand and Mathews, 1780/10/05; HP 21,772, p. 223. The date on the original reads 8/5, but this is a mistake.
30 Wills Crofts to Haldimand, 1780/10/07, HP 21,777, p. 248.
31 Powell to Haldimand 1780/10/04, 21,793, p. 308.
32 Underwood, *Indian and Tory Raids,* 198, 206; Fraser, *Skulking for the King*, 43.
33 Wells, *History of Newbury*, 91; Frederic Chase, *A History of Dartmouth College and the Town of Hanover, New Hampshire* (Brattleboro: Vermont Printing Company, 1928), 411, mentions the possibility of such an attack.
34 McCallum, *Eleazar Wheelock,* 198.
35 Fraser, *Skulking for the King*, 68. Hamilton is mentioned in many of the Royalton narratives as "a despicable villain by the name of Hamilton," or "the base Hamilton"; for Tories in war paint, see Underwood, *Indian and Tory Raids,* 198, 206; Fraser, *Skulking for the King*, 43.
36 Haldimand to Carleton, 1780/11/09, HP 21,795, reel 63, p. 238.
37 Allen to Carleton, 1780/10/29, HP 21,835, reel 88, p. 31; Allen to Alexander Webster, Oct. 29 and 31, 1780, GWPLC; Allen to Haldimand, 1780/11/04, HP 21,835, reel 88, p. 38; Allen to Carleton, 1780/11/24, ibid., p. 48.
38 *Records of Governor and Council of the State of Vermon*t, vol. II, p. 244.
39 Justus Sherwood, "Journal," *Vermont History,* 24 (April, 1956).
40 Langan to Claus, 1780/10/31, PAC vol. 25, Claus Family Papers, roll C1485, pp. 235–38; Allen to Carleton, 1780/11/24, HP 21,835, reel 88, p. 48; Carleton to Allen, Oct. 26, 1780, GWPLC.
41 Ethan Allen to Alexander Webster, Oct. 29, 1780, GWPLC; Ebenezer Allen to Jesse Safford, Oct. 30, 1780, GWPLC.
42 Haldimand to Carleton, 1780/11/09, HP 21,795, reel 63, p. 238.
43 Joseph Marsh to Washington, Nov. 3, 1780, GWPLC; Schuyler to Washington, Oct. 31, 1780, GWPLC; Washington to Schuyler, Nov. 6, 1780, GWPLC.
44 Carleton to Allen, 1780/11/15, HP 21,793, reel 61, p. 364.
45 Burgoyne to Germaine, Aug. 20, 1777, see James P. Millard, *War in the Northern Department: The British Campaign of 1777*, January 1777–June 1777, America's Historic Lakes, http://www.historiclakes.org/Timelines/timeline4b.html.
46 Washington to Schuyler, May 14, 1781, GWPLC.

PART III: THE PRISON

10. MONTRÉAL

1 Hadfield, *Englishman in America,* 51, 110; Green, *New People in an Age of War,* 298.
2 Anburey, *With Burgoyne from Québec,* 101.
3 Joseph Havens, pension application Vermont, New York, reel 1225, #R4757, frames 408-451, USNA.
4 Haldimand to Germaine, Oct. 25, 1780, from the *London Gazette*, Jan. 6, 1781.
5 David Waller Pension Application, roll 2481, frames 0331-0349, VT S14.793, USNA.
6 List of Supplies for the Indians from Sep. 25, 1780 to Jul. 1781, HP 21,770, reel 49, p. 14; Campbell to Haldimand, requisition for Indian Presents for 1781, 1779/02/01, 21,772, reel 49, p. 49.
7 Foster, *Captor's Narrative*, 2.
8 Steele, *Narrative*, 67.
9 See Returns of Prisoners, HP 21,843; *Rebel Prisoners at Québec, 1778–1783: Being a List of American Prisoners Held by the British During the Revolutionary War,* Chris McHenry, compiler (Lawrenceburg, Ind.: C. McHenry, 1981).
10 Steele, *Narrative*, 67; Samuel Blowers Pension Application, roll 0274, frames 0756-0784, NY S.12245, USNA. It is clear from a number of narratives that this was a large stone building outside the city wall, downstream a short distance from Montréal. The building does not appear on contemporaneous maps, nor does it exist today.
11 Steele, *Narrative*, 69.
12 Hollister, *Journal of Josiah Hollister,* 23. For descriptions of the building, see Rockwell, *Catskill Mountains and the Region Around,* ch. 6, p. 3.
13 For daily diet, see Steele, *Narrative*, 68; Henry Brace, "The Capture of David Abeel," *The Catskill Examiner,* 1876, article #19.
14 Kelvin Duncan, "Spruce Beer History," *Alcohol and Seniors,* http://www.agingincanada.ca/trivia.htm.
15 Larry Bowman, *Captive Americans: Prisoners During the American Revolution* (Athens: Ohio University Press, 1976), 4.
16 Steele, *Narrative*, 69; The previous winter there had been ample supplies of firewood for far fewer prisoners. Richard Murray, the Commissary of Prisoners in Montréal, contracted with woodcutters to keep the prisons well supplied in 1779–80: HP 21,843, reel 93, p. 66.
17 Rockwell, *Catskill Mountains and the Region Around.*

11. THE PROVOST

1 David Waller Pension Application, roll 2481, frames 0331-0349, VT S14.793, USNA; on Jones's marriage, see Brace, "Capture of David Abeel."
2 Bowman, *Captive Americans,* 30–31; Charles H. Metzger, *The Prisoner in the American Revolution* (Chicago: Loyola University Press, 1971), 37–38.
3 Bowman, *Captive Americans,* 4–6.
4 Metzger, *Prisoner in the American Revolution*, 7.
5 British Prisoner returns, HP 21,843, 1778–1783; McHenry, *Rebel Prisoners at Québec.*
6 Metzger, *Prisoner in the American Revolution,* 17; Bowman, *Captive Americans,* 23–25.
7 Metzger, ibid., 17, 211–213; Bowman, ibid., 24–25.
8 Bowman, ibid., 21, 48.
9 Jones to Haldimand, 1795/05/27, HP 21,843, reel 93, p. 25.
10 Jones to St. Leger, 1782/11/11, HP 21,790, reel 60, p. 104.
11 Commissary of Prisoner's Expenses, 1779/12/24, HP 21,843, reel 93, pp. 50, 130; POW expenses from Richard Murray, Commissary of Prisoners, 1780/06/24, p. 66.
12 Steele, *Narrative*, 68.
13 Brace, "Capture of David Abeel."
14 Ibid.
15 Murray's expense report, 1780/12/24, HP 21,843, p. 130.
16 Hutchinson, *Memoir of Abijah Hutchinson,* 15.
17 Abstract of Disbursements for Prisoners, 1780/12/25–1781/06/24, HP 21,843, p. 161.
18 Scudder, *The Journal of William Scudder*, p. 125.
19 *Journal of William Twiss,* May 1, 1779-Jul. 31, 1781, Public Archives of Canada, Mg23 B54.
20 Campbell to Haldimand and Mathews, 1780/12/11, HP 21,772, reel 49, p. 258; James Rogers Narrative, *Asa Fitch Papers,* 3 vols., *Oral Histories of the Mohawk Valley,* vol. 2 (Fort Campbell, Ky.: The Sleeper Co., 1997): 40.
21 Steele, *Narrative*, 69.
22 Campbell to Haldimand and Mathews, 1780/12/11, p. 258, HP 21,772, reel 49, p. 49.
23 Steele, *Narrative*, 69.
24 Royster, *Revolutionary People at War*, 60; Colonial Society of Massachusetts, *Medicine in Colonial Massachusetts, 1620–1820: a conference held 25 & 26 May 1978* (Boston: The Society; [Charlottesville]: Distributed by the University Press of Virginia, 1980), 347–382.

25 Rockwell, *Catskill Mountains and the Region Around*, ch. 6.
26 Expenses for Prisoners, 1780/06/25–1780/12/24, HP 21,843, p. 130.

12. WINTER

1 Rann, *History of Chittenden County*, 670; Anburey, *With Burgoyne from Québec*, 190.
2 Anburey, ibid., 140–144.
3 Rockwell, *Catskill Mountains and the Region Around*, ch. 6.
4 Anburey, *With Burgoyne from Québec*, 140.
5 Maj. Nairne to le Maistre, 1780/05/26, quoting Washington and Washington, *Carleton's Raid*, 65, 70.
6 James Rogers Narrative, *Asa Fitch Papers*, 2: 40.
7 General Orders/Court Martial, Announcement of Court Martial at Montréal 1781/05/28, for The Trial, HP 21,743, reel 36, pp. 79–84.
8 Watt, *Burning of the Valleys*, 241.
9 General Orders/Court Martial, HP 21,743, reel 36, pp. 79–84.
10 May 1, 1781 entry, *Journal of William Twiss.*
11 Steele, *Narrative*, 71.
12 Personal communication with Dr. Norman Selverstone, November 2004.
13 "Journal of Thomas Johnson," June 26, 1781 entry, in Wells, *History of Newbury.*
14 Steele, *Narrative*, 72.
15 James Rogers, "His Capture, Imprisonment," *Asa Fitch Papers*, 2: 40; Yarnes and Carswell Narratives, *Asa Fitch Papers*, vol. 2, 76.
16 Steele, *Narrative*, 72.
17 Ibid.
18 Royster, *Revolutionary People at War*, 79.
19 Personal communication with Gavin Watt, March 2, 2004.
20 General Orders/Court Martial, HP 21,743, reel 36, pp. 79–84.
21 At least one of them, Peter Sharp, survived 1,000 lashes and turned up at home in Hebron, New York, after the war: *Asa Fitch Papers*, 2: 108.

13. EXCHANGE 1781

1 Petition from Ephenetus White and Daniel Rumsey, 1781/07/16, HP 21,843, reel 93, p. 166; Metzger, *Prisoner in the American Revolution*, 17, 18, 211.
2 Metzger, ibid, 17; Bowman, *Captive Americans*, 25.

3 Metzger, ibid., 209, 213, 219.
4 *Asa Fitch Papers*, 2: 76, 176; William Fraser to Mathews, 1781/07/26, HP 21,734, reel 31, p. 76.
5 Mathews (for Haldimand) to Alan MacLean, 1781/07/16, HP 21,791, reel 60, p. 146; also PAC B 131, p. 164.
6 Ira Allen to Haldimand, 1781/05/06, HP 21,835, reel 88, p. 62.
7 Col. Dundas to Ira Allen, 1781/05/21, ibid., p. 70.
8 Samuel Blowers, Abna Boileau (Abner Barlow), Charles Brown, William Evans, Joseph Griffen, and John Gifford all appeared once on POW returns for October 1780, then never again. The boys: Garner Rix had been taken in by a private family; Edward Kneeland was with the Indians, or was a British re-enlistee; David Waller was with a man named John Beach; Nathaniel Gilbert had enlisted; Adan Durkee had probably died by now, unless he was still with the Indians; according to the town history, he died in jail. Ephraim Downer may have died or may still have been with the Indians; the town history simply says he remained in Canada.
9 Return of British Prisoners Exchanged, 1781/09/19 HP 21,836, reel 88, pp. 228–232.
10 Mathews, internal report, 1781/09/19, HP 21,792, reel 61, p. 167; Dundas to Mathews, 1781/09/24, HP 21,836, reel 88, p. 232.
11 Mathews to Justus Sherwood, 1781/11/15, HP 21,839, p. 153.
12 Vermont State Archives; Nye Index, 1781/09/30, series: A-274; vol. 1; record ID: 5175, p. 481.
13 Haldimand to George Smyth, 1781/11/26, HP 21,839, p. 157; Azariah Pritchard to unnamed correspondent, 1781/08/17, HP 21,836, reel 88, p. 187; Thomas Johnson to Haldimand, 1781/10/04, HP 21,835, p. 111. On plot to kidnap Bayley, see Wells, *History of Newbury*, letter from Moses Dow to Meshech Weare, June 6, 1782; Pritchard to Mathews, 10/21/81, HP 21,821, reel 81, p. 305; Sherwood to Henry Watson Powell, 1780/08/24, HP 21,842, p. 114. On political rivalry, see Williamson, *Vermont in Quandary*, 79.
14 Mathews to Sherwood, 1781/11/15, HP 21,839, p. 153.
15 John Stuart to Haldimand, 1781/10/10, HP 21,836, reel 88, p. 249.
16 Pritchard to Mathews, 1781/10/21, HP 21,821, reel 81, p. 305; Benjamin Patterson's instructions for gathering intelligence: HP 21,836, reel 88, p. 259.
17 Sosin, *Revolutionary Frontier*, 131–134; Ray Raphael, *A People's History of the American Revolution* (New York: The New Press, 2001), 205.

PART IV: THE RIVER

14. PRISON ISLAND

1 Royalton men: Samuel Pember, Peter Mason, Prince Haskell, Abraham Weldon, Joseph Rowley, Timothy Miles, Daniel Downer, Sr., Joseph Havens, Cotton Evans, Elias Curtis, John Kent, Experience Davis, John Hutchinson, Silas Cleveland, Jonathan Brown, Moses Parsons.
2 Cometti, ed., *American Journals of Lt. John Enys*, 94.
3 DeSpeth to Haldimand, 1781/10/16, HP 21,789, reel 59. p. 271; George Lawe to Mathews, 1781/10/15, HP 21,843, reel 93; Return of Rebel Prisoners, 1781/11/01, HP 21,843, reel 93, p. 279.
4 Steele, *Narrative*, 72.
5 George C. Ingram, *A Narrative History of the Fort at Coteau-du-Lac*, Manuscript Report Series: No. 186 (Ottawa: Parks Canada, 1977), vol. I: 5.
6 Ibid.
7 Hector Besner, personal communication, Jan. 16, 2005.
8 National Historic Parks of Canada; "The Fort at Coteau-du-Lac," Manuscript Report #186, vol. II, "Plan de l'Isle Prison," 130.
9 Steele, *Narrative*, 73.
10 See British Prisoner of War Returns. HP 21,843, reel 93, p. 227.
11 George C. Ingram and William D. Folan, *The Fort at Coteau-du-Lac: Structures and Other Features*, Manuscript Report Series: No. 186 (Ottawa: Parks Canada, 1977), vol. II: 101-246, Prison Island sections.
12 Lawe to DeSpeth 1781/10/15, HP 21,843, p. 71.
13 War Office 17/1575, Monthly Returns 1781/10/01, KRRNY.
14 Capt. Joseph Anderson, Capt. Archibald McDonell, Lts. John Prentice, Richard Lipscomb, John Munro.
15 Mary B. Fryer and William A. Smy, *Rolls of the Provincial Loyalist Corps, Canadian Command, American Revolutionary Period* (Toronto: Dundurn Press, 1981), 24; Captain Joseph Anderson and his brother, Samuel, held land, now confiscated, in Pownal, Vermont.
16 Various letters, PAC 1782/06/12–1783/12/24, War Office 28/5 (6), microfilm reel B-2863, 2864, pp. 57–102.
17 Hollister, *Journal of Josiah Hollister*, 27. This is possibly Charles Grandison, a Negro captured at Fort George in 1779. Intelligence from St. John's, 1779/09/13, HP 21,841, reel 92, p. 170.
18 Mathews (for Haldimand) to DeSpeth, 1781/11/05, HP 21,791, reel 60, p. 185.
19 Joseph Anderson to James Gray, 1781/10/30, HP 21,789, reel 59, p. 279.

20 Twiss to Haldimand, in Ingram and Folan, *Fort at Coteau-du-Lac: Structures and Other Features*, vol. II: 101-246, Prison Island sections.
21 Mathews (for Haldimand) to DeSpeth, 1781/11/05, HP 21,791, p. 185; Mathews (for Haldimand) to DeSpeth, 1781/11/15, ibid., p. 191.
22 Steele, *Narrative*, p. 74.
23 James Rogers Narrative, "His Capture, Imprisonment," *Asa Fitch Papers*, 2: 40; "David Carswell Story," ibid., 3: 51.
24 Smyth to Mathews, 1781/12/12, HP 21,836, reel 88, p. 203: "Snow is 3' deep on the level" in northern Vermont.
25 Pritchard to Matthews, 1781/10/21, HP 21,821, p. 305.
26 Williamson, *Vermont in Quandary*, 109.
27 Ibid., 116.
28 Lanctot, *Canada and the American Revolution*, 205.

15. McDONELL, ANDERSON AND McALPIN

1 Steele, *Narrative*, 74.
2 Ibid., 75.
3 Ibid.
4 Ibid., 76.
5 Ibid., 77.
6 Ernest Cruikshank and Gavin Watt, *The History and Muster Roll of the King's Royal Regiment of New York* (Campbellville, Ont.: Global Heritage Press, 2006), 270.
7 Fraser, *Skulking for the King*, 12.
8 The Steele narrative is at odds with British military records. He never mentions John Prentice, and remembers McDonell as being in command on the island during the early winter. British "Returns of Officers" show James McDonell at Coteau-du-Lac for only the month of October 1781. John Prentice is named as the ensign-in-command at Coteau for the month of November 1781. Though not named specifically, he is probably the ensign listed in service at Coteau-du-Lac for December. By the first of January 1782, two ensigns are listed for Coteau-du-Lac, presumably Prentice and a new addition, James McAlpin. PAC War Office 17/1576, Monthly Returns 1780–82, KRRNY.
9 Richard Dorrough and Heritage Hunters of Saratoga County, Saratoga NYGenWeb Project Saratoga County, New York. http://saratoganygenweb.com/mcalpin.htm
10 John Johnson to Haldimand, 1780/07/22, HP 21,818, reel 79, p. 165.
11 Haldimand to Johnson, 1780/07/27, HP 21,819, reel 80, p. 115.

12 Steele, *Narrative*, 78.
13 National Historic Parks Of Canada, Manuscript Report #186, Prison Island section.
14 Jacob Bitely Narrative in *Asa Fitch Papers*, 2: 69.
15 Letter from Richard Murray to Mathews, 1782/06/27, HP 21,843, reel 93, p. 270.
16 Dorrough and Heritage Hunters of Saratoga County, http://saratoganygenweb.com/mcalpin.htm.
17 For January–March, British returns list two ensigns at Coteau-du-Lac, but do not indicate whether one or both were on Prison Island. Both Steele and Hollister mention only one.
18 On drunkenness, see Gray to Richard Lernoult, 1782/06/12, WO 28/5, p. 81.
19 Steele, *Narrative*, 79.
20 Ibid., 80.
21 Ibid.
22 Ibid.
23 Hollister, *Journal of Josiah Hollister*, 27.
24 Steele, *Narrative*, 80.
25 On investigating McAlpin, see Gray to Lernoult, 1782/06/24, WO 28/5 (6), microfilm reel B-2863, 2864 PAC, p. 81.
26 Hollister, *Journal of Josiah Hollister*, 26.
27 David Carswell Narrative, *Asa Fitch Papers*, 3: 51.
28 Hollister, *Journal of Josiah Hollister*, 26.
29 Ibid.; Return of Prisoners, HP 21,843, reel 93, p. 295.
30 Hollister, *Journal of Josiah Hollister*, 27.
31 Steele, *Narrative*, 84.
32 Hollister, *Journal of Josiah Hollister*, 27.
33 Gray to Lernoult, 1782/06/24, WO 28/5 (6), microfilm reel B-2863, 2864 PAC, p. 81.
34 Steele, *Narrative*, 85.
35 Hollister, *Journal of Josiah Hollister*, 27.
36 Timothy Duerden, *A History of Delaware County, New York: A Catskill Land and Its People, 1797–2007*, "Freegift Patchen Narrative" (Fleischmanns, N.Y.: Purple Mountain Press, 2007).
37 On the investigation of the charges against McAlpin, see Gray to Lernoult, 1782/06/24, War Office 28/5 (6), microfilm reel B-2863, 2864 PAC, 81.
38 Ibid.
39 Cruikshank and Watt, *History and Muster Roll of the King's Royal Regiment of New York*, 287.

40 *Québec Gazette*, Aug. 30 and Nov. 15, 1781.
41 Hollister, *Journal of Josiah Hollister*, 28.
42 Steele, *Narrative*, 89.
43 Gray to Mathews, 1782/08/05, War Office 28/5 (6), microfilm reel B-2863, 2864 PAC, 90. Ens. Joseph Anderson is referred to in this letter as being stationed along with Lt. William Coffin at Coteau-du-Lac, and it is very likely he had been there for some time.
44 Davies, *Documents of the American Revolution, Colonial Office*; The Earl of Shelburne (Home Secretary) to Haldimand, 1782/04/22, 219.
45 Bowman, *Captive Americans,* 114.
46 Mathews, 1782/05/16, 1782/05/20, 1782/07/22, HP 21,843, reel 93, pp. 238, 240, 278.

16. NEW ARRIVALS

1 Hollister, *Journal of Josiah Hollister*, 28.
2 Steele, *Narrative*, 90.
3 Westcott, *Life of John Fitch,* ch. 7.
4 Murray to Mathews, 1782/05/16, HP 21,843, reel 93, p. 238. The letter refers to three Vermont prisoners at Coteau-du-Lac and three in Montréal, but does not name them. The letter also refers to a return from Lawe of Dec. 1782, but no such return exists in HP. Sam Blowers was released from Prison Island on May 10, 1782. He was from New York and captured at Fort Ann on Oct. 10, 1780, but was listed on one British return as captured on the White River. This mistake could have gone uncorrected and he may have been taking advantage of it to pass for a Vermonter. It is known that some did.
5 Mathews to Murray, 1782/05/13, ibid., p. 236.
6 That this is the same number as those released in late 1781 is coincidental. These are different lists. There are in fact more than 14—according to prisoner returns, there are 21. Mathews to Murray, 1782/05/16–20, ibid., pp. 24, 242, 244: The letter refers to this list, but it is not attached and is presumed lost.
7 John Fitch's experience on Prison Island is reconstructed from a biography and an autobiography: Westcott, *Life of John Fitch;* Fitch, *Autobiography of John Fitch.*
8 Guy Johnson to Alex McKee, 1780/08/12, PAC vol. 25, Claus Family Papers, roll C1485, pp. 225–227.
9 Sosin, *Revolutionary Frontier*, 136.
10 Allen, *British Indian Department and Frontier North America*, 26; Fryer, *King's Men,* 117.

11 The friction between Fitch and his fellow captives from Pennsylvania, Parkerson and Hopkins, is apparent throughout the two books about Fitch. They resented his prescient caution while on the river before capture. They resented the way in which his skills ingratiated him with both Indian captors and the British. They spread rumors about him as a Tory sympathizer and a collaborator on Prison Island. See Westcott, *Life of John Fitch;* Fitch, *Autobiography of John Fitch.*

12 Grandfather clocks with wooden gears were not uncommon at this time. See Dodge, *Vermont by Choice*, 64.

13 Segar, *Captivity and Sufferings of Lt. Nathaniel Segar*, 35.

14 Steele, *Narrative*, 90.

15 Letter from Mathews to Murray about prisoner exchange, 1782/06/21, HP 21,843, reel 93, p. 260.

16 Westcott, *Life of John Fitch*, ch. 7.

17 Ibid.

18 Ibid., 93.

19 Steele, *Narrative*, 91.

20 DeSpeth to Haldimand, 1782/06/10, 1782/06/17 HP 21,790, reel 60, pp. 10, 14.

21 DeSpeth to Haldimand, 1782/06/17, ibid., p. 14. According to the correspondence between DeSpeth and Haldimand's office, the five escapees were Coyle, Watson, Worthington, Gates and an unnamed man, possibly Allbright. Although Allbright was not named by DeSpeth, Hollister's narrative names him as the man beaten by McAlpin and examined by Connor. Gray's Jun. 24, 1782, letter to Lernoult refers to the "three rebel prisoners taken last," who could only have been the three mentioned in DeSpeth's Jun. 17 letter to Haldimand and who were the ones who made the accusation against McAlpin.

22 Hollister, *Journal of Josiah Hollister*, 27.

23 Gray to Lernoult, 1782/06/24, PAC, WO 28/5 (6), microfilm reel B-2863, 2864, p. 81.

24 Ibid.

25 General Orders, HP 21,743, reel 36, pp. 195–197.

17. SUMMER OF DISCONTENT

1 War Office 17/1576 Monthly Returns 1782; KRRNY, 1782/07/01.

2 Wearing a sprig of green in the hatband was originally one of the customs of the Green Mountain Boys of Vermont—an insult to the British in general, and to New York Tories in particular. The gesture had become one

of defiance toward Great Britain. See Ezra Swain, New York Pension, series M805, roll 784.

3 Hollister, *Journal of Josiah Hollister*, 28.
4 Section 15, Article 23 of the 1778 Articles of War.
5 The verdict of the court martial: 1792/07/29, HP 21,743, reel 36, p. 100.
6 Steele, *Narrative*, 89.
7 DeSpeth to Haldimand, 1782/07/15, HP 21,790, reel 60, p. 25.
8 Mathias Fisher Pension, Nov. 20, 1832, series: M805, file: S22239, roll: 322, image: 488, USNA.
9 Claus to Mathews, 1782/07/18, PAC vol. 25, Claus Family Papers, roll C1485, pp. 281–283.
10 Ibid., 276; Houghton to Riedesel, 1782/04/20, HP 21,797, reel 65, p. 86.
11 Steele, Narrative, 91.
12 *Mathias Fisher Narrative.* http://www.pa-roots.com/~Westmoreland/ffolder/fisher.htm. Fisher was a member of the Lochry Battalion.
13 Steele, *Narrative*, 92.
14 DeSpeth to Haldimand, relaying Anderson's report, 1782/08/22, HP 21,790, reel 60, p. 50.
15 Steele, *Narrative*, 93.

18. THE PLAN

1 Steele, *Narrative*, 94.
2 This is an educated guess. Hollister mentions John Bunnell, but there is no John Bunnell in British returns. It is quite possible that Hollister means Joseph Bonnett. He was captured at Fort Ann, had gone to the Montréal Prevost, then to Prison Island, and by the time of transfer to Prison Island was probably well known to this group of men, and was likely to have bunked in with them.
3 Zarah Norton Pension Application, roll 1830, frames 1171-end of reel, VT W.1889/ BLWt26649-160-55, USNA. Thomas Hunter, Nahum Powers, and Nathaniel Martin were captured in Corinth only a few days earlier. There were several scouts out in northern Vermont at the time looking for captives. HP 21,836, reel 88, p. 180.
4 Burnett is mentioned in Hollister's narrative.
5 Hollister, *Journal of Josiah Hollister*, 29.
6 Steele, *Narrative*, 95.
7 Ibid.
8 The Steele narrative says there were clay pits under the barracks.
9 Steele, *Narrative*, 96.

10 Ibid.
11 Ibid.
12 Ibid.
13 Hutchinson, *Memoir of Abijah Hutchinson*, 15–16
14 Hollister, *Journal of Josiah Hollister*, 29.
15 Ibid., 31. Everet Van Epps (listed as "Vinaps" in British returns) was captured in the Mohawk Valley on Oct. 24, 1781, and is listed at Coteau-du-Lac as of Jul. 22, 1782: HP 21,843, reel 93, p. 281.
16 DeSpeth to Haldimand, 1782/09/05, HP 21,790, reel 60, p. 62.
17 Ibid.
18 Knieskern's escape was successful and he survived to reach his home in New York State. William E. Roscoe, *History of Schoharie County* (Syracuse, N.Y.: D. Mason & Co., 1882), Chapter XV, "History of the Town of Sharon." Knieskern was captured in New York State on Oct. 24, 1781, HP 21,843, reel 93, p. 279.
19 Hollister, *Journal of Josiah Hollister*, p. 32. McNutt was captured at Fort Ann on Oct. 10, 1780, HP 21,843 reel 93, p. 279.
20 Mathews (for Haldimand) to DeSpeth, 1782/09/02, 21,791, reel 60, p. 239; DeSpeth to Haldimand, HP 21,790, reel 60, p. 68.
21 Steele, *Narrative*, 98.
22 Brannan (Branning in British returns) is mentioned by name in Hollister's narrative.

19. RAIN

1 Steele, *Narrative*, 97.
2 Ibid., 98.
3 Ibid.
4 Ibid.
5 Ibid.
6 Ibid., 100.
7 Ibid.
8 Ibid.
9 Ibid.
10 Hutchinson, *Memoir of Abijah Hutchinson*, 16.
11 Ibid.
12 Steele, *Narrative*, 101.
13 Ibid., 102.
14 Ibid.

PART V: GONE

20. THE ESCAPE

1 Hollister, *Journal of Josiah Hollister*, 31.
2 Steele, *Narrative*, 103.
3 Hollister, *Journal of Josiah Hollister*, 32.
4 Hollister says it took two hours for the 19 men to leave.
5 Steele, *Narrative*, 104.
6 Ibid.
7 Hollister, *Journal of Josiah Hollister*, 31.
8 Ibid.
9 Abijah Hutchinson's *Narrative* says they split into groups of three, but there were several groups of four, making four groups of four and one of three the most likely.
10 Steele, *Narrative*, 104.
11 Hollister, *Journal of Josiah Hollister*, 31.
12 The phase of the moon for this date was between a new and a quarter moon.
13 Steele, *Narrative*, 105.
14 Hutchinson, *Memoir of Abijah Hutchinson*, 16.
15 Steele, *Narrative*, 105.
16 William Twiss's journal confirms bad weather from the 12th to the end of the month; Haldimand to Riedesel, 1782/09/12, HP 21,799, reel 67, p. 323.
17 Steele, *Narrative*, 106.
18 Hollister, *Journal of Josiah Hollister*, 32.
19 Ibid., 33.
20 Ibid.

21. ZADOCK AT LARGE

1 Steele, *Narrative*, 106.
2 DeSpeth to Haldimand, 1782/09/16, HP 21,790, reel 60, p. 70.
3 Hollister, *Journal of Josiah Hollister*, 31. Four caught confirmed: DeSpeth to Haldimand, 1782/09/16, HP 21,790, reel 60, p. 70.
4 DeSpeth to Haldimand, 1782/07/15, ibid., p. 25.
5 Mathews to DeSpeth, 1782/09/19, HP 21,791, reel 60, p. 247.
6 Steele, *Narrative*, 108.
7 DeSpeth to Haldimand, 1782/09/24, HP 21,790, reel 60, p. 79.

8 Steele, *Narrative*, 108.
9 Ibid., 109.
10 Ibid., 111.

22. HUTCHINSON

1 Hutchinson's narrative says 18 reached the shore together with him, but both Zadock's narrative and British returns say there were 19 altogether. There were four in Zadock's party, and another party of four was caught in the water, leaving Hutchinson with 11, not 18.
2 This scenario is based on the logical supposition that anyone planning such a hazardous escape would know that he might be faced with the necessity of leaving an ill or injured man behind so that the others could survive.
3 Hutchinson, *Memoir of Abijah Hutchinson*, 18.

23. ZADOCK IN THE WOODS

1 Roger Stevens to Mathews, 1782/10/15, HP 21,821, p. 414; See Mathews, *Frontier Spies*, 97, for more personal information on Roger Stevens, a loyalist Vermonter in the British Secret Service: He was a braggart, careless, unreliable.
2 Mathews (for Haldimand) to DeSpeth, 1782/09/12, HP 21,791, p. 244.
3 Houghton to Riedesel, 1782/04/20, HP 21,797, reel 65, p. 86.
4 Steele, *Narrative*, 114.
5 Statement that he will be in residence for the winter here. Sherwood to Mathews, 1782/09/06, HP 21,837, reel 89, p. 331.
6 Riedesel to Haldimand, 1782/09/16, HP 21,797, reel 65, p. 25; Smyth to Mathews, 1782/09/07, HP 21,837, reel 89, p. 333; William Chambers to Mathews, 1782/09/08, HP 21,802, reel 69, p. 267.
7 Steele, *Narrative*, 115.
8 Ibid., 116.
9 October Return of Prisoners, HP 21,843, reel 93, p. 295.
10 Hadden, *Hadden's Journal*, entry for Jun. 20, 1777, 56.
11 Riedesel tô Haldimand, HP 21,797, reel 65, pp. 80, 84, 94.
12 Names of the prisoners, clearly identified as escapees from Prison Island, are not given in British records. Chambers to Mathews, 1782/05/08, HP 21,802, reel 69, p. 185.
13 Steele, *Narrative*, 117.

14 This vessel could be any one of: *Royal George, Inflexible,* Chambers to Mathews, 1782/10/03, HP 21,802, reel 69, p. 276; *The Maria*, Riedesel to Haldimand, 1782/09/26, HP 21,797, reel 65, p. 284; *Carleton, Trumbull, Lee,* or *Washington*, Chambers to Mathews, 1782/04/19, HP 21,802, reel 69, p. 165.
15 Steele, *Narrative*, 117.

24. VERMONT

1 Caverly, *History of the Town of Pittsford*, 170, 175.
2 Lt. McAllen to Chambers, 1782/08/24, HP 21,802, reel 69, p. 258.
3 Roger Stevens to Mathews, 1782/10/15, HP 21,821, reel 81, p. 414.
4 Underwood, *Indian and Tory Raids,* 210; Mathews, *Frontier Spies*, 96–97.
5 Steele, *Narrative*, 118.
6 Rann, *History of Chittenden County*, 394.
7 Spikenard, related to the ginseng family, has a root more notable for its aromatic, spicy flavor than for nourishment. *Encyclopedia Britannica.*
8 Steele, *Narrative*, 119.
9 Letter from Sherwood, 1782/08/27, HP 21,837, reel 89, p. 328; Chambers to Mathews, 1782/11/09, HP 21,802, reel 69, p. 286; Return of Men on the Lakes, HP 21,805, reel 71, p. 90.
10 Riedesel to Haldimand, 1782/09/16, HP 21,797, reel 65; Chambers to Mathews, 1782/09/08, HP 21,802, reel 69, p. 267.
11 If Zadock passed through these townships, he was very close to the highest crest of the Green Mountains, but probably never crossed to the east slope.
12 Steele, *Narrative*, 122.
13 Ibid., 123. Psalm 107, King James Bible.

25. FOUND

1 Steele, *Narrative*, 123.
2 Ibid., 125.
3 Ibid., 127.
4 Caverly, *History of the Town of Pittsford*, 151; Mathews, *Frontier Spies*, 123.
5 Caverly, ibid., 170.
6 Chambers to Mathews, 1782/10/03, HP 21,802, reel 69, p. 276; Jessup to Riedesel, 1782/07/28, HP 21,797, reel 65, p. 204; Stevens to Mathews, 1782/10/15, HP 21,821, reel 81, p. 414.
7 Steele, *Narrative*, 127.

8 Isaac Webster and Silas Canfield in 1779 and Jacob Sammons in 1780.
9 James Butterfield Pension Application, MA, NH, & NY S44351, USNA.
10 They were Mathias Fisher, Ezekiel Lewis, Samuel Murphy, James Dougherty, and George Bailey. Mathias Fisher Pension Application, series M805, roll 322, image 488, file S22239, USNA.
11 This figure comes from analysis of pension applications, journals and diaries, British military correspondence, and prisoner returns.
12 See the *Diary of Isaac Anderson*, unpublished manuscript, Cincinnati Historical Society; for Anthony Abeel's experiences, see Rockwell, *Catskill Mountains and the Region Around,* ch. 5, "Suffering and Escapes Of Prisoners—Ravages of Tories and Indians."
13 Steele, *Narrative*, 127.
14 Ibid., 129.
15 Riedesel to Haldimand, 1782/08/31, HP 21,797, reel 65, p. 242; Instructions from Riedesel to John Nairne, 1782/10/31, ibid., p. 314; Haldimand to Riedesel, 1782/09/30, ibid., reel 67, p. 329.
16 Bayley to Washington, Sep. 19, 1782, in Wells, *History of Newbury*, 401; Moses Dow to Meshech Weare, Jun. 16, 1782, ibid; Bayley to Washington, Aug. 19, 1782, Johnson Family Papers, VHS, folder 574:20.
17 Washington seriously considered an invasion of Canada in May 1782, but abandoned it when Parliament decided to seek a peace. See Lanctot, *Canada and the American Revolution*, 207.
18 Oct. 7 Letter from New Jersey in the *New York Gazetteer*, Oct. 21, 1782, 3.
19 See *A Chorographical Map of the Province of New York in North America,* by Claude Joseph Sauthier, 1779, Library of Congress Geography and Map Division, Call Number G3800 1779.S2 Vault.
20 Steele, *Narrative*, 129.
21 Ibid., 130.
22 William M. Newton, *Richard Newton of Sudbury, Massachusetts, 1638–9: Also An Account of the Indian Raid in Barnard, Vermont, August 9, 1780* (Compiled for private distribution by William M. Newton. [Woonsocket, R.I.: W. M. Newton & Son], 1912), 39.
23 Allan Everest, "Early Roads and Taverns in the Champlain Valley," *Vermont History* 37(Autumn1969): 247.
24 Steele, *Narrative*, 131.
25 Ibid., 132. Luke: 15, King James Bible.

26. BACK AT PRISON ISLAND

1 Hollister, *Journal of Josiah Hollister*, 35.
2 Mathews to DeSpeth, 1782/10/10, HP 21,791, reel 60, p. 253.
3 Names of Prisoners to be Sent to Québec for Exchange, Oct. 1782, HP 21,843, roll 93, p. 295.
4 Hollister, *Journal of Josiah Hollister*, 35.
5 Haldimand to Capt. Tongue, master of the cartel ship, *Baker and Atley*, 1782/11/11, HP 21,803, reel 70, pp. 323–24.
6 Hollister, *Journal of Josiah Hollister*, 37.
7 Return of Prisoners for Exchange, Québec, Oct. 1782, HP 21,843, roll 93, p. 295.
8 Bowman, *Captive Americans*, 22–23; Metzger, *Prisoner in the American Revolution*, 16; quote, 296.
9 On Hancock, see David Hackett Fischer, *Washington's Crossing* (Oxford: Oxford University Press, 2004), 369. Hollister was in the 1775 Invasion of Canada and siege of St. John's: Hollister's Pension Application, series M805, roll 437, image 223, file R5158, USNA. Hutchinson served at Bunker Hill and later on privateers: Abijah Hutchinson, Military Service Records, in Henry P. Johnston, *Record of Conn. Men of the Military and Naval Service During the Revolutionary War* (Hartford: 1886).
10 Steele, *Narrative*, 135.
11 The Petition of Zadock Steele, Oct. 13, 1794, Montpelier: VSA, Manuscript Collection.
12 Steele, *Narrative*, 137.

PART VI: AFTER THE WAR

27. THE CAPTIVES

1 Return of Prisoners Forwarded from Ticonderoga to Their Respective States, 1783/07/10, HP 21,843, reel 93, p. 329.
2 Dr. Warren Vincent Sprague, *Sprague Families in America* (Rutland, Vt.: The Tuttle Company, 1913); Stephen Whitney Phoenix, *The Whitney Family of Connecticut* (New York: Private Printing [Bradford press], 1878), 103.
3 Steele, *Narrative*, 137.
4 Ibid., 140.
5 Calloway, ed., *Dawnland Encounters*, 22; Calloway, "Uncertain Destiny," 201–202, 209.

6 Steele, *Narrative*, 140.
7 Calloway, "Uncertain Destiny," 209.
8 See Priest, *Life and Adventures of Isaac Hubbell.*
9 Steele, *Narrative*, 140.
10 Ibid.
11 *John Polley's Journal 1775*, PAC; for 1782 Letter from Gen. Carleton referring to the "civil war between peoples of one empire," see Metzger, *Prisoner in the American Revolution,* 230; Fischer, *Washington's Crossing*, 435.
12 See George Avery's Narrative, and David Waller's pension application (Pension Application, roll 2481, frames 0331-0349, VT S14.793, USNA), among others.
13 Lovejoy, *History of Royalton,* 2: 810–11.
14 Dunklee, *Burning of Royalton,* 86–88.

28. THE LAND — INDIANS AND SETTLERS

1 "Thomas Johnson's Diary/Journal, March 5, 1783," Johnson Family Papers, VHS, folder 574:42; Return of Prisoners Forwarded from Ticonderoga to Their Respective States, 1783/07/10, HP 21,843, reel 93, p. 329.
2 Calloway, *Western Abenakis of Vermont*, 224.
3 Ibid., 225.
4 Raphael, *People's History of the American Revolution*, quoting from Charles Jellison, *Ethan Allen: Frontier Rebel* (1969), 137.
5 Calloway, *Western Abenakis of Vermont,* 224–231; Lampee, "Mississquoi Loyalists," 97–99.
6 Taylor, *Divided Ground*, 106, quoting Brant to Johnson, Dec. 15, 1782.
7 Sturtevant, *Handbook of North American Indians*, 475–476; Taylor, *Divided Ground*, 113–137; Graymont, *Iroquois in the American Revolution*, 265, 293; Raphael, *People's History of the American Revolution*, 204–205.
8 Foster, *Captor's Narrative,* 50.
9 Stillwell, *Migrations from Vermont*, 70, quoting Benjamin Silliman, 1819.
10 Ibid., 83; Scudder, *The Journal of William Scudder*, entry for Jun. 14, 1782, 211; *Journal of William Twiss,* entry for Jul. 13, 1781; Wells, *History of Newbury,* 398, "Thomas Johnson Journal."
11 Michael Sherman, Gene Sessions, and P. Jeffrey Potash, *Freedom and Unity: A History of Vermont* (Barre: Vermont Historical Society, 2004), 132; Stillwell, *Migrations from Vermont,* 95. Note that p. 66 has very different figures: in 1800 one-third were under 26. See also, Harold A. Meeks, *Time and Change in Vermont: A Human Geography* (Chester, Ct.: Globe Pequot Press, 1986), 23.

12 The man was Johnson Taplin. Hubbard, *Forests and Clearings,* republished in *Stanstead Historical Society Red Journal 1973,* 5: 216–217.
13 Ibid.

29. LOYALISTS

1 Raphael, *People's History of the American Revolution*, 145, referring to Paul H. Smith, "The American Loyalists: Notes on Their Organization and Numerical Strength," *William and Mary Quarterly*, 3rd Series, 25(1968): 269.
2 Raphael, *People's History of the American Revolution*, 169, quoting from Pauline Maier, *From Resistance to Revolution* (1974), 278.
3 Nye, *Sequestrations, Confiscations and Sale of Estates*, 9.
4 Stillwell, *Migrations from Vermont*, 90.
5 Lovejoy Papers, Revolutionary War Notebook 8; Governor and Council, 26th of March, 1778.
6 St. Leger to Mathews, 1781/01/01, St. John's, HP 21,794, reel 62, p. 3; June, 1780 Records of Governor and Council of the State of Vermont, vol. II (Montpelier, 1874), 32.
7 Among them, Abel Davis, Levi Sylvester, Col. John Taplin, Azariah Pritchard and John Peters.
8 Letter from Moses Dow to Meshech Weare, 1782/06/16, in Wells, *History of Newbury, Vermont*, 401; Johnson Family Papers, VHS, folder 574:20.
9 Nye, *Sequestrations, Confiscations and Sale of Estates*, Appendices, 430.
10 Ibid., 10.
11 Mathews, *Frontier Spies*, 160; Caverly, *History of the Town of Pittsford*, 726. Stevens settled on the Rideau River, south of Ottawa.
12 Fryer, *King's Men*, 225.
13 Ibid., 211.
14 Williamson, *Vermont in Quandary,* 293; Taplin, "The Vermont Problem in the Continental Congress," 278–282.
15 Williamson, ibid., 121, 124.

30. THE FOURTEENTH STATE

1 Bayley to Washington, Apr. 6, 1783, Johnson Family Papers, VHS, folder 574:20.
2 Ira Allen, May 1781, Justus Sherwood's *Journal* at Isle aux Noix, quoted in Taplin, "The Vermont Problem in the Continental Congress," 205.
3 Ibid., 281–282.

4 Ibid., 252.
5 Washington to George Clinton, Jun. 21, 1781; Washington to Schuyler, Jan. 8, 1782; Washington to Schuyler, Feb. 6, 1782; Washington to Schuyler, Mar. 4, 1782, all in GWPLC.
6 Washington to Schuyler, May 14, 1781; Washington to Roger Enos, Oct. 6, 1781, GWPLC.
7 Washington to Chittenden, Jan. 1, 1782, GWPLC.
8 Taplin, "The Vermont Problem in the Continental Congress," 276.
9 Haldimand to Shelburne, no. 2, Jul. 17, 1782, p. 96, XLI; Shelburne to Haldimand (most secret) XXII, Apr. 22, 1782, p. 57; Germain to Clinton, no. 96, I, Jan. 1, 1782, all in *Documents of the American Revolution 1770–1782, Colonial Office.*
10 Haldimand to Clinton, XXIII, Apr. 28, 1782, p. 60, *Documents of the American Revolution 1770–1782, Colonial Office.*
11 Williamson, *Vermont in Quandary*, 121; Caverly, *History of the Town of Pittsford*, 177.
12 Sherwood, Apr. 10, 1783, in Williamson, *Vermont in Quandary*, 124.
13 Bayley to Washington, Apr. 6, 1783, Johnson Family Papers, VHS, folder 574:20.
14 Williamson, *Vermont in Quandary*, 124.
15 Ibid., 295.

INDEX

Notes: End note information is indicated by the letter n following the page number. Illustrations and maps are indicated by italicized page numbers.